THE OFFICIAL BLUE BOOK®

HANDBOOK OF

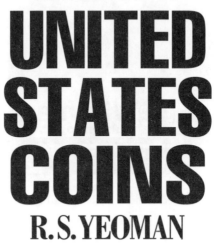

UNITED STATES COINS

R.S.YEOMAN

SENIOR EDITOR
JEFF GARRETT

RESEARCH EDITOR
Q. DAVID BOWERS

EDITOR EMERITUS
KENNETH BRESSETT

77th Edition
2020

An Illustrated Catalog of Prices Generally Paid
by Dealers for All American Coins—1616 to Date

Containing Mint records and wholesale prices for U.S. coins from 1616 to the
present time, including colonials, regular issues, commemoratives, territorials,
gold, bullion coins, Proof sets, and Mint sets. Information on collecting coins—
how coins are produced—mints and mintmarks—grading of coins—location
of mintmarks—preserving coins—starting a collection—history of mints—and
interesting descriptions of all U.S. copper, nickel, silver, and gold coins. Illustrated.

Handbook of United States Coins™
THE OFFICIAL BLUE BOOK OF UNITED STATES COINS™

THE OFFICIAL BLUE BOOK and OFFICIAL BLUE BOOK OF UNITED
STATES COINS are trademarks of Whitman Publishing, LLC.

Printed in the United States of America.

© 2019 Whitman Publishing, LLC
1974 Chandalar Drive • Suite D • Pelham, AL 35124

Scan the QR code at left or visit us at
www.whitman.com for a complete
listing of numismatic reference books,
supplies, and storage products.

CONTENTS

CONTRIBUTORS TO THIS EDITION

Senior Editor: Jeff Garrett. Research Editor: Q. David Bowers.
Editor Emeritus: Kenneth Bressett.

Whitman Publishing extends its thanks to these members of the coin-buying community who have contributed pricing for this year's *Handbook of United States Coins.* Their data were compiled and then reviewed by senior editor Jeff Garrett and consultants Phil Bressett and Kenneth Bressett. This process ensures input from a broad range of dealers and auctioneers from across the country—experts who buy, sell, and trade coins every day and know the market inside and out.

Gary Adkins	Thomas Hallenbeck	Mike Orlando
Buddy Alleva	James Halperin	Joseph Parrella
Mitchell Battino	Stephen Hayden	Robert M. Paul
Lee J. Bellisario	Brian Hendelson	Robert Rhue
William Bugert	John W. Highfill	Steve Roach
H. Robert Campbell	Brian Hodge	Maurice Rosen
Elizabeth Coggan	Jack Howes	Gerald R. Scherer Jr.
Gary and Alan Cohen	Steve Ivy	Harry Schultz
Stephen M. Cohen	Amandeep Jassal	Jeff Shevlin
Steve Contursi	Joseph Jones	Roger Siboni
Adam Crum	Donald H. Kagin	James Simek
Steven Ellsworth	Jim Koenings	David M. Sundman
Gerry Fortin	Julian M. Leidman	Barry Sunshine
Pierre Fricke	Denis W. Loring	Anthony Terranova
John Frost	Dwight N. Manley	Troy Thoreson
Mike Fuljenz	Syd Martin	Frank VanValen
Dennis M. Gillio	David McCarthy	Fred Weinberg
Ronald J. Gillio	Lee S. Minshull	Mark S. Yaffe
Rusty Goe	Charles Morgan	
Kenneth M. Goldman	Paul Nugget	

Special credit is due to the following for service and data in this book: Frank J. Colletti, Charles Davis, David Fanning, George F. Kolbe, Christopher McDowell, and P. Scott Rubin.

Special credit is due to the following for service in past editions: Stewart Blay, Scott Barman, Roger W. Burdette, Tom DeLorey, Bill Fivaz, Chuck Furjanic, James C. Gray, Charles Hoskins, R.W. Julian, Richard Kelly, David W. Lange, G.J. Lawson, Andy Lustig, J.P. Martin, Eric P. Newman, Ken Potter, Paul Rynearson, Mary Sauvain, Richard J. Schwary, Robert W. Shippee, Craig Smith, Jerry Treglia, Mark R. Vitunic, Holland Wallace, Weimar White, John Whitney, Raymond Williams, and John Wright.

Special photo credits are due to the following: Al Adams, David Akers, James Bevill, Heritage Auctions (ha.com), Ira & Larry Goldberg Coins & Collectibles, Ron Karp, Massachusetts Historical Society, Christopher McDowell, Tom Mulvaney, Ken Potter, John Scanlon, Roger Siboni, the Smithsonian Institution, Stack's Bowers Galleries, Richard Stinchcomb, and the U.S. Mint.

Since 1942, annually revised editions of the *Official Blue Book of United States Coins*™ have aided thousands of people who have coins to sell or are actively engaged in collecting United States coins. The popular coin-folder method of collecting by date has created ever-changing premium values, based on the supply and demand of each date and mint. Through its panel of contributors, the Blue Book has, over the years, reported these changing values. It also serves as a source of general numismatic information to all levels of interest in the hobby.

The values shown are representative prices paid by dealers for various United States coins. These are averages of prices assembled from many widely separated sources. On some issues slight differences in price among dealers may result from proximity to the various mints or heavily populated centers. Other factors, such as local supply and demand or dealers' stock conditions, may also cause deviations from the prices listed. While many coins bring no premium in circulated grades, they usually bring premium prices in Mint State and Proof. Extremely rare and valuable coins are usually sold at public auction, and prices vary according to current demand.

THIS BOOK LISTS PRICES MANY COIN DEALERS WILL PAY.

Premium prices are the average amount dealers will pay for coins (according to condition) if required for their stock. This book is not a retail price list.

IF YOU HAVE COINS TO SELL

Whitman Publishing, LLC, is not in the rare-coin business; however, chances are that the dealer from whom you purchased this book is engaged in the buying and selling of rare coins—contact them first. In the event that you purchased this book from a source other than a numismatic establishment, consult your local telephone directory for the names of coin dealers (they will be found sometimes under the heading of "Stamp and Coin Dealers"). If you live in a city or town that does not have any coin dealers, obtain a copy of one of the trade publications (such as *Coin World* [www.coinworld.com] or *Numismatic News* [www.numismaticnews.net]) or check the Internet in order to obtain the names and addresses of many of the country's leading dealers. Coin dealers who belong to the congressionally chartered American Numismatic Association (and who must abide by its code of ethics) are listed at www.money.org.

You will find current average *retail* valuations of American coins (the prices you can expect to pay a professional coin dealer) in the latest edition of *A Guide Book of United States Coins*™ by R.S. Yeoman, edited by Jeff Garrett. Coin collectors popularly call this the "Red Book." Pricing in even greater detail is included in Mega Red—*A Guide Book of United States Coins, Deluxe Edition.*

HOW TO READ THE CHARTS

A dash in a price column indicates that coins in that grade exist even though there are no current sales or auction records for them. (The dash does *not* necessarily mean that such coins are exceedingly rare.) Italicized prices indicate unsettled or speculative values. A number of listings of rare coins do not have prices or dashes in certain grades. This indicates that they are not available or not believed to exist in those grades.

Mintages of Proof coins are listed in parentheses.

Italicized mintages are estimates.

Numismatics or coin collecting is one of the world's oldest hobbies, dating back several centuries. Coin collecting in America did not develop to any extent until about 1840, as our pioneer forefathers were too busy carving a country out of wilderness to afford the luxury of a hobby. The discontinuance of the large-sized cent in 1857 encouraged many people to attempt to accumulate a complete set of the pieces while they were still in circulation. One of the first groups of collectors to band together for the study of numismatics was the American Numismatic Society, founded in 1858 and still a dynamic part of the hobby (www.numismatics.org). Lack of an economical method to house a collection held the number of devotees of coin collecting to a few thousand until Whitman Publishing and other manufacturers placed low-priced coin boards and folders on the market in the 1930s. Since that time, the number of Americans collecting coins has increased many-fold.

THE PRODUCTION OF COINS

To collect coins intelligently it is necessary to have some knowledge of the manner in which they are produced. Coins are made in factories called "mints." The Mint of the United States was established at Philadelphia by a resolution of Congress dated April 2, 1792. The act also provided for the coinage of gold eagles ($10), half eagles, and quarter eagles; silver dollars, half dollars, quarter dollars, dimes (originally spelled "disme"), and half dismes or half dimes; and copper cents and half cents. The first coins struck were one-cent and half-cent pieces, in March of 1793 on a hand-operated press. Most numismatic authorities consider the half disme of 1792 the first United States coinage, quoting the words of George Washington as their authority. Washington, in his annual address, November 6, 1792, said, "There has been a small beginning in the coining of the half dimes, the want of small coins in circulation calling the first attention to them." Though the half disme is considered America's first coinage, it was not the first coinage produced by the Mint; these coins were produced off premises in July of 1792 before the mint was completed. In the new Philadelphia Mint are a number of implements from the original mint, and some coins discovered when the old building was wrecked. These coins included half dismes, and the placard identifying them states that Washington furnished the silver and gave some of the pieces to his friends as souvenirs.

Prior to the adoption of the Constitution, the Continental Congress arranged for the issuance of copper coins under private contract. These are known as the 1787 *Fugio coppers* from their design, which shows a sundial and the Latin word "fugio"—"I Fly" or, in connection with the sundial, "Time Flies." The ever-appropriate motto "Mind Your Business" is also on the coin.

In the manufacture of a coin, the first step is die preparation. Dies for early federal coinage were prepared by hand; generally, letters and numbers were added with punches, while portraits and other designs were engraved into the die. Eventually, eagles, Liberty heads, and the like were also added with hubs and punches. After about 1836, many dies were made from masters, which contained all elements except the date and, if applicable, the mintmark. The addition of an element to a master die ensured its consistent placement throughout the life of the die. Today, many design tasks are performed with three-dimensional computer graphics. Mint artists are either sculptor-engravers or medallic sculptors, and their work takes place mainly at the Philadelphia Mint. The dies are made of soft steel, which is hardened after the impression is received. The die is then dressed or finished to remove imperfections and make it suitable for coining. A typical die for production coinage can be used to strike hundreds of thousands of pieces. Dies for special issues such as Proofs are replaced more often.

The hand method of cutting dies accounts for the many die varieties of early United States coins. Where the amount of coinage of a given year was large enough to wear out many dies, each new die placed in the coining press created another die variety of that year. The dies being cut by hand, no two were exactly alike in every detail, even though some of the major elements such as the head or wreath, were sunk into the die by individual master punches. Of the cents dated 1794, more than sixty different die varieties have been discovered.

Thousands of dies are now used by the mints of the United States each year, but they are all made from one master die, which is produced in the following manner:

After the design is settled upon, the plaster of paris or wax model is prepared several times the actual size of the coin. When this model is finished an electrotype (an exact duplicate in metal) is made and prepared for the reducing lathe. The reducing lathe is a machine that works on the principle of the pantograph, only in this case the one point traces or follows the form of the model while another much smaller point in the form of a drill cuts away the steel and produces a reduced-size die of the model. The die is finished and details are sharpened or worked over by an engraver with chisel and graver. The master die is used to make duplicates in soft steel which are then hardened and ready for the coining press. To harden dies, they are placed in cast-iron boxes packed with carbon to exclude the air, and when heated to a bright red are cooled suddenly with water.

In the coinage operations the first step is to prepare the metal. Among the alloys that have been used are the following: silver coins, 90% silver and 10% copper; five-cent pieces, 75% copper and 25% nickel; one-cent pieces, 95% copper and 5% zinc. (The 1943 cent consists of steel coated with zinc; and the five-cent piece of 1942–1945 contains 35% silver, 56% copper, and 9% manganese.) Under the Coinage Act of 1965, the composition of dimes, quarters, and half dollars was changed to eliminate or reduce the silver content of these coins. The copper-nickel "clad" dimes, quarters, half dollars, and dollars are composed of an outer layer of copper-nickel (75% copper and 25% nickel) bonded to an inner core of pure copper. The silver clad half dollar and dollar have an outer layer of 80% silver bonded to an inner core of 21% silver, with a total content of 40% silver. Current cents are made from a core of 99.2% zinc, 0.8% copper, with a plating of pure copper. Dollars are composed of a pure copper core with outer layers of manganese-brass.

Alloys are melted in crucibles and poured into molds to form ingots. The ingots are in the form of thin bars and vary in size according to the denomination of the coin. The width is sufficient to allow three or more coins to be cut from the strips.

The ingots are next put through rolling mills to reduce the thickness to required limits. The strips are then fed into cutting presses which cut circular blanks of the approximate size of the finished coin. The blanks are run through annealing furnaces to soften them; next they move through tumbling barrels, rotating cylinders containing cleaning solutions which clean and burnish the metal; and finally into centrifugal drying machines.

The blanks are next fed into a milling machine which produces the raised or upset rim. The blank, now called a *planchet,* is now ready for the coining press.

The planchet is held firmly by a collar, as it is struck under heavy pressure varying from 40 tons for the one-cent pieces and dimes to 170 tons for silver dollars. Upper and lower dies impress the design on both sides of the coin. The pressure is sufficient to produce a raised surface level with that of the milled rim. The collar holding the blank for silver or clad coins is grooved. The pressure forces the metal into the grooves of the collar, producing the "reeding" on the edge of the finished coin.

HOW A PROOF COIN IS MADE

Selected dies are inspected for perfection and are highly polished and cleaned. They are again wiped clean or polished after every 15 to 25 impressions and are replaced frequently to avoid imperfections from wear. Coinage blanks are polished and cleaned to assure high quality in striking. They are then hand fed into the coinage press one at a time, each blank receiving two blows from the dies to bring up sharp, high-relief details. The coinage operation is done at slow speed. Finished Proofs are individually inspected and are handled by gloves or tongs. They also receive a final inspection by packers before being sonically sealed in special plastic cases.

Certain coins, including Lincoln cents, Buffalo nickels, quarter eagles, half eagles, eagles, and double eagles, between the years 1908 and 1916, were made with Matte Proof (nickel and silver) and Sand Blast and Satin Proof (gold) finishes. These later Proofs have a dull frosted surface which was either applied to the dies, or produced by special treatment after striking.

MINTS AND MINTMARKS

In addition to the Philadelphia Mint, the U.S. government has from time to time established branch mints in various parts of the country. At present, branch mints operate in Denver, West Point, and San Francisco. Starting in 1968, Proof sets as well as some of the regular coins were produced at the San Francisco Mint and Assay Office. The Denver Mint has operated since 1906. A mint was operated at New Orleans from 1838 to 1861 and again from 1879 to 1909. Mints were also in service at Carson City, Nevada, from 1870 to 1893; at Charlotte, North Carolina, from 1838 to 1861; at Dahlonega, Georgia, from 1838 to 1861; and at San Francisco since 1854. The U.S. government also supplied a mint in the Philippines (M mintmark) in the early 1900s.

Coins struck at Philadelphia before 1979 (except 1942 to 1945 five-cent pieces) do not bear a mintmark. Historically the mintmark was used only for branch mints. Modern exceptions include the Lincoln cent and the Kennedy half dollar, which both use the P for Philadelphia. All coins struck after 1967 have the mintmark on the obverse. The letters signifying the various mints are as follows:

C—Charlotte, North Carolina (gold coins only; 1838–1861)
CC—Carson City, Nevada (1870–1893)
D—Dahlonega, Georgia (gold coins only; 1838–1861)
D—Denver, Colorado (1906 to date)
O—New Orleans, Louisiana (1838–1861; 1879–1909)
P—Philadelphia, Pennsylvania (1793 to date; P not used in early years)
S—San Francisco, California (1854 to date)
W—West Point, New York (1984 to date)

The mintmark is of utmost importance to collectors because, historically, coinage of the branch mints has often been much smaller than quantities struck at Philadelphia. Many early coins of the branch mints are very scarce.

SLABBED VERSUS UNSLABBED COINS

In this handbook, values from under $1 up to several hundred dollars are for "raw" coins—that is, coins that have not been graded and encapsulated by a professional third-party grading service. Coins valued near or above $500 are assumed to be third-party graded. A high-value coin that has not been professionally certified as authentic, graded, and encapsulated by an independent firm is apt to be valued lower than the prices indicated.

The general effect of third-party grading and authentication has been to increase buyers' and sellers' comfort levels with the perceived quality of rare coins in the marketplace.

Coins in high grades that have been certified (professionally graded and guaranteed authentic) and encapsulated ("slabbed") may be valued significantly higher than similar coins that have not been so treated. In today's marketplace, "raw" or non-certified coins, are usually valued at less, except for modern U.S. Mint and bullion products.

DISTINGUISHING MARKS

The illustrations and explanations in this section will help the collector identify certain well-known varieties.

Half Cents of 1795–1796 Showing Location of Pole to Cap

The end of the pole lies parallel with the lines of the bust, which is pointed. On some coins, the pole is missing due either to engraver error (while cutting the die) or to an error in "relapping" (when the die is ground to remove wear, clash marks, etc.).

Pole to Cap   **No Pole to Cap**

Stemless Wreath Variety of Half Cents and Large Cents

For this variety, the difference is on the reverse side. Illustrations show both Stemless and Stems to Wreath types for comparison—stemless wreath found on the 1804, 1805, and 1806 half cents; and on the 1797, 1802, and 1803 large cents.

Stemless Wreath   **Stems to Wreath**

1864 Bronze Indian Head Cent With "L" on Ribbon

A small "L," the initial of the designer James B. Long-acre, was added to the Indian Head design late in 1864 and was continued through 1909. For coins in less than Fine condition, this small letter will often be worn away. The point of the bust is rounded on the 1864 variety without "L"; the bust is pointed on the variety with "L." The initial must be visible, however, for the 1864 variety to bring the higher premium. If the coin is turned slightly so that the portrait faces the observer, the highlighted details will usually appear to better advantage.

Designer Initials, Overstrikes, Die-Doublings, and Date Varieties

During 1909, initials appeared on the reverse of the Lincoln cent.
Starting in 1918, they appear below the shoulder.

Prior to 1990, mintmarks for all mints were usually applied directly to working dies at Philadelphia in a hand-punching operation. Occasionally, a die was accidentally marked with one letter on top of another.

Dies are produced by impressing the raised coin design of a hub into the end of a cylinder of steel. In early years the Mint made use of old dies by repunching the dates on their dies with new numbers. That practice was stopped prior to 1909. Since that time, all overdated coins have been the result of errors that occur when two different-dated hubs have been used in die preparation, and one is impressed over the other by accident.

1938-D, D Over S, Buffalo Nickel

1918-S, 8 Over 7, Standing Liberty Quarter
A variety of this kind is rarely found in coinage of the 20th century.

1942, 2 Over 1, Mercury Dime

1955, Doubled-Die Obverse Lincoln Cent

Large Date Cent (1960)

Small Date Cent (1960)

Large Date Cent (1982)

Small Date Cent (1982)

COUNTERFEIT COINS

Recognizing a spurious coin can be made easier through the use of common sense and an elementary knowledge of the techniques used by counterfeiters. It is well to keep in mind that the more popular a coin is among collectors and the public, the more likely it is that counterfeits and replicas will abound. Until recently, collector coins valued at under $100 were rarely replicated because of the high cost of making such items. The same was true of counterfeits made to deceive the public. Few counterfeit coins were made because it was more profitable for the fakers to print paper money. Today, however, counterfeiters in Asia and elsewhere create fakes of a surprising variety of coins, most notably silver dollar types, but also other denominations.

Coin dealers will rarely buy coins of exceptional rarity or value without being 100% certain of authenticity. Professional authentication of rare coins for a fee is offered by commercial grading services, and by some dealers.

Replicas

Reproductions of famous and historical coins have been distributed for decades by marketing firms and souvenir vendors. Most replicas are poorly made by the casting method, and are virtually worthless. They can sometimes be identified by a seam that runs around the edge of the piece where the two halves of the casting mold were joined together.

Counterfeits

For many centuries, counterfeiters have produced base-metal forgeries of gold and silver coins to deceive the public in the normal course of trade. These pieces are usually

11

crudely made and easily detected on close examination. Crudely cast counterfeit copies of older coins are the most prevalent. These can usually be detected by the casting bubbles or pimples that can be seen with low-power magnification. Pieces struck from handmade dies are more deceptive, but the engravings do not match those of genuine Mint products.

Die-struck gold coin counterfeits have been mass produced overseas since 1950. Forgeries exist of most U.S. gold coins dated between 1870 and 1933, as well as all issues of the gold dollar and three-dollar gold piece. Most of these are very well made, as they were intended to pass the close scrutiny of collectors. Many gold coins of earlier dates have been counterfeited, and all coins dated before 1930 should be carefully examined.

Silver dollars dated 1804, Lafayette dollars, several of the low-mintage commemorative half dollars, and the 1795 half dimes have been forged in quantity. Minor-coin forgeries made in recent years are the 1909-S V.D.B.; 1914-D and 1955 doubled-die Lincoln cents; 1877 Indian Head cents; 1856 Flying Eagle cents; and, on a much smaller scale, a variety of dates of half cents and large cents. Nineteenth-century copies of colonial coins are also sometimes encountered.

Alterations

Coins are occasionally altered by the addition, removal, or change of a design feature (such as a mintmark or date digit) or by the polishing, sandblasting, acid etching, toning, or plating of the surface of a genuine piece. Among U.S. gold coins, only the 1927-D double eagle is commonly found with a spuriously added mintmark. On $2.50 and $5 gold coins, 1839 through 1856, New Orleans O mintmarks have been deceptively altered to C (for Charlotte, North Carolina) in a few instances.

Over a century ago, five-dollar gold pieces were imitated by gold plating 1883 Liberty Head five-cent coins without the word CENTS on the reverse. Other coins commonly created fraudulently through alteration include the 1799 large cent and the 1909-S; 1909-S V.D.B.; 1914-D; 1922, No D; and 1943, Copper, cents. The 1913 Liberty Head nickel has been extensively replicated by alteration of 1903 and 1912 nickels. Scarce, high-grade Denver and San Francisco Buffalo nickels of the 1920s; 1916-D and 1942, 42 Over 41, dimes; 1918-S, 8 Over 7, quarters; 1932-D and -S quarters; and 1804 silver dollars have all been made by the alteration of genuine coins of other dates or mints.

Detection

The best way to detect counterfeit coins is to compare suspected pieces with others of the same issue. Look at the photographs in this book for comparisons. Carefully check size, color, luster, weight, edge devices, and design details. Replicas generally have less detail than their genuine counterparts when studied under magnification. Modern struck counterfeits made to deceive collectors are an exception to this rule. Any questionable gold coin should be referred to an expert for verification.

Cast forgeries are usually poorly made and of incorrect weight. Base metal is often used in place of gold or silver, and the coins are lightweight and often incorrect in color and luster. Deceptive cast pieces have been made using real metal content and modern dental techniques, but these too usually vary in quality and color. Detection of alterations sometimes involves comparative examination of the suspected areas of a coin (usually mintmarks and date digits) at magnification ranging from 10x to 40x.

CONDITIONS OF COINS
Essential Elements of the Official ANA Grading System

Proof—A specially made coin distinguished by sharpness of detail and usually with a brilliant, mirrorlike surface. *Proof* refers to the method of manufacture and is not a condition, but normally the term implies nearly perfect condition unless otherwise noted.

    Gem Proof (PF-65)—Brilliant surfaces with no noticeable blemishes or flaws. A few scattered, barely noticeable marks or hairlines.

    Choice Proof (PF-63)—Reflective surfaces with only a few blemishes in secondary focal places. No major flaws.

    Proof (PF-60)—Surface may have several contact marks, hairlines, or light rubs. Luster may be dull and eye appeal lacking.

Mint State—The terms *Mint State (MS)* and *Uncirculated (Unc.)* are used interchangeably to describe coins showing no trace of wear. Such coins may vary to some degree because of blemishes, toning, or slight imperfections, as described in the following subdivisions:

    Perfect Uncirculated (MS-70)—Perfect new condition, showing no trace of wear. The finest quality possible, with no evidence of scratches, handling, or contact with other coins. Very few circulation-issue coins are ever found in this condition.

    Gem Uncirculated (MS-65)—An above average Uncirculated coin that may be brilliant or lightly toned and that has very few contact marks on the surface or rim. MS-67 through MS-62 indicate slightly higher or lower grades of preservation.

    Choice Uncirculated (MS-63)—Has some distracting contact marks or blemishes in prime focal areas. Luster may be impaired.

    Uncirculated (MS-60)—Has no trace of wear but may show a number of contact marks, and surface may be spotted or lack some luster.

Choice About Uncirculated (AU-55)—Evidence of friction on high points of design. Most of the mint luster remains.

About Uncirculated (AU-50)—Traces of light wear on many of the high points. At least half of the mint luster is still present.

Choice Extremely Fine (EF-45)—Light overall wear on highest points. All design details are very sharp. Some of the mint luster is evident.

Extremely Fine (EF-40)—Light wear on design throughout, but all features sharp and well defined. Traces of luster may show.

Choice Very Fine (VF-30)—Light, even wear on the surface and highest parts of the design. All lettering and major features are sharp.

Very Fine (VF-20)—Moderate wear on high points. All major details are clear.

Fine (F-12)—Moderate to considerable even wear. Entire design is bold with overall pleasing appearance.

Very Good (VG-8)—Well worn with main features clear and bold, although rather flat.

Good (G-4)—Heavily worn, with design visible but faint in areas. Many details are flat.

About Good (AG-3)—Very heavily worn with portions of lettering, date, and legend worn smooth. The date may be barely readable.

Important: Damaged coins, such as those that are bent, corroded, scratched, holed, nicked, stained, or mutilated, are worth less than those without defects. Flawless Uncirculated coins are generally worth more than values quoted in this book. Slightly worn coins ("sliders") that have been cleaned and conditioned ("buffed") to simulate Uncirculated luster are worth considerably less than perfect pieces.

Unlike damage inflicted after striking, manufacturing defects do not always lessen values. Examples include colonial coins with planchet flaws and weakly struck designs; early silver and gold with weight-adjustment "file marks" (parallel cuts made prior to striking); and coins with "lint marks" (surface marks due to the presence of dust or other foreign matter during striking).

Brief guides to grading are placed before each major coin type. Grading standards are not scientific and often vary among collectors, dealers, and certification services. For more on grading, consult the *Official ANA Grading Standards for United States Coins.*

PRESERVING AND CLEANING COINS

Most numismatists will tell you to "never clean a coin" and it is good advice! Cleaning coins almost always reduces their value. Collectors prefer coins in their original condition.

Some effort should be made to protect Uncirculated and Proof coins so they won't need cleaning. Tarnish on a coin is purely a chemical process caused by oxygen in the air acting on the metal, or by chemicals with which the coin comes in contact. One of the most common chemicals causing tarnish is sulphur; most paper, with the exception of specially manufactured "sulphur-free" kinds, contains sulphur due to the sulphuric acid that is used in paper manufacture; therefore do not wrap coins in ordinary paper. Also keep Uncirculated and Proof coins away from rubber bands (a rubber band placed on a silver coin for a few days will eventually produce a black stripe on the coin where the band touched). The utmost in protection is obtained by storing the coin in an airtight box, away from moisture and humidity, and by using holders made of inert materials.

Many coins become marred by careless handling. Always hold the coin by the edge. The accompanying illustration shows the right and wrong way to handle numismatic specimens. It is a breach of numismatic etiquette to handle another collector's coin except by the edge, even if it is not an Uncirculated or Proof piece.

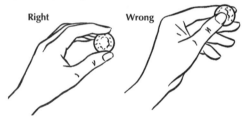

Right   Wrong

STARTING A COLLECTION

One may start a collection of United States coins with very little expense by systematically assembling the various dates and mintmarks of all the types and denominations that are now in general circulation, using Whitman's many different coin folders and albums, especially those for quarters and dollars with various designs.

With the exception of the price paid for the coin folder, collecting coins received in everyday business transactions entails no expense whatsoever; a Jefferson nickel taken out of circulation, for example, can always be spent for five cents if the occasion arises. Filling an album or two with coins found in circulation is probably the best method of determining whether coin collecting appeals to you. Not everyone can be a successful coin collector. It requires patience, intelligence of a high order, and a certain desire to know the meaning behind a lot of things that at first glance appear meaningless. You may not be cut out to be a collector but you'll never know until you look further into the subject, and if by the time an album or two of coins are collected you have no burning desire to acquire many more different coins, you will probably never be a collector. However, chances are that you will be, because if you have read this far in this book, it shows that you are interested in the subject.

High quality is the goal of every endeavor and coin collecting is no exception. After an album has been filled with circulated specimens, the next step will be to replace them with coins in Uncirculated condition, or perhaps to start collecting an obsolete series; in either case, it will be necessary to purchase some coins from dealers or other collectors. The most logical way to keep abreast of the market, or obtain the addresses of the country's leading dealers, is to subscribe to one or more of the trade publications. These magazines carry advertisements of various dealers listing coins for sale. Moreover, through these sources the beginner may obtain price lists and catalogs from the dealers.

There are several good reference books available at reasonable prices which will be helpful to the collector who wishes to know more about U.S. coins and paper money. R.S. Yeoman's *A Guide Book of United States Coins*™ (the "Red Book") lists retail values of all regular U.S. coins and also lists all coins of the U.S. colonial period and private and territorial gold coins, plus tokens, pattern coins, errors, and other numismatic collectibles.

Most coin, book, and hobby dealers can supply the following titles:

The Official Red Book®: A Guide Book of United States Coins™—R.S. Yeoman, edited by Jeff Garrett

The Official Red Book®: A Guide Book of United States Coins™, *Deluxe Edition*—R.S. Yeoman, edited by Q. David Bowers

A Guide Book of Morgan Silver Dollars—Q. David Bowers

The Expert's Guide to Collecting and Investing in Rare Coins—Q. David Bowers

Coin Collecting: A Beginner's Guide to the World of Coins—Kenneth Bressett

History of the United States Mint and Its Coinage—David W. Lange

The Official ANA Grading Standards for United States Coins—Kenneth Bressett, et al.

A Guide Book of United States Type Coins—Q. David Bowers

Join a Coin Club

Beginners should join a "coin club" if they live in a city which has one. Associating with more experienced collectors will be of great benefit. Practically all larger cities have one or more clubs and they are being rapidly organized in smaller towns. Trade publications carry information about coin clubs and events such as coin shows and conventions.

The American Numismatic Association is a national organization that collectors can join. The ANA Web site (www.money.org) has a list of member coin clubs throughout the United States. Contact the ANA by mail at 818 North Cascade Avenue, Colorado Springs, CO 80903, or by phone at 800-367-9723.

SELLING YOUR COINS

Is it time to sell your coins? Perhaps you've inherited some of them; or maybe you've collected for years, and you want to explore a new pastime or you need to cash in on your investment. In any case, you have some decisions to make. Will you sell your collection privately, or at a public auction—or perhaps sell it yourself on the Internet? Will you sell locally or to dealers nationwide? What are the benefits of each path, and which will bring the greatest profits? To get started, ask yourself:

What Am I Selling?

Rolls of Modern Coins; Proof Sets; Modern Commemoratives; Bullion; Etc.
This includes bulk investment coins, such as American Eagle bullion pieces, bags of

common circulated coins, and so on. It also includes modern commemoratives and coin sets, not all of which have increased in value in the secondary market. Such accumulations are best sold privately to a coin dealer or to another collector. Auctioning them yourself, on the Internet, is another route. Consigning them to an auction house is not likely to be your best option; this venue is typically reserved for scarcer coins.

Coins With Sentimental—but Not Necessarily High-Dollar—Value. You might have inherited an accumulation (as opposed to a studiously compiled collection) of coins—for example, a coffee can full of Wheat cents. Your local coin dealer can make you an offer, either buying the entire lot or searching through them to "cherrypick" the better pieces. If you have the time, you might sell them yourself, through an Internet auction site. Also, you might donate them to a local Boy Scout troop or similar organization (this may be tax-deductible).

Rare and/or Significant Coins. For rare, valuable, and historically significant coins, public consigned auctions are often the best way to sell—dedicated collectors know they're good sources for scarce coins. A coin consigned to a well-established auction house with numismatic experience will be carefully studied, cataloged, and presented to a serious audience. You save the time and effort of searching for potential buyers. The auction firm makes money by collecting a commission on each sale.

Another option for selling your rare and significant coins is to approach a dealer nationally recognized as an expert in the field—for example, a specialist who focuses on colonial coins. You may also receive tax benefits from donating your coins to the American Numismatic Association (ANA), the American Numismatic Society, or a museum.

Selling to a Coin Shop

Your local coin shop has the advantage of the personal touch. Good coin-shop proprietors are happy to educate and advise their customers. An active coin dealer stays up to date on the hobby and the market, knows about tax and estate laws that might affect your sale, and can study your collection and make educated decisions. Many dealers have a wide audience for selling coins—which provides the leverage to offer you a good price.

A coin shop can be a venue for selling numismatic items of any value. The owner can often make you an offer and write you a check on the spot. Of course, very rare or specialized coins will likely fetch a higher price at public auction.

You should feel comfortable with the integrity of the shop's proprietor and staff. Talk to coin-collector friends, inquire at the local coin club, and check with the Better Business Bureau. Look at the shop's Web site, advertisements, and flyers or publications—do they project fairness and professionalism?

Coin shops can be found in a phone book or online business directory. Call to make sure the owner or a qualified assistant will be there to examine your coins. A busy dealer can schedule a convenient time to meet with you. Solicit at least two quotes before you decide to sell.

Selling Through the Mail

You can ship your coins to a dealer for their offer; again, trust is important. Does the dealer belong to the ANA or the Professional Numismatists Guild (www.pngdealers. com)? Does he advertise in hobby newspapers such as *Coin World* and *Numismatic News?* Search the dealer's name on the Internet: do you find satisfied customers, or complaints and concerns?

Inquire by mail, email, or phone before shipping any coins. The dealer might request a list beforehand, and should be able to give you a general idea of value without seeing the coins in person. Once you're comfortable and have decided to sell, ask the dealer for advice on shipping and insurance. Keep in mind that the dealer will need to examine your coins before making a firm offer.

Even if you live near a coin shop, you can broaden the playing field if you're open to selling your coins through the mail to established, respected dealers. This is a good option if you have the time. The entire transaction (finding dealers; packing and shipping; waiting for the check) will likely take longer than getting a local offer.

Selling to a Dealer at a Coin Show

Between the national coin shows and the hundreds of coin clubs that sponsor city and regional shows, chances are a show is held somewhere near you at least once a year. With dozens or even hundreds of dealers in one venue, you can shop your coins around before you sell; and, as at a coin shop, payment is immediate.

For best results, decide in advance which dealers would be best to appproach, especially if you'll have to travel a long way or you're interested in a narrow specialty.

Remember, a coin show is a public venue. Be alert; use common sense. Outside the show, do not publicize the fact that you're carrying valuable coins.

Most shows list participating dealers in their programs. Decide in advance the ones you want to approach (e.g., the silver-dollar specialists, if you have Morgan dollars to sell). Or simply stroll the aisles and introduce yourself to dealers who sell items similar to those in your collection. This is all part of the fun of a coin show.

Consigning at a Public Auction

Numismatic auction firms are often connected to larger retailers that also sell through the mail, online, etc. As always, reputation is important. Study a potential auctioneer's Web site; learn about their staff, past sales results, any media coverage they might receive. Look at their catalogs: are they professionally made? The effort and experience an auction firm brings to its work will affect how much your coins sell for.

Selling Online

Selling your coins yourself online can be fun, but it requires time and (usually) some skill with scanning or photography. Each auction site has its own rules, policies, and rates; read them carefully. Be security-conscious (e.g., rent a Post Office box instead of using your home address, and insist on full, guaranteed payment before you ship any coins). You can also use the Internet to sell your coins at a fixed price, through a bulletin-board posting or other announcement. Any online sale to the public requires you to take on responsibilities similar to those of a coin shop or auction firm. There is work involved, but the experience can be enjoyable and profitable.

Early American coins are rare in conditions better than those listed and consequently dealers pay much more for them.

BRITISH NEW WORLD ISSUES

Sommer Islands (Bermuda)

This coinage, issued around 1616, was the first struck for England's colonies in the New World. The coins were known as "Hogge Money" or "Hoggies."

The pieces were made of copper lightly silvered, in four denominations: shilling, sixpence, threepence, and twopence, indicated by Roman numerals. The hog is the main device and appears on the obverse side of each. SOMMER ISLANDS is inscribed within beaded circles. The reverse shows a full-rigged galleon with the flag of St. George on each of four masts.

Shilling

	AG	G	VG	F	VF	EF
Twopence	$2,000	$3,000	$5,000	$9,000	$20,000	$40,000
Threepence			50,000			
Sixpence	1,750	2,500	4,000	8,000	19,000	30,000
Shilling	2,500	3,750	5,500	18,000	37,500	50,000

Massachusetts

"New England" Coinage (1652)

In 1652 the General Court of Massachusetts ordered the first metallic currency to be struck in the British Americas, the New England silver threepence, sixpence, and shilling. These coins were made from silver bullion procured principally from the West Indies. Joseph Jenks made the punches for the first coins at his Iron Works in Saugus, Massachusetts, close to Boston where the mint was located. John Hull was appointed mintmaster; his assistant was Robert Sanderson.

NE Shilling (1652)

	G	VG	F	VF	EF
NE Threepence *(unique)*			—		
NE Sixpence *(8 known)*	$30,000	$50,000	$100,000	$150,000	$250,000
NE Shilling	26,000	45,000	70,000	100,000	155,000

Willow Tree Coinage (1653–1660)

The simplicity of the design on the N.E. coins invited counterfeiting and clipping of the edges. Therefore, they were soon replaced by the Willow Tree, Oak Tree, and Pine Tree series. The Willow Tree coins were struck from 1653 to 1660, the Oak Trees 1660 to 1667, and the Pine Trees 1667 to 1682. All of them (with the exception of the Oak Tree twopence) bore the date 1652. Many varieties of all of these coins exist. Values shown are for the most common types.

Sixpence

	Fair	G	VG	F	VF	EF
1652 Willow Tree Threepence *(3 known)*......				—	—	—
1652 Willow Tree Sixpence *(14 known)*.......	$6,500	$14,000	$20,000	$40,000	$90,000	$150,000
1652 Willow Tree Shilling..................	6,500	14,000	20,000	30,000	75,000	125,000

Oak Tree Coinage (1660–1667)

Twopence   Threepence

	G	VG	F	VF	EF	AU	Unc.
1662 Oak Tree Twopence	$310	$450	$800	$1,500	$3,000	$4,200	$7,000
1652 Oak Tree Threepence	350	500	1,500	3,200	5,250	10,000	25,000
1652 Oak Tree Sixpence	400	700	1,600	3,750	6,000	10,000	20,000
1652 Oak Tree Shilling...........	400	700	1,600	4,000	6,500	8,000	15,000

Pine Tree Coinage (1667–1682)

The first Pine Tree coins were minted on the same size planchets as the Oak Tree pieces. Subsequent issues of the shilling were narrower and thicker, to conform to the size of English coins.

Shilling, Large Planchet (1667–1674)   Shilling, Small Planchet (1675–1682)

See next page for chart.

	G	VG	F	VF	EF	AU	Unc.
1652 Pine Tree Threepence	$300	$475	$800	$1,500	$3,200	$5,000	$10,000
1652 Pine Tree Sixpence	350	500	1,000	1,950	3,400	6,000	11,000
1652 Pine Tree Shilling, Large Planchet	450	725	1,200	2,750	4,750	8,000	17,000
1652 Pine Tree Shilling, Small Planchet	375	525	1,000	2,100	3,500	6,250	16,000

Maryland
Lord Baltimore Coinage

In 1659, Cecil Calvert, Lord Baltimore and Lord Proprietor of Maryland, had coinage struck in England for use in Maryland. There were four denominations: shilling, sixpence, fourpence (groat) in silver, and copper penny (denarium). The silver coins have the bust of Lord Baltimore on the obverse, and the Baltimore family arms with the denomination in Roman numerals on the reverse.

Fourpence (groat)   Lord Baltimore Shilling

	G	VG	F	VF	EF	AU
Penny copper *(9 known)*	—	—	$40,000	$60,000	$90,000	—
Fourpence	$1,500	$3,000	6,000	12,000	17,500	$30,000
Sixpence	800	1,300	2,500	5,000	8,000	12,000
Shilling	1,000	2,000	3,750	7,000	10,000	17,000

New Jersey
St. Patrick or Mark Newby Coinage

Mark Newby, who came to America from Dublin, Ireland, in November 1681, brought copper pieces believed by numismatists to have been struck in England circa 1663 to 1672. These are called St. Patrick coppers. The coin received wide circulation in the New Jersey Province, having been authorized to pass as legal tender by the General Assembly in May 1682. The smaller piece, known as a farthing, was never specifically authorized for circulation in the colonies.

St. Patrick Farthing

	G	VG	F	VF	EF	AU
St. Patrick "Farthing"	$90	$160	$450	$1,600	$3,500	$7,500
St. Patrick "Halfpenny"	150	350	600	1,800	5,250	9,500

COINAGE AUTHORIZED BY BRITISH ROYAL PATENT
American Plantations Tokens

These pieces struck in nearly pure tin were the first royally authorized coinage for the British colonies in America. They were made under a franchise granted in 1688 to Richard Holt. Restrikes were made circa 1828 from original dies.

	G	VG	F	VF	EF	AU	Unc.
(1688) James II Plantation Token Farthing . .							
1/24 Part Real.	$125	$150	$300	$600	$800	$1,900	$3,500
1/24 Part Real, Restrike.	50	75	150	225	325	475	800

Coinage of William Wood
Rosa Americana Coins

William Wood, an Englishman, obtained a patent from King George I to make coins for Ireland and the American colonies. The Rosa Americana pieces were issued in three denominations—halfpenny, penny, and twopence—and were intended for use in America.

Penny

	VG	F	VF	EF	AU	Unc.
(No date) Twopence, Motto in Ribbon.	$90	$170	$375	$600	$1,500	$2,500
1722 Halfpenny, DEI GRATIA REX UTILE DULCI . . .	55	125	210	400	725	1,700
1722 Penny.	55	125	210	400	725	1,700
1722 Twopence	75	140	250	500	800	2,000

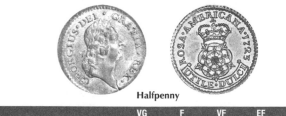

Halfpenny

	VG	F	VF	EF	AU	Unc.
1723 Halfpenny.	$35	$100	$150	$325	$700	$1,500

Entry continued on next page.

Twopence

	VG	F	VF	EF	AU	Unc.
1723 Penny............................	$40	$60	$140	$250	$400	$1,000
1723 Twopence *(illustrated)*................	75	110	175	400	700	1,250

Wood's Hibernia Coinage

The type intended for Ireland had a seated figure with a harp on the reverse side and the word HIBERNIA. Denominations struck were the halfpenny and the farthing with dates 1722, 1723, and 1724. Although these have no association with the Americas, because of the connection with William Wood many American collectors desire to obtain them.

1722, Hibernia Halfpenny   **First Type**   **Second Type**

	G	VG	F	VF	EF	AU	Unc.
1722 Farthing, first type	$75	$200	$300	$850	$1,500	$3,500	$6,000
1722 Halfpenny (first or second type) ...	12	35	50	100	175	300	700

1723, Hibernia Farthing   **1724, Hibernia Halfpenny**

	G	VG	F	VF	EF	AU	Unc.
1723 Farthing	$10	$20	$35	$70	$100	$200	$320
1723 Halfpenny...................	10	20	30	65	90	175	300
1724 Farthing	15	40	95	250	450	750	1,500
1724 Halfpenny...................	12	35	60	170	325	500	950

Virginia Halfpennies

In 1773, coinage of a copper halfpenny was authorized for Virginia by the British Crown. The style is similar to the regular English coinage. These pieces did not arrive in Virginia until 1775, but after then they did circulate on a limited basis. Most examples known today are Uncirculated, by virtue of a hoard of several thousand pieces that came to light in the 19th century and was distributed in numismatic channels.

	G	VG	F	VF	EF	AU	Unc.
1773 Halfpenny.................	$10	$30	$50	$90	$200	$280	$550

EARLY AMERICAN AND RELATED TOKENS

Elephant Tokens

London Elephant Tokens

The London Elephant tokens were struck circa 1672 to 1694. Although they were undated, two examples are known to have been struck over 1672 British halfpennies. Most are struck in copper, but one is made of brass. The legend on this piece, GOD PRESERVE LONDON, is probably just a general plea for divine aid and not a specific reference to the outbreak of plague in 1665 or the great fire of 1666.

These pieces were not struck for the colonies, and probably did not circulate in America, although a few may have been carried there by colonists. They are associated with the 1694 Carolina and New England Elephant tokens, through a shared obverse die.

	VG	F	VF	EF	AU	Unc.
(1694) Halfpenny, GOD PRESERVE LONDON,						
Thick or Thin Planchet................	$175	$325	$500	$850	$1,600	$2,250

Carolina Elephant Tokens

Although no law is known authorizing coinage for Carolina, very interesting pieces known as Elephant tokens were made with the date 1694. These copper tokens were of halfpenny denomination. The reverse reads GOD PRESERVE CAROLINA AND THE LORDS PROPRIETERS 1694.

The Carolina pieces were probably struck in England and perhaps intended as advertising to heighten interest in the Carolina Plantation.

	VG	F	VF	EF	AU	Unc.
1694 CAROLINA.	$2,500	$4,500	$10,000	$20,000	$35,000	$60,000

New England Elephant Tokens

Like the Carolina Tokens, the New England Elephant tokens were believed to have been struck in England as promotional pieces to increase interest in the American colonies.

	F	VF	EF
1694 NEW ENGLAND	$70,000	$90,000	$150,000

New Yorke in America Token

Little is known about the origin of this token. The design of a heraldic eagle on a regulated staff with oak leaf finials is identical to the crest found on the arms of William Lovelace, governor of New York, 1668 to 1673. It seems likely that this piece is a token farthing struck by Lovelace for use in New York.

	VG	F
(Undated) Brass or Copper	$4,000	$10,000
(Undated) Pewter	—	—

Gloucester Tokens

This token appears to have been a private coinage by a merchant of Gloucester (county), Virginia. The only specimens known are struck in brass. The exact origin and use of these pieces are unknown.

	F
1714 Shilling, brass *(2 known)*	$80,000

Higley or Granby Coppers

The Higley coppers were private issues. All the pieces were made of pure copper. There were seven obverse and four reverse dies. The first issue, in 1737, bore the legend THE VALUE OF THREEPENCE. After a time the quantity exceeded the local demand, and a protest arose against the stated value of the piece. The inscription was changed to VALUE ME AS YOU PLEASE.

	AG	G	VG	F
1737 THE VALVE OF THREE PENCE, CONNECTICVT, 3 Hammers..........	$6,500	$10,000	$17,000	$30,000
1737 THE VALVE OF THREE PENCE, I AM GOOD COPPER, 3 Hammers	6,500	11,000	19,000	35,000
1737 VALUE ME AS YOU PLEASE, I AM GOOD COPPER, 3 Hammers.......	6,500	10,500	17,500	30,000
(1737) VALUE ME AS YOU PLEASE, J CUT MY WAY THROUGH, Broad Axe...	6,500	10,500	17,500	30,000
1739 VALUE ME AS YOU PLEASE, J CUT MY WAY THROUGH, Broad Axe....	7,500	13,500	24,000	38,000

Hibernia–Voce Populi Coins

These coins, struck in the year 1760, were made in Dublin. Although these have no connection with America, they have been listed in numismatic publications in the United States for a long time and are collected by tradition.

Farthing (1760)   Halfpenny (1760)

	G	VG	F	VF	EF	AU	Unc.
1760 Farthing	$100	$160	$250	$650	$1,000	$1,750	$3,500
1760 Halfpenny................	37	60	100	160	260	450	650

Pitt Tokens

British politician William Pitt is the subject of these pieces, probably intended as commemorative medalets. He was a friend to the interests of America. The so-called halfpenny served as currency in England during a shortage of regular coinage.

	VG	F	VF	EF	AU	Unc.
1766 Farthing	$2,500	$5,000	$15,000	$22,000		
1766 Halfpenny	200	325	650	1,100	$2,000	$4,250

Rhode Island Ship Medals

Although this medal has a Dutch inscription, the spelling and design indicate an English or Anglo-American origin. It is believed that this token was struck in England circa 1779 for the Dutch market. Specimens are known in brass and pewter. As with many colonial issues, modern copies exist.

1778–1779, Rhode Island Ship Medal

Values shown are for brass pieces. Those struck in pewter are rare and valued higher.

	VF	EF	AU	Unc.
Rhode Island Ship Medal	$450	$850	$1,500	$3,000

John Chalmers Issues

John Chalmers, a silversmith, struck a series of silver tokens at Annapolis in 1783. Certain of the dies were by Thomas Sparrow, who also engraved bank-note plates. As most examples show wear today, these pieces seem to have served well in commerce.

	VG	F	VF	EF	AU
1783 Threepence	$1,000	$2,000	$4,000	$8,500	$17,000

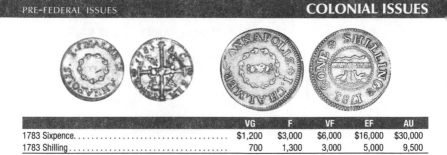

	VG	F	VF	EF	AU
1783 Sixpence	$1,200	$3,000	$6,000	$16,000	$30,000
1783 Shilling	700	1,300	3,000	5,000	9,500

FRENCH NEW WORLD ISSUES

None of the coins of the French regime is strictly American. They were all general issues for the French colonies of the New World. The copper of 1717 to 1722 was authorized by edicts of 1716 and 1721 for use in New France, Louisiana, and the French West Indies.

Copper Sou or Nine Deniers

	VG	F	VF	EF
1721-B (Rouen)	$225	$450	$1,800	$4,500
1721-H (La Rochelle)	50	110	350	1,200
1722-H	50	110	350	1,200

French Colonies in General

Coined for use in the French colonies, these circulated only unofficially in Louisiana, along with other foreign coins and tokens. Most were counterstamped RF (République Française) for use in the West Indies. The mintmark A signifies the Paris Mint.

	VG	VF	EF	AU
1767 French Colonies, Sou	$45	$125	$350	$700
1767 French Colonies, Sou, counterstamped RF	40	90	150	275

27

SPECULATIVE ISSUES, TOKENS, AND PATTERNS

Nova Constellatio Coppers

The Nova Constellatio pieces were struck supposedly by order of Gouverneur Morris. Evidence indicates that they were all struck in Birmingham, England, and imported for American circulation as a private business venture.

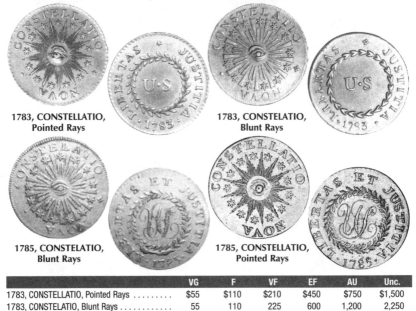

1783, CONSTELLATIO, Pointed Rays

1783, CONSTELLATIO, Blunt Rays

1785, CONSTELATIO, Blunt Rays

1785, CONSTELLATIO, Pointed Rays

	VG	F	VF	EF	AU	Unc.
1783, CONSTELLATIO, Pointed Rays	$55	$110	$210	$450	$750	$1,500
1783, CONSTELATIO, Blunt Rays	55	110	225	600	1,200	2,250
1785, CONSTELLATIO, Pointed Rays	55	110	210	450	750	1,500
1785, CONSTELATIO, Blunt Rays	55	110	225	650	1,400	2,750

Immune Columbia Pieces

Nearly all of these are very rare. Many if not most seem to be unofficial, including pieces produced at the private Machin's Mills mint in Newburgh, New York.

1785, Copper, Star Reverse

1785, George III Obverse

	G	VG	F	VF	EF	AU
1785 Copper, Star Reverse			$8,500	$14,000	$20,000	
1785, George III Obverse	$2,500	$4,750	6,000	9,000		

1787, IMMUNIS COLUMBIA, Eagle Reverse

	G	VG	F	VF	EF	AU
1785, VERMON AUCTORI Obverse, IMMUNE COLUMBIA ..	$3,200	$5,500	$7,500	$20,000		
1787, IMMUNIS COLUMBIA, Eagle Reverse	150	375	850	1,800	$2,500	$4,000

Confederatio Coppers

Some Confederatio coppers may have been patterns, but others seem to have been used in limited numbers for general circulation. This will explain why the die with the CONFEDERATIO legend was combined with other designs such as a bust of George Washington, Libertas et Justitia of 1785, Immunis Columbia of 1786, the New York "Excelsiors," Inimica Tyrannis Americana, and others. In all there were 12 dies struck in 13 combinations. There are two types of the Confederatio reverse. In one instance the stars are contained in a small circle; in the other, larger stars are in a larger circle.

Typical Obverse	**Small Circle Reverse**	**Large Circle Reverse**

	VF
1785, Stars in Small Circle, various obverses	$29,000
1785, Stars in Large Circle, various obverses	35,000

Speculative Patterns

1786, IMMUNIS COLUMBIA	**Eagle Reverse**	**Shield Reverse**

	VF	EF
1786, IMMUNIS COLUMBIA, Eagle Reverse	$30,000	$37,500
1786, IMMUNIS COLUMBIA, Shield Reverse...................................	20,000	27,500

Chart continued on next page.

29

	VF	EF
(No date) (1786) Washington Obverse, Shield Reverse	$40,000	
1786, Eagle Obverse, Shield Reverse	30,000	
1786, Washington Obverse, Eagle Reverse *(2 known)*	—	

COINAGE OF THE STATES
New Hampshire

New Hampshire was the first of the states to consider the subject of coinage following the Declaration of Independence.

William Moulton was empowered to make a limited quantity of coins of pure copper, authorized by the State House of Representatives in 1776.

	G	VG
1776 New Hampshire Copper	$50,000	$75,000

Massachusetts

The coinage of Massachusetts copper cents and half cents in 1787 and 1788 was under the direction of Joshua Witherle. These were the first coins bearing the denomination *cent* as later established by Congress. Many varieties exist, the most valuable being the cent with arrows in the eagle's right talon (on the left side of the coin).

1787 Half Cent   1787 Cent

1788 Half Cent   1788 Cent

	G	F	VF	EF	AU	Unc.
1787 Half Cent	$45	$120	$270	$400	$700	$1,500
1787 Cent, Arrows in Right Talon	4,500	12,000	25,000			
1787 Cent, Arrows in Left Talon *(illustrated)*	50	125	300	750	1,350	2,750

	G	F	VF	EF	AU	Unc.
1788 Half Cent	$50	$130	$300	$500	$900	$1,700
1788 Cent	50	130	325	550	1,000	2,100

Connecticut

Authority for establishing a mint near New Haven was granted by the state to Samuel Bishop, Joseph Hopkins, James Hillhouse, and John Goodrich in 1785. Today, well over 300 different die varieties are known of Connecticut coppers dated from 1785 to 1788. These pieces circulated widely and effectively; most are seen with significant evidence of circulation.

1785, Bust
Facing Right

1785, Bust
Facing Left

1786–1787,
Mailed Bust
Facing Right

1786–1787,
Mailed Bust
Facing Left

1787, Draped
Bust Facing Left

1788, Mailed
Bust Facing Right

Entry continued on next page.

31

	AG	G	VG	F	VF	EF	AU
1785, Bust Facing Left	$30	$75	$150	$275	$800	$1,500	$3,750
1785, Bust Facing Right	12	30	40	80	275	750	1,750
1786, Mailed Bust Facing Right	15	40	50	100	275	650	1,500
1786, Mailed Bust Facing Left	12	30	40	90	200	550	1,400
1787, Mailed Bust Facing Right	15	40	65	175	475	800	1,800
1787, Mailed Bust Facing Left	10	25	35	75	200	500	1,400
1787, Draped Bust Facing Left	10	25	35	75	200	500	1,200
1788, Mailed Bust Facing Right	10	25	50	100	300	700	1,400
1788, Mailed Bust Facing Left	10	25	32	80	210	550	1,350
1788, Draped Bust Facing Left	10	25	35	100	250	600	1,900

1788, Mailed Bust Facing Left

1788, Draped Bust Facing Left

New York and Related Issues

Brasher Doubloons

Perhaps the most famous pieces coined before the establishment of the U.S. Mint at Philadelphia were those produced by a well-known goldsmith and jeweler, Ephraim Brasher of New York.

Brasher produced a gold piece weighing about 408 grains, approximately equal in value to a Spanish doubloon (about $15.00 in New York currency).

The punch-mark EB appears in either of two positions as illustrated. This mark is found on some foreign gold coins as well, and probably was so used by Brasher as evidence of his testing of their value. Many modern forgeries exist.

	EF
1787 New York gold doubloon, EB on Breast	*$2,000,000*
1787 New York gold doubloon, EB on Wing	*1,500,000*

New York Copper Coinage

No coinage was authorized by the State of New York following the Revolutionary War, although several propositions were considered. The only coinage laws passed were those regulating coins already in use. Private mints struck several unauthorized coppers.

	G	VG	F	VF	EF
1786, NON VI VIRTUTE VICI	$2,500	$4,250	$8,500	$18,000	$30,000

	G	VG	F	VF	EF
1787 EXCELSIOR Copper, Eagle on Globe Facing Right	$1,000	$2,000	$4,000	$12,500	$25,000
1787 EXCELSIOR Copper, Eagle on Globe Facing Left	1,000	1,800	3,500	9,500	18,000

1787, George Clinton and New York Arms   **1787, Indian and New York Arms**   **1787, Indian and Eagle on Globe**

	G	VG	F	VF	EF
1787, George Clinton and New York Arms	$4,500	$10,000	$23,000	$45,000	$110,000
1787, Indian and New York Arms	4,000	6,000	12,000	20,000	50,000
1787, Indian and Eagle on Globe	4,000	6,000	12,000	18,000	35,000

Georgivs/Britannia
"Machin's Mills" Copper Halfpennies Made in America

During the era of American state coinage, James F. Atlee and other coiners minted unauthorized, lightweight, imitation British halfpence. These American-made false coins have the same devices, legends, and, in some cases, dates as genuine regal halfpence, but contain less copper. Overall quality of these pieces is similar to that of British-made imitations, but details are more often poorly rendered or missing. Identification of American-made imitations has been confirmed by identifying punch marks and matching them to those of known engravers.

Dates used on these pieces were often evasive, and are as follows: 1771, 1772, and 1774 through 1776 for the first group; 1747 and 1787 for the second group; and 1776, 1778, 1787, and 1788 for the third group. Pieces generally attributed to Atlee can be identified by a single outline in the crosses (British Union) of Britannia's shield and large triangular dentils along the coin circumference. The more-valuable American-made pieces are not to be confused with the similar English-made George III counterfeits (some of which have identical dates), or with genuine British halfpence dated 1770 to 1775.

Group I coins dated 1771, 1772, and 1774 through 1776 have distinctive bold designs but lack the fine details of the original coins. Planchets are generally of high quality. Group II coins dated 1747 and 1787 are generally poorly made. The 1 in the date is not J-shaped, and the dentils are of various sizes. There are no outlines to the stripes in the shield. Group III coins dated 1776, 1778, 1787, and 1788, struck at Machin's Mills in Newberg, New York, are similar to coins of Group II, with their triangular-shaped dentils. Most have wide dates and berries in the wreath.

	AG	G	VG	F	VF	EF	AU
1747, GEORGIVS II. Group II	$80	$125	$200	$450	$2,000	$4,000	—
1771, GEORGIVS III. Group I	30	50	110	200	750	1,200	$3,000
1772, GEORGIVS III. Group I	35	75	150	300	900	1,800	4,750
1772, GEORGIUS III. Group I	40	100	180	400	1,500	3,000	—
1774, GEORGIVS III. Group I	25	40	75	150	420	1,200	2,750
1774, GEORGIUS III. Group I	35	75	135	260	1,000	2,500	—
1775, GEORGIVS III. Group I	25	40	75	150	400	1,000	2,500
1776, GEORGIVS III. Group III	90	150	250	500	1,400	3,500	—
1776, GEORCIVS III, Small Date	600	1,200	2,500	5,000	10,000	—	—
1778, GEORGIVS III. Group III	25	50	85	200	450	1,250	2,000
1784, GEORGIVS III	100	200	500	900	1,800	2,750	4,000
1787, GEORGIVS III. Group II	25	40	75	120	350	800	1,750
1787, GEORGIVS III. Group III	25	40	75	120	350	800	1,750
1788, GEORGIVS III. Group III	30	45	85	150	375	900	1,800

Note: Values shown are what coin dealers pay for the most common varieties in each category. Rare pieces can be worth significantly more. Also see related George III combinations under Connecticut, Vermont, and New York.

Nova Eborac Coinage for New York

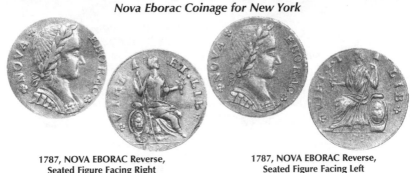

| | 1787, NOVA EBORAC Reverse, Seated Figure Facing Right | | 1787, NOVA EBORAC Reverse, Seated Figure Facing Left | |

	AG	G	F	VF	EF	AU
1787, NOVA EBORAC, Seated Figure Facing Right . . .	$30	$60	$150	$400	$900	$2,000
1787, NOVA EBORAC, Seated Figure Facing Left	27	45	125	325	700	1,450

New Jersey

On June 1, 1786, the New Jersey General Assembly granted to Thomas Goadsby, Albion Cox, and Walter Mould authority to coin some three million coppers no later than June 1788, on condition that they delivered to the treasurer of the state "one-tenth part of the full sum they shall strike and coin," in quarterly installments. These coppers were to pass current at 15 to the shilling. Produced in significant quantities, these coins are often seen in the market today and are widely collectible, although certain varieties can be rare and especially valuable.

Narrow Shield　　　　　　　Wide Shield

	AG	G	F	VF	EF	AU
1786, Narrow Shield	$12	$22	$85	$200	$375	$750
1786, Wide Shield	15	35	125	300	850	2,000

Small Planchet

	AG	G	F	VF	EF	AU
1787, Horse's Head Facing Right.	$12	$22	$85	$200	$375	$750

Fox Before Legend

	AG	G	F	VF	EF	AU
1788, Horse's Head Facing Right............	$12	$27	$100	$275	$450	$800
1788, Similar, Fox in Legend	30	75	275	900	2,000	4,500
1788, Horse's Head Facing Left.............	85	200	800	2,250	6,000	—

Vermont

Reuben Harmon Jr. was granted permission to coin copper pieces beginning July 1, 1785. The franchise was extended for eight years in 1786. However, in 1787 production was shifted to Machin's Mills, Newburgh, New York, in which Harmon had a proprietary interest. Although the Vermont coins were legally issued there, most other products of Machin's Mills were counterfeits, some dies for which were combined with Vermont pieces, creating several illogical pieces below, including the 1785 Immune Columbia and the 1788 Georgivs III Rex.

1785, IMMUNE COLUMBIA	1785–1786, Plow Type	1786, Baby Head

	AG	G	VG	F	VF	EF
1785, IMMUNE COLUMBIA..................	$1,900	$3,200	$5,500	$7,500	$20,000	—
1785, Plow Type, VERMONTS...............	80	150	300	425	1,400	$2,600
1786, Plow Type, VERMONTENSIUM	65	125	220	325	800	1,900
1786, Baby Head.......................	85	170	325	600	1,900	5,000

| | 1786–1787, Bust Left | | 1787, BRITANNIA | | 1787, Bust Right | |

	AG	G	VG	F	VF	EF
1786, Bust Left	$30	$75	$180	$400	$1,200	$2,000
1787, Bust Left	1,200	2,500	5,500	12,500	22,000	—
1787, BRITANNIA.	20	55	85	115	225	700
1787, Bust Right *(several varieties)*	25	70	135	245	600	1,250

| | 1788, Bust Right | | 1788, GEORGIVS III REX | |

	AG	G	VG	F	VF	EF
1788, Bust Right *(several varieties)*	$20	$60	$110	$225	$450	$900
1788, GEORGIVS III REX.	125	250	475	1,200	2,400	6,000

Note: This piece should not be confused with the common British halfpence with similar design and reverse legend BRITANNIA.

PRIVATE TOKENS AFTER CONFEDERATION
North American Tokens

This piece was struck in Dublin, Ireland. The obverse shows the seated figure of Hibernia facing left. Although dated 1781, it is believed to have been struck early in the next century.

Entry continued on next page.

	VG	F	VF	EF
1781, Copper or brass....................................	$25	$50	$100	$300

Bar Coppers

The Bar copper is undated and of uncertain origin. It has 13 parallel and unconnected bars on one side. On the other side is the large roman-letter USA monogram. The design was supposedly copied from a Continental Army uniform button.

	VG	F	VF	EF	AU
(Undated) (Circa 1785) Bar Copper	$925	$1,750	$3,000	$4,750	$6,750

Auctori Plebis Tokens

This token is sometimes included with the coins of Connecticut as it greatly resembles issues of that state. It was struck in England by an unknown maker.

	G	VG	F	VF	EF	AU	Unc.
1787, AUCTORI PLEBIS	$40	$75	$125	$250	$450	$900	$3,750

Mott Store Cards

This 19th century store card has long been considered an early token because of its date (1789). Most scholars believe it was most likely produced circa 1830 as a commemorative of the founding of the Mott Company, and probably served as a business card.

	VG	F	VF	EF	AU	Unc.
"1789," Mott Token......................	$45	$90	$175	$250	$320	$600

Standish Barry Threepence

Standish Barry, a Baltimore silversmith, circulated a silver threepence in 1790. The tokens were believed to have been an advertising venture at a time when small change was scarce.

	VG	F	VF	EF
1790 Threepence	$5,000	$11,000	$25,000	$47,000

Kentucky Tokens

These tokens were struck in England about 1795. Each star in the triangle represents a state, identified by its initial letter. These pieces are usually called *Kentucky cents* because the letter K (for Kentucky) happens to be at the top. In the 19th century these were often called *triangle tokens,* from the arrangement of the stars. Values are for the normal issue with plain edge; lettered-edge varieties exist and are scarcer.

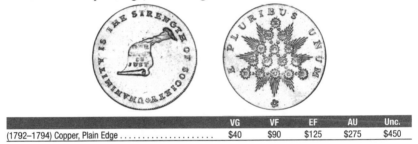

	VG	VF	EF	AU	Unc.
(1792–1794) Copper, Plain Edge	$40	$90	$125	$275	$450

Franklin Press Tokens

This piece is an English tradesman's token, but, being associated with Benjamin Franklin, has accordingly been included in American collections.

	VG	VF	EF	AU	Unc.
1794, Franklin Press Token	$50	$100	$150	$300	$480

Talbot, Allum & Lee Cents

Talbot, Allum & Lee, engaged in the India trade and located in New York, placed a large quantity of English-made coppers in circulation during 1794 and 1795. ONE CENT appears on the 1794 issue and on the edge of the 1795 issue.

Entry continued on next page.

39

1794 Cent, With NEW YORK	1795 Cent

	G	VG	VF	EF	AU	Unc.
1794 Cent, With NEW YORK	$30	$40	$125	$175	$300	$750
1794 Cent, Without NEW YORK	200	300	1,300	2,500	3,500	8,000
1795 Cent	25	35	120	150	250	450

WASHINGTON PORTRAIT PIECES

An interesting series of coins and tokens dated from 1783 to 1795 bear the portrait of George Washington. The likenesses in most instances were faithfully reproduced and were designed to honor Washington. Many of these pieces were of English origin and made later than the dates indicate.

1783, Military Bust	1783, Draped Bust

	F	VF	EF	AU	Unc.
1783, Military Bust	$40	$90	$180	$375	$950
1783, Draped Bust	45	100	200	400	1,200

1783, UNITY STATES

	VG	F	VF	EF	AU	Unc.
1783, UNITY STATES	$30	$60	$100	$200	$300	$800

Undated Double-Head Cent

	VG	F	VF	EF	AU	Unc.
(Undated) Double-Head Cent	$30	$50	$100	$200	$400	$1,200

Obverse	Large Eagle Reverse	Small Eagle Reverse

	F	VF	EF	AU	Unc.
1791 Cent, Large Eagle (Date on Obverse)	$200	$250	$350	$600	$1,300
1791 Cent, Small Eagle (Date on Reverse).	225	300	400	650	1,500

	F	VF	EF	AU
1791 Liverpool Halfpenny, Lettered Edge.	$700	$850	$1,600	$2,500

1792, Eagle With Stars, copper	—
1792, Eagle With Stars, silver	—
1792, Eagle With Stars, gold *(unique)*	—

**(1792) Undated Cent,
WASHINGTON BORN VIRGINIA**

**1792 Cent,
WASHINGTON PRESIDENT**

	VG	F	VF
(1792) Undated Cent, WASHINGTON BORN VIRGINIA, copper	$550	$1,000	$2,200
1792 Cent, WASHINGTON PRESIDENT, Plain Edge	1,500	3,750	7,500

1792 Getz Pattern

1793 Ship Halfpenny

1795 Halfpenny, Grate Token

	VG	F	VF	EF	AU	Unc.
1792, Getz Pattern, copper	$3,500	$6,500	$14,000	$25,000		
1793 Ship Halfpenny, Lettered Edge	35	100	200	300	$450	$1,600
1795, Grate Token, Lettered Edge	40	80	150	360	750	1,100
1795, Grate Token, Reeded Edge.	25	40	80	150	200	350

	F	VF	EF	AU	Unc.
1795, LIBERTY AND SECURITY Halfpenny, Plain Edge	$70	$150	$300	$600	$1,500
1795, LIBERTY AND SECURITY Halfpenny, Lettered Edge . . .	65	125	275	550	1,500
(1795) Undated, LIBERTY AND SECURITY Penny.	150	250	400	750	1,500

	G	F	VF	EF	AU
(1795) NORTH WALES Halfpenny	$50	$100	$250	$750	$1,500

	F	VF	EF	AU	Unc.
SUCCESS Medal, Large, Plain or Reeded Edge.	$100	$200	$350	$650	$1,400
SUCCESS Medal, Small, Plain or Reeded Edge.	125	250	425	700	1,500

CONTINENTAL CURRENCY

The Continental Currency pieces are believed to have been made to circulate in lieu of paper dollars at their time of issue. The exact nature of their monetary role is uncertain; they might have been experimental, or they might have seen circulation. At any rate, this might have been the first dollar-sized coin proposed for the United States. They were possibly struck in Philadelphia from dies engraved by Elisha Gallaudet. As with many early pieces, numerous replicas exist.

	G	F	VF	EF	AU	Unc.
1776, CURENCY, pewter *(2 varieties)*	$4,000	$7,000	$14,000	$19,000	$27,500	$40,000
1776, CURENCY, silver *(2 known)*.		175,000				
1776, CURRENCY, pewter.	4,000	7,000	14,000	20,000	30,000	45,000
1776, CURRENCY, EG FECIT, pewter	4,500	8,000	15,000	23,000	32,500	47,000

FUGIO COPPERS

The first coins issued by authority of the United States were the 1787 "Fugio" coppers. The legends have been credited to Benjamin Franklin by many, and the coins, as a consequence, have been referred to as *Franklin cents.*

1787, With Pointed Rays

1787, With Club Rays

	G	VG	F	VF	EF	AU	Unc.
Pointed Rays, STATES UNITED at Side of Circle *(illustrated)*	$60	$150	$275	$450	$900	$1,200	$2,250
Pointed Rays, UNITED STATES at Side of Circle	60	150	275	450	1,000	1,300	2,400
Club Rays, Rounded Ends	100	200	400	750	1,500	3,250	—

The half cent was authorized to be coined April 2, 1792. Originally the weight was to have been 132 grains, but this was changed to 104 grains by the Act of January 14, 1793, before coinage commenced. The weight was again changed to 84 grains January 26, 1796, by presidential proclamation in conformity with the Act of March 3, 1795. Coinage was discontinued by the Act of February 21, 1857. All were coined at the Philadelphia Mint.

LIBERTY CAP (1793–1797)

AG-3 About Good: Clear enough to identify.
G-4 Good: Outline of bust of Liberty clear, no details. Date readable. Reverse lettering incomplete.
VG-8 Very Good: Some hair details. Reverse lettering complete.
F-12 Fine: Most of hair detail visible. Leaves worn, but all visible.
VF-20 Very Fine: Hair near ear and forehead worn, other areas distinct. Some details in leaves visible.
EF-40 Extremely Fine: Light wear on highest parts of head and wreath.
AU-50 About Uncirculated: Only a trace of wear on Liberty's face.

Head Facing Left (1793)

	Mintage	AG-3	G-4	VG-8	F-12	VF-20	EF-40	AU-50
1793 35,334		$1,600	$2,750	$4,500	$7,000	$11,000	$15,000	$22,500

Head Facing Right (1794–1797)

Pole to Cap | Punctuated Date | No Pole to Cap

	Mintage	AG-3	G-4	VG-8	F-12	VF-20	EF-40	AU-50
1794 81,600		$225	$400	$650	$1,100	$1,500	$4,000	$7,500
1795, All kinds. 139,690								
1795, Lettered Edge, With Pole	145	400	575	850	1,350	3,000	6,000
1795, Lettered Edge, Punctuated Date	165	425	600	1,000	1,550	4,000	7,500
1795, Plain Edge, Punctuated Date . . .	225	500	650	1,100	1,650	4,250	7,500
1795, Plain Edge, No Pole	125	400	550	800	1,350	2,700	5,500
1796, With Pole 1,390	7,000	14,000	17,500	27,500	40,000	55,000	75,000
1796, No Pole . . . .*	12,000	22,500	30,000	80,000	110,000	150,000	200,000

* Included in number above.

1797, 1 Above 1, Plain Edge **1797, Plain Edge**

	Mintage	AG-3	G-4	VG-8	F-12	VF-20	EF-40	AU-50
1797, All kinds. 127,840								
1797, 1 Above 1, Plain Edge	$125	$325	$500	$800	$1,350	$2,400	$4,500
1797, Plain Edge	145	325	500	1,100	1,500	2,750	4,750
1797, Lettered Edge	350	850	1,500	3,500	10,000	35,000	
1797, Gripped Edge.	17,000	40,000	55,000	75,000	95,000		

DRAPED BUST (1800–1808)

AG-3 About Good: Clear enough to identify.
G-4 Good: Outline of bust of Liberty clear, few details, date readable. Reverse lettering worn and incomplete.
VG-8 Very Good: Some drapery visible. Date and legends complete.
F-12 Fine: Shoulder drapery and hair over brow worn smooth.
VF-20 Very Fine: Only slight wear in previously mentioned areas. Slight wear on reverse.
EF-40 Extremely Fine: Light wear on highest parts of head and wreath.
AU-50 About Uncirculated: Wear slight on hair above forehead.

1st Reverse **2nd Reverse**

	Mintage	AG-3	G-4	VG-8	F-12	VF-20	EF-40	AU-50
1800 202,908	$30	$60	$80	$115	$165	$300	$500
1802, 2 Over 0 20,266	300	550	1,500	3,500	6,500	15,000	
1803 92,000	30	60	80	100	225	550	1,000

Plain 4 **Crosslet 4** **Stems to Wreath** **Stemless Wreath**

	Mintage	AG-3	G-4	VG-8	F-12	VF-20	EF-40	AU-50
1804, All kinds. 1,055,312								
1804, Plain 4, Stems to Wreath	$25	$55	$80	$100	$200	$650	$1,250
1804, Plain 4, Stemless Wreath.	25	55	80	95	175	275	550
1804, Crosslet 4, Stemless Wreath . . .	25	55	80	95	175	275	550
1804, Crosslet 4, Stems to Wreath . . .	25	55	80	95	175	275	550

| 1804, "Spiked Chin" | Small 5 | Large 5 |

	Mintage	AG-3	G-4	VG-8	F-12	VF-20	EF-40	AU-50
1804, "Spiked Chin" ....*		$25	$60	$95	$115	$170	$275	$750
1805, All kinds.............814,464								
1805, Medium 5, Stemless Wreath ...		25	55	60	85	150	250	500
1805, Small 5, Stems to Wreath		250	600	1,150	2,500	5,500	10,000	20,000
1805, Large 5, Stems to Wreath		25	55	60	85	165	250	500

* Included in "1804, All kinds" mintage (previous page).

| Small 6 | Large 6 | 1808, 8 Over 7 | Normal Date |

	Mintage	AG-3	G-4	VG-8	F-12	VF-20	EF-40	AU-50
1806, All kinds..............356,000								
1806, Small 6, Stems to Wreath		$55	$140	$250	$425	$800	$2,000	$3,500
1806, Small 6, Stemless Wreath		25	55	60	85	150	250	500
1806, Large 6, Stems to Wreath		25	55	60	85	150	250	500
1807......................476,000		25	55	60	85	150	300	550
1808, Normal Date 400,000		25	55	60	85	150	300	500
1808, 8 Over 7 ....*		45	70	125	300	1,100	2,500	6,500

* Included in number below.

CLASSIC HEAD (1809–1836)

G-4 Good: LIBERTY only partly visible on hair band. Lettering, date, and stars worn but visible.
VG-8 Very Good: LIBERTY entirely visible on hair band. Lower curls worn.
F-12 Fine: Only partial wear on LIBERTY, and hair at top worn in spots.
VF-20 Very Fine: Lettering clear-cut. Hair only slightly worn.
EF-40 Extremely Fine: Light wear on highest points of hair and leaves.
AU-50 About Uncirculated: Sharp hair detail with only a trace of wear on higher points.
MS-60 Uncirculated: Typical brown to red surface. No trace of wear.
MS-63 Choice Uncirculated: Well-defined color, brown to red. No traces of wear.

1828, 13 Stars   1828, 12 Stars

Dealers often pay more than the prices shown for brilliant or red Uncirculated coins, and less for spotted, cleaned, or discolored pieces.

	Mintage	AG-3	G-4	VG-8	F-12	VF-20	EF-40	AU-50	MS-60	MS-63
1809.............1,154,572		$15	$35	$50	$60	$70	$105	$150	$400	$800
1810...............215,000		15	35	50	65	110	350	550	1,000	1,600
1811................63,140		125	225	450	1,000	1,500	3,500	7,500	25,000	55,000

Chart continued on next page.

	Mintage	G-4	VG-8	F-12	VF-20	EF-40	AU-50	MS-60	MS-63	PF-63
1825	63,000	$35	$50	$60	$75	$100	$200	$500	$1,250	
1826	234,000	35	50	60	70	85	125	275	475	
1828, 13 Stars	606,000	35	50	60	70	75	120	190	325	
1828, 12 Stars . . . . *		35	50	75	100	125	175	650	1,100	
1829	487,000	35	50	60	70	85	125	225	350	
1831	2,200									—
1832	51,000	35	50	60	70	80	100	175	300	$8,500
1833	103,000	35	50	60	70	80	100	175	300	4,500
1834	141,000	35	50	60	70	80	100	175	300	3,000
1835	398,000	35	50	60	70	80	100	175	300	3,000
1836										7,500

* Included in number above.

BRAIDED HAIR (1840–1857)

VG-8 Very Good: Beads in hair uniformly distinct. Hair lines visible in spots.
F-12 Fine: Hair lines above ear worn. Beads sharp.
VF-20 Very Fine: Lowest curl worn; hair otherwise distinct.
EF-40 Extremely Fine: Light wear on highest points of hair and on leaves.
AU-50 About Uncirculated: Very slight trace of wear on hair above Liberty's ear.
MS-60 Uncirculated: No trace of wear. Clear luster.
MS-63 Choice Uncirculated: No trace of wear.
PF-63 Choice Proof: Nearly perfect; only light blemishes.

Dealers often pay more than the prices shown for brilliant or red Uncirculated coins, and less for spotted, cleaned, or discolored pieces.

	Mintage	PF-63			Mintage	PF-63
1840, Original		$6,500		1845, Original		$9,500
1840, Restrike		5,500		1845, Restrike		5,500
1841, Original		6,500		1846, Original		7,500
1841, Restrike		5,500		1846, Restrike		5,500
1842, Original		6,500		1847, Original		5,000
1842, Restrike		5,500		1847, Restrike		4,000
1843, Original		6,500		1848, Original		8,500
1843, Restrike		5,500		1848, Restrike		4,500
1844, Original		6,500		1849, Original, Small Date		5,000
1844, Restrike		5,500		1849, Restrike, Small Date		5,000

Small Date **Large Date**

	Mintage	G-4	VG-8	F-12	VF-20	EF-40	AU-50	MS-60	MS-63	PF-63
1849, Large Date	39,864	$35	$45	$50	$60	$75	$110	$225	$300	—
1850	39,812	35	45	50	60	75	110	225	350	$4,500
1851	147,672	35	45	50	60	65	85	150	250	3,000
1852										3,500
1853	129,694	35	45	50	60	65	85	150	250	
1854	55,358	35	45	50	60	65	85	150	250	4,500
1855	56,500	35	45	50	60	65	85	150	250	3,000
1856	40,430	35	45	50	60	65	90	165	275	3,000
1857	35,180	35	45	50	80	100	130	225	320	3,000

Cents and half cents were the first coins struck at the United States Mint. Coinage began in 1793 with laws stating that the cent should weigh exactly twice as much as the half cent. Large cents are dated every year from 1793 to 1857 with the exception of 1815, when a lack of copper prevented production. All were coined at the Philadelphia Mint. Varieties listed are those most significant to collectors. Numerous other die varieties may be found, as each of the early dies was individually made.

FLOWING HAIR (1793)

AG-3 About Good: Date and devices clear enough to identify.
G-4 Good: Lettering worn but readable. No detail on bust.
VG-8 Very Good: Date and lettering distinct, some details of head visible.
F-12 Fine: About half of hair and other details visible.
VF-20 Very Fine: Ear visible, most details visible.
EF-40 Extremely Fine: Wear evident on highest points of hair and back of temple.

Chain Reverse (1793)

AMERI. Reverse | AMERICA Reverse

	Mintage	AG-3	G-4	VG-8	F-12	VF-20	EF-40
1793, Chain, All kinds	.36,103						
1793, AMERI. in Legend		$3,500	$6,500	$11,000	$18,000	$32,500	$55,000
1793, AMERICA.....................		2,500	5,000	7,500	14,000	24,000	47,500

Wreath Reverse (1793)

Strawberry Leaf Variety

	Mintage	AG-3	G-4	VG-8	F-12	VF-20	EF-40
1793, Wreath, All kinds	.63,353						
1793, Vine and Bars Edge		$1,050	$2,350	$3,500	$5,750	$8,500	$16,000
1793, Lettered Edge		1,050	2,600	3,750	5,750	8,500	18,000
1793, Strawberry Leaf..........	*(4 known)*	—	—	—			

LIBERTY CAP (1793–1796)

1793, Vine and Bars Edge
Chain and Wreath types only.

Lettered Edge (1793–1795)
ONE HUNDRED FOR A DOLLAR

Entry continued on next page.

Beaded Border (1793)

Head of 1793 (1793–1794) *Head in high, rounded relief.*	**Head of 1794 (1794)** *Well-defined hair;* *hook on lowest curl.*	**Head of 1795 (1794–1796)** *Head in low relief;* *no hook on lowest curl.*

	Mintage	AG-3	G-4	VG-8	F-12	VF-20	EF-40
1793, Liberty Cap 11,056		$3,000	$6,500	$9,500	$15,000	$27,000	$50,000
1794, All kinds. 918,521							
1794, "Head of 1793".		325	750	1,250	2,000	4,500	10,000
1794, "Head of 1794".		125	175	225	750	1,000	3,000
1794, "Head of 1795".		125	175	225	750	1,000	2,500
1795, Lettered Edge 37,000		125	185	225	750	1,200	2,400
1795, Plain Edge 501,500		125	195	250	600	1,000	2,000
1796, Liberty Cap 109,825		150	200	300	700	1,250	2,800

DRAPED BUST (1796–1807)

AG-3 About Good: Clear enough to identify.
G-4 Good: Lettering worn, but clear; date clear. Bust lacking in detail.
VG-8 Very Good: Drapery on Liberty partly visible. Less wear in date and lettering.
F-12 Fine: Hair over brow smooth; some detail showing in other parts of hair.
VF-20 Very Fine: Hair lines slightly worn. Hair over brow better defined.
EF-40 Extremely Fine: Hair above forehead and left of eye outlined and detailed. Only slight wear on olive leaves.

LIHERTY Error

	Mintage	AG-3	G-4	VG-8	F-12	VF-20	EF-40
1796, Draped Bust 363,375		$125	$175	$225	$500	$1,500	$5,500
1796, LIHERTY Error . . . . *		400	800	1,200	1,650	3,500	8,500

* Included in number above.

LARGE CENTS

Gripped Edge		With Stems		Stemless	
Mintage	**AG-3**	**G-4**	**VG-8**	**F-12**	**VF-20**	**EF-40**
1797, All kinds. 897,510						
1797, Gripped Edge, 1795-Style Reverse . . .	$80	$125	$250	$450	$950	$2,500
1797, Plain Edge, 1795-Style Reverse.	55	75	145	230	750	3,000
1797, 1797 Reverse, With Stems.	65	80	135	200	750	1,700
1797, 1797 Reverse, Stemless	55	75	155	250	750	2,300

1798, 8 Over 7	1799, 9 Over 8	1800 Over 1798	1800, 80 Over 79

	Mintage	**AG-3**	**G-4**	**VG-8**	**F-12**	**VF-20**	**EF-40**
1798, All kinds. 1,841,745							
1798, 8 Over 7		$100	$300	$450	$750	$1,200	$3,000
1798.		55	100	125	175	350	1,350
1799, 9 Over 8 . . . . *		3,000	5,500	8,500	17,500	37,000	125,000
1799, Normal Date . . . . *		2,000	4,000	6,500	11,000	27,500	100,000
1800, All kinds. 2,822,175							
1800, 1800 Over 1798		45	55	70	115	500	1,850
1800, 80 Over 79		45	55	70	100	250	1,200
1800, Normal Date		45	55	70	100	225	1,100

* Included in "1798, All kinds," mintage.

Fraction 1/000		Corrected Fraction		1801 Reverse, 3 Errors	

	Mintage	**AG-3**	**G-4**	**VG-8**	**F-12**	**VF-20**	**EF-40**
1801, All kinds. 1,362,837							
1801, Normal Reverse.		$35	$25	$30	$75	$200	$750
1801, 3 Errors: 1/000, One Stem, and IINITED		55	125	350	650	1,500	4,000
1801, Fraction 1/000.		40	65	85	200	275	825
1801, 1/100 Over 1/000		35	45	65	125	300	950
1802, All kinds. 3,435,100							
1802, Normal Reverse.		35	45	65	125	200	750
1802, Fraction 1/000.		35	45	75	150	250	1,500
1802, Stemless Wreath		35	45	65	125	200	750

1803, Small Date, Blunt 1	1803, Large Date, Pointed 1

Small Fraction	Large Fraction

See next page for chart.

51

	Mintage	AG-3	G-4	VG-8	F-12	VF-20	EF-40
1803, All kinds.	3,131,691						
1803, Small Date, Small Fraction.		$35	$55	$75	$200	$350	$850
1803, Small Date, Large Fraction		35	55	75	185	300	750
1803, Large Date, Small Fraction		3,000	5,500	10,000	17,000	30,000	
1803, Large Date, Large Fraction		85	125	250	550	1,250	2,500
1803, 1/100 Over 1/000		55	75	150	250	500	1,200
1803, Stemless Wreath		55	65	85	200	350	1,000

Broken Dies

All genuine 1804 cents have crosslet 4 in date and a large fraction.
The 0 in date is in line with O in OF on reverse.

	Mintage	AG-3	G-4	VG-8	F-12	VF-20	EF-40
1804 (a)	.96,500	$800	$1,500	$2,500	$3,500	$7,000	$12,000
1805	.941,116	35	65	80	125	250	800
1806	.348,000	35	55	75	100	235	950

a. Values shown are for coins with normal or broken dies.

Small 1807, 7 Over 6
(Blunt 1)

Large 1807, 7 Over 6
(Pointed 1)

	Mintage	AG-3	G-4	VG-8	F-12	VF-20	EF-40
1807, All kinds.	.829,221						
1807, Small 7 Over 6, Blunt 1		$800	$1,650	$3,500	$6,000	$15,000	$45,000
1807, Large 7 Over 6		35	65	75	85	200	750
1807, Small Fraction		35	65	75	85	225	800
1807, Large Fraction		35	65	75	85	200	750

CLASSIC HEAD (1808–1814)

AG-3 About Good: Details clear enough to identify.
G-4 Good: Legends, stars, and date worn, but plain.
VG-8 Very Good: LIBERTY all readable. Liberty's ear visible. Details worn but plain.
F-12 Fine: Hair on forehead and before ear nearly smooth. Ear and hair under ear sharp.
VF-20 Very Fine: Some detail in all hair lines. Slight wear on leaves on reverse.
EF-40 Extremely Fine: All hair lines sharp. Very slight wear on high points.

	Mintage	AG-3	G-4	VG-8	F-12	VF-20	EF-40
1808	1,007,000	$45	$80	$125	$300	$700	$1,500
1809	222,867	45	80	135	325	700	1,600

1810, 10 Over 09   1810, Normal Date   1811, Last 1 Over 0   1811, Normal Date

	Mintage	AG-3	G-4	VG-8	F-12	VF-20	EF-40
1810, All kinds	1,458,500						
1810, 10 Over 09		$45	$65	$125	$350	$750	$1,600
1810, Normal Date		45	65	125	350	725	1,500
1811, All kinds	218,025						
1811, Last 1 Over 0		125	175	300	550	1,100	3,500
1811, Normal Date		100	125	200	400	850	1,850
1812	1,075,500	45	65	125	250	650	1,400
1813	418,000	45	65	125	250	650	1,500
1814	357,830	45	65	125	250	650	1,400

MODIFIED LIBERTY HEAD (1816–1857)

G-4 Good: Details on Liberty's head partly visible. Even wear in date and legends.
VG-8 Very Good: LIBERTY, date, stars, and legends clear. Part of hair cord visible.
F-12 Fine: All hair lines visible. Hair cords uniformly visible.
VF-20 Very Fine: Hair cords only slightly worn. Hair lines only partly worn, all well defined.
EF-40 Extremely Fine: Both hair cords stand out sharply. All hair lines sharp.
AU-50 About Uncirculated: Only traces of wear on hair and highest points on leaves and bow.
MS-60 Uncirculated: Typical brown surface. No trace of wear.
MS-63 Choice Uncirculated: Some distracting contact marks or blemishes in prime focal areas. Impaired luster possible.

Matron Head (1816–1835)

1817, 13 Stars

1817, 15 Stars

Dealers often pay more than the prices shown for brilliant or red Uncirculated coins, and less for spotted, cleaned, or discolored pieces.

	Mintage	G-4	VG-8	F-12	VF-20	EF-40	AU-50	MS-60	MS-63
1816	2,820,982	$20	$25	$35	$55	$125	$175	$250	$500
1817, 13 Stars	3,948,400	20	25	35	45	75	145	240	500
1817, 15 Stars	*	20	30	45	125	400	650	1,500	3,000
1818	3,167,000	20	25	35	45	75	145	240	500

* Included in number above.

1819, 9 Over 8

1820, 20 Over 19

	Mintage	G-4	VG-8	F-12	VF-20	EF-40	AU-50	MS-60	MS-63
1819 2,671,000		$20	$25	$30	$40	$65	$125	$200	$450
1819, 9 Over 8 . . . . *		25	30	35	40	150	175	300	550
1820 4,407,550		20	25	30	40	60	100	200	350
1820, 20 Over 19 . . . . *		25	30	35	55	150	225	500	700
1821 **(a)** 389,000		25	30	60	185	650	1,500	4,500	—
1822 2,072,339		20	25	30	50	100	275	475	775

* Included in number above. **a.** Wide and closely spaced AMER varieties are valued the same.

1823, 3 Over 2   **1824, 4 Over 2**   **1826, 6 Over 5**

	Mintage	G-4	VG-8	F-12	VF-20	EF-40	AU-50	MS-60	MS-63
1823, 3 Over 2 . . . . *		$35	$55	$150	$300	$1,000	$1,900	$10,000	—
1823, Normal Date . . . . *		45	70	175	425	1,500	3,000	10,000	—
1824, 4 Over 2 . . . . *		35	45	50	200	750	1,500	3,500	$7,500
1824, Normal Date . 1,262,000		30	35	45	75	210	350	950	1,650
1825 1,461,100		30	35	45	45	150	250	800	1,500
1826, 6 Over 5 1,517,425		30	45	65	110	425	600	1,500	3,500
1826, Normal Date . . . . **		30	35	45	55	110	190	500	1,000
1827 2,357,732		30	35	45	65	80	150	400	1,000

* Included in number below. ** Included in number above.

Date Size, Through 1828   **Date Size, 1828 and Later**

	Mintage	G-4	VG-8	F-12	VF-20	EF-40	AU-50	MS-60	MS-63
1828, Large Narrow Date 2,260,624		$25	$30	$35	$45	$70	$150	$400	$700
1828, Small Wide Date . . . . *		25	30	40	55	120	250	550	1,200
1829 1,414,500		25	30	35	45	70	110	250	525
1830 1,711,500		25	30	35	45	60	100	200	400
1831 3,359,260		25	30	35	45	50	100	200	350
1832 2,362,000		25	30	35	45	50	80	175	325
1833 2,739,000		25	30	35	45	50	80	175	325
1834 1,855,100		25	30	35	45	70	100	200	350
1835 3,878,400		25	30	35	45	65	90	200	350

* Included in number above.

Matron Head Modified (1835–1839) and Braided Hair (1837–1857)

G-4 Good: Considerably worn. LIBERTY readable.
VG-8 Very Good: Hairlines smooth but visible; outline of ear clearly defined.
F-12 Fine: Hairlines at top of head and behind ear worn but visible. Braid over brow plain; ear clear.
VF-20 Very Fine: All details sharper than for F-12. Only slight wear on hair over brow.
EF-40 Extremely Fine: Hair above ear detailed, but slightly worn.
AU-50 About Uncirculated: Trace of wear on high points of hair above ear and eye and on highest points on leaves and bow.
MS-60 Uncirculated: Typical brown surface. No trace of wear.
MS-63 Choice Uncirculated: Some distracting contact marks or blemishes in prime focal areas. Impaired luster possible.

1839, 1839 Over 1836

Dealers often pay more than the prices shown for brilliant or red Uncirculated coins, and less for spotted, cleaned, or discolored pieces.

	Mintage	G-4	VG-8	F-12	VF-20	EF-40	AU-50	MS-60	MS-63
1836	2,111,000	$20	$25	$30	$40	$55	$85	$160	$300
1837	5,558,300	20	25	30	40	65	90	160	275
1838	6,370,200	20	25	30	40	50	85	150	275
1839	3,128,661	20	25	30	40	45	80	150	275
1839, 1839 Over 1836, Plain Cords . . . . . . *	250	450	750	1,500	4,000	10,000	—	—
1840	2,462,700	20	25	30	35	40	75	150	300
1841	1,597,367	20	25	30	35	40	75	150	300
1842	2,383,390	20	25	30	35	40	75	150	300

* Included in number above.

"Head of 1840"
Petite Head (1839–1843)

"Head of 1844"
Mature Head (1843–1857)

Small Letters

Large Letters

	Mintage	G-4	VG-8	F-12	VF-20	EF-40	AU-50	MS-60	MS-63
1843, Petite, Small Letters	2,425,342	$20	$25	$30	$28	$30	$60	$145	$185
1843, Petite, Large Letters . . . . *		20	25	35	45	70	125	325	600
1843, Mature, Large Letters . . . . *		20	25	30	40	50	90	160	400
1844, Normal Date	2,398,752	20	25	30	40	45	65	120	200
1844, 44 Over 81 . . . . *		55	70	100	150	300	500	1,000	2,500
1845	3,894,804	20	25	30	35	45	70	125	200
1846	4,120,800	20	25	30	35	45	70	125	200
1847	6,183,669	20	25	30	35	45	70	125	200
1847, 7 Over "Small 7" . . . . *		20	25	30	45	75	200	550	1,000

* Included in number above.

Mintage	G-4	VG-8	F-12	VF-20	EF-40	AU-50	MS-60	MS-63
1848 6,415,799	$20	$25	$30	$35	$45	$70	$110	$150
1849 4,178,500	20	25	30	35	45	70	125	225
1850 4,426,844	20	25	30	35	45	70	100	200

1844, 44 Over 81   **1851, 51 Over 81**   **1847, 7 Over "Small" 7**

Dealers often pay more than the prices shown for brilliant or red Uncirculated coins, and less for spotted, cleaned, or discolored pieces.

Mintage	G-4	VG-8	F-12	VF-20	EF-40	AU-50	MS-60	MS-63
1851, Normal Date . . 9,889,707	$20	$25	$30	$35	$40	$70	$100	$150
1851, 51 Over 81 . . . . *	20	25	30	35	75	110	250	450
1852 5,063,094	20	25	30	35	40	70	100	200
1853 6,641,131	20	25	30	35	40	70	100	200
1854 4,236,156	20	25	30	35	40	70	100	200

* Included in number above.

1855, Upright 5's   **1855, Slanting 5's**   **1855, Knob on Ear**

Mintage	G-4	VG-8	F-12	VF-20	EF-40	AU-50	MS-60	MS-63
1855, All kinds. 1,574,829								
1855, Upright 5's.	$20	$25	$30	$35	$40	$70	$100	$125
1855, Slanting 5's	20	25	30	35	40	70	115	200
1855, Slanting 5's, Knob on Ear.	20	25	30	35	45	90	160	300
1856, Upright 5 2,690,463	20	25	30	35	40	70	100	200
1856, Slanting 5 . . . . *	20	25	30	35	40	70	100	200

* Included in number above.

1857, Large Date   **1857, Small Date**

Mintage	G-4	VG-8	F-12	VF-20	EF-40	AU-50	MS-60	MS-63
1857, Large Date. . . . 333,546	$20	$20	$35	$40	$50	$120	$200	$325
1857, Small Date. . . . . *	20	35	40	45	60	130	220	350

* Included in number above.

FLYING EAGLE (1856–1858)

The Act of February 21, 1857, provided for the coinage of the new copper-nickel small cent. The 1856 Flying Eagle cent was not an authorized Mint issue, as the law governing the new-size coin was enacted after the date of issue. It is believed that nearly 1,000 original strikings and 1,500 or more restrikes were made of the 1856. They are properly referred to as *patterns*.

G-4 Good: All details worn, but readable.
VG-8 Very Good: Details in eagle's feathers and eye evident, but worn.
F-12 Fine: Eagle-head details and feather tips sharp.
VF-20 Very Fine: Considerable detail visible in feathers in right wing and tail.
EF-40 Extremely Fine: Slight wear, all details sharp.
AU-50 About Uncirculated: Slight wear on eagle's left wing and breast.
MS-60 Uncirculated: No trace of wear. Light blemishes.
MS-63 Choice Uncirculated: Some distracting contact marks or blemishes in prime focal areas. Some impairment of luster possible.
PF-63 Choice Proof: Nearly perfect.

| 1858, 8 Over 7 | 1856–1858, Large Letters | 1858, Small Letters |

Dealers often pay more than the prices shown for brilliant Uncirculated and Proof coins, and less for spotted, cleaned, or discolored pieces.

	Mintage	G-4	VG-8	F-12	VF-20	EF-40	AU-50	MS-60	MS-63	PF-63
1856	2,000	$5,000	$6,000	$7,500	$8,500	$9,500	$10,000	$12,000	$15,000	$15,000
1857	17,450,000	15	25	30	35	80	100	350	750	
	(100)									5,000
1858, Large Letters	24,600,000	15	25	30	35	80	100	350	750	
	(100)									5,000
1858, 8 Over 7	*	25	50	115	250	450	850	2,000	5,500	
1858, Small Letters	*	15	25	30	35	80	100	350	750	
	(200)									4,000

* Included in mintage for 1858, Large Letters.

INDIAN HEAD (1859–1909)

The small cent was redesigned in 1859, and a representation of Miss Liberty wearing an Indian war bonnet was adopted as the obverse device. The 1859 reverse was also changed to represent a laurel wreath. In 1860 the reverse was modified to display an oak wreath with a small shield at the top. From 1859 into 1864, cents were struck in copper-nickel. In 1864 the composition was changed to bronze, although copper-nickel cents were also struck during that year.

SMALL CENTS

G-4 Good: No LIBERTY visible.
VG-8 Very Good: At least some letters of LIBERTY readable on head band.
F-12 Fine: LIBERTY mostly visible.
VF-20 Very Fine: Slight but even wear on LIBERTY.
EF-40 Extremely Fine: LIBERTY sharp. All other details sharp. Only slight wear on ribbon end.
AU-50 About Uncirculated: Very slight trace of wear above the ear and the lowest curl of hair.
MS-60 Uncirculated: No trace of wear. Light blemishes.
MS-63 Choice Uncirculated: Some distracting contact marks or blemishes in prime focal areas. Impaired luster possible.
PF-63 Choice Proof: Nearly perfect.

Without Shield at Top of Wreath (1859 Only)

With Shield on Reverse (1860–1909)

Variety 1 – Copper-Nickel, Laurel Wreath Reverse (1859)

Dealers often pay more than the prices shown for brilliant Uncirculated coins, and less for spotted, cleaned, or discolored pieces.

	Mintage	G-4	VG-8	F-12	VF-20	EF-40	AU-50	MS-60	MS-63	PF-63
1859 . . . . . . *(800)*. . .	36,400,000	$7	$10	$15	$30	$65	$100	$140	$500	$1,000

Variety 2 – Copper-Nickel, Oak Wreath With Shield (1860–1864)

	Mintage	G-4	VG-8	F-12	VF-20	EF-40	AU-50	MS-60	MS-63	PF-63
1860 . . . . . . *(1,000)*	20,566,000	$6.00	$7	$8	$12	$32	$65	$100	$200	$575
1861 . . . . . . *(1,000)*	10,100,000	15.00	20	25	35	65	85	125	225	650
1862 *(1,500–2,000)*	28,075,000	5.50	6	10	15	30	45	100	150	500
1863 . . *(800–1,000)*	49,840,000	5.50	6	10	15	30	45	100	150	500
1864 . . *(800–1,000)*	13,740,000	10.00	15	20	40	55	75	125	225	550

Variety 3 – Bronze (1864–1909)

1864, Indian Head Cent With "L"

	Mintage	G-4	VG-8	F-12	VF-20	EF-40	AU-50	MS-60	MS-63	PF-63
1864, All kinds.	39,233,714									
1864, No L *(150)*.		$5	$10	$15	$25	$35	$45	$55	$85	$300
1864, With L *(20)*.		35	55	75	100	170	190	225	375	—
1865 . . *(750–1,000)*. .	35,429,286	5	6	9	12	20	35	50	100	200
1866 . . *(725–1,000)*. . .	9,826,500	30	40	55	75	100	150	175	275	220
1867 . . *(850–1,100)*. . .	9,821,000	30	40	55	75	100	150	175	275	220
1868 . . *(750–1,000)*. .	10,266,500	30	40	55	75	100	150	175	275	200
1869 . . *(850–1,100)*. . .	6,420,000	45	55	90	150	225	275	300	450	210
1870 . . . . . . *(1,000)*. . .	5,275,000	30	35	85	135	200	275	300	400	175
1871 . . . . *(960)*. .	3,929,500	35	45	125	185	225	300	365	500	175
1872 . . *(850–1,100)*. . .	4,042,000	55	85	185	250	300	450	550	700	250
1873 *(1,500–2,000)*. .	11,676,500	12	15	25	40	80	100	120	250	175
1874 *(1,000–1,200)*. .	14,187,500	10	15	20	30	50	75	110	175	175
1875 *(1,000–1,250)*. .	13,528,000	10	15	20	35	55	85	115	175	175
1876 *(1,500–2,000)*. . .	7,944,000	15	20	30	60	100	145	185	275	175
1877 *(1,250–1,500)*.	852,500	325	425	650	750	1,500	2,000	2,500	3,500	2,250

Dealers often pay more than the prices shown for brilliant or red Uncirculated coins, and less for spotted, cleaned, or discolored pieces.

	Mintage	G-4	VG-8	F-12	VF-20	EF-40	AU-50	MS-60	MS-63	PF-63
1878 .... (2,350).... 5,797,500		$15.00	$20.00	$25.00	$65.00	$100	$145	$165	$250	$175
1879 .... (3,200)... 16,228,000		4.00	6.00	8.00	18.00	40	45	50	80	150
1880 .... (3,955)... 38,961,000		1.75	2.00	3.00	6.00	15	25	40	70	150
1881 .... (3,575)... 39,208,000		1.75	2.00	3.00	5.00	10	16	26	37	150
1882 .... (3,100)... 38,578,000		1.75	2.00	3.00	5.00	10	16	26	37	150
1883 .... (6,609)... 45,591,500		1.75	2.00	3.00	5.00	10	16	26	37	150
1884 .... (3,942)... 23,257,800		2.25	2.50	3.50	6.00	14	20	30	60	150
1885 .... (3,790)... 11,761,594		3.00	4.00	6.00	14.00	35	45	60	100	150
1886 .... (4,290)... 17,650,000		1.75	3.00	8.00	24.00	65	85	100	125	150
1887 .... (2,960)... 45,223,523		1.25	1.50	1.75	2.25	8	14	25	35	150
1888 .... (4,582)... 37,489,832		0.85	1.10	1.80	2.75	8	14	25	40	150
1889 .... (3,336)... 48,866,025		0.85	1.10	1.80	2.75	6	12	25	35	150
1890 .... (2,740)... 57,180,114		0.85	1.10	1.80	2.75	6	12	25	35	150
1891 .... (2,350)... 47,070,000		0.85	1.10	1.80	2.75	6	12	25	35	150
1892 .... (2,745)... 37,647,087		0.85	1.10	1.80	2.75	6	12	25	35	150
1893 .... (2,195)... 46,640,000		0.85	1.10	1.80	2.75	6	12	25	35	150
1894 .... (2,632)... 16,749,500		2.00	3.00	4.75	8.50	25	30	40	50	150
1895 .... (2,062)... 38,341,574		0.85	1.10	1.30	2.00	6	11	25	30	150
1896 .... (1,862)... 39,055,431		0.85	1.10	1.30	2.00	6	11	25	30	150
1897 .... (1,938)... 50,464,392		0.85	1.10	1.30	2.00	6	11	25	30	150
1898 .... (1,795)... 49,821,284		0.85	1.10	1.30	2.00	6	11	25	30	150
1899 .... (2,031)... 53,598,000		0.85	1.10	1.30	2.00	6	11	25	30	150
1900 .... (2,262)... 66,831,502		0.80	1.00	1.10	1.50	5	10	20	25	150
1901 .... (1,985)... 79,609,158		0.80	1.00	1.10	1.50	5	10	20	25	150
1902 .... (2,018)... 87,374,704		0.80	1.00	1.10	1.50	5	10	20	25	150
1903 .... (1,790)... 85,092,703		0.80	1.00	1.10	1.50	5	10	20	25	150
1904 .... (1,817)... 61,326,198		0.80	1.00	1.10	1.50	5	10	20	25	150
1905 .... (2,152)... 80,717,011		0.80	1.00	1.10	1.50	5	10	20	25	150
1906 .... (1,725)... 96,020,530		0.80	1.00	1.10	1.50	5	10	20	25	150
1907 .... (1,475).. 108,137,143		0.80	1.00	1.10	1.50	5	10	20	25	150

Location of Mintmark S on Reverse of Indian Head Cent (1908 and 1909 Only)

	Mintage	G-4	VG-8	F-12	VF-20	EF-40	AU-50	MS-60	MS-63	PF-63
1908 ... (1,620)... 32,326,367		$0.80	$1.10	$1.25	$1.50	$5	$10	$18	$25	$125
1908S 1,115,000		60.00	70.00	100.00	125.00	150	175	200	300	
1909 .... (2,175)... 14,368,470		5.00	6.00	8.00	10.00	12	16	25	35	150
1909S 309,000		200.00	225.00	300.00	400.00	450	550	750	900	

LINCOLN, WHEAT EARS REVERSE (1909–1958)

Victor D. Brenner designed this cent, which was issued to commemorate the 100th anniversary of Abraham Lincoln's birth. The designer's initials (V.D.B.) appear on the reverse of a limited quantity of cents of 1909. Later in the year they were removed from the dies but restored in 1918 as very small incuse letters beneath the shoulder. The Lincoln type was the first cent to have the motto IN GOD WE TRUST.

G-4 Good: Date worn but apparent. Lines in wheat heads missing. Full rims.
VG-8 Very Good: Half of lines visible in upper wheat heads.
F-12 Fine: Wheat lines worn but visible.
VF-20 Very Fine: Lincoln's cheekbone and jawbone worn but separated. No worn spots on wheat heads.
EF-40 Extremely Fine: Slight wear. All details sharp.
AU-50 About Uncirculated: Slight wear on cheek and jaw and on wheat stalks.
MS-60 Uncirculated: No trace of wear. Light blemishes. Brown or red-brown color.
MS-63 Choice Uncirculated: No trace of wear. Slight blemishes. Red-brown color.
MS-65 Gem Uncirculated: No trace of wear. Barely noticeable blemishes. Nearly full red color.
PF-63 Choice Proof: Reflective surfaces with only a few blemishes in secondary focal places. No major flaws.

Location of mintmark S or D
on obverse of Lincoln cent.

**Designer's Initials
V.D.B. (1909 Only)**

**No V.D.B.
on Reverse
(1909–1958)**

Dealers often pay more than the prices shown for brilliant Uncirculated coins, and less for spotted, cleaned, or discolored pieces.

	Mintage	G-4	VG-8	F-12	VF-20	EF-40	AU-50	MS-60	MS-63	MATTE PF-63
1909, V.D.B.										
. . . . (1,194). . .27,995,000	$6.00	$6.50	$7.00	$8.00	$9.00	$10.00	$13.00	$20	$2,000	
1909S, V.D.B. 484,000	400.00	450.00	500.00	550.00	600.00	750.00	900.00	1,100		
1909 . . . (2,618). . .72,702,618	1.00	1.25	1.60	2.00	2.50	6.00	8.50	15	300	
1909S 1,825,000	45.00	55.00	65.00	85.00	100.00	150.00	225.00	275		
1910 . . . (4,083). .146,801,218	0.10	0.12	0.15	0.30	1.00	2.50	9.00	15	270	
1910S 6,045,000	8.00	10.00	12.00	14.00	25.00	40.00	55.00	70		
1911 . . . (1,725). .101,177,787	0.10	0.15	0.30	0.50	1.50	3.50	11.00	25	275	
1911D 12,672,000	2.40	3.00	4.50	9.00	21.00	35.00	50.00	70		
1911S 4,026,000	20.00	25.00	30.00	35.00	50.00	65.00	110.00	150		
1912 . . . (2,172). . .68,153,060	0.15	0.25	0.70	2.00	2.50	8.00	17.00	25	275	
1912D 10,411,000	2.75	3.50	4.25	10.00	25.00	40.00	75.00	120		
1912S 4,431,000	11.00	13.00	15.00	18.00	35.00	47.00	90.00	125		
1913 . . . (2,983). . .76,532,352	0.15	0.20	0.50	1.50	8.00	12.00	16.00	25	275	
1913D 15,804,000	0.75	1.00	1.50	3.50	20.00	26.00	50.00	100		
1913S 6,101,000	5.50	6.75	9.00	12.00	27.00	50.00	85.00	135		
1914 . . . (1,365). . .75,238,432	0.20	0.30	0.75	2.00	6.50	17.00	25.00	37	275	
1914D **(a)** 1,193,000	85.00	100.00	145.00	180.00	450.00	1,000.00	1,500.00	2,500		
1914S 4,137,000	11.00	14.00	16.00	19.00	40.00	90.00	175.00	350		
1915 . . . (1,150). . .29,092,120	0.40	1.00	2.00	8.00	26.00	35.00	46.00	65	300	
1915D 22,050,000	0.50	1.00	1.50	2.25	9.00	22.00	45.00	60		
1915S 4,833,000	10.00	12.00	15.00	18.00	35.00	65.00	110.00	150		
1916 . . . (1,050). .131,833,677	0.10	0.15	0.25	0.50	2.00	5.00	10.00	15	1,000	
1916D 35,956,000	0.30	0.50	0.85	2.00	5.50	12.00	35.00	65		
1916S 22,510,000	0.50	0.75	1.50	3.00	10.00	20.00	45.00	90		
1917 196,429,785	0.05	0.07	0.10	0.25	0.60	3.00	10.00	15		
1917D 55,120,000	0.25	0.40	0.75	1.50	14.00	19.00	39.00	70		
1917S 32,620,000	0.10	0.15	0.25	0.50	2.75	12.00	35.00	65		

a. Beware of altered date or mintmark. No V.D.B. on shoulder of genuine 1914-D cent.

SMALL CENTS

Designer's initials placed on Lincoln's shoulder next to rim, starting in 1918.

For brilliant Unc. coins before 1934, dealers usually pay more than the prices shown. They pay less for spotted, cleaned, or discolored pieces.

Mintage	G-4	VG-8	F-12	VF-20	EF-40	AU-50	MS-60	MS-63
1918 288,104,634	$0.04	$0.05	$0.10	$0.20	$1.00	$3.00	$6.00	$15.00
1918D 47,830,000	0.20	0.25	0.60	1.25	6.00	12.00	33.00	68.00
1918S . . . 34,680,000	0.15	0.20	0.50	1.00	4.00	15.00	35.00	75.00
1919 392,021,000	0.04	0.05	0.07	0.15	0.75	1.50	5.00	14.00
1919D 57,154,000	0.10	0.12	0.15	0.40	2.50	15.00	28.00	55.00
1919S 139,760,000	0.05	0.06	0.10	0.30	1.35	7.00	18.00	60.00
1920 310,165,000	0.03	0.05	0.07	0.15	0.50	1.50	6.00	12.00
1920D 49,280,000	0.20	0.40	0.80	2.00	6.00	15.00	35.00	55.00
1920S 46,220,000	0.10	0.20	0.30	0.70	3.50	17.00	45.00	90.00
1921 39,157,000	0.06	0.08	0.15	0.35	1.50	6.00	22.00	40.00
1921S 15,274,000	0.35	0.50	0.70	1.50	15.00	35.00	55.00	100.00
1922D 7,160,000	7.00	8.00	9.00	11.00	17.00	28.00	45.00	75.00
1922, No D **(b)** . . . . . . *	300.00	350.00	450.00	550.00	1,000.00	2,500.00	6,500.00	17,500.00
1923 74,723,000	0.04	0.05	0.07	0.15	1.00	2.50	7.00	14.00
1923S 8,700,000	1.25	1.50	2.00	3.00	15.00	35.00	100.00	225.00
1924 75,178,000	0.04	0.05	0.07	0.15	1.50	3.50	15.00	25.00
1924D 2,520,000	18.00	20.00	25.00	30.00	55.00	95.00	150.00	210.00
1924S 11,696,000	0.40	0.50	0.80	1.10	9.00	30.00	55.00	100.00
1925 139,949,000	0.03	0.04	0.05	0.15	0.50	2.00	5.00	10.00
1925D 22,580,000	0.10	0.15	0.50	1.00	4.50	11.00	27.00	38.00
1925S 26,380,000	0.05	0.06	0.10	0.25	3.00	14.00	40.00	95.00
1926 157,088,000	0.03	0.04	0.05	0.15	0.50	2.00	5.00	8.00
1926D 28,020,000	0.25	0.35	0.70	1.10	3.00	10.00	35.00	50.00
1926S 4,550,000	3.00	3.50	4.50	6.00	14.00	32.00	65.00	145.00
1927 144,440,000	0.03	0.04	0.05	0.20	0.50	1.00	5.00	10.00
1927D 27,170,000	0.10	0.15	0.50	1.00	2.00	6.00	26.00	42.00
1927S 14,276,000	0.25	0.30	0.50	1.25	4.00	11.00	35.00	70.00
1928 134,116,000	0.03	0.04	0.05	0.15	0.50	1.00	4.50	10.00
1928D 31,170,000	0.05	0.10	0.15	0.25	0.85	4.00	15.00	34.00
1928S 17,266,000	0.10	0.12	0.25	0.50	1.50	5.00	34.00	55.00
1929 185,262,000	0.03	0.04	0.05	0.15	0.35	1.50	4.00	6.00
1929D 41,730,000	0.04	0.06	0.10	0.25	1.00	2.00	12.00	15.00
1929S 50,148,000	0.03	0.05	0.10	0.20	0.60	1.75	7.00	11.00
1930 157,415,000	0.03	0.04	0.05	0.15	0.25	0.75	2.00	3.50
1930D 40,100,000	0.04	0.06	0.10	0.25	0.60	1.00	5.00	10.00
1930S 24,286,000	0.03	0.05	0.10	0.15	0.40	2.00	3.50	5.00
1931 19,396,000	0.15	0.20	0.30	0.40	0.60	2.00	10.00	15.00
1931D 4,480,000	2.00	2.25	3.00	3.50	5.00	14.00	30.00	42.00
1931S 866,000	45.00	50.00	60.00	70.00	75.00	85.00	100.00	125.00
1932 9,062,000	0.40	0.50	0.60	1.00	1.25	3.75	10.00	13.00
1932D 10,500,000	0.25	0.35	0.40	0.50	1.00	3.25	10.00	15.00
1933 14,360,000	0.30	0.40	0.50	0.70	1.25	3.75	10.00	15.00
1933D 6,200,000	1.00	1.25	1.50	2.50	4.25	7.00	13.00	16.00

* Included in number above. **b.** 1922 cents with a weak or missing mintmark were made from extremely worn dies that originally struck normal 1922-D cents. Three different die pairs were involved; two of them produced "Weak D" coins. One die pair (no. 2, identified by a "strong reverse") is acknowledged as striking "No D" coins. Weak D cents are worth considerably less. Beware of removed mintmark.

Chart continued on next page.

	Mintage	G-4	VG-8	F-12	VF-20	EF-40	AU-50	MS-60	MS-63	PF-63
1934	219,080,000	$0.03	$0.03	$0.03	$0.03	$0.10	$1.00	$3.00	$4.50	
1934D	28,446,000	0.04	0.06	0.08	0.15	0.50	2.00	9.00	15.00	
1935	245,388,000	0.03	0.03	0.03	0.04	0.06	0.20	2.00	3.00	
1935D	47,000,000	0.03	0.03	0.03	0.04	0.20	0.50	3.00	4.00	
1935S	38,702,000	0.03	0.04	0.04	0.04	0.12	1.25	4.00	6.00	
1936 . . . . (5,569) . .	309,632,000	0.03	0.03	0.03	0.04	0.06	0.25	1.00	3.00	$100
1936D	40,620,000	0.03	0.03	0.03	0.04	0.08	0.20	1.00	3.00	
1936S	29,130,000	0.03	0.03	0.03	0.04	0.10	0.20	1.00	3.00	
1937 . . . . (9,320) . .	309,170,000	0.02	0.03	0.03	0.03	0.05	0.20	0.50	3.00	35
1937D	50,430,000	0.02	0.03	0.03	0.03	0.06	0.30	0.80	4.00	
1937S	34,500,000	0.03	0.03	0.03	0.04	0.06	0.30	0.80	4.00	
1938 . . . (14,734) . .	156,682,000	0.02	0.03	0.03	0.03	0.05	0.30	0.75	2.00	25
1938D	20,010,000	0.02	0.03	0.05	0.06	0.15	0.50	1.00	5.00	
1938S	15,180,000	0.06	0.08	0.10	0.12	0.15	0.30	1.00	4.00	
1939 . . . (13,520) . .	316,466,000	0.02	0.03	0.03	0.03	0.03	0.20	0.30	2.50	23
1939D	15,160,000	0.06	0.08	0.10	0.12	0.15	0.35	1.00	4.00	
1939S	52,070,000	0.03	0.03	0.05	0.08	0.10	0.30	1.00	4.00	
1940 . . . (15,872) . .	586,810,000	0.02	0.03	0.03	0.03	0.03	0.20	0.30	2.00	15
1940D	81,390,000	0.02	0.03	0.03	0.03	0.03	0.20	0.40	2.00	
1940S	112,940,000	0.02	0.03	0.03	0.03	0.04	0.20	0.40	2.75	
1941 . . . (21,100) . .	887,018,000	0.02	0.03	0.03	0.03	0.03	0.20	0.30	2.00	15
1941D	128,700,000	0.02	0.03	0.03	0.03	0.03	0.40	0.80	3.00	
1941S	92,360,000	0.02	0.03	0.03	0.03	0.04	0.35	1.00	4.00	
1942 . . . (32,600) . .	657,796,000	0.02	0.03	0.03	0.03	0.03	0.10	0.15	1.00	15
1942D	206,698,000	0.02	0.03	0.03	0.03	0.03	0.10	0.25	1.50	
1942S	85,590,000	0.02	0.03	0.03	0.03	0.10	1.00	2.25	6.00	

Variety 2 – Zinc-Coated Steel (1943)

	Mintage	F-12	VF-20	EF-40	MS-60	MS-63	MS-65
1943	684,628,670	$0.05	$0.10	$0.15	$0.70	$1.25	$3.25
1943D	217,660,000	0.05	0.10	0.15	0.90	2.00	4.50
1943S	191,550,000	0.06	0.12	0.20	1.20	2.75	9.00

Variety 1 (Bronze) Resumed (1944–1958)

1944-D, D Over S

1955, Doubled-Die Obverse

	Mintage	VF-20	EF-40	MS-63	MS-65	PF-65
1944	1,435,400,000	$0.03	$0.03	$0.25	$1.60	
1944D	430,578,000	0.03	0.03	0.20	1.50	
1944D, D Over S . . . . *		60.00	80.00	200.00	350.00	
1944S	282,760,000	0.03	0.03	0.20	1.50	

* Included in number above.

	Mintage	VF-20	EF-40	MS-63	MS-65	PF-65
1945	1,040,515,000	$0.03	$0.03	$0.20	$0.50	
1945D	266,268,000	0.03	0.03	0.15	0.50	
1945S	181,770,000	0.03	0.03	0.10	1.00	
1946	991,655,000	0.03	0.03	0.10	0.50	
1946D	315,690,000	0.03	0.03	0.15	1.00	
1946S	198,100,000	0.03	0.03	0.15	1.25	
1947	190,555,000	0.03	0.03	0.25	0.75	
1947D	194,750,000	0.03	0.03	0.12	0.50	
1947S	99,000,000	0.03	0.03	0.15	1.50	
1948	317,570,000	0.03	0.03	0.15	0.50	
1948D	172,637,500	0.03	0.03	0.12	0.60	
1948S	81,735,000	0.03	0.03	0.20	1.50	
1949	217,775,000	0.03	0.03	0.30	0.75	
1949D	153,132,500	0.03	0.03	0.20	0.75	
1949S	64,290,000	0.04	0.05	0.50	2.00	
1950 (51,386)	272,635,000	0.03	0.03	0.25	0.50	$37
1950D	334,950,000	0.03	0.03	0.10	0.50	
1950S	118,505,000	0.03	0.03	0.25	0.80	
1951 (57,500)	284,576,000	0.03	0.03	0.25	0.80	35
1951D	625,355,000	0.03	0.03	0.10	0.50	
1951S	136,010,000	0.03	0.03	0.25	0.60	
1952 (81,980)	186,775,000	0.03	0.03	0.15	0.60	25
1952D	746,130,000	0.03	0.03	0.15	0.60	
1952S	137,800,004	0.03	0.03	0.50	1.50	
1953 (128,800)	256,755,000	0.03	0.03	0.10	0.50	18
1953D	700,515,000	0.03	0.03	0.10	0.50	
1953S	181,835,000	0.03	0.04	0.12	0.75	
1954 (233,300)	71,640,050	0.03	0.06	0.15	0.85	10
1954D	251,552,500	0.03	0.03	0.05	0.30	
1954S	96,190,000	0.03	0.03	0.05	0.30	
1955 (378,200)	330,958,200	0.03	0.03	0.06	0.30	9
1955, Doubled-Die Obverse	*	850.00	1,000.00 (a)	1,750.00	7,500.00	
1955D	563,257,500	0.03	0.03	0.05	0.25	
1955S	44,610,000	0.10	0.15	0.15	0.50	
1956 (669,384)	420,745,000	0.03	0.03	0.05	0.25	3
1956D	1,098,201,100	0.03	0.03	0.05	0.30	
1957 (1,247,952)	282,540,000	0.03	0.03	0.05	0.30	3
1957D	1,051,342,000	0.03	0.03	0.05	0.30	
1958 (875,652)	252,525,000	0.03	0.03	0.05	0.30	3
1958D	800,953,300	0.03	0.03	0.05	0.30	

* Included in number above. **a.** For MS-60 Uncirculated coins, dealers usually pay $1,400.

LINCOLN, MEMORIAL REVERSE (1959–2008)

Small Date   Large Date

	Mintage	MS-63	MS-65	PF-65
1959 (1,149,291)	609,715,000	$0.02	$0.10	$1.00

Entry continued on next page.

1969-S, Doubled-Die Obverse

Small Date, Numbers Aligned at Top

Large Date, Low 7 in Date

Enlarged Detail of 1972 Doubled-Die Obverse

	Mintage	MS-63	MS-65	PF-63
1959D	1,279,760,000	$0.02	$0.10	
1960, Lg Dt	586,405,000	0.02	0.10	
	(1,691,602)			$0.75
1960, Sm Dt	*	1.00	2.70	
	*			9.50
1960D, Lg Dt	1,580,884,000	0.02	0.10	
1960D, Sm Dt	*	0.02	0.10	
1961	753,345,000	0.02	0.10	
	(3,028,244)			0.50
1961D	1,753,266,700	0.02	0.10	
1962	606,045,000	0.02	0.10	
	(3,218,019)			0.50
1962D	1,793,148,140	0.02	0.10	
1963	754,110,000	0.02	0.10	
	(3,075,645)			0.50
1963D	1,774,020,400	0.02	0.10	
1964	2,648,575,000	0.02	0.10	
	(3,950,762)			0.50
1964D	3,799,071,500	0.02	0.10	
1965	1,497,224,900	0.03	0.12	
1966	2,188,147,783	0.04	0.12	
1967	3,048,667,100	0.03	0.12	
1968	1,707,880,970	0.03	0.12	
1968D	2,886,269,600	0.02	0.12	
1968S	258,270,001	0.02	0.15	
	(3,041,506)			0.35
1969	1,136,910,000	0.05	0.20	
1969D	4,002,832,200	0.03	0.15	
1969S	544,375,000	0.03	0.15	
	(2,934,631)			0.35
1969S, DDO	*	—	—	
1970	1,898,315,000	0.05	0.20	
1970D	2,891,438,900	0.02	0.10	
1970S, Sm Dt				
(High 7)	(a)	20.00	30.00	
	(b)			20.00
1970S, Lg Dt				
(Low 7)	690,560,004	0.03	0.20	
	(2,632,810)			0.25

	Mintage	MS-63	MS-65	PF-63
1971	1,919,490,000	$0.05	$0.20	
1971D	2,911,045,600	0.03	0.20	
1971S	525,133,459	0.03	0.20	
	(3,220,733)			$0.25
1972, DDO	**	225.00	350.00	
1972	2,933,255,000	0.02	0.10	
1972D	2,665,071,400	0.02	0.10	
1972S	376,939,108	0.02	0.10	
	(3,260,996)			0.25
1973	3,728,245,000	0.02	0.10	
1973D	3,549,576,588	0.02	0.10	
1973S	317,177,295	0.02	0.15	
	(2,760,339)			0.25
1974	4,232,140,523	0.02	0.10	
1974D	4,235,098,000	0.02	0.10	
1974S	409,426,660	0.03	0.20	
	(2,612,568)			0.25
1975	5,451,476,142	0.02	0.10	
1975D	4,505,275,300	0.02	0.10	
1975S	(2,845,450)			1.60
1976	4,674,292,426	0.02	0.10	
1976D	4,221,592,455	0.02	0.10	
1976S	(4,149,730)			1.25
1977	4,469,930,000	0.02	0.10	
1977D	4,194,062,300	0.02	0.10	
1977S	(3,251,152)			1.00
1978	5,558,605,000	0.02	0.10	
1978D	4,280,233,400	0.02	0.10	
1978S	(3,127,781)			1.00
1979	6,018,515,000	0.02	0.10	
1979D	4,139,357,254	0.02	0.10	
1979S, Type 1	(3,677,175)			1.75
1979S, Type 2	*			2.00
1980	7,414,705,000	0.02	0.10	
1980D	5,140,098,660	0.02	0.10	
1980S	(3,554,806)			1.00
1981	7,491,750,000	0.02	0.10	
1981D	5,373,235,677	0.02	0.10	
1981S, Type 1	(4,063,083)			1.50
1981S, Type 2	*			14.00

* Included in number above. **a.** Included in circulation-strike mintage for 1970-S, Large Date (Low 7). **b.** Included in Proof mintage for 1970-S, Large Date (Low 7).

Large Date

Small Date

	Mintage	MS-63	MS-65	PF-63
1982, Lg Dt.	.10,712,525,000	$0.02	$0.10	
1982, Sm Dt	.............*	0.03	0.12	

* Included in number above.

	Mintage	MS-63	MS-65	PF-63
1982D, Lg Dt.	.6,012,979,368	$0.02	$0.10	
1982S, Sm Dt	.. (3,857,479)			$1.60

Copper-Plated Zinc (1982–2008)

Close AM

Wide AM

*1995, Doubled Die showing strong
doubling on word LIBERTY.*

	Mintage	MS-63	MS-65	PF-63
1982, Lg Dt	.............*	$0.02	$0.25	
1982, Sm Dt	.............*	0.02	0.30	
1982D, Lg Dt	.............*	0.05	0.20	
1982D, Sm Dt	...........*	0.01	0.10	
1983	7,752,355,000	0.01	0.10	
1983D	6,467,199,428	0.01	0.10	
1983S	.... (3,279,126)	0.01	0.05	$1.10
1984	8,151,079,000	0.01	0.05	
1984, Dbl Ear	..........**	50.00	100.00	
1984D	5,569,238,906	0.01	0.10	
1984S	.... (3,065,110)			1.10
1985	5,648,489,887	0.01	0.05	
1985D	5,287,339,926	0.01	0.05	
1985S	.... (3,362,821)			1.25
1986	4,491,395,493	0.01	0.06	
1986D	4,442,866,698	0.01	0.05	
1986S	.... (3,010,497)			2.00
1987	4,682,466,931	0.01	0.05	
1987D	4,879,389,514	0.01	0.05	
1987S	.... (4,227,728)			1.10
1988	6,092,810,000	0.01	0.05	
1988D	5,253,740,443	0.01	0.05	
1988S	.... (3,262,948)			2.00
1989	7,261,535,000	0.01	0.05	
1989D	5,345,467,111	0.01	0.05	
1989S	.... (3,220,194)			2.00
1990	6,851,765,000	0.01	0.05	
1990D	4,922,894,533	0.01	0.05	
1990S	.... (3,299,559)			2.00
1990, Pf, No S	..........**			—
1991	5,165,940,000	0.01	0.05	
1991D	4,158,446,076	$0.01	$0.05	
1991S	.... (2,867,787)			$6.75
1992	4,648,905,000	0.01	0.05	
1992, Close AM (a)	......**	—	—	
1992D	4,448,673,300	0.01	0.05	
1992D, Close AM (a)	.....**	—	—	
1992S	.... (4,176,560)			1.10
1993	5,684,705,000	0.01	0.05	
1993D	6,426,650,571	0.01	0.05	
1993S	.... (3,394,792)			3.00
1994	6,500,850,000	0.01	0.05	
1994D	7,131,765,000	0.01	0.05	
1994S	.... (3,269,923)			3.00
1995	6,411,440,000	0.01	0.05	
1995, DblDie Obv	..........**	5.00	20.00	
1995D	7,128,560,000	0.01	0.05	
1995S	.... (2,797,481)			3.00
1996	6,612,465,000	0.01	0.05	
1996D	6,510,795,000	0.01	0.05	
1996S	.... (2,525,265)			1.25
1997	4,622,800,000	0.01	0.05	
1997D	4,576,555,000	0.01	0.05	
1997S	.... (2,796,678)			4.00
1998	5,032,155,000	0.01	0.05	
1998, Wide AM (b)	........**	2.00	10.00	
1998D	5,225,353,500	0.01	0.05	
1998S	.... (2,086,507)			3.00
1998S, Close AM (a)	.....**			150.00
1999	5,237,600,000	0.01	0.05	
1999, Wide AM (b)	........**			—
1999D	6,360,065,000	0.01	0.05	

* Included in previous section's mintages. ** Included in number above. **a.** The circulation-strike hub adopted in 1993, with AM almost touching, was accidentally used on these cents. **b.** Varieties were made using Proof dies that have a wide space between AM in AMERICA. The letters nearly touch on other Uncirculated cents.

Chart continued on next page.

	Mintage	MS-63	MS-65	PF-63
1999S . . . . (3,347,966)				$2.00
1999S, Close AM (a) . . . . .**				30.00
2000 5,503,200,000	$0.01	$0.05		
2000, Wide AM (b). . . . . . .**	2.00	5.00		
2000D 8,774,220,000	0.01	0.05		
2000S . . . . (4,047,993)				1.20
2001 4,959,600,000	0.01	0.05		
2001D 5,374,990,000	0.01	0.05		
2001S . . . . (3,184,606)				1.20
2002 3,260,800,000	0.01	0.05		
2002D 4,028,055,000	0.01	0.05		
2002S . . . . (3,211,995)				1.20
2003 3,300,000,000	0.01	0.05		
2003D 3,548,000,000	0.01	0.05		
2003S . . . . (3,298,439)				1.20

	Mintage	MS-63	MS-65	PF-63
2004 3,379,600,000	$0.01	$0.05	
2004D 3,456,400,000	0.01	0.05	
2004S . . . . (2,965,422)			$1.20
2005 3,935,600,000	0.01	0.05	
2005D 3,764,450,500	0.01	0.05	
2005S . . . . (3,344,679)			1.20
2006 4,290,000,000	0.01	0.05	
2006D 3,944,000,000	0.01	0.05	
2006S . . . . (3,054,436)			1.20
2007 3,762,400,000	0.01	0.05	
2007D 3,638,800,000	0.01	0.05	
2007S . . . . (2,577,166)			1.20
2008 2,558,800,000	0.01	0.05	
2008D 2,849,600,000	0.01	0.05	
2008S . . . . (2,169,561)			1.20

** Included in number above. **a.** The circulation-strike hub adopted in 1993, with AM almost touching, was accidentally used on these cents. **b.** Varieties were made using Proof dies that have a wide space between AM in AMERICA. The letters nearly touch on other Uncirculated cents.

LINCOLN, BICENTENNIAL (2009)

One-cent coins issued during 2009 are a unique tribute to President Abraham Lincoln, recognizing the bicentennial of his birth and the 100th anniversary of the first issuance of the Lincoln cent. These coins use four different design themes on the reverse to represent the four major aspects of President Lincoln's life. The obverse of each of these coins carries the traditional portrait of Lincoln that has been in use since 1909.

The special reverse designs, released as quarterly issues throughout 2009, are described as: Birth and Early Childhood in Kentucky (designer, Richard Masters; sculptor, Jim Licaretz); Formative Years in Indiana (designer and sculptor, Charles Vickers); Professional Life in Illinois (designer, Joel Iskowitz; sculptor, Don Everhart); and Presidency in Washington (designer, Susan Gamble; sculptor, Joseph Menna). Those issued for commercial circulation are made of the exact same copper-plated composition used since 1982. Special versions included in collector sets are made of the same metallic composition as was used for the original 1909 cents (95% copper, 5% tin and zinc).

2009 Lincoln cent reverse designs

	Mintage	MS-63	MS-65	PF-65
2009, Birth and Early Childhood. 284,400,000	$0.05	$0.10	
2009, Birth and Early Childhood, copper, Satin finish. 784,614		4.00	
2009D, Birth and Early Childhood 350,400,000	0.05	0.10	
2009D, Birth and Early Childhood, copper, Satin finish. 784,614		4.00	
2009S, Birth and Early Childhood . . . . (2,995,615)			$2
2009, Formative Years. 376,000,000	0.05	0.10	
2009, Formative Years, copper, Satin finish 784,614		4.00	
2009D, Formative Years. 363,600,000	0.05	0.10	

	Mintage	MS-63	MS-65	PF-65
2009D, Formative Years, copper, Satin finish	784,614		$4.00	
2009S, Formative Years	(2,995,615)			$2
2009, Professional Life	316,000,000	$0.05	0.10	
2009, Professional Life, copper, Satin finish	784,614		4.00	
2009D, Professional Life	336,000,000	0.05	0.10	
2009D, Professional Life, copper, Satin finish	784,614		4.00	
2009S, Professional Life	(2,995,615)			2
2009, Presidency	129,600,000	0.05	0.10	
2009, Presidency, copper, Satin finish	784,614		4.00	
2009D, Presidency	198,000,000	0.05	0.10	
2009D, Presidency, copper, Satin finish	784,614		4.00	
2009S, Presidency	(2,995,615)			2

LINCOLN, SHIELD REVERSE (2010 TO DATE)

Since the conclusion of the 2009 Bicentennial One-Cent Program, one-cent coins feature a reverse that has "an image emblematic of President Lincoln's preservation of the United States of America as a single and united country."

	Mintage	MS-65	PF-63		Mintage	MS-65	PF-63
2010	1,963,630,000	$0.01		2015	4,691,300,000	$0.01	
2010D	2,047,200,000	0.01		2015D	4,674,000,000	0.01	
2010S	(1,689,216)		$2	2015S	(1,050,164)		$2
2011	2,402,400,000	0.01		2016	4,698,000,000	0.01	
2011D	2,536,140,000	0.01		2016D	4,420,400,000	0.01	
2011S	(1,673,010)		2	2016S	(1,011,624)		2
2012	3,132,000,000	0.01		2017P	4,361,220,000	0.01	
2012D	2,883,200,000	0.01		2017D	4,272,800,000	0.01	
2012S	(1,239,148)		2	2017S	(979,477)		2
2013	3,750,400,000	0.01		2018P	4,066,800,000	0.01	
2013D	3,319,600,000	0.01		2018D	3,736,400,000	0.01	
2013S	(1,274,505)		2	2018S	(844,220)		2
2014	3,990,800,000	0.01		2019P (a)		0.01	
2014D	4,155,600,000	0.01		2019D (a)		0.01	
2014S	(1,190,369)		2	2019S (a)			2

a. In 2019, the Mint also issued three one-cent coins from the West Point Mint, adding them as premiums to annual U.S. Mint products: one Proof, included with the 2019 Proof Set; one Reverse Proof, included with the 2019 Silver Proof Set; and one Burnished coin, included with the 2019 Uncirculated Set.

TWO-CENT PIECE (1864–1873)

The Act of April 22, 1864, which changed the copper-nickel cent to a lighter-weight bronze composition, included a provision for a new coin, the two-cent piece. Its weight was specified as 96 grains, and its bronze alloy the same as for the cent. The two-cent piece was the nation's first circulating coin to bear the motto IN GOD WE TRUST.

There are two varieties for 1864, the first year of issue: the scarcer Small Motto, and the Large Motto. The differences are illustrated in the close-ups below. On the Small Motto variety, the stem to the cluster of leaves below TRUST is plainly visible, the D in GOD is wide, the first T in TRUST is close to the ribbon crease, and the U in TRUST is squat. On the Large Motto variety there is no stem, the D is narrow, the first T is farther from the crease, and the U is tall and narrow.

1864, Small Motto

1864, Large Motto

G-4 Good: At least part of IN GOD visible.
VG-8 Very Good: WE weakly visible.
F-12 Fine: Complete motto visible. The word WE weak.
VF-20 Very Fine: WE is clear, but not strong.
EF-40 Extremely Fine: The word WE bold.
AU-50 About Uncirculated: Traces of wear visible on leaf tips, arrow points, and the word WE.
MS-60 Uncirculated: No trace of wear. Light blemishes.
MS-63 Choice Uncirculated: Some distracting contact marks or blemishes in prime focal areas. Some impairment of luster possible.
PF-63 Choice Proof: Reflective surfaces with only a few blemishes in secondary focal places. No major flaws.

Dealers often pay more than the prices shown for brilliant red choice Uncirculated and Proof coins, and less for cleaned or discolored pieces.

	Mintage	G-4	VG-8	F-12	VF-20	EF-40	AU-50	MS-60	MS-63	PF-63
1864, Small Motto . . . . *		$150	$185	$250	$375	$500	$750	$1,000	$1,250	$17,500
1864, Large Motto *(100+)* . .	19,822,500	10	12	15	20	30	45	70	115	500
1865 . . . . *(500+)* . .	13,640,000	10	12	15	20	30	45	70	115	375
1866 . . . . *(725+)* . .	3,177,000	10	12	15	20	30	45	70	115	375
1867 . . . . *(625+)* . .	2,938,750	10	12	15	20	30	45	70	115	375
1868 . . . . *(600+)* . .	2,803,750	10	12	15	25	35	50	75	125	375
1869 . . . . *(600+)* . .	1,546,500	15	20	25	30	45	75	100	125	375
1870 . . . . *(1,000+)*	861,250	17	25	30	35	50	85	125	200	375
1871 . . . . *(960+)*	721,250	20	30	35	40	75	100	175	250	450
1872 . . . . *(950+)*	65,000	250	300	400	500	650	1,000	1,500	2,250	600
1873 . . . . *(600)*										2,250

* Included in number below.

SILVER THREE-CENT PIECES (TRIMES) (1851–1873)

This smallest of United States silver coins was authorized by Congress March 3, 1851. The first three-cent silver pieces had no lines bordering the six-pointed star. From 1854 through 1858 there were two lines, while issues of the last 15 years show only one line. Issues from 1854 through 1873 have an olive sprig over the III and a bundle of three arrows beneath.

G-4 Good: Star worn smooth. Legend and date readable.
VG-8 Very Good: Outline of shield defined. Legend and date clear.
F-12 Fine: Only star points worn smooth.
VF-20 Very Fine: Only partial wear on star ridges.
EF-40 Extremely Fine: Ridges on star points visible.
AU-50 About Uncirculated: Trace of wear visible at each star point. Center of shield possibly weak.
MS-60 Uncirculated: No trace of wear. Light blemishes.
MS-63 Choice Uncirculated: Some distracting contact marks or blemishes in prime focal areas. Some impairment of luster possible.
PF-63 Choice Proof: Reflective surfaces with only a few blemishes in secondary focal places. No major flaws.

Mintmark location.

| No Outline Around Star (1851–1853) | Three Outlines to Star, Large Date (1854–1858) | Two Outlines to Star, Small Date (1859–1873) | 1862, 2 Over 1 |

Dealers usually pay higher prices for well-struck examples.

	Mintage	G-4	VG-8	F-12	VF-20	EF-40	AU-50	MS-60	MS-63	PF-63
1851	5,447,400	$20	$25	$30	$40	$45	$100	$125	$200	—
1851O	720,000	30	40	50	65	125	175	350	650	
1852	18,663,500	20	25	30	40	45	100	125	200	—
1853	11,400,000	20	25	30	40	45	100	125	200	
1854	671,000	30	35	40	50	75	125	175	450	$6,000
1855	139,000	30	35	40	60	100	150	450	1,100	3,250
1856	1,458,000	30	35	40	50	75	125	150	450	3,000
1857	1,042,000	30	35	40	50	75	125	150	450	2,200
1858 . . . . (210) . .	1,603,700	30	35	40	50	75	125	150	450	15,000
1859 . . . . (800)	364,200	30	35	40	50	65	100	125	200	550
1860 . . . . . .(1,000) 286,000		30	35	40	50	65	100	125	200	750
1861 . . . . . .(1,000) 497,000		30	35	40	50	65	100	125	200	550
1862, 2/1 . . . .*		30	35	40	50	70	125	110	250	
1862 . . . . (550) 343,000		30	35	40	50	65	100	125	200	550
1863 . . . . (460) 21,000					400	475	550	750	1,000	550
1864 . . . . (470) 12,000					375	450	525	700	950	550

	Mintage	VF-20	EF-40	AU-50	MS-60	MS-63	PF-63
1865 . . . .(500) 8,000		$425	$450	$500	$1,000	$1,750	$650
1866 . . . .(725) . . .22,000		425	450	450	550	750	650
1867 . . . .(625) 4,000		425	450	550	750	1,200	650
1868 . . . .(600) 3,500		1,000	1,200	1,500	2,500	4,000	650
1869 . . . .(600) 4,500		425	450	600	800	1,500	650
1870 . . . . (1,000) 3,000		425	450	550	650	750	650
1871 . . . .(960) 3,400		425	450	550	650	850	650
1872 . . . .(950) 1,000		900	1,200	1,450	1,750	2,250	650
1873, Proof only . . . .(600)							1,200

* Included in number below.

NICKEL THREE-CENT PIECES (1865–1889)

Three-cent pieces struck in a nickel alloy were intended to replace the earlier silver three-cent coins, which were hoarded by the public during the Civil War. The Mint struck more than 11 million three-cent coins of the new composition (75% copper and 25% nickel) in 1865, their first year of issue, compared to only 8,000 silver pieces. The nickel coins were all made at the Philadelphia Mint. They have a plain (non-reeded) edge.

G-4 Good: Date and legends complete though worn. III smooth.
VG-8 Very Good: III half worn. Rims complete.
VF-20 Very Fine: Three-quarters of hair details visible.
EF-40 Extremely Fine: Slight, even wear.
AU-50 About Uncirculated: Slight wear on hair curls, above forehead, and on wreath and numeral III.
MS-60 Uncirculated: No trace of wear. Light blemishes.
MS-63 Choice Uncirculated: Some distracting contact marks or blemishes in prime focal areas. Some impairment of luster possible.
PF-63 Choice Proof: Reflective surfaces with only a few blemishes in secondary focal places. No major flaws.

Dealers often pay more than the prices shown for brilliant choice Unc. and Proof coins, and less for spotted, cleaned, or discolored pieces.

	Mintage	G-4	VG-8	F-12	VF-20	EF-40	AU-50	MS-60	MS-63	PF-63
1865 . . . . *(500+)* . .	11,382,000	$10	$12	$14	$16	$25	$35	$75	$100	$650
1866 . . . . *(725+)* . .	4,801,000	10	12	14	16	25	35	75	100	225
1867 . . . . *(625+)* . .	3,915,000	10	12	14	16	25	35	75	100	225
1868 . . . . *(600+)* . .	3,252,000	10	12	14	16	25	35	85	100	225
1869 . . . . *(600+)* . .	1,604,000	10	12	14	16	25	35	85	100	225
1870 . . . . . *(1,000+)* . .	1,335,000	10	12	14	16	25	35	85	145	225
1871 . . . . *(960+)* . . .	604,000	10	12	14	16	25	35	85	165	225
1872 . . . . *(950+)* . . .	862,000	10	12	14	16	25	35	85	175	225
1873 . . . . . *(1,100+)* . . .	390,000	10	12	14	16	25	35	85	165	225
1874 . . . . *(700+)* . . .	790,000	10	12	14	16	25	35	85	150	225
1875 . . . . *(700+)* . . .	228,000	10	12	14	16	25	35	100	150	225
1876 . . . . . *(1,150+)* . . .	162,000	10	12	14	16	25	35	110	175	250
1877, Pf only . . (900)					800	1,000				1,500
1878, Pf only (2,350)					425	550				650
1879 . . . . . . (3,200)	38,000	20	25	30	40	60	75	150	250	250
1880 . . . . . . (3,955)	21,000	40	45	50	60	70	85	175	250	250
1881 . . . . . . (3,575) . .	1,077,000	10	12	14	16	25	35	65	125	225
1882 . . . . . . (3,100)	22,200	35	45	50	75	85	125	225	400	225
1883 . . . . . . (6,609)	4,000	75	85	100	135	175	250	750	1,500	235
1884 . . . . . . (3,942)	1,700	450	650	750	1000	1450	2200	3,000	4,500	300
1885 . . . . . . (3,790)	1,000	550	750	850	1,150	1,500	2,000	2,500	4,000	275
1886, Pf only (4,290)					175	200				250
1887 . . . . . . (2,960)	5,001	120	140	150	160	175	250	300	350	250
1887, 7/6 . . . . *					180	225				350
1888 . . . . . . (4,582)	36,501	20	23	27	35	45	60	175	250	225
1889 . . . . . . (3,436)	18,125	35	45	60	75	100	125	175	275	225

* Included in number above.

SHIELD (1866–1883)

The Shield type nickel was made possible by the Act of May 16, 1866. Its weight was set at 77-16/100 grains with the same composition as the nickel three-cent piece.

G-4 Good: All letters in motto readable.
VG-8 Very Good: Motto clear and stands out. Rims slightly worn but even. Part of shield lines visible.
F-12 Fine: Half of each olive leaf worn smooth.
EF-40 Extremely Fine: Slight wear to leaf tips and cross over shield.
AU-50 About Uncirculated: Traces of light wear on only the high design points. Half of mint luster present.
MS-60 Uncirculated: No trace of wear. Light blemishes.
MS-63 Choice Uncirculated: Some distracting blemishes in prime focal areas. Impaired luster possible.
PF-63 Choice Proof: Reflective surfaces. Only a few blemishes in secondary focal areas. No major flaws.

With Rays (1866–1867)

Without Rays (1867–1883)

1873, Close 3	1873, Open 3	Typical Example of 1883, 3 Over 2

Other varieties exist.

Dealers often pay more than the prices shown for brilliant choice Unc. and Proof coins, and less for spotted, cleaned, or discolored pieces.

	Mintage	G-4	VG-8	F-12	VF-20	EF-40	AU-50	MS-60	MS-63	PF-63
1866, Rays . . . . . . *(600+)* . .14,742,500		$20	$25	$30	$50	$85	$135	$225	$350	$1,200
1867, Rays . . . . *(25+)* . . .2,019,000		25	30	35	60	90	150	250	325	20,000
1867, Without Rays . . . . *(600+)* . .28,890,500		20	22	25	30	40	50	100	150	275
1868 . . . . *(600+)* . .28,817,000		20	22	25	30	40	50	100	150	250
1869 . . . . *(600+)* . .16,395,000		20	22	25	30	40	50	100	150	250
1870 . . . .*(1,000+)* . . .4,806,000		20	22	25	30	40	50	100	150	250
1871 . . . . *(960+)* 561,000		45	55	85	125	185	245	375	600	250
1872 . . . . *(950+)* . .6,036,000		20	22	25	30	55	100	175	200	250
1873, Close 3 . . .*(1,100+)* 436,050		20	22	25	30	40	60	135	250	250
1873, Open 3 4,113,950		20	30	40	65	100	150	275	550	
1874 . . . . *(700+)* . . .3,538,000		20	22	25	30	50	100	175	250	250
1875 . . . . *(700+)* . . .2,097,000		25	30	35	40	80	115	185	265	250
1876 . . . .*(1,150+)* . . .2,530,000		20	25	30	45	55	85	175	250	250
1877, Pf only . . . . . *(900)*.			1,250	1,500	1,650					2,250
1878, Pf only . . . *(2,350)*.			600	750	850					1,000
1879 . . . . *(3,200)*. 25,900		250	350	450	500	600	750	1,250	1,650	300
1880 . . . . *(3,955)*. 16,000		1,250	1,500	1,650	2,000	3,500	4,500	10,000	13,500	275
1881 . . . . *(3,575)*. 68,800		150	200	275	325	400	550	850	1,000	275
1882 . . . . *(3,100)*. . . .11,472,900		15	20	22	25	35	55	100	150	250
1883 . . . . *(5,419)*. 1,451,500		15	20	22	25	35	55	100	150	250
1883, 3 Over 2 . . . .*		125	175	300	450	600	750	1,250	1,750	

* Included in number above.

LIBERTY HEAD (1883–1913)

In 1883 the design was changed to the "Liberty head." This type first appeared without the word CENTS on the coin, merely a large letter V. These "CENTS-less" coins were goldplated by fraudsters and passed as $5 pieces. Later in that year the word CENTS was added.

G-4 Good: No details in head. LIBERTY obliterated.
VG-8 Very Good: Some letters in LIBERTY legible.
F-12 Fine: All letters in LIBERTY legible.
VF-20 Very Fine: LIBERTY bold, including letter L.
EF-40 Extremely Fine: LIBERTY sharp. Corn grains at bottom of wreath visible on reverse.
AU-50 About Uncirculated: Traces of light wear on only high points of design. Half of mint luster present.
MS-60 Uncirculated: No trace of wear. Contact marks possible. Surface may be spotted, or luster faded.
MS-63 Choice Uncirculated: No trace of wear. Light blemishes.
PF-63 Choice Proof: Reflective surfaces. Only a few blemishes in secondary focal areas. No major flaws.

Variety 1, Without CENTS (1883 Only)   Variety 2, With CENTS (1883–1913)   Mintmark Location

Dealers often pay more than the prices shown for brilliant choice Unc. and Proof coins, and less for spotted, cleaned, or discolored pieces.

	Mintage	G-4	VG-8	F-12	VF-20	EF-40	AU-50	MS-60	MS-63	PF-63
1883, Without CENTS..(5,219)...5,474,300		$2.75	$3.25	$3.75	$6	$6.50	$9	$18	$26	$200
1883, CENTS (6,783)..16,026,200		7.00	15.00	20.00	35	50.00	75	100	135	150
1884.......(3,942)..11,270,000		8.00	15.00	20.00	35	50.00	75	115	165	150
1885.......(3,790)...1,472,700		200.00	350.00	450.00	700	800.00	1,150	1,350	2,250	800
1886.......(4,290)...3,326,000		140.00	165.00	225.00	325	425.00	500	850	1,350	400
1887.......(2,960)..15,260,692		5.00	10.00	15.00	25	50.00	65	85	110	150
1888.......(4,582)..10,167,901		15.00	20.00	30.00	60	85.00	125	175	225	150
1889.......(3,336)..15,878,025		8.00	10.00	15.00	30	45.00	65	100	165	150
1890.......(2,740)..16,256,532		4.00	8.00	12.00	20	35.00	65	100	145	150
1891.......(2,350)..16,832,000		3.00	4.00	12.00	20	35.00	65	100	145	150
1892.......(2,745)..11,696,897		3.00	4.00	10.00	15	25.00	30	100	125	150
1893.......(2,195)..13,368,000		3.00	4.00	10.00	15	30.00	35	100	135	150
1894.......(2,632)...5,410,500		10.00	20.00	55.00	100	135.00	200	225	225	165
1895.......(2,062)...9,977,822		3.00	2.50	7.00	10	25.00	30	100	130	150
1896.......(1,862)...8,841,058		2.00	5.00	15.00	20	35.00	50	130	165	150
1897.......(1,938)..20,426,797		2.00	5.00	9.00	12	22.00	30	60	125	150
1898.......(1,795)..12,530,292		2.00	5.00	9.00	12	22.00	30	95	125	150
1899.......(2,031)..26,027,000		1.00	1.25	2.50	6	15.00	30	65	100	150
1900.......(2,262)..27,253,733		1.00	1.25	2.50	6	15.00	30	55	100	150
1901.......(1,985)..26,478,228		1.00	1.25	2.50	6	15.00	30	55	100	150
1902.......(2,018)..31,480,579		1.00	1.25	2.50	6	15.00	30	55	100	150
1903.......(1,790)..28,004,935		1.00	1.25	2.50	6	15.00	30	55	100	150
1904.......(1,817)..21,403,167		1.00	1.25	2.50	6	15.00	30	55	100	150
1905.......(2,152)..29,825,124		1.00	1.25	2.50	6	15.00	30	55	100	150
1906.......(1,725)..38,612,000		1.00	1.25	2.50	6	15.00	30	55	100	150
1907.......(1,475)..39,213,325		1.00	1.25	2.50	6	15.00	30	55	100	150
1908.......(1,620)..22,684,557		1.00	1.25	2.50	6	15.00	30	55	100	150

	Mintage	G-4	VG-8	F-12	VF-20	EF-40	AU-50	MS-60	MS-63	PF-63
1909 .... (4,763)...	11,585,763	$1.00	$1.50	$2.50	$8	$18	$35	$55	$95	$150
1910 .... (2,405)...	30,166,948	1.00	1.25	2.25	5	15	30	45	80	150
1911 .... (1,733)...	39,557,639	1.00	1.25	2.25	5	15	30	45	80	150
1912 .... (2,145)...	26,234,569	1.00	1.25	2.25	5	15	30	45	80	150
1912D............	8,474,000	1.50	2.00	6.00	20	50	100	185	225	
1912S..............	238,000	65.00	100.00	120.00	250	475	850	1,100	1,350	
1913 Liberty Head *(5 known)*....									2,750,000	

INDIAN HEAD OR BUFFALO (1913–1938)

The Buffalo nickel was designed by James E. Fraser, whose initial F is below the date. He modeled the bison after Black Diamond in the New York Central Park Zoo.

G-4 Good: Legends and date readable. Buffalo's horn does not show.
VG-8 Very Good: Horn worn nearly flat.
F-12 Fine: Horn and tail smooth but partially visible. Obverse rim intact.
VF-20 Very Fine: Much of horn visible. Indian's cheekbone worn.
EF-40 Extremely Fine: Horn lightly worn. Slight wear on Indian's hair ribbon.
AU-50 About Uncirculated: Traces of light wear on high points of design. Half of mint luster present.
MS-60 Uncirculated: No trace of wear. May have several blemishes.
MS-63 Choice Uncirculated: No trace of wear. Light blemishes.
Matte PF-63 Choice Proof: Crisp surfaces. Only a few blemishes in secondary focal areas. No major flaws.

Variety 1 – FIVE CENTS on Raised Ground (1913)

Dealers often pay more than the prices shown for brilliant choice Unc. coins, and less for spotted, cleaned, weakly struck, or discolored pieces.

	Mintage	G-4	VG-8	F-12	VF-20	EF-40	AU-50	MS-60	MS-63	MATTE PF-63
1913, Variety 1 .. (1,520) ..	30,992,000	$5	$8	$10	$12	$15	$18	$22	$35	$1,000
1913D, Variety 1	5,337,000	8	10	12	15	20	25	35	45	
1913S, Variety 1	2,105,000	20	25	30	35	45	60	75	115	

Variety 2 – FIVE CENTS in Recess (1913–1938)

Mintmark Below FIVE CENTS   **1916, Doubled-Die Obverse**   **1918-D, 8 Over 7**

	Mintage	G-4	VG-8	F-12	VF-20	EF-40	AU-50	MS-60	MS-63	MATTE PF-63
1913, Variety 2	29,857,186	$5	$7	$8	$10	$12	$15	$22	$32	
................(1,514)										$750
1913D, Variety 2	4,156,000	65	85	100	115	135	165	200	240	
1913S, Variety 2	1,209,000	150	200	225	275	300	450	550	800	
1914.............	20,664,463	10	11	12	14	16	22	35	50	
................(1,275)										750

Chart continued on next page.

Dealers often pay more than the prices shown for brilliant choice Unc. coins, and less for spotted, cleaned, weakly struck, or discolored pieces.

	Mintage	G-4	VG-8	F-12	VF-20	EF-40	AU-50	MS-60	MS-63	MATTE PF-63
1914D	3,912,000	$55.00	$65.00	$85.00	$110.00	$150	$200	$285	$350	
1914S	3,470,000	15.00	20.00	25.00	35.00	50	85	125	250	
1915	20,986,220	2.50	3.00	4.00	7.00	12	30	45	50	
	(1,050)									$750
1915D	7,569,000	10.00	15.00	25.00	35.00	75	95	150	250	
1915S	1,505,000	20.00	35.00	40.00	80.00	200	300	425	650	
1916	63,497,466	2.00	2.50	3.00	3.50	5	10	28	35	
	(600)									850
1916, DblDie Obv	* 3,000.00	4,000.00	6,000.00	8,000.00	12,500	20,000	45,000	100,000	
1916D	13,333,000	7.00	10.00	11.00	25.00	45	60	100	150	
1916S	11,860,000	5.00	8.00	12.00	25.00	45	65	135	185	
1917	51,424,019	2.00	2.50	3.00	4.00	7	16	30	60	
1917D	9,910,000	10.00	15.00	25.00	45.00	85	150	250	400	
1917S	4,193,000	10.00	20.00	40.00	55.00	115	165	400	800	
1918	32,086,314	1.50	2.00	2.50	6.00	16	22	85	165	

* Included in number above.

	Mintage	G-4	VG-8	F-12	VF-20	EF-40	AU-50	MS-60	MS-63
1918D, 8 Over 7	** $500.00	$750.00	$1,600.00	$3,000.00	$5,500.00	$8,500	$25,000	$40,000
1918D	8,362,000	12.00	20.00	30.00	70.00	150.00	200	300	750
1918S	4,882,000	8.00	15.00	25.00	55.00	115.00	250	450	1,500
1919	60,868,000	0.50	0.55	0.80	2.00	7.00	15	35	60
1919D (a)	8,006,000	10.00	15.00	45.00	70.00	140.00	225	450	1,000
1919S (a)	7,521,000	4.00	10.00	25.00	60.00	145.00	225	400	1,100
1920	63,093,000	0.45	0.60	1.25	2.50	6.00	15	35	70
1920D (a)	9,418,000	4.00	10.00	20.00	65.00	175.00	250	375	1,000
1920S	9,689,000	1.50	5.00	10.00	45.00	115.00	150	375	1,050
1921	10,663,000	0.80	2.00	3.00	10.00	25.00	35	70	140
1921S	1,557,000	40.00	60.00	90.00	200.00	500.00	750	1,200	1,850
1923	35,715,000	0.45	0.60	0.80	4.00	7.50	18	35	80
1923S (a)	6,142,000	3.00	5.00	10.00	55.00	150.00	200	350	550
1924	21,620,000	0.40	0.60	0.80	4.00	9.00	25	40	80
1924D	5,258,000	3.50	5.00	15.00	50.00	120.00	195	275	550
1924S	1,437,000	10.00	25.00	55.00	200.00	600.00	1,200	1,500	3,000
1925	35,565,100	0.75	1.25	2.00	4.00	8.00	16	25	47
1925D (a)	4,450,000	5.00	12.00	25.00	45.00	100.00	200	300	500
1925S	6,256,000	2.00	5.00	10.00	40.00	115.00	200	350	1,350
1926	44,693,000	0.35	0.45	0.60	3.00	5.00	12	22	35
1926D (a)	5,638,000	3.00	10.00	15.00	55.00	100.00	200	250	400
1926S	970,000	15.00	25.00	50.00	145.00	450.00	1,650	2,750	6,000
1927	37,981,000	0.50	0.55	0.60	1.50	6.00	10	25	40
1927D	5,730,000	0.85	2.00	2.50	15.00	40.00	55	85	160
1927S	3,430,000	0.60	0.90	1.75	18.00	45.00	115	500	1,650
1928	23,411,000	0.40	0.45	0.60	2.00	5.00	10	22	30
1928D	6,436,000	0.45	0.85	1.75	6.00	20.00	25	30	50
1928S	6,936,000	0.60	0.75	1.25	5.00	15.00	55	185	350
1929	36,446,000	0.35	0.40	0.60	2.00	5.00	10	16	35
1929D	8,370,000	0.45	0.60	0.80	3.00	15.00	20	35	65
1929S	7,754,000	0.40	0.60	0.75	0.90	5.50	12	25	45

** Included in number below. **a.** Dealers pay considerably more for Uncirculated pieces with full, sharp details.

1937-D, "3-Legged" Variety   **1938-D, D Over S**

Dealers often pay more than the prices shown for brilliant choice Unc. coins, and less for spotted, cleaned, weakly struck, or discolored pieces.

	Mintage	G-4	VG-8	F-12	VF-20	EF-40	AU-50	MS-60	MS-63	PF-63
1930	22,849,000	$0.40	$0.50	$0.70	$0.80	$5.00	$11.00	$16	$35	
1930S	5,435,000	0.40	0.50	0.70	0.80	6.00	15.00	25	60	
1931S	1,200,000	7.00	8.00	8.80	9.25	15.00	25.00	30	45	
1934	20,213,003	0.35	0.45	0.55	0.75	3.00	9.00	16	30	
1934D	7,480,000	0.50	0.75	1.25	3.00	9.00	21.00	35	55	
1935	58,264,000	0.35	0.45	0.55	0.75	1.25	4.25	10	25	
1935D	12,092,000	0.35	0.50	1.00	3.00	6.00	20.00	30	40	
1935S	10,300,000	0.35	0.45	0.55	0.75	2.00	7.50	15	36	
1936 . . . . (4,420) . .	118,997,000	0.35	0.45	0.55	0.75	1.25	4.00	10	25	$600
1936D	24,814,000	0.45	0.60	0.75	0.95	1.75	4.50	15	20	
1936S	14,930,000	0.35	0.45	0.55	0.75	1.25	4.50	15	15	
1937 . . . . (5,769) . . .	79,480,000	0.35	0.45	0.55	0.75	1.25	3.00	15	20	625
1937D	17,826,000	0.35	0.45	0.55	0.75	1.25	4.00	10	15	
1937D, 3-Legged . . . .*	300.00	325.00	350.00	400.00	450.00	550.00	1,250	2,500	
1937S	5,635,000	0.35	0.45	0.55	0.75	1.25	4.00	11	20	
1938D	7,020,000	1.00	1.10	1.50	1.75	2.00	4.00	11	15	
1938D, D Over S . . . .*	1.50	2.00	4.00	5.00	8.00	12.00	25	36	

* Included in number above.

JEFFERSON (1938–2003)

This nickel was originally designed by Felix Schlag. He won an award of $1,000 in a competition with some 390 artists. It established the definite public approval of portrait and pictorial rather than symbolic devices on our coinage. On October 8, 1942, the wartime five-cent piece composed of copper (56%), silver (35%), and manganese (9%) was introduced to eliminate nickel, a critical war material. A larger mintmark was placed above the dome. The letter P (Philadelphia) was used for the first time, indicating the change of alloy. The designer's initials FS were added below the bust starting in 1966. The mintmark position was moved to the obverse starting in 1968.

VG-8 Very Good: Second porch pillar from right nearly gone, other three still visible but weak.

F-12 Fine: Jefferson's cheekbone worn flat. Hair lines and eyebrow faint. Second pillar weak, especially at bottom.

VF-20 Very Fine: Second pillar plain and complete on both sides.

EF-40 Extremely Fine: Cheekbone, hair lines, eyebrow slightly worn but well defined. Base of triangle above pillars visible but weak.

MS-63 Select Uncirculated: No trace of wear. Slight blemishes.

MS-65 Choice Uncirculated: No trace of wear. Barely noticeable blemishes.

PF-65 Gem Proof: Brilliant surfaces. No noticeable blemishes or flaws. May have a few barely noticeable marks or hairlines.

Mintmark located at right of building.

Mintmark, starting in 1968.

See next page for chart.

Coin dealers usually pay more than the Mint State prices shown for Uncirculated Jefferson nickels with fully struck steps visible in Monticello.

	Mintage	VG-8	F-12	VF-20	EF-40	MS-63	MS-65	PF-65
1938 . . . . . (19,365). . . 19,496,000		$0.10	$0.12	$0.20	$0.25	$1.10	$6.00	$55
1938D 5,376,000		0.25	0.35	0.75	1.00	2.25	7.00	
1938S 4,105,000		0.40	0.60	0.85	1.50	2.75	8.00	
1939 . . . . . (12,535). . 120,615,000		0.08	0.10	0.12	0.25	1.00	2.00	55
1939D 3,514,000		1.20	1.60	3.00	5.00	30.00	45.00	
1939S 6,630,000		0.25	0.30	0.50	1.50	14.00	30.00	
1940 . . . . . (14,158). . 176,485,000		0.05	0.05	0.05	0.10	1.00	2.00	55
1940D 43,540,000		0.05	0.05	0.05	0.10	1.25	3.50	
1940S 39,690,000		0.05	0.05	0.05	0.10	1.25	3.50	
1941 . . . . . (18,720). . 203,265,000		0.05	0.05	0.05	0.10	0.50	2.00	45
1941D 53,432,000		0.05	0.05	0.05	0.10	1.25	3.00	
1941S 43,445,000		0.05	0.05	0.05	0.10	1.50	3.50	
1942 . . . . . (29,600). . . 49,789,000		0.05	0.05	0.05	0.10	1.25	4.00	45
1942D 13,938,000		0.10	0.15	0.25	1.00	16.00	23.00	

Wartime Silver Alloy (1942–1945)

Mintmark Location

1943-P, 3 Over 2

	Mintage	VG-8	F-12	VF-20	EF-40	MS-63	MS-65	PF-65
1942P . . . . (27,600). . . 57,873,000		$1	$1.10	$1.20	$1.40	$4	$8	$100
1942S 32,900,000		1	1.10	1.20	1.40	4	9	
1943P, 3 Over 2 . . . . *			15.00	20.00	38.00	130	320	
1943P 271,165,000		1	1.10	1.20	1.40	3	8	
1943D 15,294,000		1	1.10	1.20	1.40	5	8	
1943S 104,060,000		1	1.10	1.20	1.40	3	8	
1944P 119,150,000		1	1.10	1.20	1.40	5	9	
1944D 32,309,000		1	1.10	1.20	1.40	5	9	
1944S 21,640,000		1	1.10	1.20	1.40	4	8	
1945P 119,408,100		1	1.10	1.20	1.40	3	8	
1945D 37,158,000		1	1.10	1.20	1.40	3	8	
1945S 58,939,000		1	1.10	1.20	1.40	3	8	

* Included in number below.

Prewar Composition, Mintmark Style Resumed (1946–1965)

1954-S, S Over D   **1955-D, D Over S**

	Mintage	VF-20	EF-40	MS-63	MS-65	PF-65
1946 161,116,000		$0.05	$0.05	$0.60	$5	
1946D 45,292,200		0.05	0.05	0.60	4	
1946S 13,560,000		0.05	0.06	0.35	4	

NICKEL FIVE-CENT PIECES

	Mintage	VF-20	EF-40	MS-63	MS-65	PF-65
1947	95,000,000	$0.05	$0.05	$0.35	$4.00	
1947D	37,822,000	0.05	0.05	0.35	4.00	
1947S	24,720,000	0.05	0.06	0.35	5.00	
1948	89,348,000	0.05	0.05	0.35	3.00	
1948D	44,734,000	0.05	0.06	0.75	2.00	
1948S	11,300,000	0.05	0.06	0.50	2.00	
1949	60,652,000	0.05	0.10	2.00	5.00	
1949D	36,498,000	0.05	0.05	0.75	3.00	
1949D, D Over S	*	18.00	30.00	125.00	250.00	
1949S	9,716,000	0.05	0.10	0.50	3.00	
1950	(51,386) 9,796,000	0.05	0.10	0.50	2.50	$30.00
1950D	2,630,030	3.00	3.50	8.50	12.50	
1951	(57,500) 28,552,000	0.05	0.06	1.25	5.00	25.00
1951D	20,460,000	0.05	0.06	1.50	4.00	
1951S	7,776,000	0.05	0.10	1.50	4.00	
1952	(81,980) 63,988,000	0.05	0.05	0.35	3.00	18.00
1952D	30,638,000	0.05	0.05	2.00	5.00	
1952S	20,572,000	0.05	0.05	0.55	4.00	
1953	(128,800) 46,644,000	0.05	0.05	0.25	2.50	18.00
1953D	59,878,600	0.05	0.05	0.25	2.75	
1953S	19,210,900	0.05	0.05	0.30	3.00	
1954	(233,300) 47,684,050	0.05	0.05	0.50	4.00	9.00
1954D	117,183,060	0.05	0.05	0.40	10.00	
1954S	29,384,000	0.05	0.05	0.50	5.00	
1954S, S Over D	*	2.50	5.00	18.00	35.00	
1955	(378,200) 7,888,000	0.06	0.08	0.40	5.00	6.00
1955D	74,464,100	0.05	0.05	0.25	7.00	
1955D, D Over S **(a)**	*	3.00	5.00	30.00	100.00	
1956	(669,384) 35,216,000	0.05	0.05	0.25	7.00	1.00
1956D	67,222,940	0.05	0.05	0.25	7.00	
1957	(1,247,952) 38,408,000	0.05	0.05	0.25	5.00	1.00
1957D	136,828,900	0.05	0.05	0.25	5.00	
1958	(875,652) 17,088,000	0.05	0.05	0.20	4.00	1.50
1958D	168,249,120	0.05	0.05	0.15	4.00	
1959	(1,149,291) 27,248,000	0.05	0.05	0.15	3.00	0.85
1959D	160,738,240	0.05	0.05	0.15	2.50	
1960	(1,691,602) 55,416,000	0.05	0.05	0.15	2.50	0.85
1960D	192,582,180	0.05	0.05	0.15	3.00	
1961	(3,028,144) 73,640,100	0.05	0.05	0.15	4.00	0.85
1961D	229,342,760	0.05	0.05	0.15	4.00	
1962	(3,218,019) 97,384,000	0.05	0.05	0.15	3.00	0.85
1962D	280,195,720	0.05	0.05	0.15	7.00	
1963	(3,075,645) 175,776,000	0.05	0.05	0.15	3.00	0.85
1963D	276,829,460	0.05	0.05	0.15	8.00	
1964	(3,950,762) 1,024,672,000	0.05	0.05	0.15	2.50	0.85
1964D	1,787,297,160	0.05	0.05	0.15	1.00	
1965	136,131,380	0.05	0.05	0.15	1.00	

* Included in number above. **a.** Varieties exist. Values are for the variety illustrated on previous page.

1966 Through 2003

	Mintage	MS-63	MS-65	PF-65		Mintage	MS-63	MS-65	PF-65
1966	156,208,283	$0.10	$1		1968D	91,227,880	$0.10	$1	
1967	107,325,800	0.10	1		1968S	100,396,004	0.10	1	

Chart continued on next page.

	Mintage	MS-63	MS-65	PF-65
1968S, Proof	(3,041,506)			$0.75
1969D	202,807,500	$0.10	$1.00	
1969S	120,165,000	0.10	0.80	
	(2,934,631)			0.75
1970D	515,485,380	0.10	3.00	
1970S	238,832,004	0.10	2.00	
	(2,632,810)			0.75
1971	106,884,000	0.25	0.80	
1971D	316,144,800	0.10	0.80	
1971S	(3,220,733)			0.75

	Mintage	MS-63	MS-65	PF-65
1972	202,036,000	$0.10	$0.80	
1972D	351,694,600	0.10	0.80	
1972S	(3,260,996)			$1.00
1973	384,396,000	0.10	0.80	
1973D	261,405,000	0.10	0.80	
1973S	(2,760,339)			0.75
1974	601,752,000	0.10	0.80	
1974D	277,373,000	0.10	0.80	
1974S	(2,612,568)			1.00

	Mintage	MS-65	PF-65
1975	181,772,000	$0.75	
1975D	401,875,300	0.75	
1975S	(2,845,450)		$0.85
1976	367,124,000	0.75	
1976D	563,964,147	0.75	
1976S	(4,149,730)		0.85
1977	585,376,000	0.75	
1977D	297,313,422	0.75	
1977S	(3,251,152)		0.75
1978	391,308,000	0.75	
1978D	313,092,780	0.75	
1978S	(3,127,781)		0.75
1979	463,188,000	0.75	
1979D	325,867,672	1.00	
1979S, Type 1	(3,677,175)		0.75
1979S, Type 2	*		1.00
1980P	593,004,000	0.50	
1980D	502,323,448	0.50	
1980S	(3,554,806)		0.75
1981P	657,504,000	0.50	
1981D	364,801,843	0.50	
1981S, Type 1	(4,063,083)		1.00
1981S, Type 2	*		2.00
1982P	292,355,000	3.00	
1982D	373,726,544	2.00	
1982S	(3,857,479)		1.00
1983P	561,615,000	3.00	
1983D	536,726,276	1.50	
1983S	(3,279,126)		1.00
1984P	746,769,000	1.25	
1984D	517,675,146	0.75	
1984S	(3,065,110)		1.50
1985P	647,114,962	0.50	
1985D	459,747,446	0.50	
1985S	(3,362,821)		1.25
1986P	536,883,483	0.50	
1986D	361,819,140	0.50	
1986S	(3,010,497)		2.75
1987P	371,499,481	0.70	
1987D	410,590,604	0.75	

	Mintage	MS-65	PF-65
1987S	(4,227,728)		$1.00
1988P	771,360,000	$0.60	
1988D	663,771,652	0.60	
1988S	(3,262,948)		2.00
1989P	898,812,000	0.50	
1989D	570,842,474	0.50	
1989S	(3,220,194)		1.75
1990P	661,636,000	0.50	
1990D	663,938,503	0.50	
1990S	(3,299,559)		1.75
1991P	614,104,000	0.50	
1991D	436,496,678	0.50	
1991S	(2,867,787)		2.00
1992P	399,552,000	0.75	
1992D	450,565,113	0.50	
1992S	(4,176,560)		1.25
1993P	412,076,000	0.30	
1993D	406,084,135	0.30	
1993S	(3,394,792)		1.50
1994P	722,160,000	0.50	
1994D	715,762,110	0.30	
1994S	(3,269,923)		1.25
1995P	774,156,000	0.30	
1995D	888,112,000	0.30	
1995S	(2,797,481)		2.00
1996P	829,332,000	0.30	
1996D	817,736,000	0.30	
1996S	(2,525,265)		1.00
1997P	470,972,000	0.30	
1997D	466,640,000	0.50	
1997S	(2,796,678)		1.75
1998P	688,272,000	0.30	
1998D	635,360,000	0.30	
1998S	(2,086,507)		1.75
1999P	1,212,000,000	0.30	
1999D	1,066,720,000	0.30	
1999S	(3,347,966)		2.00
2000P	846,240,000	0.30	
2000D	1,509,520,000	0.30	
2000S	(4,047,993)		1.75

* Included in number above.

	Mintage	MS-65	PF-65
2001P	675,704,000	$0.20	
2001D	627,680,000	0.20	
2001S	(3,184,606)		$1.75
2002P	539,280,000	0.20	
2002D	691,200,000	0.20	

	Mintage	MS-65	PF-65
2002S	(3,211,995)		$1.50
2003P	441,840,000	$0.20	
2003D	383,040,000	0.20	
2003S	(3,298,439)		1.50

WESTWARD JOURNEY (2004–2005)

The Westward Journey Nickel Series™ commemorates the bicentennial of the Louisiana Purchase and the journey of Meriwether Lewis and William Clark to explore that vast territory. **2004**—*Obverse:* traditional portrait of Jefferson. *Reverses:* Louisiana Purchase / Peace Medal reverse, by Mint sculptor Norman E. Nemeth. Keelboat reverse, by Mint sculptor Al Maletsky. **2005**—*Obverse:* new portrait of Jefferson, designed by Joe Fitzgerald after a 1789 marble bust by Jean-Antoine Houdon, and rendered by Mint sculptor Don Everhart. *Reverses:* American Bison reverse, designed by Jamie Franki and produced by Norman E. Nemeth. "Ocean in View" reverse, designed by Joe Fitzgerald and produced by Mint sculptor Donna Weaver.

2004 Obverse   **2005 Obverse**

Peace Medal   **Keelboat**   **American Bison**   **Ocean in View**

	Mintage	MS-65	PF-65
2004P, Peace Medal	361,440,000	$0.25	
2004D, Peace Medal	372,000,000	0.25	
2004S, Peace Medal	(2,992,069)		$1.25
2004P, Keelboat	366,720,000	0.25	
2004D, Keelboat	344,880,000	0.25	
2004S, Keelboat	(2,965,422)		1.25
2005P, American Bison	448,320,000	0.30	
2005D, American Bison	487,680,000	0.30	
2005S, American Bison	(3,344,679)		1.35
2005P, Ocean in View	394,080,000	0.25	
2005D, Ocean in View	411,120,000	0.25	
2005S, Ocean in View	(3,344,679)		1.25

JEFFERSON MODIFIED (2006 TO DATE)

In 2006 the Monticello design of 1938 to 2003 was returned to the reverse of the nickel five-cent coin. A new obverse motif featured a facing portrait of Thomas Jefferson, designed by Jamie Franki and sculpted by Donna Weaver. These designs have continued in use to date.

Felix Schlag's initials moved to reverse

	Mintage	MS-65	PF-63		Mintage	MS-65	PF-63
2006P, Monticello	693,120,000	$0.25		2013P	607,440,000	$0.20	
2006D, Monticello	809,280,000	0.25		2013D	615,600,000	0.20	
2006S, Monticello	(3,054,436)		$1.25	2013S	(1,274,505)		$1.10
2007P	571,680,000	0.20		2014P	635,520,000	0.20	
2007D	626,160,000	0.20		2014D	570,720,000	0.20	
2007S	(2,577,166)		1.10	2014S	(1,190,369)		1.10
2008P	279,840,000	0.20		2015P	752,880,000	0.20	
2008D	345,600,000	0.20		2015D	846,720,000	0.20	
2008S	(2,169,561)		1.10	2015S	(1,050,164)		1.10
2009P	39,840,000	0.50		2016P	786,960,000	0.20	
2009D	46,800,000	0.50		2016D	759,600,000	0.20	
2009S	(2,179,867)		1.10	2016S	(1,011,624)		1.10
2010P	260,640,000	0.20		2017P	710,160,000	0.20	
2010D	229,920,000	0.20		2017D	663,120,000	0.20	
2010S	(1,689,216)		1.10	2017S (a)	(979,477)		1.10
2011P	450,000,000	0.20		2018P	629,520,000	0.20	
2011D	540,240,000	0.20		2018D	626,880,000	0.20	
2011S	(1,673,010)		1.10	2018S	(844,220)		1.10
2012P	464,640,000	0.20		2019P		0.20	
2012D	558,960,000	0.20		2019D		0.20	
2012S	(1,239,148)		1.10	2019S			1.10

a. For its 225th anniversary, the Mint issued a special set of Enhanced Uncirculated coins from the San Francisco Mint; they are not included here.

The half dime types present the same general characteristics as larger United States silver coins. Authorized by the Act of April 2, 1792, they were not coined until February 1795, although dated 1794. At first the weight was 20.8 grains, and fineness .8924. By the Act of January 18, 1837, the weight was slightly reduced to 20-5/8 grains and the fineness changed to .900. Finally, the weight was reduced to 19.2 grains by the Act of February 21, 1853.

FLOWING HAIR (1794–1795)

AG-3 About Good: Details clear enough to identify.
G-4 Good: Eagle, wreath, bust outlined but lack details.
VG-8 Very Good: Some details on face. All lettering legible.
F-12 Fine: Hair ends visible. Hair at top smooth.
VF-20 Very Fine: Hair lines at top visible. Hair about ear defined.
EF-40 Extremely Fine: Hair above forehead and at neck well defined but shows some wear.

AU-50 About Uncirculated: Slight wear on high waves of hair, near ear and face, and on head and tips of eagle's wings.
MS-60 Uncirculated: No trace of wear. Light blemishes.
MS-63 Choice Uncirculated: Some distracting marks or blemishes in prime focal areas. Some impairment of luster possible.

For Uncirculated examples, coin dealers usually pay less than the prices shown for pieces that are weakly struck.

	Mintage	AG-3	G-4	VG-8	F-12	VF-20	EF-40	AU-50	MS-60	MS-63
1794	86,416	$500	$1,200	$1,400	$2,250	$3,000	$5,500	$8,000	$12,000	$25,000
1795	*	400	1,000	1,150	1,500	2,250	4,750	6,000	8,500	12,500

* Included in number above.

DRAPED BUST (1796–1805)

AG-3 About Good: Details clear enough to identify.
G-4 Good: Date, stars, LIBERTY readable. Bust of Liberty outlined, but no details.
VG-8 Very Good: Some details visible.
F-12 Fine: Hair and drapery lines worn, but visible.
VF-20 Very Fine: Only left side of drapery indistinct.
EF-40 Extremely Fine: Details visible in all hair lines.
AU-50 About Uncirculated: Slight wear on bust, shoulder, and hair; wear on eagle's head and top of wings.
MS-60 Uncirculated: No trace of wear. Light blemishes.
MS-63 Choice Uncirculated: Some distracting marks or blemishes in prime focal areas. Impaired luster possible.

Small Eagle Reverse (1796–1797)

	Mintage	AG-3	G-4	VG-8	F-12	VF-20	EF-40	AU-50	MS-60	MS-63
1796, 6 Over 5	10,230	$750	$1,500	$2,000	$3,000	$4,000	$6,000	$9,500	$17,500	$25,000
1796, LIBERTY	*	500	1,000	1,250	2,250	3,250	6,000	8,000	13,500	22,500
1797, 15 Stars	44,527	500	1,000	1,250	2,250	3,250	6,000	7,000	10,000	14,000
1797, 16 Stars	*	500	1,000	1,250	2,250	3,250	5,250	7,500	10,000	14,500
1797, 13 Stars	750	1,750	2,500	3,250	4,500	10,000	17,500	32,500	45,000

* Included in number above.

Heraldic Eagle Reverse (1800–1805)

1800 LIBEKTY

	Mintage	AG-3	G-4	VG-8	F-12	VF-20	EF-40	AU-50	MS-60	MS-63
1800	24,000	$350	$850	$1,000	$1,500	$1,750	$4,000	$5,000	$8,500	$13,000
1800, LIBEKTY	16,000	350	850	1,000	1,800	2,000	4,500	5,750	10,000	17,500
1801	27,760	350	850	1,000	1,500	2,000	5,000	6,500	11,500	16,500
1802	3,060	20,000	55,000	85,000	110,000	125,000	150,000	250,000	—	—
1803	37,850	400	1,000	1,150	1,500	1,750	4,500	6,250	9,000	12,500
1805	15,600	400	1,000	1,150	1,500	2,250	7,500	17,500	—	—

CAPPED BUST (1829–1837)

G-4 Good: Bust of Liberty outlined, no detail. Date and legend legible.
VG-8 Very Good: Complete legend and date plain. At least three letters
of LIBERTY on edge of cap show clearly.
F-12 Fine: All letters in LIBERTY visible.
VF-20 Very Fine: Full rims. Ear and shoulder clasp show plainly.
EF-40 Extremely Fine: Ear very distinct; eyebrow and hair well defined.

AU-50 About Uncirculated: Traces of light wear on many of the high points. At least half of mint luster still present.
MS-60 Uncirculated: No trace of wear. Light blemishes.
MS-63 Choice Uncirculated: No trace of wear. Light blemishes. Attractive mint luster.

	Mintage	G-4	VG-8	F-12	VF-20	EF-40	AU-50	MS-60	MS-63
1829	1,230,000	$35	$55	$60	$80	$120	$175	$275	$650
1830	1,240,000	35	50	55	75	110	150	250	650
1831	1,242,700	35	50	55	75	110	150	250	650
1832	965,000	35	50	55	75	110	150	250	650
1833	1,370,000	35	50	55	75	110	150	250	650
1834	1,480,000	35	50	55	75	110	150	250	650
1835	2,760,000	35	50	55	75	110	150	250	650
1836	1,900,000	35	50	55	75	110	150	250	650
1837, Small 5 C.	871,000	35	55	65	100	150	300	850	1,650
1837, Large 5 C. . . . . *		35	45	55	80	110	175	275	650

* Included in number above.

LIBERTY SEATED (1837–1873)

G-4 Good: LIBERTY on shield smooth. Date and letters legible.
VG-8 Very Good: At least three letters in LIBERTY visible.
F-12 Fine: Entire LIBERTY visible, weak spots.
VF-20 Very Fine: Entire LIBERTY strong and even.
EF-40 Extremely Fine: LIBERTY and scroll edges distinct.
AU-50 About Uncirculated: Traces of light wear on many of the high points. At least half of mint luster still present.
MS-60 Uncirculated: No trace of wear. Light blemishes.
MS-63 Choice Uncirculated: No trace of wear. Light blemishes. Attractive mint luster.

Variety 1 – No Stars on Obverse (1837–1838)

	Mintage	G-4	VG-8	F-12	VF-20	EF-40	AU-50	MS-60	MS-63
1837	1,405,000	$25	$30	$55	$100	$150	$275	$425	$625
18380, No Stars	70,000	65	115	225	400	1,150	1,750	3,000	6,500

Variety 2 – Stars on Obverse (1838–1853)

From 1838 through 1859 the mintmark was located above the bow on the reverse. Large, medium, or small mintmark varieties occur for several dates.

	Mintage	G-4	VG-8	F-12	VF-20	EF-40	AU-50	MS-60	MS-63
1838	2,255,000	$10	$12	$15	$20	$50	$125	$150	$275
1839	1,069,150	10	12	15	20	50	125	150	275
18390	1,291,600	12	15	20	25	60	125	325	1,000
1840	1,344,085	10	12	15	40	50	125	150	275
18400	935,000	12	15	20	25	75	250	850	2,000
1841	1,150,000	10	12	15	20	30	85	110	175
18410	815,000	12	15	20	25	65	115	450	750
1842	815,000	10	12	15	20	40	85	110	175
18420	350,000	15	20	35	150	450	650	1,000	1,650
1843	815,000	10	12	15	20	40	85	110	175
1844	430,000	10	12	15	20	40	85	110	175
18440	220,000	55	100	200	500	950	1,500	4,750	6,500
1845	1,564,000	10	12	15	20	40	85	110	175
1846	27,000	500	850	1,250	1,750	2,500	4,000	12,500	18,500
1847	1,274,000	10	12	15	20	40	85	110	200
1848	668,000	10	12	15	20	40	85	125	275
18480	600,000	12	15	20	30	65	125	275	550
1849, 9 Over 6 . . . .*		13	15	20	35	65	150	375	750
1849, 9 Over Widely Placed 6 . . . .*		18	22	30	40	75	150	375	750
1849, Normal Date . . .	1,309,000	10	12	15	30	40	85	110	240
18490	140,000	25	45	75	150	350	650	1,350	2,500
1850	955,000	10	12	16	20	40	85	110	175
18500	690,000	12	15	20	35	80	175	450	1,000
1851	781,000	10	12	16	20	40	85	110	175
18510	860,000	12	15	20	25	75	140	300	500
1852	1,000,500	10	12	16	20	40	85	110	175
18520	260,000	16	20	40	75	150	300	450	1,250
1853, No Arrows	135,000	25	40	60	130	200	375	450	700
18530, No Arrows	160,000	150	275	400	500	1,400	2,500	6,500	10,000

* Included in number below.

Variety 3 – Arrows at Date (1853–1855)

As on the dimes, quarters, and halves, arrows were placed at the sides of the date for a short period starting in 1853 to denote the reduction of weight.

	Mintage	G-4	VG-8	F-12	VF-20	EF-40	AU-50	MS-60	MS-63	PF-63
1853	13,210,020	$10	$12	$15	$20	$40	$100	$140	$225	—
18530	2,200,000	12	14	16	22	40	85	175	575	
1854	5,740,000	10	12	15	20	35	80	135	200	$5,000

Chart continued on next page.

	Mintage	G-4	VG-8	F-12	VF-20	EF-40	AU-50	MS-60	MS-63	PF-63
1854O	1,560,000	$12	$14	$16	$20	$40	$90	$140	$450	
1855	1,750,000	10	12	15	20	35	80	135	225	$5,000
1855O	600,000	12	14	16	35	85	120	400	700	

Variety 2 Resumed, with Weight Standard of 1853 (1856–1859)

1858 Over Inverted Date

	Mintage	G-4	VG-8	F-12	VF-20	EF-40	AU-50	MS-60	MS-63	PF-63
1856	4,880,000	$10	$12	$15	$20	$35	$80	$100	$175	$2,500
1856O	1,100,000	10	12	15	30	50	140	325	625	
1857	7,280,000	10	12	15	20	35	80	100	175	1,500
1857O	1,380,000	10	12	15	22	35	100	200	225	
1858 . . . . . . *(300)*	3,500,000	10	12	15	20	35	80	100	175	500
1858, Over Inverted Date . . . .*		18	25	40	55	110	175	400	750	
1858O	1,660,000	10	12	15	25	40	80	125	225	
1859 . . . . . . *(800)*	340,000	10	12	15	20	40	80	125	200	500
1859O	560,000	10	12	17	25	65	110	150	225	

* Included in number above.

Variety 4 – Legend on Obverse (1860–1873)

	Mintage	G-4	VG-8	F-12	VF-20	EF-40	AU-50	MS-60	MS-63	PF-63
1860 . . . . . . (1,000) . . .	798,000	$10	$12	$15	$17	$30	$45	$100	$175	$350
1860O	1,060,000	10	12	15	17	30	50	110	200	
1861 . . . . . . (1,000) . .	3,360,000	10	12	15	17	30	45	100	175	350
1862 . . . . (550) . .	1,492,000	10	15	25	35	40	50	110	200	350
1863 . . . . (460)	18,000	120	165	225	275	350	400	450	600	350
1863S	100,000	15	30	65	80	125	200	425	625	
1864 . . . . (470)	48,000	225	300	500	675	800	950	1,000	1,100	350
1864S	90,000	30	50	90	125	300	375	500	750	
1865 . . . . (500)	13,000	200	250	450	525	600	700	800	850	350
1865S	120,000	15	25	35	50	125	375	800	1,500	
1866 . . . . (725)	10,000	200	250	475	500	600	675	700	800	350
1866S	120,000	15	25	35	50	120	225	300	650	
1867 . . . . (625)	8,000	300	375	575	700	775	825	875	1,000	350
1867S	120,000	10	20	30	50	100	200	375	625	
1868 . . . . (600)	88,600	30	40	80	125	180	300	400	525	350
1868S	280,000	10	12	16	20	35	70	175	325	
1869 . . . . (600)	208,000	10	12	16	20	35	70	125	200	350
1869S	230,000	10	12	16	20	30	70	175	450	
1870 . . . . . . (1,000) . . .	535,000	10	12	15	17	30	45	100	175	350
1870S *(unique)*								1,000,000		
1871 . . . . (960) . .	1,873,000	10	12	15	17	30	45	100	175	350
1871S	161,000	10	15	20	35	45	100	150	250	
1872 . . . . (950) . .	2,947,000	10	12	15	17	30	45	100	175	350
1872S	837,000	10	12	15	17	30	45	100	175	
1873 . . . . (600) . .	7,126,000	10	12	15	17	30	45	100	175	350
1873S	324,000	10	12	15	17	30	45	100	175	

The designs of the dimes, first coined in 1796, follow closely those of the half dimes up through the Liberty Seated type. The dimes in each instance weigh twice as much as the half dimes.

DRAPED BUST (1796–1807)
Small Eagle Reverse (1796–1797)

AG-3 About Good: Details clear enough to identify.
G-4 Good: Date legible. Bust outlined, but no detail.
VG-8 Very Good: All but deepest drapery folds worn smooth. Hair lines nearly gone and curls lacking in detail.
F-12 Fine: All drapery lines visible. Hair partly worn.
VF-20 Very Fine: Only left side of drapery indistinct.
EF-40 Extremely Fine: Hair well outlined with details visible.
AU-50 About Uncirculated: Traces of light wear on many of the high points. At least half of mint luster still present.
MS-60 Uncirculated: No trace of wear. Light blemishes.
MS-63 Choice Uncirculated: Some distracting marks or blemishes in prime focal areas. Impaired luster possible.

1797, 16 Stars   1797, 13 Stars

	Mintage	AG-3	G-4	VG-8	F-12	VF-20	EF-40	AU-50	MS-60	MS-63
1796	22,135	$1,000	$2,000	$2,500	$3,500	$4,500	$7,500	$11,000	$17,500	$30,000
1797, All kinds	25,261									
1797, 16 Stars		1,000	2,250	2,600	3,750	5,000	8,500	12,000	20,000	35,000
1797, 13 Stars		1,100	2,250	2,750	4,000	6,500	10,000	12,500	37,500	55,000

Heraldic Eagle Reverse (1798–1807)

	Mintage	AG-3	G-4	VG-8	F-12	VF-20	EF-40	AU-50	MS-60	MS-63
1798, All kinds	27,550									
1798, 8 Over 7, 16 Stars on Reverse		$250	$550	$850	$1,000	$1,500	$2,250	$3,750	$5,000	$12,000
1798, 8 Over 7, 13 Stars on Reverse		500	1,250	2,250	3,500	5,500	8,500	12,000		
1798		250	550	750	1,000	1,500	2,250	3,500	5,000	10,000
1800	21,760	250	600	950	1,200	1,650	2,500	5,000	17,500	30,000
1801	34,640	250	600	800	1,000	2,200	3,250	7,000	27,500	35,000
1802	10,975	450	1,000	1,500	2,000	2,500	4,750	9,000	25,000	
1803	33,040	200	850	1,200	1,500	1,800	3,000	6,500	45,000	
1804	8,265	1,250	2,500	3,500	7,500	10,000	22,500	45,000	—	
1805	120,780	225	450	750	1,000	1,350	2,250	3,000	5,000	8,000
1807	165,000	225	500	675	850	1,100	1,750	2,600	4,250	7,500

CAPPED BUST (1809–1837)

G-4 Good: Date, letters, and stars discernible. Bust outlined, no details.
VG-8 Very Good: Legends and date plain. Some letters in LIBERTY visible.
F-12 Fine: Clear LIBERTY. Ear and shoulder clasp visible. Part of rim visible on both sides.
VF-20 Very Fine: LIBERTY distinct. Full rim. Ear and clasp plain and distinct.
EF-40 Extremely Fine: LIBERTY sharp. Ear distinct. Hair above eye well defined.
AU-50 About Uncirculated: Traces of light wear on only the high points of the design. Half of mint luster present.
MS-60 Uncirculated: No trace of wear. Light blemishes.
MS-63 Choice Uncirculated: Some distracting marks or blemishes in prime focal areas. Impaired luster possible.

Variety 1 – Wide Border (1809–1828)

| 1823, 3 Over 2 | 1824, 4 Over 2 | 1828, Large Date | 1828, Small Date |

	Mintage	G-4	VG-8	F-12	VF-20	EF-40	AU-50	MS-60	MS-63
1809	51,065	$450	$650	$1,000	$1,750	$2,500	$3,500	$4,500	$5,500
1811, 11 Over 09	65,180	100	150	200	500	1,000	1,500	2,500	4,750
1814	421,500	50	75	100	175	400	500	1,000	2,000
1820	942,587	50	75	100	175	375	450	900	1,800
1821	1,186,512	50	75	100	150	375	450	900	1,800
1822	100,000	1,400	2,000	2,750	5,000	7,500	10,000	15,000	22,000
1823, 3 Over 2, All kinds	440,000								
1823, 3 Over 2, Small E's		30	50	80	140	375	500	1,000	1,800
1823, 3 Over 2, Large E's		30	50	80	140	375	500	1,000	1,800
1824, 4 Over 2	510,000	50	100	150	350	675	750	1,000	2,250
1825	*	30	50	80	140	375	450	900	1,800
1827	1,215,000	30	50	80	140	375	450	950	1,800
1828, Large Date, Curl Base 2	125,000	55	75	100	350	550	1,000	2,500	4,500

* Included in number above.

Variety 2 – Modified Design (1828–1837)

| 1829, Small 10 C. | 1829, Large 10 C. | 1830, 30 Over 29 |

	Mintage	G-4	VG-8	F-12	VF-20	EF-40	AU-50	MS-60	MS-63
1828, Small Date, Square Base 2	*	$25	$35	$50	$75	$220	$350	$650	$1,500
1829, Small 10 C.	770,000	20	30	40	65	200	300	650	1,500
1829, Medium 10 C.	*	20	30	40	65	200	300	650	1,500
1829, Large 10 C.	*	20	30	40	65	200	300	650	1,500
1830, 30 Over 29	510,000	20	30	50	90	225	375	675	1,750

* Included in number above.

	Mintage	G-4	VG-8	F-12	VF-20	EF-40	AU-50	MS-60	MS-63
1830, Large 10 C. . . . *	$20	$30	$40	$65	$200	$300	$650	$1,350
1830, Small 10 C. . . . *	20	30	40	65	200	300	650	1,350
1831 771,350	20	30	40	65	200	300	650	1,350
1832 522,500	20	30	40	65	200	300	650	1,350
1833 485,000	20	30	40	65	200	300	650	1,350
1834 635,000	20	30	40	65	200	300	650	1,350
1835 1,410,000	20	30	40	65	200	300	650	1,350
1836 1,190,000	20	30	40	65	200	300	650	1,350
1837 359,500	20	30	40	65	200	300	650	1,350

* Included in mintage for 1830, 30 Over 29 (previous page).

LIBERTY SEATED (1837–1891)
Variety 1 – No Stars on Obverse (1837–1838)

G-4 Good: LIBERTY on shield not readable. Date and letters legible.
F-12 Fine: LIBERTY visible, weak spots.
VF-20 Very Fine: LIBERTY strong and even.
EF-40 Extremely Fine: LIBERTY and scroll edges distinct.
AU-50 About Uncirculated: Wear on Liberty's shoulder and hair high points.
MS-60 Uncirculated: No trace of wear. Light blemishes.
MS-63 Choice Uncirculated: Some distracting marks or blemishes in focal areas. Impaired luster possible.

**No Drapery From Elbow
No Stars on Obverse**

*Mintmarks on Liberty Seated dimes on
reverse, within or below the wreath.
Size of mintmark varies on many dates.*

	Mintage	G-4	F-12	VF-20	EF-40	AU-50	MS-60	MS-63
1837 682,500	$20	$55	$160	$275	$450	$700	$1,200
1838O . . . . *406,034+*	45	65	150	250	700	2,500	3,500

Variety 2 – Stars on Obverse (1838–1853)

**No Drapery From Elbow, Tilted Shield
(1838–1840)**

**Drapery From Elbow, Upright Shield
(1840–1891)**

1838, Small Stars   **1838, Large Stars**

	Mintage	G-4	F-12	VF-20	EF-40	AU-50	MS-60	MS-63
1838, All kinds. 1,992,500							
1838, Small Stars	$10	$25	$50	$100	$225	$400	$700
1838, Large Stars	10	12	25	80	175	275	550
1838, Partial Drapery	12	18	35	75	210	425	1,000
1839 1,053,115	10	15	25	80	175	275	550
1839O 1,291,600	12	20	25	90	185	325	750
1840, No Drapery 981,500	10	15	25	80	185	275	550
1840O, No Drapery 1,175,000	30	75	100	300	650	3,000	7,500
1840, Drapery 377,500	35	85	125	450	750	1,500	6,500

Chart continued on next page.

	Mintage	G-4	F-12	VF-20	EF-40	AU-50	MS-60	MS-63
1841 1,622,500		$10	$12	$18	$25	$80	$175	$400
1841O 2,007,500		12	20	35	80	125	525	1,000
1842 1,887,500		10	12	18	25	80	175	375
1842O 2,020,000		20	55	100	250	700	2,250	3,000
1843 1,370,000		10	12	18	25	80	175	475
1843O 150,000		125	400	850	2,000	6,500	45,000	
1844 72,500		115	200	400	750	1,100	2,500	6,500
1845 1,755,000		10	12	18	25	80	175	450
1845O 230,000		45	150	300	550	1,250	5,500	—
1846 31,300		125	350	750	1,650	5,000	12,000	22,500
1847 245,000		10	16	35	100	200	850	1,650
1848 451,500		10	12	30	45	85	325	475
1849 839,000		10	12	20	40	100	250	550
1849O 300,000		15	35	100	200	500	1,250	3,500
1850 1,931,500		10	12	18	30	90	200	375
1850O 510,000		15	30	55	75	125	550	1,500
1851 1,026,500		10	12	18	25	80	200	500
1851O 400,000		12	20	45	100	275	1,100	2,000
1852 1,535,500		10	12	18	25	80	175	375
1852O 430,000		15	25	75	150	300	1,000	2,000
1853, No Arrows 95,000		60	200	325	450	525	675	1,000

Variety 3 – Arrows at Date (1853–1855)

	Mintage	G-4	F-12	VF-20	EF-40	AU-50	MS-60	MS-63	PF-63
1853, With Arrows . . 12,173,000		$10	$12	$20	$25	$100	$225	$450	$12,500
1853O 1,100,000		10	20	75	200	325	1,100	1,750	
1854 4,470,000		10	12	20	25	100	200	400	5,500
1854O 1,770,000		10	12	20	35	125	250	600	
1855 2,075,000		10	12	20	25	100	225	550	5,500

Variety 2 Resumed, With Weight Standard of Variety 3 (1856–1860)

Small Date, Arrows Removed (1856–1860)

	Mintage	G-4	F-12	VF-20	EF-40	AU-50	MS-60	MS-63	PF-63
1856, All kinds 5,780,000									
1856, Large Date		$7	$10	$18	$25	$80	$175	$375	
1856, Small Date		7	10	15	20	80	175	350	$2,000
1856O 1,180,000		8	10	18	35	125	500	825	
1856S 70,000		150	375	650	1,200	1,500	4,500	9,500	

	Mintage	G-4	F-12	VF-20	EF-40	AU-50	MS-60	MS-63	PF-63
1857	5,580,000	$7	$10	$15	$25	$80	$175	$375	$1,800
1857O	1,540,000	8	10	15	25	100	225	400	
1858 . . . . . . (300+) . . .	1,540,000	7	10	15	25	80	175	375	1,000
1858O	200,000	8	15	40	90	175	325	600	
1858S	60,000	100	225	450	850	1,500	4,500	8,000	
1859 . . . . . . (800+)	429,200	7	10	15	25	80	175	375	700
1859O	480,000	8	10	20	45	125	200	375	
1859S	60,000	100	300	650	1,500	3,000	12,000	20,000	
1860S	140,000	35	100	150	350	600	1,450	5,000	

Variety 4 – Legend on Obverse (1860–1873)

	Mintage	G-4	F-12	VF-20	EF-40	AU-50	MS-60	MS-63	PF-63
1860 . . . . . . (1,000)	606,000	$7	$10	$18	$20	$50	$125	$175	$450
1860O	40,000	350	1,000	2,000	3,500	5,500	12,000	25,000	
1861 . . . . . . (1,000) . . .	1,883,000	7	10	15	20	40	100	175	450
1861S	172,500	100	250	400	550	850	3,500	12,000	
1862 . . . . (550) . . .	847,000	7	10	15	20	50	120	175	450
1862S	180,750	85	200	350	550	1,500	2,500	5,500	
1863 . . . . (460) . . .	14,000	300	550	650	750	850	1,000	1,500	450
1863S	157,500	75	200	300	550	750	1,950	5,500	
1864 . . . . (470)	11,000	185	400	550	650	750	850	1,350	475
1864S	230,000	65	125	250	550	750	1,000	1,450	
1865 . . . . (500)	10,000	250	500	600	750	850	1,000	1,200	450
1865S	175,000	55	225	450	650	2,000	4,500	10,000	
1866 . . . . . . (725)	8,000	475	650	750	950	1,000	1,200	1,750	450
1866S	135,000	55	150	250	400	850	2,000	4,500	
1867 . . . . (625)	6,000	350	600	700	800	1,000	1,150	1,500	350
1867S	140,000	55	150	250	450	1,000	1,250	3,000	
1868 . . . . (600) . . .	464,000	10	15	25	40	90	175	425	350
1868S	260,000	10	15	60	325	375	450	600	
1869 . . . . (600) . . .	256,000	10	15	55	65	100	225	450	350
1869S	450,000	10	15	20	150	200	300	500	
1870 . . . . . (1,000)	470,500	10	12	15	20	55	150	250	350
1870S	50,000	150	400	500	600	800	1,100	1,500	
1871 . . . . (960) . . .	906,750	10	12	15	20	80	150	225	350
1871CC	20,100	2,000	4,000	6,000	8,500	17,500	—	—	
1871S	320,000	15	60	100	150	200	400	750	
1872 . . . . (950) . .	2,395,500	10	12	15	20	45	100	175	350
1872CC	35,480	650	2,000	2,500	7,500	15,000	—	—	
1872S	190,000	15	55	80	150	275	700	1,500	
1873, Close 3 (600) . . .	*1,507,400*	10	12	15	20	45	100	175	350
1873, Open 3	*60,000*	10	30	45	80	110	325	750	
1873CC *(unique)*	12,400							—	

Variety 5 – Arrows at Date (1873–1874)

In 1873, the dime was increased in weight from 2.49 grams to 2.50 grams. Arrows at the date in 1873 and 1874 indicate this change.

	Mintage	G-4	F-12	VF-20	EF-40	AU-50	MS-60	MS-63	PF-63
1873 . . . . (500). . . 2,377,700		$10	$18	$30	$100	$175	$275	$575	$600
1873CC 18,791		2,500	3,000	6,000	11,500	27,500	—	—	
1873S 455,000		10	20	35	110	275	525	1,100	
1874 . . . . (700). . . 2,940,000		10	16	30	100	175	285	575	600
1874CC 10,817		4,500	8,500	14,000	25,000	35,000	—	—	
1874S 240,000		11	40	65	125	275	500	1,100	

Variety 4 Resumed, With Weight Standard of Variety 5 (1875–1891)

	Mintage	G-4	F-12	VF-20	EF-40	AU-50	MS-60	MS-63	PF-63
1875 . . . . (700). . 10,350,000		$7	$10	$12	$20	$45	$100	$150	$350
1875CC 4,645,000		12	25	30	50	80	150	300	
1875S 9,070,000		7	10	12	20	45	100	150	
1876 . . . .(1,250). . 11,460,000		7	10	12	20	45	100	150	350
1876CC 8,270,000		12	25	30	45	80	150	245	
1876S 10,420,000		7	10	12	20	45	100	175	
1877 . . . . (510). . . 7,310,000		7	10	12	20	45	100	150	350
1877CC 7,700,000		12	25	30	55	80	125	325	
1877S 2,340,000		7	10	12	20	45	100	175	
1878 . . . . (800). . . 1,677,200		7	10	12	20	45	100	175	350
1878CC 200,000		100	200	250	300	475	850	1,500	
1879 . . . . . .(1,100). 14,000		100	175	225	400	425	450	500	350
1880 . . . .(1,355). 36,000		80	160	200	250	275	375	450	350
1881 . . . . (975). 24,000		95	175	225	250	300	325	400	350
1882 . . . . . .(1,100). . . 3,910,000		7	10	12	20	45	100	150	350
1883 . . . . . .(1,039). . . 7,674,673		7	10	12	20	45	100	150	350
1884 . . . . (875). . . 3,365,505		7	10	12	20	45	100	150	350
1884S 564,969		10	15	30	60	175	400	625	
1885 . . . . (930). . . 2,532,497		7	10	12	20	45	110	150	350
1885S 43,690		350	750	950	1,650	2,750	4,000	5,500	
1886 . . . . (886). . . 6,376,684		7	10	12	20	45	100	150	350
1886S 206,524		12	25	40	65	95	300	625	
1887 . . . . (710). . 11,283,229		7	10	12	20	45	100	150	350
1887S 4,454,450		7	10	12	20	45	100	150	
1888 . . . . (832). . . 5,495,655		7	10	12	20	45	100	150	350
1888S 1,720,000		7	10	12	25	45	125	375	
1889 . . . . (711). . . 7,380,000		7	10	12	20	45	100	150	350
1889S 972,678		10	15	25	40	75	225	525	
1890 . . . . (590). . . 9,910,951		7	10	12	20	45	100	150	350
1890S 1,423,076		7	12	20	40	75	180	375	
1891 . . . . (600). . 15,310,000		7	10	12	20	45	100	150	350
18910 4,540,000		7	15	18	20	45	125	165	
1891S 3,196,116		7	10	12	20	45	100	150	

BARBER OR LIBERTY HEAD (1892–1916)

This type was designed by Charles E. Barber, chief engraver of the Mint. His initial B is at the truncation of the neck. He also designed the quarters and half dollars of the same period.

G-4 Good: Date and letters plain. LIBERTY obliterated.

VG-8 Very Good: Some letters visible in LIBERTY.

F-12 Fine: Letters in LIBERTY visible, though some weak.

VF-20 Very Fine: Letters of LIBERTY evenly plain.

EF-40 Extremely Fine: All letters in LIBERTY sharp, distinct. Headband edges distinct.

AU-50 About Uncirculated: Slight traces of wear on hair cheekbone and on leaf tips in wreath.

MS-60 Uncirculated: No trace of wear. Light blemishes.

MS-63 Choice Uncirculated: Some distracting blemishes in prime focal areas. Impaired luster possible.

Mintmark location is on reverse, below wreath.

	Mintage	G-4	VG-8	F-12	VF-20	EF-40	AU-50	MS-60	MS-63	PF-63
1892 .... (1,245)...	12,120,000	$3.00	$4.00	$8	$12	$15	$35	$75	$145	$350
1892O	3,841,700	4.00	6.00	15	25	35	45	90	175	
1892S	990,710	35.00	55.00	110	125	160	180	240	450	
1893, 3/2 ....*		45.00	65.00	85	100	120	175	650	1,250	—
1893 ...... (792)....	3,339,940	3.00	5.00	10	15	24	35	95	145	350
1893O	1,760,000	12.00	25.00	75	85	100	125	175	350	
1893S (a)	2,491,401	6.00	12.00	18	25	40	75	150	375	
1894 ...... (970)....	1,330,000	10.00	20.00	65	85	100	125	175	275	350
1894O	720,000	30.00	45.00	110	160	250	400	925	1,500	
1894S	24 (b)								1,500,000	
1895 ...... (880).....	690,000	35.00	75.00	180	275	325	400	475	675	350
1895O	440,000	250.00	350.00	600	1,000	1,750	2,250	4,000	8,000	
1895S	1,120,000	20.00	30.00	75	100	125	175	300	625	
1896 ......(762)....	2,000,000	4.50	10.00	28	36	50	55	95	225	350
1896O	610,000	50.00	85.00	175	225	280	400	850	1,750	
1896S	576,056	50.00	70.00	160	200	275	310	500	900	
1897 ...... (731)...	10,868,533	2.00	2.50	3	6	12	35	75	145	350
1897O	666,000	40.00	65.00	175	250	300	400	675	1,000	
1897S	1,342,844	8.00	16.00	50	75	90	140	250	625	
1898 ......(735)...	16,320,000	2.00	2.50	3	5	12	35	75	145	350
1898O	2,130,000	5.00	10.00	38	75	80	150	275	650	
1898S	1,702,507	2.00	5.00	16	25	35	75	200	650	
1899 ...... (846)...	19,580,000	2.00	2.50	3	5	12	35	75	145	350
1899O	2,650,000	4.00	7.00	35	45	70	125	225	600	
1899S	1,867,493	2.00	5.00	12	16	20	55	175	375	
1900 ......(912)...	17,600,000	1.75	2.00	3	5	12	35	75	145	350

* Included in number below. **a.** Boldy doubled mintmark is valued slightly higher. **b.** Five of these were reserved for assay.

Chart continued on next page.

	Mintage	G-4	VG-8	F-12	VF-20	EF-40	AU-50	MS-60	MS-63	PF-63
1900O	2,010,000	$10.00	$20	$65.00	$100.00	$150	$200	$350	$600	
1900S	5,168,270	1.75	2	5.00	7.00	14	35	95	225	
1901 (813)	18,859,665	1.75	2	2.50	5.00	12	35	75	150	$350
1901O	5,620,000	1.75	2	6.00	10.00	30	85	275	500	
1901S	593,022	50.00	100	225.00	300.00	400	500	1,000	1,500	
1902 (777)	21,380,000	1.75	2	2.50	4.00	12	35	75	150	350
1902O	4,500,000	1.75	2	6.00	12.00	30	70	250	525	
1902S	2,070,000	3.00	8	25.00	40.00	60	100	225	525	
1903 (755)	19,500,000	1.75	2	2.50	4.00	12	35	75	150	350
1903O	8,180,000	1.75	2	7.00	10.00	20	40	150	325	
1903S	613,300	50.00	85	225.00	350.00	450	550	800	1,000	
1904 (670)	14,600,357	1.75	2	2.50	4.00	12	35	75	150	350
1904S	800,000	25.00	45	100.00	150.00	200	350	500	1,200	
1905 (727)	14,551,623	1.75	2	2.50	4.00	12	35	75	150	350
1905O	3,400,000	1.75	4	16.00	25.00	50	75	150	225	
1905S	6,855,199	1.75	2	3.00	7.00	18	40	125	175	
1906 (675)	19,957,731	1.75	2	2.50	4.00	12	35	75	150	350
1906D	4,060,000	1.75	2	2.50	6.00	15	35	95	200	
1906O	2,610,000	2.00	5	22.00	35.00	47	65	125	185	
1906S	3,136,640	1.75	2	5.00	10.00	18	55	135	250	
1907 (575)	22,220,000	1.75	2	2.50	4.00	12	35	75	150	350
1907D	4,080,000	1.75	2	4.00	6.00	18	55	150	500	
1907O	5,058,000	1.75	3	15.00	22.00	24	50	100	185	
1907S	3,178,470	1.75	2	6.00	10.00	25	65	225	425	
1908 (545)	10,600,000	1.75	2	2.50	4.00	12	35	75	150	350
1908D	7,490,000	1.75	2	2.50	4.00	14	35	75	150	
1908O	1,789,000	2.00	4	22.00	30.00	45	65	160	325	
1908S	3,220,000	1.75	2	4.00	8.00	18	75	175	400	
1909 (650)	10,240,000	1.75	2	2.50	3.50	12	35	75	150	350
1909D	954,000	3.00	7	35.00	50.00	75	125	275	600	
1909O	2,287,000	1.75	3	5.00	8.00	25	85	175	375	
1909S	1,000,000	3.00	8	40.00	60.00	90	175	300	675	
1910 (551)	11,520,000	1.75	2	2.50	3.50	12	35	75	150	350
1910D	3,490,000	1.75	2	3.00	6.00	20	45	125	250	
1910S	1,240,000	2.00	3	25.00	35.00	50	100	250	400	
1911 (543)	18,870,000	1.75	2	2.50	3.50	12	35	75	150	350
1911D	11,209,000	1.75	2	2.50	3.50	12	35	75	150	
1911S	3,520,000	1.75	2	3.00	8.50	16	45	120	200	
1912 (700)	19,349,300	1.75	2	2.50	3.50	12	35	75	150	350
1912D	11,760,000	1.75	2	2.50	3.50	12	35	75	150	
1912S	3,420,000	1.75	2	2.50	3.50	16	45	95	165	
1913 (622)	19,760,000	1.75	2	2.50	3.50	12	35	75	150	350
1913S	510,000	20.00	35	75.00	100.00	150	225	450	750	
1914 (425)	17,360,230	1.75	2	2.50	3.50	12	35	75	150	350
1914D	11,908,000	1.75	2	2.50	3.50	12	35	75	150	
1914S	2,100,000	1.75	2	3.00	7.00	15	35	85	150	
1915 (450)	5,620,000	1.75	2	2.50	3.50	12	35	75	150	350
1915S	960,000	2.00	4	15.00	20.00	32	70	140	275	
1916	18,490,000	1.75	2	2.50	3.50	12	35	75	150	
1916S	5,820,000	1.75	2	2.50	3.50	12	35	75	150	

WINGED LIBERTY HEAD
OR "MERCURY" (1916–1945)

Although this coin is commonly called the *Mercury* dime, the main device is in fact a representation of Liberty. The wings crowning her cap are intended to symbolize liberty of thought. Designer Adolph Weinman's monogram, AW, is at the right of the neck. A Centennial Gold issue was struck in 2016.

G-4 Good: Letters and date clear. Lines and bands in fasces obliterated.
VG-8 Very Good: Half of sticks discernible in fasces.
F-12 Fine: All sticks in fasces defined. Diagonal bands worn nearly flat.
VF-20 Very Fine: Diagonal bands definitely visible.
EF-40 Extremely Fine: Only slight wear on diagonal bands. Braids and hair before ear clearly visible.
AU-50 About Uncirculated: Slight trace of wear. Most mint luster present.
MS-63 Choice Uncirculated: No trace of wear. Light blemishes. Attractive mint luster.
MS-65 Gem Uncirculated: Only light, scattered, non-distracting marks. Strong luster, good eye appeal.

Mintmark location is on reverse, left of fasces.

The Mint State prices shown are what coin dealers pay for average Uncirculated pieces with minimum blemishes. For coins with sharp strikes and split horizontal bands on the reverse, they usually pay much more.

	Mintage	G-4	VG-8	F-12	VF-20	EF-40	MS-60	MS-63	MS-65
1916	22,180,080	$2.00	$2.50	$3	$4.00	$5.00	$18	$24	$55
1916D	264,000	550.00	950.00	1,750	2,750.00	4,250.00	8,000	10,000	17,000
1916S	10,450,000	2.00	2.50	4	6.00	10.00	20	35	120
1917	55,230,000	1.50	1.50	2	2.50	4.00	15	26	85
1917D	9,402,000	2.00	3.00	5	10.00	22.00	65	180	700
1917S	27,330,000	1.50	1.50	2	3.00	6.00	30	100	275
1918	26,680,000	1.50	1.50	3	5.00	13.00	40	75	225
1918D	22,674,800	1.50	1.50	3	5.00	12.00	55	140	400
1918S	19,300,000	1.50	1.50	2	4.00	9.00	60	125	525
1919	35,740,000	1.50	1.50	2	2.50	6.00	20	100	200
1919D	9,939,000	1.50	1.50	5	12.00	22.00	105	250	900
1919S	8,850,000	1.50	1.50	4	8.00	20.00	105	270	1,000
1920	59,030,000	1.50	1.50	2	2.50	5.00	16	35	150
1920D	19,171,000	1.50	1.50	2	3.00	11.00	65	200	475
1920S	13,820,000	1.50	1.50	3	3.00	10.00	65	175	800
1921	1,230,000	25.00	40.00	60	150.00	325.00	650	1,250	2,000
1921D	1,080,000	35.00	65.00	120	200.00	425.00	700	1,350	2,250
1923	50,130,000	1.50	1.50	2	2.50	3.00	16	24	65
1923S	6,440,000	1.50	1.50	4	8.00	32.00	90	220	750
1924	24,010,000	1.50	1.50	2	2.50	6.00	23	45	105
1924D	6,810,000	1.50	1.50	3	9.00	26.00	95	280	600
1924S	7,120,000	1.50	1.50	2	5.00	24.00	120	300	775
1925	25,610,000	1.50	1.50	2	2.50	4.00	16	40	140
1925D	5,117,000	2.00	2.50	5	22.00	60.00	200	425	1,000
1925S	5,850,000	1.50	1.50	3	7.00	35.00	90	275	800
1926	32,160,000	1.50	1.50	2	2.50	3.00	15	30	130
1926D	6,828,000	1.50	1.50	2	6.00	16.00	60	150	350
1926S	1,520,000	4.00	6.00	12	32.00	140.00	550	950	2,500
1927	28,080,000	1.50	1.50	2	2.50	3.00	15	32	80
1927D	4,812,000	1.50	1.50	2	12.00	35.00	100	225	750

Chart continued on next page.

	Mintage	G-4	VG-8	F-12	VF-20	EF-40	MS-60	MS-63	MS-65
1927S	4,770,000	$1.10	$1.10	$2.00	$4.00	$15.00	$150	$300	$800
1928	19,480,000	1.10	1.10	2.00	2.50	3.00	15	30	75
1928D	4,161,000	1.10	1.10	4.00	10.00	24.00	100	225	500
1928S	7,400,000	1.10	1.10	2.00	3.00	8.00	75	175	265
1929	25,970,000	1.10	1.10	2.00	2.50	3.00	13	20	40
1929D	5,034,000	1.10	1.10	2.00	3.00	8.00	16	17	40
1929S	4,730,000	1.10	1.10	2.00	2.50	3.00	18	20	60
1930	6,770,000	1.10	1.10	2.00	2.50	3.00	15	25	60
1930S	1,843,000	1.10	1.10	3.00	3.50	8.00	35	75	110
1931	3,150,000	1.10	1.10	2.00	2.50	5.00	20	40	80
1931D	1,260,000	3.00	4.00	6.00	8.00	18.00	46	75	160
1931S	1,800,000	2.00	3.00	3.00	4.00	9.00	40	75	160

	Mintage	VG-8	F-12	VF-20	EF-40	MS-60	MS-63	MS-65	PF-63
1934	24,080,000	$1.10	$1.10	$1.30	$1.40	$10.00	$15	$25	
1934D	6,772,000	1.10	1.10	1.30	1.40	20.00	30	45	
1935	58,830,000	1.10	1.10	1.30	1.40	5.00	8	15	
1935D	10,477,000	1.10	1.10	1.30	1.40	16.00	25	50	
1935S	15,840,000	1.10	1.10	1.30	1.40	10.00	16	20	
1936	(4,130).. 87,500,000	1.10	1.10	1.30	1.40	5.00	8	15	$500
1936D	16,132,000	1.10	1.10	1.30	1.40	14.00	20	30	
1936S	9,210,000	1.10	1.10	1.30	1.40	12.00	15	20	
1937	(5,756). 56,860,000	1.10	1.10	1.30	1.40	4.00	7	15	250
1937D	14,146,000	1.10	1.10	1.30	1.40	12.00	16	24	
1937S	9,740,000	1.10	1.10	1.30	1.40	12.00	15	20	
1938	(8,728). 22,190,000	1.10	1.10	1.30	1.40	6.00	7	15	125
1938D	5,537,000	1.10	1.10	1.30	1.40	9.00	10	16	
1938S	8,090,000	1.10	1.10	1.30	1.40	8.00	9	20	
1939	(9,321). 67,740,000	1.10	1.10	1.30	1.40	4.00	6	15	125
1939D	24,394,000	1.10	1.10	1.30	1.40	4.00	6	15	
1939S	10,540,000	1.10	1.10	1.30	1.40	12.00	15	20	
1940	(11,827). 65,350,000	1.10	1.10	1.30	1.40	4.00	6	15	100
1940D	21,198,000	1.10	1.10	1.30	1.40	4.00	6	16	
1940S	21,560,000	1.10	1.10	1.30	1.40	4.00	6	16	
1941	(16,557). 175,090,000	1.10	1.10	1.30	1.40	4.00	6	15	100
1941D	45,634,000	1.10	1.10	1.30	1.40	4.00	6	16	
1941S	43,090,000	1.10	1.10	1.30	1.40	4.00	6	16	
1942, 42 Over 41	*	285.00	290.00	300.00	400.00	1,500.00	3,250	8,000	
1942	(22,329) 205,410,000	1.10	1.10	1.30	1.40	4.00	6	15	100
1942D, 42 Over 41	*	275.00	280.00	290.00	375.00	1,500.00	3,250	8,000	
1942D	60,740,000	1.10	1.10	1.30	1.40	5.00	7	16	
1942S	49,300,000	1.10	1.10	1.30	1.40	6.00	7	16	
1943	191,710,000	1.10	1.10	1.30	1.40	4.00	6	15	
1943D	71,949,000	1.10	1.10	1.30	1.40	5.00	7	16	
1943S	60,400,000	1.10	1.10	1.30	1.40	5.00	7	15	
1944	231,410,000	1.10	1.10	1.30	1.40	4.00	6	15	
1944D	62,224,000	1.10	1.10	1.30	1.40	5.00	7	15	
1944S	49,490,000	1.10	1.10	1.30	1.40	5.00	7	15	
1945	159,130,000	1.10	1.10	1.30	1.40	4.00	6	15	
1945D	40,245,000	1.10	1.10	1.30	1.40	4.00	6	16	
1945S	41,920,000	1.10	1.10	1.30	1.40	5.00	7	16	
1945S, Micro S	*	1.50	1.50	1.60	2.00	12.50	18	45	

* Included in number above.

ROOSEVELT (1946 TO DATE)

John R. Sinnock (whose initials, JS, are at the truncation of the neck) designed this dime showing a portrait of Franklin D. Roosevelt. The design has heavier lettering and a more modernistic character than preceding types.

VF-20 Very Fine: Moderate wear on high points of design. All major details are clear.

EF-40 Extremely Fine: All lines of torch, flame, and hair very plain.

MS-63 Choice Uncirculated: Some distracting contact marks or blemishes in prime focal areas. Impaired luster possible.

MS-65 Gem Uncirculated: Only light, non-distracting scattered marks. Strong luster, good eye appeal.

PF-65 Gem Proof: Nearly perfect.

Mintmark on reverse,
1946–1964.

Silver Coinage (1946–1964)

	Mintage	VF-20	EF-40	MS-63	MS-65	PF-65
1946	255,250,000	$1.10	$1.10	$2.50	$6.00	
1946D	61,043,500	1.10	1.10	2.50	7.00	
1946S	27,900,000	1.10	1.10	4.00	10.00	
1947	121,520,000	1.10	1.10	2.50	6.00	
1947D	46,835,000	1.10	1.10	2.50	6.00	
1947S	34,840,000	1.10	1.10	2.50	6.00	
1948	74,950,000	1.10	1.10	2.50	6.00	
1948D	52,841,000	1.10	1.10	2.50	6.00	
1948S	35,520,000	1.10	1.10	2.50	6.00	
1949	30,940,000	1.10	1.10	14.00	19.00	
1949D	26,034,000	1.10	1.10	5.00	9.00	
1949S	13,510,000	1.10	1.10	22.00	32.50	
1950	(51,386)	50,130,114	1.10	1.10	6.50	8.00	$25
1950D	46,803,000	1.10	1.10	2.50	6.00	
1950S	20,440,000	1.10	1.10	20.00	30.00	
1951	(57,500)	103,880,102	1.10	1.10	2.00	5.00	25
1951D	56,529,000	1.10	1.10	2.00	5.00	
1951S	31,630,000	1.10	1.10	7.50	14.00	
1952	(81,980)	99,040,093	1.10	1.10	2.00	5.00	18
1952D	122,100,000	1.10	1.10	2.00	4.00	
1952S	44,419,500	1.10	1.10	3.75	6.25	
1953	(128,800)	53,490,120	1.10	1.10	2.50	4.50	20
1953D	136,433,000	1.10	1.10	2.50	4.50	
1953S	39,180,000	1.10	1.10	2.50	4.50	
1954	(233,300)	114,010,203	1.10	1.10	2.00	4.00	10
1954D	106,397,000	1.10	1.10	2.00	4.00	
1954S	22,860,000	1.10	1.10	2.00	4.00	

Chart continued on next page.

	Mintage	VF-20	EF-40	MS-63	MS-65	PF-65
1955 . . . . (378,200)	12,450,181	$1.10	$1.10	$1.75	$5.00	$8
1955D	13,959,000	1.10	1.10	1.75	4.00	
1955S	18,510,000	1.10	1.10	1.75	4.00	
1956 . . . . (669,384)	108,640,000	1.10	1.10	1.75	4.00	4
1956D	108,015,100	1.10	1.10	1.75	3.50	
1957 . . . . (1,247,952)	160,160,000	1.10	1.10	1.75	3.50	3
1957D	113,354,330	1.10	1.10	1.75	3.25	
1958 . . . . (875,652)	31,910,000	1.10	1.10	1.75	4.00	3
1958D	136,564,600	1.10	1.10	1.75	4.00	
1959 . . . . (1,149,291)	85,780,000	1.10	1.10	1.75	3.50	3
1959D	164,919,790	1.10	1.10	1.75	3.50	
1960 . . . . (1,691,602) . . .	70,390,000	1.10	1.10	1.75	3.50	3
1960D	200,160,400	1.10	1.10	1.75	3.00	
1961 . . . . (3,028,244)	93,730,000	1.10	1.10	1.75	3.00	3
1961D	209,146,550	1.10	1.10	1.75	3.00	
1962 . . . . (3,218,019)	72,450,000	1.10	1.10	1.75	3.00	3
1962D	334,948,380	1.10	1.10	1.75	3.00	
1963 . . . . (3,075,645) . . .	123,650,000	1.10	1.10	1.75	3.00	3
1963D	421,476,530	1.10	1.10	1.75	3.00	
1964 . . . . (3,950,762) . . .	929,360,000	1.10	1.10	1.75	3.00	3
1964D	1,357,517,180	1.10	1.10	1.75	3.00	

Clad Coinage and Silver Proofs (1965 to Date)

*Mintmark on obverse,
starting in 1968.*

	Mintage	MS-63	MS-65	PF-65
1965	1,652,140,570	$0.15	$1.00	
1966	1,382,734,540	0.15	0.90	
1967	2,244,007,320	0.15	0.80	
1968	424,470,400	0.15	0.80	
1968D	480,748,280	0.15	0.80	
1968S	(3,041,506)			$0.80
1969	145,790,000	0.25	1.00	
1969D	563,323,870	0.15	0.75	
1969S	(2,394,631)			0.80
1970	345,570,000	0.15	0.50	
1970D	754,942,100	0.15	0.50	
1970S	(2,632,810)			0.80
1971	162,690,000	0.18	0.75	
1971D	377,914,240	0.16	0.65	
1971S	(3,220,733)			0.80
1972	431,540,000	0.15	0.50	
1972D	330,290,000	0.15	0.50	
1972S	(3,260,996)			0.80
1973	315,670,000	0.15	0.50	
1973D	455,032,426	0.15	0.50	
1973S	(2,760,339)			$0.80
1974	470,248,000	$0.15	$0.50	
1974D	571,083,000	0.15	0.50	
1974S	(2,612,568)			0.80
1975	585,673,900	0.15	0.50	
1975D	313,705,300	0.15	0.50	
1975S	(2,845,450)			1.00
1976	568,760,000	0.15	0.50	
1976D	695,222,774	0.15	0.50	
1976S	(4,149,730)			1.00
1977	796,930,000	0.15	0.50	
1977D	376,607,228	0.15	0.50	
1977S	(3,251,152)			0.80
1978	663,980,000	0.15	0.50	
1978D	282,847,540	0.15	0.50	
1978S	(3,127,781)			0.80
1979	315,440,000	0.15	0.50	
1979D	390,921,184	0.15	0.50	
1979S, Type 1 . .	(3,677,175)			2.75
1979S, Type 2 . . . .*				4.00

* Included in number above.

Mintage	MS-63	MS-65	PF-65
1980P 735,170,000	$0.15	$0.50	
1980D 719,354,321	0.15	0.50	
1980S . . . . (3,554,806)			$0.80
1981P 676,650,000	0.15	0.50	
1981D 712,284,143	0.15	0.50	
1981S, Type 1 . . (4,063,083)			2.75
1981S, Type 2 . . . .*			14.00
1982, No Mmk.	30.00	50.00	
1982P 519,475,000	1.50	2.75	
1982D 542,713,584	0.60	1.50	
1982S . . . . (3,857,479)			1.50
1983P 647,025,000	1.25	2.75	
1983D 730,129,224	0.50	1.75	
1983S . . . . (3,279,126)			1.00
1984P 856,669,000	0.15	0.60	
1984D 704,803,976	0.20	0.75	
1984S . . . . (3,065,110)			1.00
1985P 705,200,962	0.15	0.60	
1985D 587,979,970	0.15	0.60	
1985S . . . . (3,362,821)			1.00
1986P 682,649,693	0.25	0.75	
1986D 473,326,970	0.25	0.75	
1986S . . . . (3,010,497)			1.75
1987P 762,709,481	0.15	0.60	
1987D 653,203,402	0.15	0.60	
1987S . . . . (4,227,728)			1.25
1988P 1,030,550,000	0.12	0.50	
1988D 962,385,489	0.12	0.50	
1988S . . . . (3,262,948)			1.75
1989P 1,298,400,000	0.10	0.50	
1989D 896,535,597	0.10	0.50	
1989S . . . . (3,220,194)			1.75
1990P 1,034,340,000	0.10	0.50	
1990D 839,995,824	0.10	0.50	
1990S . . . . (3,299,559)			1.00
1991P 927,220,000	0.10	0.50	
1991D 601,241,114	0.12	0.50	
1991S . . . . (2,867,787)			1.70
1992P 593,500,000	0.10	0.50	
1992D 616,273,932	0.10	0.50	
1992S . . . . (2,858,981)			1.50
1992S, Silver . . . (1,317,579)			3.00
1993P 766,180,000	0.10	0.50	
1993D 750,110,166	0.10	0.50	
1993S . . . . (2,633,439)			2.25
1993S, Silver . . . . . (761,353)			3.50
1994P 1,189,000,000	0.10	0.50	
1994D 1,303,268,110	0.10	0.50	
1994S . . . . (2,484,594)			2.25
1994S, Silver . . . . . (785,329)			3.75

Mintage	MS-63	MS-65	PF-65
1995P 1,125,500,000	$0.10	$0.50	
1995D 1,274,890,000	0.15	0.50	
1995S . . . . (2,117,496)			$5.50
1995S, Silver . . . . . (679,985)			7.50
1996P 1,421,163,000	0.10	0.50	
1996D 1,400,300,000	0.10	0.50	
1996W 1,457,000	6.00	11.00	
1996S . . . . (1,750,244)			1.25
1996S, Silver . . . . . (775,021)			3.50
1997P 991,640,000	0.10	0.50	
1997D 979,810,000	0.10	0.50	
1997S . . . . (2,055,000)			3.50
1997S, Silver . . . . . (741,678)			7.00
1998P 1,163,000,000	0.10	0.50	
1998D 1,172,250,000	0.10	0.50	
1998S . . . . (2,086,507)			1.75
1998S, Silver . . . . . (878,792)			3.00
1999P . . . 2,164,000,000	0.10	0.50	
1999D 1,397,750,000	0.10	0.50	
1999S . . . . (2,543,401)			1.75
1999S, Silver . . . . . (804,565)			3.50
2000P 1,842,500,000	0.10	0.50	
2000D 1,818,700,000	0.10	0.50	
2000S . . . . (3,082,572)			1.00
2000S, Silver . . . . . (965,421)			3.00
2001P 1,369,590,000	0.10	0.50	
2001D 1,412,800,000	0.10	0.50	
2001S . . . . (2,294,909)			0.75
2001S, Silver . . . . . (889,697)			3.00
2002P 1,187,500,000	0.10	0.50	
2002D 1,379,500,000	0.10	0.50	
2002S . . . . (2,319,766)			0.75
2002S, Silver . . . . . (892,229)			3.00
2003P 1,085,500,000	0.10	0.50	
2003D 986,500,000	0.10	0.50	
2003S . . . . (2,172,684)			0.75
2003S, Silver . . . (1,125,755)			3.00
2004P 1,328,000,000	0.10	0.50	
2004D 1,159,500,000	0.10	0.50	
2004S . . . . (1,789,488)			0.75
2004S, Silver . . . (1,175,934)			3.00
2005P 1,412,000,000	0.10	0.50	
2005D 1,423,500,000	0.10	0.50	
2005S . . . . (2,275,000)			0.75
2005S, Silver . . . (1,069,679)			3.00
2006P 1,381,000,000	0.10	0.50	
2006D 1,447,500,000	0.10	0.50	
2006S . . . . (2,000,428)			0.75
2006S, Silver . . . (1,054,008)			3.00
2007P 1,047,500,000	0.10	0.50	

* Included in number above.

Chart continued on next page.

	Mintage	MS-63	MS-65	PF-65
2007D 1,042,000,000		$0.10	$0.50	
2007S . . . . (1,702,116)				$0.75
2007S, Silver . . . . . (875,050)				3.00
2008P 391,000,000		0.10	0.50	
2008D 624,500,000		0.10	0.50	
2008S . . . . (1,405,674)				0.75
2008S, Silver . . . . . (763,887)				3.00
2009P 96,500,000		0.20	0.50	
2009D 49,500,000		0.20	0.50	
2009S . . . . (1,482,502)				0.75
2009S, Silver . . . . . (697,365)				3.00
2010P 557,000,000		0.10	0.50	
2010D 562,000,000		0.10	0.50	
2010S . . . . (1,103,815)				0.75
2010S, Silver . . . . (585,401)				3.00
2011P 748,000,000		0.10	0.50	
2011D 754,000,000		0.10	0.50	
2011S . . . . (1,098,835)				0.75
2011S, Silver . . . . . (574,175)				3.00
2012P 808,000,000		0.10	0.50	
2012D 868,000,000		0.10	0.50	

	Mintage	MS-63	MS-65	PF-65
2012S . . . . (794,002)				$0.75
2012S, Silver . . . . . (495,315)				12.00
2013P 1,086,500,000		$0.10	$0.50	
2013D 1,025,500,000		0.10	0.50	
2013S . . . . (854,785)				0.75
2013S, Silver . . . . . (467,691)				3.00
2014P 1,125,500,000		0.10	0.50	
2014D 1,177,000,000		0.10	0.50	
2014S . . . . (760,876)				0.75
2014S, Silver . . . . . (491,157)				3.00
2015P 1,497,510,000		0.10	0.50	
2015D 1,543,500,000		0.10	0.50	
2015P, Rev Pf, Silver (a) . . . . (74,430)				10.00
2015S . . . . (662,854)				0.75
2015S, Silver . . . . . (387,310)				3.00
2015W, Silver (a) . . . (74,430)				5.00
2016P 1,517,000,000		0.10	0.50	
2016D 1,437,000,000		0.10	0.50	
2016S . . . . (641,775)				0.75
2016S, Silver . . . . . (419,469)				3.00

a. Included in March of Dimes commemorative Proof set.

	Mintage	SP-67	SP-70
2016W, Gold (a) 124,885		$160	$180

a. In 2016 the Mint issued a centennial version of the Winged Liberty Head ("Mercury") dime in gold.

	Mintage	MS-63	MS-65	PF-65
2017P 1,437,500,000		$0.10	$0.50	
2017D 1,290,500,000		0.10	0.50	
2017S . . . . (621,384)				$0.75
2017S, Silver . . . . . (406,994)				3.00
2018P 1,193,000,000		0.10	0.50	
2018D 1,006,000,000		0.10	0.50	

	Mintage	MS-63	MS-65	PF-65
2018S . . . . (535,221)				$0.75
2018S, Silver . . . . . (350,820)				3.00
2019P		$0.10	$0.50	
2019D		0.10	0.50	
201PS				0.75
201PS, Silver				3.00

LIBERTY SEATED (1875–1878)

The twenty-cent piece was a short-lived coin authorized by the Act of March 3, 1875. The edge of the coin is plain. Most of the 1876-CC coins were melted at the Mint and never released. The mintmark is on the reverse below the eagle.

G-4 Good: LIBERTY on shield obliterated. Letters and date legible.

VG-8 Very Good: One or two letters in LIBERTY barely visible. Other details bold.

F-12 Fine: Some letters of LIBERTY possibly visible.

VF-20 Very Fine: LIBERTY readable, but partly weak.

EF-40 Extremely Fine: LIBERTY mostly sharp. Only slight wear on high points of coin.

AU-50 About Uncirculated: Slight trace of wear on breast, head, and knees.

MS-60 Uncirculated: No trace of wear. Light blemishes.

MS-63 Choice Uncirculated: Some distracting blemishes in prime focal areas. Some impairment of luster possible.

PF-63 Choice Proof: Reflective surfaces with only a few blemishes in secondary focal places. No major flaws.

	Mintage	G-4	VG-8	F-12	VF-20	EF-40	AU-50	MS-60	MS-63	PF-63
1875 . . . . (1,200) 38,500		$150	$200	$225	$250	$350	$450	$650	$1,100	$1,850
1875CC 133,290		150	225	300	350	700	950	1,500	2,500	
1875S 1,155,000		75	85	105	140	175	225	475	800	
1876 . . . . (1,150) 14,750		150	160	175	200	300	350	550	1,100	1,850
1876CC 10,000							125,000	175,000	250,000	
1877 . . . . . . (510)					2,500	3,500				8,500
1878 . . . . . . (600)					1,750	2,250				3,500

Authorized in 1792, this denomination was not issued until four years later. The first type weighed 104 grains, the standard until modified to 103-1/8 grains by the Act of January 18, 1837. As with the dime and half dime, the weight was reduced and arrows placed at the date in 1853. Rays were placed in the field of the reverse during that year only.

DRAPED BUST (1796–1807)

AG-3 About Good: Details clear enough to identify.
G-4 Good: Date readable. Bust outlined, but no detail.
VG-8 Very Good: All but deepest drapery folds worn smooth. Hairlines nearly gone and curls lacking in detail.
F-12 Fine: All drapery lines visible. Hair partly worn.
VF-20 Very Fine: Only left side of drapery indistinct.
EF-40 Extremely Fine: Hair well outlined and detailed.
AU-50 About Uncirculated: Slight trace of wear on shoulder and highest waves of hair.
MS-60 Uncirculated: No trace of wear. Light blemishes.
MS-63 Choice Uncirculated: Some distracting marks or blemishes in focal areas. Impaired luster possible.

Small Eagle Reverse (1796)

	Mintage	AG-3	G-4	VG-8	F-12	VF-20	EF-40	AU-50	MS-60	MS-63
1796	6,146	$4,500	$8,000	$12,500	$17,500	$25,000	$42,000	$50,000	$60,000	$115,000

Heraldic Eagle Reverse (1804–1807)

	Mintage	AG-3	G-4	VG-8	F-12	VF-20	EF-40	AU-50	MS-60	MS-63
1804	6,738	$1,250	$2,750	$4,500	$6,500	$10,000	$24,000	$40,000	$75,000	$125,000
1805	121,394	125	350	450	650	1,100	2,500	3,750	8,500	12,500
1806, 6 Over 5	*	125	350	450	700	1,050	2,500	3,750	9,500	17,500
1806	206,124	125	350	450	650	1,100	2,750	3,750	8,500	12,500
1807	220,643	125	350	450	650	1,000	2,500	3,750	8,500	12,500

* Included in number below.

CAPPED BUST (1815–1838)
Variety 1 – Large Diameter (1815–1828)

AG-3 About Good: Details clear enough to identify.
G-4 Good: Date, letters, stars legible. Hair under Liberty's headband smooth. Cap lines worn smooth.
VG-8 Very Good: Rim well defined. Main details visible. Full LIBERTY on cap. Hair above eye nearly smooth.
F-12 Fine: All hair lines visible, but only partial detail visible in drapery. Shoulder clasp distinct.
VF-20 Very Fine: All details visible, but some wear evident. Clasp and ear sharp.
EF-40 Extremely Fine: All details distinct. Hair well outlined.
AU-50 About Uncirculated: Slight trace of wear on tips of curls and above the eye, and on the wing and claw tips.
MS-60 Uncirculated: No trace of wear. Light blemishes.
MS-63 Choice Uncirculated: Some distracting marks or blemishes in focal areas. Impaired luster possible.

	Mintage	AG-3	G-4	VG-8	F-12	VF-20	EF-40	AU-50	MS-60	MS-63
1815 89,235		$75	$125	$250	$400	$550	$1,650	$2,250	$3,500	$5,500
1818, 8 Over 5 . . . .*		35	60	100	275	500	1,000	1,350	2,500	5,000
1818, Normal Date 361,174		35	60	100	175	325	1,000	1,350	2,500	5,000
1819 144,000		35	60	100	175	325	1,000	1,500	2,750	5,250
1820 127,444		35	60	100	175	325	1,000	1,500	2,750	5,000
1821 216,851		35	60	100	175	325	1,000	1,350	2,500	5,000
1822 64,080		75	125	200	350	600	1,150	1,750	2,750	5,500
1822, 25 Over 50 C. . . . .*		1,500	4,000	7,500	15,000	20,000	27,500	35,000	45,000	
1823, 3 Over 2 17,800		15,000	35,000	40,000	55,000	75,000	100,000	135,000	—	
1824, 4 Over 2 . . . .**		250	500	700	1,200	1,600	3,500	4,750	7,500	
1825 168,000		35	75	100	175	325	1,000	1,500	2,500	4,250
1827, Original (Curl Base 2 in 25 C.) **(a)**. . .4,000										150,000
1827, Restrike (Square Base 2 in 25 C.) **(a)**. . . . . . .*										45,000
1828 102,000		35	60	100	175	325	1,000	1,500	2,500	4,250
1828, 25 Over 50 C. . . . .*		250	700	1,200	1,500	2,500	5,500	8,500	12,500	55,000

* Included in regular mintage.   ** Included in 1825 mintage.   **a.** The 7 is punched over a 3, which is punched over an earlier 2.

Variety 2 – Reduced Diameter (1831–1838), Motto Removed

G-4 Good: Bust of Liberty well defined. Hair under headband smooth. Date, letters, stars legible. Scant rims.
VG-8 Very Good: Details apparent but worn on high spots. Rims strong. Full LIBERTY.
F-12 Fine: All hair lines visible. Drapery partly worn. Shoulder clasp distinct.
VF-20 Very Fine: Only top spots worn. Clasp sharp. Ear distinct.
EF-40 Extremely Fine: Hair details and clasp bold and clear.

AU-50 About Uncirculated: Slight trace of wear on hair around forehead, on cheek, and at top and bottom tips of eagle's wings and left claw.
MS-60 Uncirculated: No trace of wear. Light blemishes.
MS-63 Choice Uncirculated: Some distracting contact marks or blemishes in prime focal areas. Impaired luster possible.

	Mintage	G-4	VG-8	F-12	VF-20	EF-40	AU-50	MS-60	MS-63
1831 398,000		$45	$75	$85	$110	$275	$500	$1,300	$2,750
1832 320,000		45	65	75	100	275	500	1,300	2,750
1833 156,000		45	65	75	110	275	500	1,300	2,750
1834 286,000		45	65	75	100	275	500	1,300	2,750
1835 1,952,000		45	65	75	100	275	500	1,300	2,750
1836 472,000		45	65	75	100	275	500	1,300	3,000
1837 252,400		45	65	75	100	275	500	1,300	2,750
1838 366,000		45	65	75	100	275	500	1,300	2,750

LIBERTY SEATED (1838–1891)

G-4 Good: Scant rim. LIBERTY on shield worn off. Date and letters legible.
VG-8 Very Good: Rim fairly defined, at least three letters in LIBERTY evident.
F-12 Fine: LIBERTY complete, but partly weak.
VF-20 Very Fine: LIBERTY strong.
EF-40 Extremely Fine: Complete LIBERTY and edges of scroll. Shoulder clasp clear on Liberty's gown.
AU-50 About Uncirculated: Slight wear on Liberty's knees and breast and on eagle's neck, wing tips, and claws.
MS-60 Uncirculated: No trace of wear. Light blemishes.
MS-63 Choice Uncirculated: Some distracting marks or blemishes in focal areas. Impaired luster possible.

Variety 1 – No Motto Above Eagle (1838–1853)

Small Date

Mintmark location is on reverse, below eagle.

Large Date

	Mintage	G-4	VG-8	F-12	VF-20	EF-40	AU-50	MS-60	MS-63
1838	466,000	$20	$25	$35	$120	$275	$600	$1,100	$2,750
1839	491,146	15	20	30	80	275	600	1,100	2,750
1840	188,127	15	22	30	65	110	200	575	2,000
1840O	425,200	20	22	40	70	125	300	650	2,250
1841	120,000	25	35	65	85	150	275	475	900
1841O	452,000	20	25	30	75	200	225	425	1,000
1842, Small Date (Proof only)									35,000
1842, Large Date	88,000	35	50	90	150	200	425	800	1,500
1842O, Small Date	*	400	850	1,200	2,000	4,500	7,500	20,000	
1842O, Large Date	769,000	18	25	30	35	100	200	650	2,500
1843	645,600	15	20	25	30	55	125	275	650
1843O	968,000	18	25	50	225	650	850	1,500	2,750
1844	421,200	15	20	25	30	50	125	300	700
1844O	740,000	18	25	30	50	100	200	850	1,200
1845	922,000	15	20	25	30	60	125	300	625
1846	510,000	15	20	25	30	75	150	300	700
1847	734,000	15	20	25	30	55	125	300	650
1847O	368,000	50	85	150	300	650	1,200	4,750	10,000
1848	146,000	15	22	40	65	125	225	750	2,500
1849	340,000	15	22	25	45	80	150	500	1,000
1849O	(a)	850	1,200	1,350	2,000	4,500	5,500	12,500	15,000
1850	190,800	22	36	50	70	115	180	850	1,500
1850O	412,000	27	35	45	70	175	400	1,200	2,600
1851	160,000	27	42	60	100	215	320	800	1,300
1851O	88,000	250	400	550	750	1,500	2,500	4,500	
1852	177,060	50	75	100	200	350	450	850	1,500
1852O	96,000	125	175	450	1,000	1,500	3,500	6,500	20,000
1853, Recut Date, No Arrows or Rays	44,200	750	1,000	1,500	2,000	2,500	3,500	4,500	5,500

* Included in number below. **a.** Mintage for 1849-O included with 1850-O.

Variety 2 – Arrows at Date, Rays Around Eagle (1853)

1853, 3 Over 4

	Mintage	G-4	VG-8	F-12	VF-20	EF-40	AU-50	MS-60	MS-63
1853	15,210,020	$15	$18	$20	$30	$115	$250	$700	$1,300
1853, 3 Over 4	*	35	55	75	125	225	375	1,100	2,500
1853O	1,332,000	20	25	35	40	200	750	2,500	5,500

* Included in number above.

Variety 3 – Arrows at Date, No Rays (1854–1855)

	Mintage	G-4	VG-8	F-12	VF-20	EF-40	AU-50	MS-60	MS-63
1854	12,380,000	$10	$15	$18	$25	$50	$160	$400	$950
1854O	1,484,000	20	25	30	35	70	200	625	1,200
1855	2,857,000	10	15	20	25	50	160	400	850
1855O	176,000	60	100	175	350	450	1,250	2,000	8,500
1855S	396,400	45	85	150	250	550	750	1,500	4,500

Variety 1 Resumed, With Weight Standard of Variety 2 (1856–1865)

	Mintage	G-4	VG-8	F-12	VF-20	EF-40	AU-50	MS-60	MS-63	PF-63
1856	7,264,000	$10	$11	$15	$25	$40	$120	$225	$400	$2,500
1856O	968,000	20	25	45	65	125	300	600	1,250	
1856S	286,000	125	200	350	450	1,000	1,750	4,500	10,000	
1857	9,644,000	10	11	15	25	40	120	225	400	2,000
1857O	1,180,000	20	25	30	35	125	275	575	1,500	
1857S	82,000	115	200	250	500	600	1,250	2,500	4,500	
1858 . . . . . (300+). . .	7,368,000	10	11	15	25	40	120	225	400	1,000
1858O	520,000	20	25	30	35	100	350	2,000	4,500	
1858S	121,000	150	225	300	550	1,500	2,750	15,000	—	
1859 . . . . . (800). . . .	1,343,200	10	11	15	25	40	120	225	525	700
1859O	260,000	20	25	30	50	150	500	1,500	4,500	
1859S	80,000	200	250	350	850	3,250	9,000	—	—	
1860 . . . . (1,000).	804,400	10	11	15	25	40	120	225	400	700
1860O	388,000	20	25	30	35	55	275	650	1,100	
1860S	56,000	600	1,000	2,000	3,500	6,000	11,000	—	—	
1861 . . . . (1,000). . . .	4,853,600	10	11	15	25	40	120	225	400	700
1861S	96,000	350	500	850	1,450	3,000	8,500	22,500	—	
1862 . . . . . (550).	932,000	10	20	25	35	45	120	225	400	700
1862S	67,000	100	200	300	400	800	1,500	2,500	3,500	
1863 . . . . . (460).	191,600	25	30	45	90	125	200	325	550	700
1864 . . . . . (470).	93,600	45	60	80	140	250	300	375	800	700
1864S	20,000	550	750	1,000	1,500	2,500	3,500	7,500	15,000	
1865 . . . . . . (500).	58,800	50	60	140	250	300	550	850	1,250	700
1865S	41,000	125	175	250	450	650	850	2,500	3,500	

Variety 4 – Motto Above Eagle (1866–1873)

	Mintage	G-4	VG-8	F-12	VF-20	EF-40	AU-50	MS-60	MS-63	PF-63
1866 . . . . . . (725).	16,800	$500	$650	$850	$1,100	$1,250	$1,400	$1,600	$2,000	$500
1866S	28,000	250	350	550	1,000	1,100	1,500	3,000	5,500	

Chart continued on next page.

103

	Mintage	G-4	VG-8	F-12	VF-20	EF-40	AU-50	MS-60	MS-63	PF-63
1867 . . . . (625) 20,000		$125	$200	$325	$400	$800	$1,000	$1,100	$2,500	$500
1867S 48,000		225	350	550	750	1,500	3,750	7,500	—	
1868 . . . . (600) 29,400		70	90	130	175	350	450	600	900	500
1868S 96,000		50	65	100	200	525	650	1,500	3,250	
1869 . . . . (600) 16,000		250	350	550	650	750	850	1,250	3,000	500
1869S 76,000		55	85	140	275	525	725	1,750	2,750	
1870 . . . . (1,000) 86,400		30	35	75	120	150	225	500	800	500
1870CC 8,340		7,000	8,500	15,000	20,000	27,500	65,000	—		
1871 . . . . (960) . . . 118,200		15	20	30	60	225	275	475	875	500
1871CC 10,890		4,500	7,500	12,000	15,000	25,000	45,000	—	—	
1871S 30,900		450	750	1,200	1,500	2,500	3,500	4,500	6,500	
1872 . . . . (950) . . . 182,000		15	20	40	55	200	275	700	1,200	500
1872CC 22,850		1,000	1,500	2,250	4,500	7,500	14,500	35,000		
1872S 83,000		1,200	1,500	2,000	2,500	3,500	4,500	6,500		
1873 . . . . (600) . . . 212,000		15	25	30	45	80	100	225	500	500
1873CC 4,000					—	60,000	—	—		

Variety 5 – Arrows at Date (1873–1874)

	Mintage	G-4	VG-8	F-12	VF-20	EF-40	AU-50	MS-60	MS-63	PF-63
1873 . . . . (500) . . 1,271,200		$15	$18	$20	$40	$125	$250	$550	$1,000	$800
1873CC 12,462		3,500	6,500	8,500	12,500	17,500	30,000	65,000	85,000	
1873S 156,000		45	65	100	150	275	375	800	1,500	
1874 . . . . (700) 471,200		15	20	20	40	125	275	550	1,000	800
1874S 392,000		15	20	35	60	150	300	550	1,000	

Variety 4 Resumed, With Weight Standard of Variety 5 (1875–1891)

1877-S, S Over Horizontal S

	Mintage	G-4	VG-8	F-12	VF-20	EF-40	AU-50	MS-60	MS-63	PF-63
1875 . . . . . . (700) 4,292,800		$15	$18	$20	$25	$40	$100	$175	$400	$500
1875CC 140,000		85	185	350	450	650	1,100	2,500	5,500	
1875S 680,000		15	18	25	40	80	160	375	600	
1876 . . . . (1,150) . . . 17,816,000		15	18	20	25	40	100	175	400	500
1876CC 4,944,000		25	40	50	60	100	125	275	600	
1876S 8,596,000		15	18	20	25	40	100	175	400	
1877 . . . . . . (510) . . . 10,911,200		15	18	20	25	40	100	175	400	500
1877CC 4,192,000		30	40	50	60	100	125	250	400	
1877S 8,996,000		15	18	20	25	40	100	175	400	

	Mintage	G-4	VG-8	F-12	VF-20	EF-40	AU-50	MS-60	MS-63	PF-63
1877S, S Over Horizontal S .....*		$15	$25	$40	$75	$125	$200	$400	$1,100	
1878 . . . . (800). . 2,260,000		15	18	20	25	40	100	200	400	$500
1878CC 996,000		35	45	55	75	100	150	300	625	
1878S 140,000		125	200	350	550	750	1,000	1,500	4,000	
1879 . . . . . (1,100). 13,600		90	110	150	175	250	400	450	550	500
1880 . . . . . . (1,355). 13,600		90	110	150	175	250	300	390	520	500
1881 . . . .(975). 12,000		115	135	200	225	250	325	420	575	500
1882 . . . . . . (1,100). 15,200		100	125	165	225	275	350	425	625	500
1883 . . . . . . (1,039). 14,400		100	125	175	200	300	350	425	625	500
1884 . . . .(875). 8,000		175	200	275	300	400	450	550	700	500
1885 . . . .(930). 13,600		100	125	175	200	250	300	415	725	500
1886 . . . .(886). 5,000		225	275	375	450	600	750	850	1,050	500
1887 . . . .(710). 10,000		150	200	250	325	375	425	485	675	500
1888 . . . .(832). 10,001		150	200	235	300	350	400	475	515	500
1888S 1,216,000		15	18	29	35	40	100	175	400	
1889 . . . .(711). 12,000		125	140	175	200	250	300	400	525	500
1890 . . . .(590). 80,000		40	50	75	100	140	225	335	515	500
1891 . . . .(600). . 3,920,000		15	18	20	25	40	130	175	400	500
1891O 68,000		200	350	650	1,000	1,750	2,500	5,000	8,000	
1891S 2,216,000		15	18	20	25	40	100	175	400	

* Included in 1877-S regular mintage (previous page).

BARBER OR LIBERTY HEAD (1892–1916)

Like other silver coins of this type, the quarter dollars minted from 1892 to 1916 were designed by U.S. Mint chief engraver Charles E. Barber. His initial B is found at the truncation of the neck of Miss Liberty.

G-4 Good: Date and legends legible. LIBERTY worn off headband.
VG-8 Very Good: Some letters in LIBERTY legible.
F-12 Fine: LIBERTY completely legible but not sharp.
VF-20 Very Fine: All letters in LIBERTY evenly plain.
EF-40 Extremely Fine: LIBERTY bold, its ribbon distinct.

AU-50 About Uncirculated: Slight trace of wear above forehead, on cheek, and on eagle's head, wings, and tail.
MS-60 Uncirculated: No trace of wear. Light blemishes.
MS-63 Choice Uncirculated: Some distracting marks or blemishes in focal areas. Impaired luster possible.
PF-63 Choice Proof: Reflective surfaces with only a few blemishes in secondary focal places. No major flaws.

	Mintage	G-4	VG-8	F-12	VF-20	EF-40	AU-50	MS-60	MS-63	PF-63
1892 . . . . . . (1,245). . 8,236,000		$6	$7	$12	$20	$30	$75	$150	$250	$500
1892O 2,460,000		8	9	15	25	40	85	200	260	
1892S 964,079		20	30	40	60	85	150	325	525	
1893 . . . .(792). . 5,444,023		6	7	12	15	30	75	150	250	500
1893O 3,396,000		6	7	12	25	45	85	150	275	
1893S 1,454,535		9	12	30	60	80	150	275	650	
1894 . . . .(972). . 3,432,000		6	7	12	15	35	75	150	250	500
1894O 2,852,000		6	7	15	30	60	125	175	400	
1894S 2,648,821		6	7	12	25	55	100	175	425	
1895 . . . .(880). . 4,440,000		6	7	12	15	30	75	150	250	500
1895O 2,816,000		6	8	15	30	60	125	225	575	
1895S 1,764,681		9	13	35	60	75	175	250	600	
1896 . . . .(762). . 3,874,000		6	7	10	15	35	75	150	250	500
1896O 1,484,000		30	40	100	160	275	450	675	1,100	

Chart continued on next page.

	Mintage	G-4	VG-8	F-12	VF-20	EF-40	AU-50	MS-60	MS-63	PF-63
1896S 188,039		$450	$1,000	$1,450	$2,250	$3,500	$4,500	$7,500	$15,000	
1897 . . . . . (731) 8,140,000		6	7	8	15	30	75	150	250	$500
1897O 1,414,800		12	30	100	160	200	275	550	1,100	
1897S 542,229		50	75	175	275	400	475	1,100	1,800	
1898 . . . . . (735) . . . 11,100,000		6	7	8	15	30	75	150	250	500
1898O 1,868,000		8	12	35	65	125	175	400	1,000	
1898S 1,020,592		6	7	20	30	45	125	250	900	
1899 . . . . . (846) 12,624,000		6	7	8	15	30	75	150	250	500
1899O 2,644,000		7	8	15	30	60	150	250	475	
1899S 708,000		10	20	45	55	65	200	350	900	
1900 . . . . . (912) 10,016,000		6	7	8	15	30	75	150	250	500
1900O 3,416,000		8	10	30	50	70	200	350	500	
1900S 1,858,585		6	7	12	20	30	75	200	650	
1901 . . . . . (813) 8,892,000		8	12	15	30	35	75	150	250	500
1901O 1,612,000		25	40	120	175	275	350	650	1,100	
1901S 72,664		2,750	5,500	10,000	15,000	20,000	25,000	30,000	35,000	
1902 . . . . . (777) . . . 12,196,967		5	6	8	15	30	75	150	250	500
1902O 4,748,000		6	7	20	30	60	125	275	800	
1902S 1,524,612		7	9	20	35	70	125	300	550	
1903 . . . . . (755) 9,759,309		5	6	8	15	30	75	150	250	500
1903O 3,500,000		5	6	15	25	50	125	250	675	
1903S 1,036,000		8	9	15	35	65	150	250	500	
1904 . . . . . (670) 9,588,143		5	6	8	15	30	75	150	250	500
1904O 2,456,000		10	16	35	75	125	250	525	750	
1905 . . . . . (727) 4,967,523		10	12	20	30	40	75	150	250	500
1905O 1,230,000		20	25	55	100	125	200	300	950	
1905S 1,884,000		12	18	30	45	55	110	200	600	
1906 . . . . . (675) 3,655,760		4	5	8	15	30	75	150	250	500
1906D 3,280,000		4	6	8	15	30	75	150	275	
1906O 2,056,000		4	5	12	20	45	100	160	325	
1907 . . . . . (575) 7,132,000		4	5	8	15	30	75	150	250	500
1907D 2,484,000		4	5	10	15	30	80	150	400	
1907O 4,560,000		5	6	8	15	30	75	150	250	
1907S 1,360,000		5	6	15	30	55	150	300	800	
1908 . . . . . (545) 4,232,000		4	5	8	15	30	75	150	250	500
1908D 5,788,000		4	5	8	15	30	75	150	250	
1908O 6,244,000		5	6	8	15	30	75	150	250	
1908S 784,000		10	25	65	70	150	275	425	650	
1909 . . . . . (650) 9,268,000		4	5	8	15	30	75	150	250	500
1909D 5,114,000		4	5	8	15	30	85	150	250	
1909O 712,000		25	55	275	650	1,500	1,500	2,000	3,000	
1909S 1,348,000		5	6	12	20	40	100	175	425	
1910 . . . . . (551) 2,244,000		4	5	10	15	30	75	150	250	500
1910D 1,500,000		4	5	15	30	50	125	200	500	
1911 . . . . . (543) 3,720,000		4	5	8	15	30	75	150	250	500
1911D 933,600		12	18	75	150	225	400	575	700	
1911S 988,000		5	6	20	35	70	125	225	425	
1912 . . . . . (700) 4,400,000		4	5	8	15	30	75	150	250	500
1912S 708,000		8	12	25	40	55	125	250	525	
1913 . . . . . (613) 484,000		10	14	40	75	185	300	550	700	500
1913D 1,450,800		5	6	12	20	35	90	150	250	
1913S 40,000		1,000	1,500	3,000	5,000	7,000	8,500	11,000	13,500	

	Mintage	G-4	VG-8	F-12	VF-20	EF-40	AU-50	MS-60	MS-63	PF-63
1914 . . . . . .(380). . . .	6,244,230	$4	$5	$7	$15	$30	$75	$150	$250	$500
1914D	3,046,000	4	5	7	15	30	75	150	250	
1914S	264,000	55	90	225	275	400	750	1,100	1,500	
1915 . . . . . .(450). . . .	3,480,000	4	5	7	15	30	75	150	250	500
1915D	3,694,000	4	5	7	15	30	75	150	250	
1915S	704,000	10	20	30	45	50	125	175	275	
1916	1,788,000	4	5	7	15	30	75	150	250	
1916D	6,540,800	4	5	7	15	30	75	150	250	

STANDING LIBERTY (1916–1930)

This design is by Hermon A. MacNeil, whose initial M is above and to the right of the date. Liberty bears a shield of protection in her left arm, while the right hand holds the olive branch of peace. There was a modification in 1917. The reverse had a new arrangement of stars and the eagle was higher. After 1924 the date was "recessed," thereby giving it greater protection from the effects of circulation. A Centennial Gold issue was struck in 2016.

G-4 Good: Date and lettering legible. Top of date worn. Liberty's right leg and toes worn off. Much wear evident on left leg and drapery lines.
VG-8 Very Good: Distinct date. Toes faintly visible. Drapery lines visible above Liberty's left leg.
F-12 Fine: High curve of right leg flat from thigh to ankle. Only slight wear evident on left leg. Drapery lines over right thigh seen only at sides of leg.
VF-20 Very Fine: Garment line across right leg worn, but visible at sides.
EF-40 Extremely Fine: Flattened only at high spots. Liberty's toes are sharp. Drapery lines across right leg evident.
AU-50 About Uncirculated: Slight trace of wear on head, kneecap, shield's center, and highest point on eagle's body.
MS-60 Uncirculated: No trace of wear, but contact marks, surface spots, or faded luster possible.
MS-63 Choice Uncirculated: No trace of wear. Light blemishes. Attractive mint luster.

Variety 1 – No Stars Below Eagle (1916–1917)

Mintmark location is on obverse, to left of date.

	Mintage	G-4	VG-8	F-12	VF-20	EF-40	AU-50	MS-60	MS-63
1916	52,000	$2,250	$3,500	$4,500	$5,250	$6,500	$8,000	$10,000	$11,500
1917, Variety 1	8,740,000	12	20	30	40	60	110	150	225
1917D, Variety 1 . . .	1,509,200	14	25	35	55	80	125	210	250
1917S, Variety 1 . . .	1,952,000	16	30	40	65	105	150	240	325

Variety 2 – Stars Below Eagle (1917–1930)
Pedestal Date (1917–1924)

1918-S, 8 Over 7

See next page for chart.   **107**

	Mintage	G-4	VG-8	F-12	VF-20	EF-40	AU-50	MS-60	MS-63
1917, Variety 2 13,880,000		$11	$20	$25	$30	$45	$75	$120	$165
1917D, Variety 2 6,224,400		18	25	35	45	65	100	160	225
1917S, Variety 2 5,552,000		18	25	35	45	70	95	150	225
1918 14,240,000		8	10	15	17	25	45	90	150
1918D 7,380,000		15	18	30	35	65	100	175	250
1918S, Normal Date . . .11,072,000		9	10	15	20	30	50	110	160
1918S, 8 Over 7 . . . .*		1,000	1,450	2,750	3,500	5,500	8,000	12,500	20,000
1919 11,324,000		18	25	30	35	40	60	100	150
1919D 1,944,000		45	50	110	225	350	500	600	1,100
1919S 1,836,000		40	50	100	200	325	475	725	1,200
1920 27,860,000		7	9	12	20	25	50	100	125
1920D 3,586,400		30	35	45	65	90	100	300	525
1920S 6,380,000		8	12	15	20	30	85	125	450
1921 1,916,000		100	125	250	375	500	675	1,000	1,250
1923 9,716,000		7	9	15	20	25	50	100	160
1923S 1,360,000		175	250	375	550	1,000	1,200	1,500	2,500
1924 10,920,000		7	9	12	20	30	55	110	160
1924D 3,112,000		25	35	50	75	100	125	175	225
1924S 2,860,000		15	18	20	30	60	125	175	525

* Included in number above.

Recessed Date (1925–1930)

	Mintage	G-4	VG-8	F-12	VF-20	EF-40	AU-50	MS-60	MS-63
1925 12,280,000		$4	$5	$6	$7	$16	$40	$80	$140
1926 11,316,000		4	5	6	7	16	40	80	125
1926D 1,716,000		4	6	10	20	45	75	100	140
1926S 2,700,000		4	5	6	10	50	125	200	475
1927 11,912,000		4	5	6	7	16	40	80	125
1927D 976,000		6	10	15	35	80	125	160	200
1927S 396,000		35	45	65	175	600	1,500	3,250	4,500
1928 6,336,000		4	5	6	7	16	40	80	125
1928D 1,627,600		4	5	6	7	16	40	80	125
1928S 2,644,000		4	5	6	7	16	40	80	125
1929 11,140,000		4	5	6	7	16	40	80	125
1929D 1,358,000		4	5	6	7	16	40	80	125
1929S 1,764,000		4	5	6	7	16	40	80	125
1930 5,632,000		4	5	6	7	16	40	80	125
1930S 1,556,000		4	5	6	7	16	40	80	125

WASHINGTON (1932 TO DATE)

This type was intended to be a commemorative issue marking the 200th anniversary of President Washington's birth. John Flanagan, a New York sculptor, was the designer. The initials JF are found at the base of the neck. The mintmark is on the reverse below the wreath for coins from 1932 to 1964. Starting in 1968, the mintmark was moved to the obverse at the right of the ribbon.

F-12 Fine: Hair lines about Washington's ear visible. Tiny feathers on eagle's breast faintly visible.
VF-20 Very Fine: Most hair details visible. Wing feathers clear.
EF-40 Extremely Fine: Hair lines sharp. Wear spots confined to top of eagle's legs and center of breast.
MS-60 Uncirculated: No trace of wear, but many contact marks, surface spotting, or faded luster possible.
MS-63 Choice Uncirculated: No trace of wear. Light blemishes. Attractive mint luster.
MS-64 Uncirculated: A few scattered contact marks. Good eye appeal and attractive luster.
MS-65 Gem Uncirculated: Only light, scattered, non-distracting marks. Strong luster, good eye appeal.
PF-65 Gem Proof: Hardly any blemishes, and no flaws.

Silver Coinage (1932–1964)

	Mintage	VG-8	F-12	VF-20	EF-40	MS-60	MS-63	MS-65	PF-63
1932	5,404,000	$3.50	$4.50	$5.00	$5.50	$13	$25	$145	
1932D	436,800	50.00	60.00	75.00	90.00	675	1,050	7,500	
1932S	408,000	50.00	60.00	75.00	90.00	275	475	2,500	
1934	31,912,052	2.75	3.25	3.50	5.00	10	18	50	
1934D	3,527,200	2.75	3.25	5.00	8.00	100	175	350	
1935	32,484,000	2.75	3.25	3.50	5.00	8	15	35	
1935D	5,780,000	2.75	3.25	3.50	8.00	100	140	275	
1935S	5,660,000	2.75	3.25	3.50	6.00	45	60	145	
1936 (3,837)	41,300,000	2.75	3.25	3.50	5.00	10	16	45	$850
1936D	5,374,000	2.75	3.25	3.50	15.00	225	350	575	
1936S	3,828,000	2.75	3.25	3.50	6.00	45	65	175	
1937 (5,542)	19,696,000	2.75	3.25	3.50	5.00	10	15	45	250
1937D	7,189,600	2.75	3.25	3.50	6.00	25	40	75	
1937S	1,652,000	2.75	3.25	3.50	8.00	70	110	180	
1938 (8,045)	9,472,000	2.75	3.25	3.50	6.00	45	50	120	140
1938S	2,832,000	2.75	3.25	3.50	6.00	45	60	110	
1939 (8,795)	33,540,000	2.75	3.25	3.50	5.00	6	11	25	120
1939D	7,092,000	2.75	3.25	3.50	5.00	16	20	45	
1939S	2,628,000	2.75	3.25	3.50	7.00	45	65	150	

	Mintage	F-12	VF-20	EF-40	MS-60	MS-63	MS-65	PF-65
1940 (11,246)	35,704,000	$2.75	$3.25	$3.50	$7	$12	$25	$70
1940D	2,797,600	2.75	3.25	6.00	50	80	125	
1940S	8,244,000	2.75	3.25	3.50	10	13	20	
1941 (15,287)	79,032,000	2.75	3.25	3.50	5	7	18	60
1941D	16,714,800	2.75	3.25	5.00	12	22	25	
1941S	16,080,000	2.75	3.25	3.50	9	18	25	
1942 (21,123)	102,096,000	2.75	3.25	3.50	5	6	10	50
1942D	17,487,200	2.75	3.25	3.50	7	11	15	
1942S	19,384,000	2.75	3.25	5.00	30	45	70	
1943	99,700,000	2.75	3.25	3.50	5	6	18	
1943D	16,095,600	2.75	3.25	3.50	10	15	20	
1943S	21,700,000	2.75	3.25	3.50	9	20	22	
1944	104,956,000	2.75	3.25	3.50	5	6	13	
1944D	14,600,800	2.75	3.25	3.50	8	9	15	
1944S	12,560,000	2.75	3.25	3.50	7	8	12	
1945	74,372,000	2.75	3.25	3.50	5	6	17	
1945D	12,341,600	2.75	3.25	3.50	8	10	17	
1945S	17,004,001	2.75	3.25	3.50	5	6	12	
1946	53,436,000	2.75	3.25	3.50	5	6	15	
1946D	9,072,800	2.75	3.25	3.50	5	6	12	
1946S	4,204,000	2.75	3.25	3.50	5	6	12	
1947	22,556,000	2.75	3.25	3.50	5	7	12	

Chart continued on next page.

	Mintage	F-12	VF-20	EF-40	MS-60	MS-63	MS-65	PF-65
1947D	15,338,400	$2.75	$3.25	$3.50	$5.00	$7.00	$14	
1947S	5,532,000	2.75	3.25	3.50	5.00	7.00	10	
1948	35,196,000	2.75	3.25	3.50	5.00	6.00	10	
1948D	16,766,800	2.75	3.25	3.50	5.00	7.00	20	
1948S	15,960,000	2.75	3.25	3.50	5.00	6.00	15	
1949	9,312,000	2.75	3.25	5.00	12.00	20.00	30	
1949D	10,068,400	2.75	3.25	3.50	7.00	12.00	15	
1950 . . . . . (51,386) . . .	24,920,126	2.75	3.25	3.50	5.00	6.00	10	$25.00
1950D	21,075,600	2.75	3.25	3.50	5.00	6.00	10	
1950D, D Over S	*	10.00	25.00	75.00	125.00	425.00	2,750	
1950S	10,284,004	2.75	3.25	4.50	5.00	6.00	10	
1950S, S Over D	*	10.00	27.00	80.00	200.00	250.00	800	
1951 . . . . . (57,500) . . .	43,448,102	2.75	3.25	3.50	4.50	6.00	10	25.00
1951D	35,354,800	2.75	3.25	3.50	4.50	6.00	10	
1951S	9,048,000	2.75	3.25	3.50	5.00	12.00	15	
1952 . . . . . (81,980) . . .	38,780,093	2.75	3.25	3.50	4.50	6.00	10	25.00
1952D	49,795,200	2.75	3.25	3.50	4.50	6.00	15	
1952S	13,707,800	2.75	3.25	3.50	5.00	10.00	15	
1953 . . . . (128,800) . . .	18,536,120	2.75	3.25	3.50	4.50	6.00	15	20.00
1953D	56,112,400	2.75	3.25	3.25	4.50	6.00	14	
1953S	14,016,000	2.75	3.25	3.50	4.50	6.00	13	
1954 . . . . (233,300) . . .	54,412,203	2.75	3.25	3.50	4.50	6.00	10	8.00
1954D	42,305,500	2.75	3.25	3.50	4.50	6.00	15	
1954S	11,834,722	2.75	3.25	3.50	4.50	6.00	13	
1955 . . . . (378,200) . . .	18,180,181	2.75	3.25	3.50	4.50	6.00	10	10.00
1955D	3,182,400	2.75	3.25	3.50	4.50	6.00	18	
1956 . . . . (669,384) . . .	44,144,000	2.75	3.25	3.50	4.50	6.00	9	7.50
1956D	32,334,500	2.75	3.25	3.50	4.50	6.00	10	
1957 . . . (1,247,952) . . .	46,532,000	2.75	3.25	3.50	4.50	6.00	10	6.00
1957D	77,924,160	2.75	3.25	3.50	4.50	6.00	9	
1958 . . . . (875,652) . . .	6,360,000	2.75	3.25	3.50	4.50	6.00	8	6.00
1958D	78,124,900	2.75	3.25	3.50	4.50	6.00	8	
1959 . . . (1,149,291) . . .	24,384,000	2.75	3.25	3.50	4.50	6.00	8	5.00
1959D	62,054,232	2.75	3.25	3.50	4.50	6.00	8	
1960 . . . (1,691,602) . . .	29,164,000	2.75	3.25	3.50	4.25	5.50	6	5.00
1960D	63,000,324	2.75	3.25	3.50	4.25	5.50	6	
1961 . . . (3,028,244) . . .	37,036,000	2.75	3.25	3.50	4.25	5.50	6	5.00
1961D	83,656,928	2.75	3.25	3.50	4.25	5.50	6	
1962 . . . (3,218,019) . . .	36,156,000	2.75	3.25	3.50	4.25	5.50	6	5.00
1962D	127,554,756	2.75	3.25	3.50	4.25	5.50	6	
1963 . . . (3,075,645) . . .	74,316,000	2.75	3.25	3.50	4.25	5.50	6	5.00
1963D	135,288,184	2.75	3.25	3.50	4.25	5.50	6	
1964 . . . (3,950,762) . .	560,390,585	2.75	3.25	3.50	4.25	5.50	6	5.00
1964D	704,135,528	2.75	3.25	3.50	4.25	5.50	6	

* Included in number above.

Clad Coinage and Silver Proofs (1965 to Date)

	Mintage	MS-63	MS-65	PF-65		Mintage	MS-63	MS-65	PF-65
1965	1,819,717,540	$0.30	$4.00		1968D	101,534,000	$0.30	$3.00	
1966	821,101,500	0.30	3.00		1968S	(3,041,506)			$1
1967	1,524,031,848	0.30	3.00		1969	176,212,000	0.75	3.50	
1968	220,731,500	0.50	3.50		1969D	114,372,000	0.50	4.00	

	Mintage	MS-63	MS-65	PF-65
1969S . . . . (2,934,631)				$1
1970 136,420,000	$0.25	$3		
1970D 417,341,364	0.25	2		
1970S . . . . (2,632,810)				1
1971 109,284,000	0.30	2		
1971D 258,634,428	0.30	2		
1971S . . . . (3,220,733)				1
1972 215,048,000	0.30	2		

	Mintage	MS-63	MS-65	PF-65
1972D 311,067,732	$0.30	$2		
1972S . . . . (3,260,996)				$1
1973 346,924,000	0.30	2		
1973D 232,977,400	0.30	2		
1973S . . . . (2,760,339)				1
1974 801,456,000	0.30	2		
1974D 353,160,300	0.30	3		
1974S . . . . (2,612,568)				1

Bicentennial (1776–1976)

	Mintage	MS-63	MS-65	PF-65
1776–1976, Copper-Nickel Clad 809,784,016	$0.30	$2	
1776–1976D, Copper-Nickel Clad 860,118,839	0.30	2	
1776–1976S, Copper-Nickel Clad . . . . (7,059,099)			$1
1776–1976S, Silver Clad. 11,000,000	2.50	3	
1776–1976S, Silver Clad. . . . . (4,000,000)			3

Note: Mintage figures for 1976-S silver clad coins are approximate; many were melted in 1982.

Eagle Reverse Resumed (1977–1998)
(Dies Slightly Modified to Lower Relief)

	Mintage	MS-63	MS-65	PF-65
1977 468,556,000	$0.27			
1977D 256,524,978	0.27	$1.00		
1977S . . . . (3,251,152)				$1
1978 521,452,000	0.27	1.50		
1978D 287,373,152	0.27	1.50		
1978S . . . . (3,127,781)				1
1979 515,708,000	0.28	1.50		
1979D 489,789,780	0.27	1.25		
1979S . . . . (3,677,175)				
Type 1.				1
Type 2.				2
1980P 635,832,000	0.27	1.50		
1980D 518,327,487	0.27	1.25		
1980S . . . . (3,554,806)				1
1981P 601,716,000	0.27	1.50		
1981D 575,722,833	0.27	1.00		
1981S . . . . (4,063,083)				
Type 1.				3
Type 2.				6
1982P 500,931,000	1.00	10.00		
1982D 480,042,788	1.00	8.00		
1982S . . . . (3,857,479)				1
1983P 673,535,000	8.00	25.00		

	Mintage	MS-63	MS-65	PF-65
1983D 617,806,446	$3.00	$20		
1983S . . . . (3,279,126)				$1
1984P 676,545,000	0.30	3		
1984D 546,483,064	0.30	3		
1984S . . . . (3,065,110)				1
1985P 775,818,962	0.50	5		
1985D 519,962,888	0.35	3		
1985S . . . . (3,362,821)				1
1986P 551,199,333	1.00	4		
1986D 504,298,660	2.00	9		
1986S . . . . (3,010,497)				1
1987P 582,499,481	0.27	3		
1987D 655,594,696	0.27	1		
1987S . . . . (4,227,728)				1
1988P 562,052,000	0.50	5		
1988D 596,810,688	0.50	4		
1988S . . . . (3,262,948)				1
1989P 512,868,000	0.30	5		
1989D 896,535,597	0.27	1		
1989S . . . . (3,220,194)				1
1990P 613,792,000	0.27	4		
1990D 927,638,181	0.28	4		
1990S . . . . (3,299,559)				1

Chart continued on next page.

	Mintage	MS-63	MS-65	PF-65
1991P	570,968,000	$0.30	$4	
1991D	630,966,693	0.30	4	
1991S	(2,867,787)			$1.25
1992P	384,764,000	0.35	5	
1992D	389,777,107	0.35	5	
1992S	(2,858,981)			1.25
1992S, Silver	(1,317,579)			5.00
1993P	639,276,000	0.30	2	
1993D	645,476,128	0.30	2	
1993S	(2,633,439)			1.25
1993S, Silver	(761,353)			5.00
1994P	825,600,000	0.30	4	
1994D	880,034,110	0.30	4	
1994S	(2,484,594)			1.25
1994S, Silver	(785,329)			5.00
1995P	1,004,336,000	0.30	4	

	Mintage	MS-63	MS-65	PF-65
1995D	1,103,216,000	$0.30	$3	
1995S	(2,117,496)			$3.00
1995S, Silver	(679,985)			5.00
1996P	925,040,000	0.25	3	
1996D	906,868,000	0.25	3	
1996S	(1,750,244)			2.00
1996S, Silver	(775,021)			5.00
1997P	595,740,000	0.25	3	
1997D	599,680,000	0.25	3	
1997S	(2,055,000)			2.00
1997S, Silver	(741,678)			5.00
1998P	896,268,000	0.25	2	
1998D	821,000,000	0.25	2	
1998S	(2,086,507)			2.50
1998S, Silver	(878,792)			5.00

State Quarters (1999–2008)

The United States Mint 50 State Quarters® Program, which began in 1999, produced a series of 50 quarter dollar coins with special designs honoring each state. Five different designs were issued each year during the period 1999 through 2008. States were commemorated in the order of their entrance into statehood.

These are all legal-tender coins of standard weight and composition. The obverse side depicting President George Washington was modified to include some of the wording previously used on the reverse. The modification was authorized by special legislation, and carried out by Mint sculptor-engraver William Cousins, whose initials were added to the truncation of Washington's neck adjacent to those of the original designer, John Flanagan.

Each state theme was proposed, and the design approved, by the governor of the state. Final designs were created by Mint personnel.

Circulation coins were made at the Philadelphia and Denver mints. Proof coins were made in San Francisco. Both copper-nickel and silver Proof coins were made each year.

	Mintage	AU-50	MS-63	PF-65
Delaware				
1999P	373,400,000	$0.25	$0.50	
1999D	401,424,000	0.25	0.50	
1999S	(3,713,359)			$1.75
1999S, Silver	(804,565)			14.00
Pennsylvania				
1999P	349,000,000	0.25	0.50	
1999D	358,332,000	0.25	0.50	
1999S	(3,713,359)			1.75
1999S, Silver	(804,565)			14.00

	Mintage	AU-50	MS-63	PF-65
New Jersey				
1999P	363,200,000	$0.25	$0.30	
1999D	299,028,000	0.25	0.35	
1999S	(3,713,359)			$1.75
1999S, Silver	(804,565)			14.00
Georgia				
1999P	451,188,000	0.25	0.30	
1999D	488,744,000	0.25	0.30	
1999S	(3,713,359)			1.75
1999S, Silver	(804,565)			14.00

QUARTER DOLLARS

	Mintage	AU-50	MS-63	PF-65
Connecticut				
1999P	688,744,000	$0.25	$0.30	
1999D	657,880,000	0.25	0.30	

	Mintage	AU-50	MS-63	PF-65
Connecticut				
1999S	(3,713,359)			$1.75
1999S, Silver	(804,565)			14.00

	Mintage	AU-50	MS-63	PF-65
Massachusetts				
2000P	628,600,000	$0.25	$0.30	
2000D	535,184,000	0.25	0.30	
2000S	(4,020,172)			$1.50
2000S, Silver	(965,421)			6.00
Maryland				
2000P	678,200,000	0.25	0.30	
2000D	556,532,000	0.25	0.30	
2000S	(4,020,172)			1.50
2000S, Silver	(965,421)			6.00
South Carolina				
2000P	742,576,000	0.25	0.32	
2000D	566,208,000	0.25	0.32	

	Mintage	AU-50	MS-63	PF-65
South Carolina				
2000S	(4,020,172)			$1.50
2000S, Silver	(965,421)			6.00
New Hampshire				
2000P	673,040,000	$0.25	$0.30	
2000D	495,976,000	0.25	0.30	
2000S	(4,020,172)			1.50
2000S, Silver	(965,421)			6.00
Virginia				
2000P	943,000,000	0.25	0.30	
2000D	651,616,000	0.25	0.30	
2000S	(4,020,172)			1.50
2000S, Silver	(965,421)			6.00

	Mintage	AU-50	MS-63	PF-65
New York				
2001P	655,400,000	$0.25	$0.30	
2001D	619,640,000	0.25	0.30	
2001S	(3,094,140)			$1.50
2001S, Silver	(889,697)			8.00
North Carolina				
2001P	627,600,000	0.25	0.30	
2001D	427,876,000	0.25	0.30	
2001S	(3,094,140)			1.50
2001S, Silver	(889,697)			8.00
Rhode Island				
2001P	423,000,000	0.25	0.30	
2001D	447,100,000	0.25	0.30	

	Mintage	AU-50	MS-63	PF-65
Rhode Island				
2001S	(3,094,140)			$1.50
2001S, Silver	(889,697)			8.00
Vermont				
2001P	423,400,000	$0.25	$0.30	
2001D	459,404,000	0.25	0.30	
2001S	(3,094,140)			1.50
2001S, Silver	(889,697)			8.00
Kentucky				
2001P	353,000,000	0.25	0.30	
2001D	370,564,000	0.25	0.30	
2001S	(3,094,140)			1.50
2001S, Silver	(889,697)			8.00

	Mintage	AU-50	MS-63	PF-65
Tennessee				
2002P	361,600,000	$0.30	$0.40	
2002D	286,468,000	0.30	0.40	
2002S	(3,084,245)			$1.50
2002S, Silver	(892,229)			6.00
Ohio				
2002P	217,200,000	0.25	0.30	
2002D	414,832,000	0.25	0.30	
2002S	(3,084,245)			1.50
2002S, Silver	(892,229)			6.00
Louisiana				
2002P	362,000,000	0.25	0.30	
2002D	402,204,000	0.25	0.30	

	Mintage	AU-50	MS-63	PF-65
Louisiana				
2002S	(3,084,245)			$1.50
2002S, Silver	(892,229)			6.00
Indiana				
2002P	362,600,000	$0.25	$0.30	
2002D	327,200,000	0.25	0.30	
2002S	(3,084,245)			1.50
2002S, Silver	(892,229)			6.00
Mississippi				
2002P	290,000,000	0.25	0.30	
2002D	289,600,000	0.25	0.30	
2002S	(3,084,245)			1.50
2002S, Silver	(892,229)			6.00

	Mintage	AU-50	MS-63	PF-65
Illinois				
2003P	225,800,000	$0.25	$0.30	
2003D	237,400,000	0.25	0.30	
2003S	(3,408,516)			$1.50
2003S, Silver	(1,125,755)			6.00
Alabama				
2003P	225,000,000	0.25	0.30	
2003D	232,400,000	0.25	0.30	
2003S	(3,408,516)			1.50
2003S, Silver	(1,125,755)			6.00
Maine				
2003P	217,400,000	0.25	0.30	
2003D	231,400,000	0.25	0.30	

	Mintage	AU-50	MS-63	PF-65
Maine				
2003S	(3,408,516)			$1.50
2003S, Silver	(1,125,755)			6.00
Missouri				
2003P	225,000,000	$0.25	$0.30	
2003D	228,200,000	0.25	0.30	
2003S	(3,408,516)			1.50
2003S, Silver	(1,125,755)			6.00
Arkansas				
2003P	228,000,000	0.25	0.30	
2003D	229,800,000	0.25	0.30	
2003S	(3,408,516)			1.50
2003S, Silver	(1,125,755)			6.00

QUARTER DOLLARS

	Mintage	AU-50	MS-63	PF-65
Michigan				
2004P	233,800,000	$0.25	$0.30	
2004D	225,800,000	0.25	0.30	
2004S	(2,740,684)			$1.50
2004S, Silver	(1,769,786)			6.00
Florida				
2004P	240,200,000	0.25	0.30	
2004D	241,600,000	0.25	0.30	
2004S	(2,740,684)			1.50
2004S, Silver	(1,769,786)			6.00
Texas				
2004P	278,800,000	0.25	0.30	
2004D	263,000,000	0.25	0.30	

	Mintage	AU-50	MS-63	PF-65
Texas				
2004S	(2,740,684)			$1.50
2004S, Silver	(1,769,786)			6.00
Iowa				
2004P	213,800,000	$0.25	$0.30	
2004D	251,400,000	0.25	0.30	
2004S	(2,740,684)			1.50
2004S, Silver	(1,769,786)			6.00
Wisconsin				
2004P	226,400,000	0.25	0.30	
2004D	226,800,000	0.25	0.30	
2004S	(2,740,684)			1.50
2004S, Silver	(1,769,786)			6.00

	Mintage	AU-50	MS-63	PF-65
California				
2005P	257,200,000	$0.25	$0.30	
2005D	263,200,000	0.25	0.30	
2005S	(3,262,960)			$1.50
2005S, Silver	(1,678,649)			6.00
Minnesota				
2005P	239,600,000	0.25	0.30	
2005D	248,400,000	0.25	0.30	
2005S	(3,262,960)			1.50
2005S, Silver	(1,678,649)			6.00
Oregon				
2005P	316,200,000	0.25	0.30	
2005D	404,000,000	0.25	0.30	

	Mintage	AU-50	MS-63	PF-65
Oregon				
2005S	(3,262,960)			$1.50
2005S, Silver	(1,678,649)			6.00
Kansas				
2005P	263,400,000	$0.25	$0.30	
2005D	300,000,000	0.25	0.30	
2005S	(3,262,960)			1.50
2005S, Silver	(1,678,649)			6.00
West Virginia				
2005P	365,400,000	0.25	0.30	
2005D	356,200,000	0.25	0.30	
2005S	(3,262,960)			1.50
2005S, Silver	(1,678,649)			6.00

	Mintage	AU-50	MS-63	PF-65
Nevada				
2006P	277,000,000	$0.25	$0.30	
2006D	312,800,000	0.25	0.30	
2006S	(2,882,428)			$1.50
2006S, Silver	(1,585,008)			6.00

	Mintage	AU-50	MS-63	PF-65
Nebraska				
2006P	318,000,000	$0.25	$0.30	
2006D	273,000,000	0.25	0.30	
2006S	(2,882,428)			$1.50
2006S, Silver	(1,585,008)			6.00

Chart continued on next pages

115

	Mintage	AU-50	MS-63	PF-65
Colorado				
2006P	274,800,000	$0.25	$0.30	
2006D	294,200,000	0.25	0.30	
2006S	(2,882,428)			$1.50
2006S, Silver	(1,585,008)			6.00
North Dakota				
2006P	305,800,000	0.25	0.30	
2006D	359,000,000	0.25	0.30	

	Mintage	AU-50	MS-63	PF-65
North Dakota				
2006S	(2,882,428)			$1.50
2006S, Silver.	(1,585,008)			6.00
South Dakota				
2006P	245,000,000	$0.25	$0.30	
2006D	265,800,000	0.25	0.30	
2006S	(2,882,428)			1.50
2006S, Silver	(1,585,008)			6.00

	Mintage	AU-50	MS-63	PF-65
Montana				
2007P	257,000,000	$0.25	$0.30	
2007D	256,240,000	0.25	0.30	
2007S	(2,374,778)			$1.50
2007S, Silver	(1,313,481)			6.00
Washington				
2007P	265,200,000	0.25	0.30	
2007D	280,000,000	0.25	0.30	
2007S	(2,374,778)			1.50
2007S, Silver	(1,313,481)			6.00
Idaho				
2007P	294,600,000	0.25	0.30	
2007D	286,800,000	0.25	0.30	

	Mintage	AU-50	MS-63	PF-65
Idaho				
2007S	(2,374,778)			$1.50
2007S, Silver	(1,313,481)			6.00
Wyoming				
2007P	243,600,000	$0.25	$0.30	
2007D	320,800,000	0.25	0.30	
2007S	(2,374,778)			1.50
2007S, Silver	(1,313,481)			6.00
Utah				
2007P	255,000,000	0.25	0.30	
2007D	253,200,000	0.25	0.30	
2007S	(2,374,778)			1.50
2007S, Silver	(1,313,481)			6.00

	Mintage	AU-50	MS-63	PF-65
Oklahoma				
2008P	222,000,000	$0.25	$0.30	
2008D	194,600,000	0.25	0.30	
2008S	(2,078,112)			$1.50
2008S, Silver	(1,192,908)			6.00
New Mexico				
2008P	244,200,000	0.25	0.30	
2008D	244,400,000	0.25	0.30	
2008S	(2,078,112)			1.50
2008S, Silver	(1,192,908)			6.00
Arizona				
2008P	244,600,000	0.25	0.30	
2008D	265,000,000	0.25	0.30	

	Mintage	AU-50	MS-63	PF-65
Arizona				
2008S	(2,078,112)			$1.50
2008S, Silver	(1,192,908)			6.00
Alaska				
2008P	251,800,000	$0.25	$0.30	
2008D	254,000,000	0.25	0.30	
2008S	(2,078,112)			1.50
2008S, Silver	(1,192,908)			6.00
Hawaii				
2008P	254,000,000	0.25	0.30	
2008D	263,600,00	0.25	0.30	
2008S	(2,078,112)			3.00
2008S, Silver	(1,192,908)			6.00

Some State quarters were accidentally made with misaligned dies and are valued higher than ordinary pieces. Normal United States coins have dies oriented in "coin alignment," such that the reverse appears upside down when the coin is rotated from right to left. Values for the rotated-die quarters vary according to the amount of shifting. The most valuable are those that are shifted 180 degrees, so that both sides appear upright when the coin is turned over (called *medal alignment*).

Manufacturing varieties showing die doubling or other minor, unintentional characteristics are of interest to collectors and are often worth premium prices.

District of Columbia and U.S. Territories Quarters (2009)

At the ending of the U.S. Mint 50 State Quarters® Program a new series of quarter-dollar reverse designs was authorized to recognize the District of Columbia and the five U.S. territories: the Commonwealth of Puerto Rico, Guam, American Samoa, the U.S. Virgin Islands, and the Commonwealth of the Northern Mariana Islands. Each of these coins, issued sequentially during 2009, has the portrait of George Washington, as in the past, and is made of the same weight and composition. Each coin commemorates the history, geography, or traditions of the place it represents.

	Mintage	AU-50	MS-63	PF-65
District of Columbia				
2009P	83,600,000	$0.25	$0.30	
2009D	88,800,000	0.25	0.30	
2009S	(2,113,478)			$1.50
2009S, Silver	(996,548)			6.00
Puerto Rico				
2009P	53,200,000	0.25	0.30	
2009D	86,000,000	0.25	0.30	
2009S	(2,113,478)			1.50
2009S, Silver	(996,548)			6.00
Guam				
2009P	45,000,000	0.25	0.30	
2009D	42,600,000	0.25	0.30	
2009S	(2,113,478)			1.50
2009S, Silver	(996,548)			6.00

	Mintage	AU-50	MS-63	PF-65
American Samoa				
2009P	42,600,000	$0.25	$0.30	
2009D	39,600,000	0.25	0.30	
2009S	(2,113,478)			$1.50
2009S, Silver	(996,548)			6.00
U.S. Virgin Islands				
2009P	41,000,000	0.25	0.40	
2009D	41,000,000	0.25	0.40	
2009S	(2,113,478)			1.50
2009S, Silver	(996,548)			6.00
Northern Mariana Islands				
2009P	35,200,000	0.25	0.30	
2009D	37,600,000	0.25	0.30	
2009S	(2,113,478)			1.50
2009S, Silver	(996,548)			6.00

America the Beautiful™ Quarters Program (2010–2021)

Following up on the popularity of the 50 State Quarters® Program, Congress has authorized the production of new circulating commemorative quarters from 2010 to

2021. The coins honor a site of "natural or historic significance" from each of the 50 states, five U.S. territories, and the District of Columbia. They continue to bear George Washington's portrait on the obverse.

Five designs will be released each year through 2020, with the final coin issued in 2021, in the order the coins' featured locations were designated national parks or national sites. At the discretion of the secretary of the Treasury, this series could be extended an additional 11 years by featuring a second national park or site from each state, district, and territory.

In addition to the circulating quarters, a series of five-ounce silver bullion pieces are being coined each year with designs nearly identical to those of the America the Beautiful™ quarters, with two main exceptions: the size, which is three inches in diameter; and the edge, which is marked .999 FINE SILVER 5.0 OUNCE, rather than reeded as on the standard quarters.

	Mintage	AU-50	MS-63	PF-65
Hot Springs National Park (Arkansas)				
2010P	35,600,000	$0.25	$0.30	
2010D	34,000,000	0.25	0.30	
2010S	(1,402,889)			$1.50
2010S, Silver	(859,417)			6.00
Yellowstone National Park (Wyoming)				
2010P	33,600,000	0.25	0.30	
2010D	34,800,000	0.25	0.30	
2010S	(1,404,259)			1.50
2010S, Silver	(859,417)			6.00
Yosemite National Park (California)				
2010P	35,200,000	0.25	0.30	
2010D	34,800,000	0.25	0.30	

	Mintage	AU-50	MS-63	PF-65
Yosemite National Park (California)				
2010S	(1,401,522)			$1.50
2010S, Silver	(859,417)			6.00
Grand Canyon National Park (Arizona)				
2010P	34,800,000	$0.25	$0.30	
2010D	35,400,000	0.25	0.30	
2010S	(1,401,462)			1.50
2010S, Silver	(859,417)			6.00
Mount Hood National Forest (Oregon)				
2010P	34,400,000	0.25	0.30	
2010D	34,400,000	0.25	0.30	
2010S	(1,398,106)			1.50
2010S, Silver	(859,417)			6.00

	Mintage	AU-50	MS-63	PF-65
Gettysburg National Military Park (Pennsylvania)				
2011P	30,800,000	$0.25	$0.30	
2011D	30,400,000	0.25	0.30	
2011S	(1,273,068)			$1.50
2011S, Silver	(722,076)			6.00

	Mintage	AU-50	MS-63	PF-65
Glacier National Park (Montana)				
2011P	30,400,000	$0.25	$0.30	
2011D	31,200,000	0.25	0.30	
2011S	(1,273,068)			$1.50
2011S, Silver	(722,076)			6.00

	Mintage	AU-50	MS-63	PF-65
Olympic National Park (Washington)				
2011P	30,400,000	$0.25	$0.30	
2011D	30,600,000	0.25	0.30	
2011S	(1,269,422)			$1.50
2011S, Silver	(722,076)			6.00
Vicksburg National Military Park (Mississippi)				
2011P	30,800,000	0.25	0.30	
2011D	33,400,000	0.25	0.30	

	Mintage	AU-50	MS-63	PF-65
Vicksburg National Military Park (Mississippi)				
2011S	(1,268,623)			$1.50
2011S, Silver	(722,076)			6.00
Chickasaw National Recreation Area (Oklahoma)				
2011P	73,800,000	$0.25	$0.30	
2011D	69,400,000	0.25	0.30	
2011S	(1,266,825)			1.50
2011S, Silver	(722,076)			6.00

	Mintage	AU-50	MS-63	PF-65
El Yunque National Forest (Puerto Rico)				
2012P	25,800,000	$0.25	$0.30	
2012D	25,000,000	0.25	0.30	
2012S	1,680,140		0.50 **(a)**	
2012S	(1,012,094)			$1.50
2012S, Silver	(608,060)			6.00
Chaco Culture National Historical Park (New Mexico)				
2012P	22,000,000	0.25	0.30	
2012D	22,000,000	0.25	0.30	
2012S	1,389,020		0.50 **(a)**	
2012S	(961,464)			1.50
2012S, Silver	(608,060)			6.00
Acadia National Park (Maine)				
2012P	24,800,000	0.25	0.30	
2012D	21,606,000	0.25	0.30	
2012S	1,409,120		0.50 **(a)**	

	Mintage	AU-50	MS-63	PF-65
Acadia National Park (Maine)				
2012S	(962,038)			$1.50
2012S, Silver	(608,060)			6.00
Hawai'i Volcanoes National Park (Hawaii)				
2012P	46,200,000	$0.25	$0.30	
2012D	78,600,000	0.25	0.30	
2012S	1,409,120		0.50 **(a)**	
2012S	(962,447)			1.50
2012S, Silver	(608,060)			6.00
Denali National Park and Preserve (Alaska)				
2012P	135,400,000	0.25	0.30	
2012D	166,600,000	0.25	0.30	
2012S	1,409,220		0.50 **(a)**	
2012S	(959,602)			1.50
2012S, Silver	(608,060)			6.00

a. Not issued for circulation.

	Mintage	AU-50	MS-63	PF-65
White Mountain National Forest (New Hampshire)				
2013P	68,800,000	$0.25	$0.30	
2013D	107,600,000	0.25	0.30	
2013S	1,606,900		0.50 **(a)**	
2013S	(989,803)			$1.50
2013S, Silver	(467,691)			6.00

	Mintage	AU-50	MS-63	PF-65
Perry's Victory and International Peace Memorial (Ohio)				
2013P	107,800,000	0.25	$0.30	
2013D	131,600,000	0.25	0.30	
2013S	1,425,860		0.50 **(a)**	
2013S	(947,815)			$1.50
2013S, Silver	(467,691)			6.00

a. Not issued for circulation.

Chart continued on next page.

	Mintage	AU-50	MS-63	PF-65
Great Basin National Park (Nevada)				
2013P	122,400,000	$0.25	$0.30	
2013D	141,400,000	0.25	0.30	
2013S	1,316,500		0.50 **(a)**	
2013S	*(945,777)*			$1.50
2013S, Silver	(467,691)			6.00
Ft. McHenry Nat'l Monument and Historic Shrine (Maryland)				
2013P	120,000,000	0.25	0.30	
2013D	151,400,000	0.25	0.30	
2013S	1,313,680		0.50 **(a)**	

	Mintage	AU-50	MS-63	PF-65
Ft. McHenry Nat'l Monument and Historic Shrine (Maryland)				
2013S	*(946,380)*			$1.50
2013S, Silver	(467,691)			6.00
Mount Rushmore National Memorial (South Dakota)				
2013P	231,800,000	$0.25	$0.30	
2013D	272,400,000	0.25	0.30	
2013S	1,373,260		0.50 **(a)**	
2013S	*(958,853)*			1.50
2013S, Silver	(467,691)			6.00

a. Not issued for circulation.

	Mintage	AU-50	MS-63	PF-65
Great Smoky Mountains National Park (Tennessee)				
2014P	73,200,000	$0.25	$0.30	
2014D	99,400,000	0.25	0.30	
2014S	1,360,780		0.50 **(a)**	
2014S	*(881,896)*			$1.50
2014S, Silver	(472,107)			6.00
Shenandoah National Park (Virginia)				
2014P	112,800,000	0.25	0.30	
2014D	197,800,000	0.25	0.30	
2014S	1,266,720		0.50 **(a)**	
2014S	*(846,441)*			1.50
2014S, Silver	(472,107)			6.00
Arches National Park (Utah)				
2014P	214,200,000	0.25	0.30	
2014D	251,400,000	0.25	0.30	
2014S	1,235,940		0.50 **(a)**	

	Mintage	AU-50	MS-63	PF-65
Arches National Park (Utah)				
2014S	*(844,775)*			$1.50
2014S, Silver	(472,107)			6.00
Great Sand Dunes National Park (Colorado)				
2014P	159,600,000	$0.25	$0.30	
2014D	171,800,000	0.25	0.30	
2014S	1,176,760		0.50 **(a)**	
2014S	*(843,238)*			1.50
2014S, Silver	(472,107)			6.00
Everglades National Park (Florida)				
2014P	157,601,200	0.25	0.30	
2014D	142,400,000	0.25	0.30	
2014S	1,180,900		0.50 **(a)**	
2014S	*(856,139)*			1.50
2014S, Silver	(472,107)			6.00

a. Not issued for circulation.

	Mintage	AU-50	MS-63	PF-65
Homestead National Monument of America (Nebraska)				
2015P	214,400,000	$0.25	$0.30	
2015D	248,600,000	0.25	0.30	
2015S	1,153,840		0.50 **(a)**	
2015S	*(778,319)*			$2.00
2015S, Silver	*(490,621)*			6.00
Kisatchie National Forest (Louisiana)				
2015P	397,200,000	0.25	0.30	
2015D	379,600,000	0.25	0.30	
2015S	1,099,380		0.50 **(a)**	
2015S	*(777,407)*			1.50
2015S, Silver	*(490,621)*			6.00
Blue Ridge Parkway (North Carolina)				
2015P	325,616,000	0.25	0.30	
2015D	505,200,000	0.25	0.30	
2015S	1,096,620		0.50 **(a)**	

	Mintage	AU-50	MS-63	PF-65
Blue Ridge Parkway (North Carolina)				
2015S	*(779,338)*			$1.50
2015S, Silver	*(490,621)*			6.00
Bombay Hook National Wildlife Refuge (Delaware)				
2015P	275,000,000	$0.25	$0.30	
2015D	206,400,000	0.25	0.30	
2015S	1,013,920		0.50 **(a)**	
2015S	*(775,610)*			1.50
2015S, Silver	*(490,621)*			6.00
Saratoga National Historical Park (New York)				
2015P	223,000,000	0.25	0.30	
2015D	215,800,000	0.25	0.30	
2015S	1,045,500		0.50 **(a)**	
2015S	*(777,129)*			1.50
2015S, Silver	*(490,621)*			6.00

a. Not issued for circulation.

	Mintage	AU-50	MS-63	PF-65
Shawnee National Forest (Illinois)				
2016P	155,600,000	$0.25	$0.30	
2016D	151,800,000	0.25	0.30	
2016S	*1,066,440*		0.50 **(a)**	
2016S	*(732,039)*			$1.50
2016S, Silver	*(515,205)*			6.00
Cumberland Gap National Historical Park (Kentucky)				
2016P	215,400,000	0.25	0.30	
2016D	223,200,000	0.25	0.30	
2016S	*1,021,120*		0.50 **(a)**	
2016S	*(701,831)*			1.50
2016S, Silver	*(515,205)*			6.00
Harpers Ferry National Historical Park (West Virginia)				
2016P	434,630,000	0.25	0.30	
2016D	424,000,000	0.25	0.30	
2016S	*1,035,840*		0.50 **(a)**	

	Mintage	AU-50	MS-63	PF-65
Harpers Ferry National Historical Park (West Virginia)				
2016S	*(701,203)*			$1.50
2016S, Silver	*(515,205)*			6.00
Theodore Roosevelt National Park (North Dakota)				
2016P	231,600,000	$0.25	$0.30	
2016D	223,200,000	0.25	0.30	
2016S	*1,057,020*		0.50 **(a)**	
2016S	*(702,930)*			1.50
2016S, Silver	*(515,205)*			6.00
Ft. Moultrie at Ft. Sumter Nat'l Monument (South Carolina)				
2016P	154,400,000	0.25	0.30	
2016D	142,200,000	0.25	0.30	
2016S	*966,260*		0.50 **(a)**	
2016S	*(717,049)*			1.50
2016S, Silver	*(515,205)*			6.00

a. Not issued for circulation.

	Mintage	SP-67	SP-70
2016W, Gold **(a)**	*91,752*	$325	$350

a. In 2016 the Mint issued a centennial version of the Standing Liberty quarter in gold.

	Mintage	AU-50	MS-63	PF-65
Effigy Mounds National Monument (Iowa)				
2017P	271,200,000	$0.25	$0.30	
2017D	210,800,000	0.25	0.30	
2017S	931,340		0.50 **(a)**	
2017S	(706,042)			$1.50
2017S, Silver	(496,626)			6.00
Frederick Douglass National Historic Site (DC)				
2017P	184,800,000	0.25	0.30	
2017D	185,800,000	0.25	0.30	
2017S	934,940		0.50 **(a)**	
2017S	(672,188)			1.50
2017S, Silver	(496,626)			6.00
Ozark National Scenic Riverways (Missouri)				
2017P	203,000,000	0.25	0.30	
2017D	200,000,000	0.25	0.30	
2017S	906,840		0.50 **(a)**	

	Mintage	AU-50	MS-63	PF-65
Ozark National Scenic Riverways (Missouri)				
2017S	(671,902)			$1.50
2017S, Silver	(496,626)			6.00
Ellis Island (Statue of Liberty Nat'l Monument) (New Jersey)				
2017P	234,000,000	$0.25	$0.30	
2017D	254,000,000	0.25	0.30	
2017S	956,200		0.50 **(a)**	
2017S	(674,537)			1.50
2017S, Silver	(496,626)			6.00
George Rogers Clark National Historical Park (Indiana)				
2017P	191,600,000	0.25	0.30	
2017D	180,800,000	0.25	0.30	
2017S	919,060		0.50 **(a)**	
2017S	(689,235)			1.50
2017S, Silver	(496,626)			6.00

a. Not issued for circulation.

	Mintage	AU-50	MS-63	PF-65
Pictured Rocks National Lakeshore (Michigan)				
2018P	186,714,000	$0.25	$0.30	
2018D	182,600,000	0.25	0.30	
2018S	917,580		0.50 **(a)**	
2018S	(688,538)			$1.50
2018S, Silver	(350,820)			6.00
Apostle Islands National Lakeshore (Wisconsin)				
2018P	223,200,000	0.25	0.30	
2018D	216,600,000	0.25	0.30	
2018S	871,820		0.50 **(a)**	
2018S	(659,633)			1.50
2018S, Silver	(350,820)			6.00
Voyageurs National Park (Minnesota)				
2018P	237,400,000	0.25	0.30	
2018D	197,800,000	0.25	0.30	
2018S	831,560		0.50 **(a)**	

	Mintage	AU-50	MS-63	PF-65
Voyageurs National Park (Minnesota)				
2018S	(659,448)			$1.50
2018S, Silver	(350,820)			6.00
Cumberland Island National Seashore (Georgia)				
2018P	138,000,000	$0.25	$0.30	
2018D	151,600,000	0.25	0.30	
2018S	816,660		0.50 **(a)**	
2018S	(658,438)			1.50
2018S, Silver	(350,820)			6.00
Block Island National Wildlife Refuge (Rhode Island)				
2018P	159,600,000	$0.25	$0.30	
2018D	159,600,000	0.25	0.30	
2018S	764,660		0.50 **(a)**	
2018S	(675,567)			1.50
2018S, Silver	(350,820)			6.00

a. Not issued for circulation.

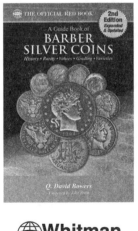

	Mintage	AU-50	MS-63	PF-65
Lowell National Historical Park (Massachusetts)				
2019P		$0.25	$0.30	
2019D		0.25	0.30	
2019S			0.50 **(a)**	
2019S				$1.50
2019S, Silver				6.00
American Memorial Park (Northern Mariana Islands)				
2019P		0.25	0.30	
2019D		0.25	0.30	
2019S			0.50 **(a)**	
2019S				1.50
2019S, Silver				6.00
San Antonio Missions National Historical Park (Texas)				
2019P		0.25	0.30	
2019D		0.25	0.30	
2019S			0.50 **(a)**	

	Mintage	AU-50	MS-63	PF-65
San Antonio Missions National Historical Park (Texas)				
2019S				$1.50
2019S, Silver				6.00
War in the Pacific National Historical Park (Guam)				
2019P		$0.25	$0.30	
2019D		0.25	0.30	
2019S			0.50 **(a)**	
2019S				1.50
2019S, Silver				6.00
Frank Church River of No Return Wilderness (Idaho)				
2019P		0.25	0.30	
2019D		0.25	0.30	
2019S			0.50 **(a)**	
2019S				1.50
2019S, Silver				6.00

a. Not issued for circulation.

The half dollar, authorized by the Act of April 2, 1792, was not minted until December 1794. The weight of the half dollar was 208 grains and its fineness .8924 when first issued. This standard was not changed until 1837 when the Act of January 18, 1837, specified 206-1/4 grains, .900 fine. This fineness continued in use until 1965.

Arrows at the date in 1853 indicate the reduction of weight to 192 grains. During that year only, rays were added to the reverse. Arrows remained in 1854 and 1855. In 1873 the weight was raised by .9 grains and arrows were again placed at the date.

FLOWING HAIR (1794–1795)

AG-3 About Good: Clear enough to identify.
G-4 Good: Date and letters sufficient to be legible. Main devices outlined, but lacking in detail.
VG-8 Very Good: Major details discernible. Letters well formed but worn.
F-12 Fine: Hair ends distinguishable. Top hair lines visible, but otherwise worn smooth.
VF-20 Very Fine: Some detail visible in hair in center; other details more bold.
EF-40 Extremely Fine: Hair above head and down neck detailed, with slight wear.
AU-50 About Uncirculated: All hair visible; slight wear on bust of Liberty and on top edges of eagle's wings, head, and breast.

1795, 2 Leaves Under Each Wing

1795, 3 Leaves Under Each Wing

	Mintage	AG-3	G-4	VG-8	F-12	VF-20	EF-40	AU-50
1794 23,464		$1,500	$3,000	$4,500	$7,500	$17,500	$27,500	$45,000
1795 299,680		350	650	1,000	1,700	2,750	8,000	12,000
1795, Recut Date. . . . .*		350	650	1,000	1,700	3,500	8,250	14,000
1795, 3 Leaves Under Each Wing . . . . . .*		800	1,600	2,000	3,250	5,000	12,000	25,000

* Included in number above.

DRAPED BUST (1796–1807)

AG-3 About Good: Clear enough to identify.
G-4 Good: Date and letters sufficiently clear to be legible. Main devices outlined, but lacking in detail.
VG-8 Very Good: Major details discernible. Letters well formed but worn.
F-12 Fine: Hair ends distinguishable. Top hair lines visible, but otherwise worn smooth.
VF-20 Very Fine: Right side of drapery slightly worn. Left side to curls smooth.
EF-40 Extremely Fine: All lines in drapery on bust distinctly visible around to hair curls.
AU-50 About Uncirculated: Slight trace of wear on cheek, hair, and shoulder.

Small Eagle Reverse (1796–1797)

1796, 16 Stars

1797, 15 Stars

	Mintage	AG-3	G-4	VG-8	F-12	VF-20	EF-40	AU-50
1796, All kinds.	3,918							
1796, 15 Stars		$12,500	$25,000	$30,000	$35,000	$50,000	$75,000	$120,000
1796, 16 Stars		12,500	25,000	30,000	35,000	50,000	75,000	120,000
1797, 15 Stars		12,500	27,000	35,000	40,000	55,000	77,500	125,000

Heraldic Eagle Reverse (1801–1807)

1805, 5 Over 4

1806, 6 Over 5

	Mintage	G-4	VG-8	F-12	VF-20	EF-40	AU-50	MS-60
1801	30,289	$650	$1,000	$1,600	$2,350	$4,000	$11,000	$45,000
1802	29,890	700	1,050	1,650	2,000	5,000	10,000	35,000
1803	188,234	150	250	350	550	1,500	2,750	14,000
1805, All kinds.	211,722							
1805, 5 Over 4		225	500	700	1,250	2,250	4,500	20,000
1805, Normal Date		125	175	250	450	1,500	3,250	16,500
1806, All kinds.	839,576							
1806, Normal Date		125	175	200	450	1,500	3,250	12,000
1806, 6 Over 5		125	175	200	450	1,500	3,250	12,000
1806, 6 Over Inverted 6.		225	325	650	1,000	2,250	4,500	9,000
1807	301,076	125	175	200	450	1,500	3,250	6,500

CAPPED BUST, LETTERED EDGE (1807–1836)

John Reich designed this capped-head concept of Liberty. Reich's design of Liberty facing left was used on all U.S. silver denominations for the next 30 years.

G-4 Good: Date and letters legible. Bust worn smooth with outline distinct.
VG-8 Very Good: LIBERTY faint. Legends distinguishable. Clasp at shoulder visible; curl above it nearly smooth.
F-12 Fine: Clasp and adjacent curl clearly outlined with slight details.
VF-20 Very Fine: Clasp at shoulder clear. Wear visible on highest point of curl. Hair over brow distinguishable.
EF-40 Extremely Fine: Clasp and adjacent curl fairly sharp. Brow and hair above distinct. Curls well defined.
AU-50 About Uncirculated: Trace of wear on hair over eye and over ear.
MS-60 Uncirculated: No trace of wear. Light blemishes. Possible slide marks from storage handling.
MS-63 Choice Uncirculated: Some distracting contact marks or blemishes in prime focal areas. Impaired luster possible.

First Style (1807–1808)

See next page for chart.   125

	Mintage	G-4	VG-8	F-12	VF-20	EF-40	AU-50	MS-60	MS-63
1807	750,500	$85	$125	$300	$450	$750	$1,600	$4,500	$6,500
1808, 8 Over 7	*	60	85	115	200	425	1,000	2,500	5,500
1808	1,368,600	40	50	55	85	225	750	2,000	3,500

* Included in number below.

Remodeled Portrait and Eagle (1809–1836)

	Mintage	G-4	VG-8	F-12	VF-20	EF-40	AU-50	MS-60	MS-63
1809	1,405,810	$40	$50	$55	$80	$250	$425	$1,100	$4,500
1810	1,276,276	40	55	65	85	250	400	1,000	4,000
1811	1,203,644	40	55	55	70	225	325	1,000	2,500

1812, 2 Over 1	1813, 50 C. Over UNI	1814, 4 Over 3

	Mintage	G-4	VG-8	F-12	VF-20	EF-40	AU-50	MS-60	MS-63
1812, All kinds	1,628,059								
1812, 2 Over 1		$45	$60	$80	$125	$250	$650	$2,000	$4,500
1812		40	50	65	80	225	525	1,000	2,500
1813	1,241,903	40	50	55	75	275	450	1,750	2,750
1813, 50 C. Over UNI	*	50	65	80	110	225	600	1,200	3,250
1814, All kinds	1,039,075								
1814, 4 Over 3		60	80	100	135	550	650	1,400	3,500
1814		40	50	60	100	550	650	1,200	2,500

* Included in number above.

1817, 7 Over 3	1817, 7 Over 4	1817, "Punctuated" Date

	Mintage	G-4	VG-8	F-12	VF-20	EF-40	AU-50	MS-60	MS-63
1815, 5 Over 2	47,150	$1,000	$1,500	$2,500	$3,000	$4,500	$7,500	$13,500	$35,000
1817, All kinds	1,215,567								
1817, 7 Over 3		65	100	225	250	750	1,500	5,500	11,000
1817, 7 Over 4 (8 known)				110,000	150,000	250,000			
1817, Dated 181.7		40	50	55	70	150	650	1,000	2,000
1817		40	50	55	70	150	650	1,000	2,000

1818, 2nd 8 Over 7   1819, 9 Over 8   1820, 20 Over 19

	Mintage	G-4	VG-8	F-12	VF-20	EF-40	AU-50	MS-60	MS-63
1818, 2nd 8 Over 7 . . . . *	$55	$65	$70	$90	$160	$550	$1,500	$4,500
1818 1,960,322	40	50	55	70	175	350	1,200	2,500
1819, 9 Over 8 . . . . *	40	55	60	120	175	400	1,500	4,000
1819 2,208,000	40	50	55	120	200	325	1,250	2,500
1820, 20 Over 19 . . . . *	55	70	80	125	225	600	2,000	4,500
1820 751,122	40	55	60	85	200	350	1,500	3,500
1821 1,305,797	40	55	60	70	225	400	1,250	2,500
1822 1,559,573	40	50	55	70	175	325	825	1,650
1823 1,694,200	40	50	55	65	175	750	1,000	2,000

* Included in number below.

"Various Dates"   1824, 4 Over 1   1828, Curl Base,   1828, Square
Probably 4 Over   Knob 2   Base 2
2 Over 0.

	Mintage	G-4	VG-8	F-12	VF-20	EF-40	AU-50	MS-60	MS-63
1824, All kinds. 3,504,954								
1824, 4 Over Various Dates	$40	$50	$55	$60	$110	$275	$825	$1,500
1824, 4 Over 1	45	55	60	70	125	275	825	2,000
1824	40	50	55	60	110	275	825	1,500
1825 2,943,166	35	50	55	60	110	250	825	1,500
1826 4,004,180	35	50	55	60	110	250	825	1,500
1827, All kinds. 5,493,400								
1827, 7 Over 6	55	60	70	80	130	250	825	1,600
1827	35	50	55	60	150	225	825	1,500
1828, All kinds. 3,075,200								
1828, Curl Base No Knob 2	40	50	55	65	110	250	825	1,550
1828, Curl Base Knob 2.	40	50	55	65	110	250	825	1,550
1828, Square Base 2.	40	50	55	65	125	250	825	1,550
1829, 9 Over 7 . . . . *	40	55	60	70	125	250	825	2,500
1829 3,712,156	35	45	50	60	110	225	800	1,350
1830 4,764,800	35	45	50	60	110	225	800	1,350
1831 5,873,660	35	45	50	60	110	225	800	1,350
1832 4,797,000	35	45	50	60	110	225	800	1,350
1833 5,206,000	35	45	50	60	110	225	800	1,350
1834 6,412,004	35	45	50	60	110	225	800	1,350
1835 5,352,006	35	45	50	60	110	225	800	1,350
1836 6,545,000	35	45	50	60	110	225	800	1,350
1836, 50 Over 00 . . . . **	50	55	65	90	175	450	1,100	2,250

* Included in number below. ** Included in number above.

CAPPED BUST, REEDED EDGE (1836–1839)

G-4 Good: LIBERTY barely discernible on headband.
VG-8 Very Good: Some letters in LIBERTY clear.
F-12 Fine: LIBERTY complete but faint.
VF-20 Very Fine: LIBERTY sharp. Shoulder clasp clear.
EF-40 Extremely Fine: LIBERTY sharp and strong. Hair details visible.
AU-50 About Uncirculated: Slight trace of wear on cap, cheek, and hair above forehead, and on eagle's claws, wing tops, and head.
MS-60 Uncirculated: No trace of wear. Light blemishes.
MS-63 Choice Uncirculated: Some distracting marks or blemishes in focal areas. Impaired luster possible.

Reverse 50 CENTS (1836–1837)

	Mintage	G-4	VG-8	F-12	VF-20	EF-40	AU-50	MS-60	MS-63
1836	1,200+	$700	$850	$1,250	$1,600	$2,500	$4,000	$7,000	$15,000
1837	3,629,820	35	45	55	75	135	275	825	1,750

Reverse HALF DOL. (1838–1839)

On half dollars of 1838 and 1839, the mintmark appears on the obverse; on those thereafter, through 1915, it is on the reverse.

	Mintage	G-4	VG-8	F-12	VF-20	EF-40	AU-50	MS-60	MS-63
1838	3,546,000	$35	$45	$55	$75	$135	$275	$825	$1,750
1838O	20					250,000	300,000	350,000	
1839	1,392,976	35	45	55	75	135	275	825	1,750
1839O	116,000	250	450	700	850	1,500	1,500	5,500	10,000

LIBERTY SEATED (1839–1891)

G-4 Good: Scant rim. LIBERTY on shield worn off. Date and letters legible.
VG-8 Very Good: Rim fairly defined. Some letters in LIBERTY evident.
F-12 Fine: LIBERTY complete, but weak.
VF-20 Very Fine: LIBERTY mostly sharp.
EF-40 Extremely Fine: LIBERTY entirely sharp. Scroll edges and clasp distinct.
AU-50 About Uncirculated: Slight wear on Liberty's breast and knees; eagle's head, claws, and wing tops.
MS-60 Uncirculated: No trace of wear. Light blemishes.
MS-63 Choice Uncirculated: Some distracting blemishes in prime focal areas. Impaired luster possible.
PF-63 Choice Proof: Reflective surfaces with only a few blemishes in secondary focal places. No major flaws.

Variety 1 – No Motto Above Eagle (1839–1853)

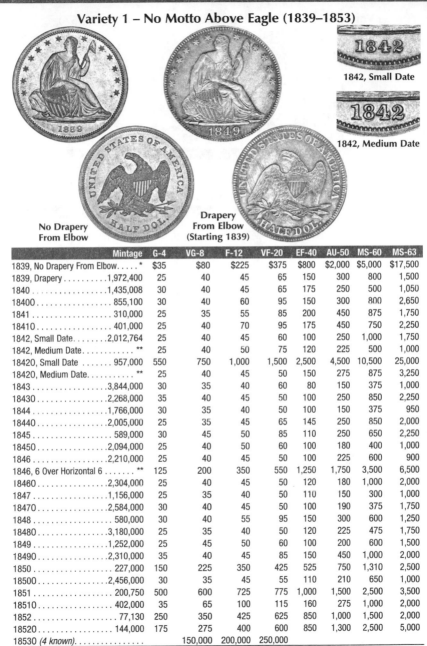

1842, Small Date

1842, Medium Date

No Drapery From Elbow

Drapery From Elbow (Starting 1839)

	Mintage	G-4	VG-8	F-12	VF-20	EF-40	AU-50	MS-60	MS-63
1839, No Drapery From Elbow.....*		$35	$80	$225	$375	$800	$2,000	$5,000	$17,500
1839, Drapery.........1,972,400		25	40	45	65	150	300	800	1,500
1840.................1,435,008		30	40	45	65	175	250	500	1,050
1840O.................855,100		30	40	60	95	150	300	800	2,650
1841.................310,000		25	35	55	85	200	450	875	1,750
1841O.................401,000		25	40	70	95	175	450	750	2,250
1842, Small Date.......2,012,764		25	40	45	60	100	250	1,000	1,750
1842, Medium Date...........**		25	40	50	75	120	225	500	1,000
1842O, Small Date......957,000		550	750	1,000	1,500	2,500	4,500	10,500	25,000
1842O, Medium Date...........**		25	40	45	50	150	275	875	3,250
1843.................3,844,000		30	35	40	60	80	150	375	1,000
1843O.................2,268,000		35	40	45	50	100	250	850	2,250
1844.................1,766,000		30	35	40	50	100	150	375	950
1844O.................2,005,000		25	35	45	65	145	250	850	2,000
1845.................589,000		30	45	50	85	110	250	650	2,250
1845O.................2,094,000		25	40	50	60	100	180	400	1,000
1846.................2,210,000		25	40	45	50	100	225	600	900
1846, 6 Over Horizontal 6.......**		125	200	350	550	1,250	1,750	3,500	6,500
1846O.................2,304,000		25	40	45	50	120	180	1,000	2,000
1847.................1,156,000		25	35	40	50	110	150	300	1,000
1847O.................2,584,000		30	40	45	50	100	190	375	1,750
1848.................580,000		30	40	55	95	150	300	600	1,250
1848O.................3,180,000		25	35	40	50	120	225	475	1,750
1849.................1,252,000		25	45	50	60	100	200	600	1,500
1849O.................2,310,000		35	40	45	85	150	450	1,000	2,000
1850.................227,000		150	225	350	425	525	750	1,310	2,500
1850O.................2,456,000		30	35	45	55	110	210	650	1,000
1851.................200,750		500	600	725	775	1,000	1,500	2,500	3,500
1851O.................402,000		35	65	100	115	160	275	1,000	2,000
1852.................77,130		250	350	425	625	850	1,000	1,500	2,000
1852O.................144,000		175	275	400	600	850	1,300	2,500	5,000
1853O (4 known)................			150,000	200,000	250,000				

* Included in number below. **Included in number above.

Variety 2 – Arrows at Date, Rays Around Eagle (1853)

	Mintage	G-4	VG-8	F-12	VF-20	EF-40	AU-50	MS-60	MS-63
1853	3,532,708	$25	$30	$45	$65	$160	$375	$1,100	$2,000
1853O	1,328,000	30	40	55	70	175	475	1,750	3,250

Variety 3 – Arrows at Date, No Rays (1854–1855)

	Mintage	G-4	VG-8	F-12	VF-20	EF-40	AU-50	MS-60	MS-63
1854	2,982,000	$25	$30	$45	$50	$80	$200	$375	$1,000
1854O	5,240,000	25	30	40	50	80	200	375	1,000
1855, Over 1854 . . . . *	40	60	125	200	325	600	1,250	2,250
1855	759,500	25	30	40	50	90	200	400	1,100
1855O	3,688,000	25	30	40	50	90	200	375	1,000
1855S	129,950	325	750	1,000	1,250	2,250	5,000	25,000	35,000

* Included in number below.

Variety 1 Resumed, With Weight Standard of Variety 2 (1856–1866)

	Mintage	G-4	VG-8	F-12	VF-20	EF-40	AU-50	MS-60	MS-63	PF-63
1856	938,000	$25	$40	$45	$55	$75	$150	$350	$700	
1856O	2,658,000	25	40	45	60	75	150	325	700	
1856S	211,000	55	100	150	225	650	1,500	3,250	8,500	
1857	1,988,000	25	35	40	55	75	150	325	700	
1857O	818,000	25	35	40	50	75	150	600	2,000	
1857S	158,000	100	125	165	250	750	1,100	2,500	6,750	
1858 . . . . . . (300+). . .	4,225,700	25	35	40	50	75	150	325	700	$1,250
1858O	7,294,000	25	35	40	50	75	150	325	700	
1858S	476,000	35	50	60	100	225	350	1,200	2,500	
1859 . . . . . . (800)	747,200	25	35	40	50	75	150	325	700	1,200
1859O	2,834,000	25	35	40	60	75	150	325	700	
1859S	566,000	35	40	45	65	125	150	800	2,000	
1860 . . . . (1,000)	302,700	30	35	45	50	80	150	450	700	1,200
1860O	1,290,000	25	35	40	55	75	150	325	700	
1860S	472,000	35	45	50	65	120	175	800	2,500	
1861 . . . . (1,000) . . .	2,887,400	25	40	50	65	100	200	325	700	1,200
1861O	2,532,633	40	45	55	65	100	175	900	2,000	
1861S	939,500	30	40	50	85	200	350	650	1,650	
1862 . . . . . . (550)	253,000	25	45	75	125	225	350	550	1,000	1,200
1862S	1,352,000	30	50	60	85	135	200	650	1,650	
1863 . . . . . . (460) . . .	503,200	25	45	55	100	150	300	550	1,000	1,200
1863S	916,000	25	45	55	100	200	350	850	1,500	
1864 . . . . . . (470) . . .	379,100	25	40	85	200	275	400	700	1,050	1,200
1864S	658,000	40	65	125	200	350	550	1,200	3,000	
1865 . . . . . . (500) . . .	511,400	40	60	80	100	250	500	1,000	1,500	1,200
1865S	675,000	45	70	100	155	250	500	1,200	1,500	
1866S, No Motto	60,000	300	400	650	800	1,500	2,000	5,000	15,000	

Variety 4 – Motto Above Eagle (1866–1873)

	Mintage	G-4	VG-8	F-12	VF-20	EF-40	AU-50	MS-60	MS-63	PF-63
1866 . . . . . . (725)	744,900	$40	$50	$50	$65	$125	$150	$500	$1,350	$850
1866S	994,000	30	40	50	100	150	250	500	1,250	
1867 . . . . . . (625)	449,300	40	50	80	125	200	300	500	1,100	850
1867S	1,196,000	35	40	55	100	200	450	850	2,000	
1868 . . . . . . (600)	417,600	30	35	50	100	200	375	550	1,250	850
1868S	1,160,000	25	35	40	55	100	175	350	1,250	
1869 . . . . . . (600)	795,300	25	35	40	60	80	175	450	1,000	850
1869S	656,000	25	35	40	60	100	175	525	1,500	
1870 . . . . (1,000)	633,900	25	35	45	60	110	150	375	700	850
1870CC	54,617	1,100	2,200	3,500	5,000	8,000	25,000	—	—	
1870S	1,004,000	45	55	85	100	300	500	1,350	2,500	
1871 . . . . . . (960)	1,203,600	30	35	50	65	100	175	450	850	850
1871CC	153,950	350	500	850	1,250	2,250	4,500	20,000	35,000	
1871S	2,178,000	25	35	45	55	100	225	550	1,200	
1872 . . . . . . (950)	880,600	25	35	40	55	125	250	550	1,000	850
1872CC	257,000	200	350	500	800	1,650	2,750	17,500	45,000	
1872S	580,000	30	40	55	100	200	400	750	1,200	
1873 . . . . . . (600)	801,200	25	30	45	50	80	175	325	1,050	850
1873CC	122,500	275	500	750	1,250	2,500	4,000	7,500	20,000	

Variety 5 – Arrows at Date (1873–1874)

	Mintage	G-4	VG-8	F-12	VF-20	EF-40	AU-50	MS-60	MS-63	PF-63
1873 . . . . . . (800)	1,815,200	$25	$30	$45	$55	$160	$300	$600	$1,250	$1,500
1873CC	214,560	175	325	500	800	1,500	2,500	6,000	15,000	
1873S	228,000	40	75	120	140	250	500	1,500	5,250	
1874 . . . . . . (700)	2,359,600	25	30	45	55	160	300	600	1,250	1,500
1874CC	59,000	850	1,200	1,500	2,000	4,000	6,000	10,000	20,000	
1874S	394,000	55	125	150	175	225	450	1,100	2,000	

Variety 4 Resumed, With Weight Standard of Variety 5 (1875–1891)

	Mintage	G-4	VG-8	F-12	VF-20	EF-40	AU-50	MS-60	MS-63	PF-63
1875......(700)....	6,026,800	$25	$30	$40	$50	$75	$140	$300	$600	$750
1875CC...........	1,008,000	50	75	150	200	350	650	1,000	2,000	
1875S............	3,200,000	25	30	45	50	75	140	300	600	
1876....(1,150)....	8,418,000	25	35	45	50	75	140	300	600	750
1876CC...........	1,956,000	35	50	65	80	110	200	450	900	
1876S............	4,528,000	25	35	40	50	75	140	275	600	
1877......(510)....	8,304,000	25	30	40	50	75	140	275	600	750
1877CC...........	1,420,000	35	50	65	110	130	175	425	900	
1877S............	5,356,000	25	30	40	50	75	140	275	600	
1878......(800)....	1,377,600	25	50	80	85	90	160	300	600	750
1878CC...........	62,000	750	1,000	1,650	2,000	3,000	4,000	8,000	15,000	
1878S............	12,000	22,500	30,000	35,000	40,000	50,000	55,000	65,000	115,000	
1879....(1,100).......	4,800	200	250	300	350	450	525	600	1,000	750
1880....(1,355).......	8,400	175	200	275	325	450	500	575	1,000	750
1881....(975).......	10,000	175	200	275	350	450	500	550	1,000	750
1882....(1,100).......	4,400	225	265	300	350	450	500	600	1,000	750
1883....(1,039).......	8,000	225	250	300	350	450	500	575	1,000	750
1884......(875).......	4,400	265	300	325	350	450	500	575	1,000	750
1885......(930).......	5,200	275	300	325	350	450	500	600	1,000	750
1886......(886).......	5,000	300	375	400	425	475	525	600	1,000	750
1887......(710).......	5,000	375	425	475	525	575	650	675	1,000	750
1888......(832).......	12,001	185	225	275	300	450	500	600	1,000	750
1889......(711).......	12,000	200	250	275	325	450	550	650	1,000	750
1890......(590).......	12,000	200	250	275	300	400	450	600	1,000	750
1891......(600)......	200,000	40	50	75	85	110	140	350	900	750

BARBER OR LIBERTY HEAD (1892–1915)

Like the dime and quarter dollar, this type was designed by U.S. Mint chief engraver Charles E. Barber, whose initial B is on the truncation of the neck.

G-4 Good: Date and legends legible. LIBERTY worn off headband.

VG-8 Very Good: Some letters legible in LIBERTY.

F-12 Fine: LIBERTY nearly completely legible, but worn.

VF-20 Very Fine: All letters in LIBERTY evenly plain.

EF-40 Extremely Fine: LIBERTY bold, and its ribbon distinct.

AU-50 About Uncirculated: Slight trace of wear above forehead, leaf tips, and cheek, and on eagle's head, tail, and wing tips.

MS-60 Uncirculated: No trace of wear. Light blemishes.

MS-63 Choice Uncirculated: Some distracting contact marks or blemishes in prime focal areas. Impaired luster possible.

PF-63 Choice Proof: Reflective surfaces with only a few blemishes in secondary focal places. No major flaws.

Mintmark location on reverse, below eagle.

	Mintage	G-4	VG-8	F-12	VF-20	EF-40	AU-50	MS-60	MS-63	PF-63
1892 . . . . (1,245) 934,000		$15	$20	$40	$75	$125	$225	$400	$700	$750
1892O 390,000		200	300	400	450	500	600	750	1,250	
1892S 1,029,028		175	225	250	400	500	650	850	1,350	
1893 . . . . . . (792) 1,826,000		15	20	55	100	150	225	400	850	750
1893O 1,389,000		25	45	85	150	250	300	600	950	
1893S 740,000		100	150	350	500	850	1,100	1,400	2,750	
1894 . . . . . (972) . . . 1,148,000		15	25	60	120	160	225	400	700	750
1894O 2,138,000		13	20	50	125	225	275	400	750	
1894S 4,048,690		13	20	40	75	135	225	400	950	
1895 . . . . . . (880) 1,834,338		13	15	40	75	125	225	400	700	750
1895O 1,766,000		20	35	70	125	175	250	500	1,000	
1895S 1,108,086		20	45	100	150	200	275	425	850	
1896 . . . . . . (762) 950,000		20	25	55	100	150	225	425	700	750
1896O 924,000		20	25	125	300	1,000	2,000	3,500	7,000	
1896S 1,140,948		45	60	115	275	750	750	1,650	2,500	
1897 . . . . . . (731) 2,480,000		13	15	30	70	125	225	400	700	750
1897O 632,000		85	110	300	500	700	850	1,250	2,500	
1897S 933,900		90	145	250	400	750	1,000	2,000	2,750	
1898 . . . . . . (735) 2,956,000		13	15	30	70	125	225	400	700	750
1898O 874,000		20	65	145	250	400	550	1,000	1,750	
1898S 2,358,550		15	20	55	100	225	350	1,000	2,350	
1899 . . . . . . (846) 5,538,000		13	15	30	70	140	225	400	700	750
1899O 1,724,000		13	20	40	115	200	300	450	1,100	
1899S 1,686,411		13	20	50	100	135	275	500	1,300	
1900 . . . . . . (912) 4,762,000		8	11	30	70	125	225	400	700	750
1900O 2,744,000		8	11	45	125	225	325	850	2,000	
1900S 2,560,322		8	11	35	75	175	225	450	1,500	
1901 . . . . . . (813) 4,268,000		8	11	30	70	125	225	400	700	750
1901O 1,124,000		8	15	40	150	850	1,100	1,650	3,000	
1901S 847,044		8	30	100	250	950	1,350	2,500	5,000	
1902 . . . . . . (777) 4,922,000		8	11	30	70	125	225	400	700	750
1902O 2,526,000		8	11	30	70	125	325	600	1,500	
1902S 1,460,670		8	11	30	90	175	225	600	1,500	
1903 . . . . . . (755) 2,278,000		8	11	30	70	125	225	400	1,000	750
1903O 2,100,000		8	11	30	70	125	225	500	1,100	
1903S 1,920,772		8	11	30	75	150	300	550	1,250	
1904 . . . . . . (670) 2,992,000		8	11	30	70	125	225	400	700	750
1904O 1,117,600		8	12	45	125	325	550	1,100	2,500	
1904S 553,038		20	50	200	500	2,000	4,500	8,500	13,500	
1905 . . . . . . (727) 662,000		10	12	50	110	150	225	500	850	750
1905O 505,000		10	20	60	125	200	225	600	1,000	
1905S 2,494,000		8	11	30	75	125	225	500	1,100	
1906 . . . . . . (675) 2,638,000		8	11	30	70	125	225	400	700	750
1906D 4,028,000		8	11	30	70	125	225	400	1,000	
1906O 2,446,000		8	11	30	70	125	225	575	950	
1906S 1,740,154		8	11	30	70	125	225	400	800	
1907 . . . . . . (575) 2,598,000		8	11	30	70	125	225	400	700	750
1907D 3,856,000		8	11	30	70	125	225	400	700	
1907O 3,946,600		8	11	30	70	125	225	400	700	
1907S 1,250,000		8	20	40	100	225	425	750	3,750	
1908 . . . . . . (545) 1,354,000		8	11	30	70	125	225	400	700	750
1908D 3,280,000		8	11	30	70	125	225	400	700	

Chart continued on next page.

	Mintage	G-4	VG-8	F-12	VF-20	EF-40	AU-50	MS-60	MS-63	PF-63
19080	5,360,000	$8	$11	$30	$70	$125	$225	$400	$700	
1908S	1,644,828	8	11	40	100	175	225	500	1,450	
1909 (650)	2,368,000	8	11	30	70	125	225	400	700	$750
19090	925,400	8	11	40	110	250	475	900	1,100	
1909S	1,764,000	8	11	35	70	125	225	400	850	
1910 (551)	418,000	10	15	45	110	200	225	400	750	750
1910S	1,948,000	8	12	30	70	125	225	650	1,000	
1911 (543)	1,406,000	8	11	30	70	125	225	400	700	750
1911D	695,080	8	11	30	70	125	225	400	700	
1911S	1,272,000	8	11	30	70	125	225	650	1,000	
1912 (700)	1,550,000	8	11	30	70	125	225	400	700	750
1912D	2,300,800	8	11	30	70	125	225	400	700	
1912S	1,370,000	8	11	30	70	125	225	400	750	
1913 (627)	188,000	40	50	125	275	400	525	1,100	1,350	750
1913D	534,000	8	15	30	70	125	225	400	700	
1913S	604,000	8	15	30	70	125	225	650	1,100	
1914 (380)	124,230	65	100	200	325	475	650	1,150	1,350	750
1914S	992,000	8	11	30	70	125	225	400	700	
1915 (450)	138,000	50	75	185	225	350	550	1,000	2,000	750
1915D	1,170,400	8	11	30	70	125	225	400	700	
1915S	1,604,000	8	11	30	70	125	225	400	700	

LIBERTY WALKING (1916–1947)

This type was designed by American sculptor Adolph A. Weinman, whose monogram, AW, appears under the tip of the tail feathers. On the 1916 coins and some of the 1917 coins, the mintmark is located on the obverse below the motto. A Centennial Gold issue was struck in 2016.

G-4 Good: Rims defined. Motto IN GOD WE TRUST legible.
VG-8 Very Good: Motto distinct. About half of skirt lines at left clear.
F-12 Fine: All skirt lines evident, but worn in spots. Clear details in sandal below motto.
VF-20 Very Fine: Skirt lines sharp, including leg area. Little wear on breast and right arm.
EF-40 Extremely Fine: All skirt lines bold.
AU-50 About Uncirculated: Slight trace of wear on Liberty's head, knee, and breast tips and on eagle's claws and head.
MS-60 Uncirculated: No trace of wear. Light blemishes.
MS-63 Choice Uncirculated: Some distracting contact marks or blemishes in prime focal areas. Impaired luster possible.
PF-63 Choice Proof: Reflective surfaces with only a few blemishes in secondary focal places. No major flaws.
PF-65 Gem Proof: Brilliant surfaces with no noticeable blemishes or flaws. A few scattered, barely noticeable marks or hairlines possible.

1916–1917

1917–1947

Mintmark Locations

Coin dealers often pay more than the Mint State prices shown for choice Uncirculated examples that are well struck.

	Mintage	G-4	VG-8	F-12	VF-20	EF-40	AU-50	MS-60	MS-63
1916	608,000	$30.00	$45	$55	$100	$155	$200	$250	$550
1916D, Obverse Mintmark	1,014,400	25.00	30	40	70	125	175	250	600
1916S, Obverse Mintmark	508,000	50.00	65	125	250	400	750	1,000	1,800
1917	12,292,000	10.00	11	13	15	20	40	75	145
1917D, Obverse Mintmark	765,400	12.00	16	40	80	150	250	550	950
1917D, Reverse Mintmark	1,940,000	10.00	12	25	65	185	375	850	1,750
1917S, Obverse Mintmark	952,000	15.00	22	75	200	575	950	2,450	4,500
1917S, Reverse Mintmark	5,554,000	10.00	13	15	17	40	150	450	1,350
1918	6,634,000	10.00	13	15	35	70	200	400	950
1918D	3,853,040	10.00	13	20	50	150	350	1,000	2,200
1918S	10,282,000	10.00	13	15	20	45	125	400	1,350
1919	962,000	15.00	18	40	150	350	750	1,750	2,750
1919D	1,165,000	15.00	20	50	175	550	1,500	3,500	9,500
1919S	1,552,000	10.00	18	35	175	650	1,100	2,750	6,500
1920	6,372,000	10.00	15	20	25	45	100	300	550
1920D	1,551,000	10.00	15	35	125	350	550	2,000	3,750
1920S	4,624,000	10.00	13	15	50	125	400	750	2,500
1921	246,000	100.00	150	200	475	1,500	2,400	4,500	6,500
1921D	208,000	150.00	200	350	575	2,250	3,750	6,500	11,500
1921S	548,000	20.00	30	125	550	2,750	5,500	15,000	27,500
1923S	2,178,000	10.00	13	15	60	350	900	2,000	3,500
1927S	2,392,000	8.00	9	10	25	100	300	850	1,650
1928S	1,940,000	8.00	9	10	35	115	500	900	2,450
1929D	1,001,200	8.00	9	10	20	50	150	300	600
1929S	1,902,000	8.00	9	10	15	60	135	350	850
1933S	1,786,000	8.00	9	10	15	40	175	500	1,100
1934	6,964,000	5.50	6	7	8	9	15	40	50
1934D	2,361,000	5.50	6	7	8	15	55	95	200
1934S	3,652,000	5.50	6	7	8	16	65	250	600
1935	9,162,000	5.50	6	7	8	9	15	25	40
1935D	3,003,800	5.50	6	7	8	15	30	75	175
1935S	3,854,000	5.50	6	7	8	25	55	150	275

	Mintage	G-4	VG-8	F-12	VF-20	EF-40	AU-50	MS-60	MS-63	PF-63	PF-65
1936 ... (3,901)	12,614,000	$5.50	$6	$7	$8	$9	$12	$25	$40	$1,000	$2,000
1936D	4,252,400	5.50	6	7	8	10	25	45	60		
1936S	3,884,000	5.50	6	7	8	15	30	80	125		
1937 ... (5,728)	9,522,000	5.50	6	7	8	10	12	25	35	325	600
1937D	1,676,000	5.50	6	7	8	15	50	120	175		
1937S	2,090,000	5.50	6	7	8	10	30	85	125		
1938 ... (8,152)	4,110,000	5.50	6	7	8	9	20	35	90	275	400
1938D	491,600	35.00	40	55	60	85	140	300	375		
1939 ... (8,808)	6,812,000	5.50	6	7	8	9	15	25	35	300	400
1939D	4,267,800	5.50	6	7	8	9	12	25	40		
1939S	2,552,000	5.50	6	7	8	10	40	90	100		

	Mintage	VG-8	F-12	VF-20	EF-40	AU-50	MS-60	MS-63	PF-63	PF-65
1940 ... (11,279)	9,156,000	$5.50	$6	$7	$8	$12	$20	$30	$250	$350
1940S	4,550,000	5.50	6	7	8	12	25	35		
1941 ... (15,412)	24,192,000	5.50	6	7	8	12	20	30	250	350
1941D	11,248,400	5.50	6	7	8	12	20	35		
1941S	8,098,000	5.50	6	7	8	12	40	55		
1942 ... (21,120)	47,818,000	5.50	6	7	8	12	20	30	250	350

Chart continued on next page.

	Mintage	VG-8	F-12	VF-20	EF-40	AU-50	MS-60	MS-63
1942D	10,973,800	$5.50	$6	$7	$8	$12	$20	$45
1942S	12,708,000	5.50	6	7	8	12	20	35
1943	53,190,000	5.50	6	7	8	12	20	30
1943D	11,346,000	5.50	6	7	8	12	22	35
1943S	13,450,000	5.50	6	7	8	12	22	30
1944	28,206,000	5.50	6	7	8	12	20	30
1944D	9,769,000	5.50	6	7	8	12	20	35
1944S	8,904,000	5.50	6	7	8	12	22	30
1945	31,502,000	5.50	6	7	8	12	20	30
1945D	9,966,800	5.50	6	7	8	12	20	30
1945S	10,156,000	5.50	6	7	8	12	22	30
1946	12,118,000	5.50	6	7	8	12	20	30
1946D	2,151,000	5.50	6	7	8	12	25	30
1946S	3,724,000	5.50	6	7	8	12	30	35
1947	4,094,000	5.50	6	7	8	12	25	30
1947D	3,900,600	5.50	6	7	8	12	25	30

FRANKLIN (1948–1963)

The Benjamin Franklin half dollar and the Roosevelt dime were both designed by U.S. Mint chief engraver John R. Sinnock. His initials appear below the shoulder.

VF-20 Very Fine: At least half of the lower and upper incused lines on rim of Liberty Bell on reverse visible.

EF-40 Extremely Fine: Wear spots at top of end of Franklin's curls and hair at back of ears. Wear evident at top and on lettering of Liberty Bell.

MS-60 Uncirculated: No trace of wear. Light blemishes.

MS-63 Choice Uncirculated: Some distracting contact marks or blemishes in prime focal areas. Impaired luster possible.

MS-65 Gem Uncirculated: Only light, scattered contact marks that are not distracting. Strong luster, good eye appeal.

PF-63 Choice Proof: Reflective surfaces with only a few blemishes in secondary focal places. No major flaws.

PF-65 Gem Proof: Brilliant surfaces with no noticeable blemishes or flaws. A few scattered, barely noticeable marks or hairlines possible.

Mintmark Location

Coin dealers usually pay more than the Mint State prices shown for well-struck Uncirculated halves with full bell lines.

	Mintage	VF-20	EF-40	MS-60	MS-63	MS-65	PF-63	PF-65
1948	3,006,814	$5.50	$6	$10	$12	$35		
1948D	4,028,600	5.50	6	10	12	60		
1949	5,614,000	5.50	6	20	30	65		
1949D	4,120,600	5.50	6	25	30	250		
1949S	3,744,000	5.50	6	40	45	75		
1950 ..... (51,386)	7,742,123	5.50	6	12	18	50	$200	$250
1950D	8,031,600	5.50	6	10	23	110		
1951 ..... (57,500)	16,802,102	5.50	6	10	12	30	175	200
1951D	9,475,200	5.50	6	15	18	85		
1951S	13,696,000	5.50	6	12	15	30		
1952 ..... (81,980)	21,192,093	5.50	6	8	10	30	80	100
1952D	25,395,600	5.50	6	8	10	60		
1952S	5,526,000	5.50	6	35	40	50		

	Mintage	VF-20	EF-40	MS-60	MS-63	MS-65	PF-63	PF-65
1953 .... (128,800).... 2,668,120		$5.50	$6	$10	$11	$35	$65	$85
1953D 20,900,400		5.50	6	10	11	55		
1953S 4,148,000		5.50	6	15	20	25		
1954 .... (233,300)... 13,188,202		5.50	6	8	10	20	25	45
1954D 25,445,580		5.50	6	8	10	40		
1954S 4,993,400		5.50	6	8	10	20		
1955 .... (378,200).... 2,498,181		5.50	6	8	13	25	25	40
1956 .... (669,384).... 4,032,000		5.50	6	8	10	15	15	20
1957 ...(1,247,952)....5,114,000		5.50	6	8	10	15	12	15
1957D 19,966,850		5.50	6	8	10	20		
1958 .... (875,652).... 4,042,000		5.50	6	8	10	15	12	17
1958D 23,962,412		5.50	6	8	10	15		
1959 ...(1,149,291)....6,200,000		5.50	6	8	10	25	12	14
1959D 13,053,750		5.50	6	8	10	40		
1960 ...(1,691,602)....6,024,000		5.50	6	8	10	45	12	14
1960D 18,215,812		5.50	6	8	10	100		
1961 ...(3,028,244)....8,290,000		5.50	6	8	10	20	12	14
1961D 20,276,442		5.50	6	8	10	60		
1962 ...(3,218,019)....9,714,000		5.50	6	8	10	40	12	14
1962D 35,473,281		5.50	6	8	10	35		
1963 ...(3,075,645)... 22,164,000		5.50	6	8	10	15	12	14
1963D 67,069,292		5.50	6	8	10	15		

KENNEDY (1964 TO DATE)

Gilroy Roberts, chief engraver of the U.S. Mint from 1948 to 1964, designed the obverse of this coin, a tribute to President John F. Kennedy, who was assassinated in November 1963. Roberts's stylized initials are on the truncation of the forceful bust of Kennedy. The reverse, which uses as its motif the eagle from the Seal of the President of the United States, is the work of assistant engraver Frank Gasparro. The Kennedy half dollar was minted in 90% silver in its first year of issue, 1964. From 1965 to 1970 its fineness was reduced to 40% silver. Since 1971 the coin has been struck in copper-nickel (except for certain silver Proofs, 1992 to date). Dates after 2001 have not been released into general circulation, instead being made available in 20-coin rolls, 200-coin bags, and coin sets sold by the Mint. In 2014 a .999 fine gold version was made for collectors, dual-dated 1964–2014 to mark the coin's 50th anniversary.

In the early 1970s an open contest was held to select a new reverse design for the Kennedy half dollar, to celebrate the nation's bicentennial. Seth G. Huntington's winning entry featured a view of Independence Hall in Philadelphia. The Bicentennial half dollars bear the dual date 1776–1976.

Mintmark Location (1964)

Mintmark Location (1968 to Date)

Entry continued on next page.

Silver Coinage (1964)

	Mintage	MS-63	PF-63	PF-65
1964	(3,950,762)....273,304,004	$7	$10	$13
1964D	156,205,446	7		

Silver Clad Coinage (1965–1970)

	Mintage	MS-63	PF-63	PF-65
1965	65,879,366	$3		
1966	108,984,932	3		
1967	295,046,978	3		
1968D	246,951,930	3		
1968S	(3,041,506)		$3.50	$5
1969D	129,881,800	$3		
1969S	(2,934,631)		$3.50	$5
1970D	2,150,000	10		
1970S	(2,632,810)		4.00	8

Clad Coinage and Silver Proofs (1971 to Date)

	Mintage	MS-63	PF-63	PF-65
1971	155,164,000	$0.55		
1971D	302,097,424	0.55		
1971S	(3,220,733)		$1.50	$3
1972	153,180,000	0.60		
1972D	141,890,000	0.60		
1972S	(3,260,996)		1.50	3
1973	64,964,000	$0.55		
1973D	83,171,400	0.55		
1973S	(2,760,339)		$1.50	$2.50
1974	201,596,000	0.55		
1974D	79,066,300	0.55		
1974S	(2,612,568)		1.50	3.00

Bicentennial (1776–1976)

	Mintage	MS-63	PF-63	PF-65
1776–1976, Clad	234,308,000	$0.55		
1776–1976D, Clad	287,565,248	0.55		
1776–1976S, Clad	(7,059,099)		$0.75	$2.50
1776–1976S, Silver	*11,000,000*	3.00		
1776–1976S, Silver	*(4,000,000)*		3.50	5.00

Note: Mintage figures for 1976-S silver coins are approximate; many were melted in 1982.

Eagle Reverse Resumed (1977 to Date)

	Mintage	MS-63	PF-63	PF-65
1977	43,598,000	$0.60		
1977D	31,449,106	0.60		
1977S	(3,251,152)		$1.00	$1.25
1978	14,350,000	0.60		
1978D	13,765,799	1.00		
1978S	(3,127,781)		1.00	1.50
1979	68,312,000	0.55		
1979D	15,815,422	0.55		
1979S	(3,677,175)			
Type 1			$1.00	$2.00
Type 2			3.00	6.00
1980P	44,134,000	$0.55		
1980D	33,456,449	0.55		
1980S	(3,554,806)		1.00	1.50
1981P	29,544,000	0.75		
1981D	27,839,533	0.75		

HALF DOLLARS

Eagle Reverse Resumed (1977 to Date)

	Mintage	MS-63	PF-63	PF-65		Mintage	MS-63	PF-63	PF-65
1981S	(4,063,083)				1996D	24,744,000	$0.50		
Type 1			$1.00	$2.00	1996S	(1,750,244)		$3.00	$5
Type 2			5.00	10.00	1996S, Silver	(775,021)		11.00	16
1982P	10,819,000	$2.50			1997P	20,882,000	0.50		
1982D	13,140,102	2.50			1997D	19,876,000	0.50		
1982S	(3,857,479)		1.00	1.50	1997S	(2,055,000)		3.00	6
1983P	34,139,000	3.00			1997S, Silver	(741,678)		20.00	25
1983D	32,472,244	3.50			1998P	15,646,000	0.50		
1983S	(3,279,126)		1.00	1.75	1998D	15,064,000	0.50		
1984P	26,029,000	0.75			1998S	(2,086,507)		3.00	6
1984D	26,262,158	0.75			1998S, Silver	(878,792)		10.00	11
1984S	(3,065,110)		1.00	2.00	1998S, Silver,				
1985P	18,706,962	2.00			Matte Finish . . .	(62,000)		75.00	85
1985D	19,814,034	1.50			1999P	8,900,000	0.55		
1985S	(3,362,821)		1.00	1.75	1999D	10,682,000	0.55		
1986P	13,107,633	3.00			1999S	(2,543,401)		3.00	5
1986D	15,336,145	2.50			1999S, Silver	(804,565)		10.00	12
1986S	(3,010,497)		3.00	4.50	2000P	22,600,000	0.60		
1987P **(a)**	2,890,758	2.50			2000D	19,466,000	0.60		
1987D **(a)**	2,890,758	2.50			2000S	(3,082,483)		2.00	3
1987S	(4,227,728)		1.00	1.75	2000S, Silver	(965,421)		8.00	11
1988P	13,626,000	1.50			2001P	21,200,000	0.55		
1988D	12,000,096	1.35			2001D	19,504,000	0.55		
1988S	(3,262,948)		2.00	2.50	2001S	(2,294,909)		3.25	4
1989P	24,542,000	1.00			2001S, Silver	(889,697)		8.00	11
1989D	23,000,216	1.10			2002P **(a)**	3,100,000	0.65		
1989S	(3,220,194)		1.50	3.00	2002D **(a)**	2,500,000	0.65		
1990P	22,278,000	1.00			2002S	(2,319,766)		2.00	3
1990D	20,096,242	1.10			2002S, Silver	(892,229)		8.00	11
1990S	(3,299,559)		1.50	2.00	2003P **(a)**	2,500,000	0.65		
1991P	14,874,000	0.70			2003D **(a)**	2,500,000	0.65		
1991D	15,054,678	1.25			2003S	(2,172,684)		2.00	3
1991S	(2,867,787)		4.00	4.00	2003S, Silver . . .	(1,125,755)		8.00	11
1992P	17,628,000	0.50			2004P **(a)**	2,900,000	0.65		
1992D	17,000,106	1.10			2004D **(a)**	2,900,000	0.65		
1992S	(2,858,981)		2.00	3	2004S	(1,789,488)		3.00	7
1992S, Silver . . .	(1,317,579)		10.00	12	2004S, Silver . . .	(1,175,934)		8.00	11
1993P	15,510,000	0.50			2005P	3,800,000	0.65		
1993D	15,000,006	0.50			2005D	3,500,000	0.65		
1993S	(2,633,439)		3.00	5	2005S	(2,275,000)		2.00	3
1993S, Silver	(761,353)		10.00	12	2005S, Silver . . .	(1,069,679)		8.00	11
1994P	23,718,000	0.50			2006P **(a)**	2,400,000	0.65		
1994D	23,828,110	0.50			2006D **(a)**	2,000,000	0.65		
1994S	(2,484,594)		3.00	4	2006S	(2,000,428)		2.00	3
1994S, Silver	(785,329)		10.00	12	2006S, Silver . . .	(1,054,008)		8.00	11
1995P	26,496,000	0.50			2007P **(a)**	2,400,000	0.65		
1995D	26,288,000	0.50			2007D **(a)**	2,400,000	0.65		
1995S	(2,117,496)		6.00	8	2007S	(1,702,116)		2.00	3
1995S, Silver	(679,985)		15.00	20	2007S, Silver	(875,050)		8.00	11
1996P	24,442,000	0.50			2008P **(a)**	1,700,000	0.65		

a. Not issued for circulation.

Entry continued on next page.

HALF DOLLARS

	Mintage	MS-63	PF-63	PF-65
2008D (a)	1,700,000	$0.65		
2008S	(1,405,674)		$4	$6
2008S, Silver	(763,887)		8	11
2009P (a)	1,900,000	0.65		
2009D (a)	1,900,000	0.65		
2009S	(1,482,502)		2	3
2009S, Silver	(697,365)		8	11
2010P (a)	1,800,000	0.65		
2010D (a)	1,700,000	0.65		
2010S	(1,103,815)		4	6
2010S, Silver	(585,401)		10	12
2011P (a)	1,750,000	0.65		
2011D (a)	1,700,000	0.65		
2011S	(1,098,835)		4	6
2011S, Silver	(574,175)		12	14
2012P (a)	1,800,000	0.65		
2012D (a)	1,700,000	0.65		
2012S	(843,705)		12	15
2012S, Silver	(445,612)		75	85
2013P (a)	5,000,000	0.65		
2013D (a)	4,600,000	0.65		
2013S	(854,785)		3	4
2013S, Silver	(467,691)		14	16

	Mintage	MS-63	PF-63	PF-65
2014P (a)	2,500,000	$0.65		
2014P, High Relief (b)		0.65		
2014P, Silver (c)	(219,173)		$18	$20
2014D (a)	2,100,000	0.65		
2014D, High Relief (b)		0.65		
2014D, Silver (c)	219,173	18.00		
2014S, Silver Enhanced (c)	219,173	20.00		
2014S	(767,977)		3	4
2014S, Silver	(472,107)		14	16
2014W, Reverse Proof, Silver (c)	(219,173)		20	22
2014W, 50th Anniversary, Gold (d)	(73,722)			650
2015P (a)	2,300,000	0.65		
2015D (a)	2,300,000	0.65		
2015S	(662,854)		3	4
2015S, Silver	(387,310)		14	16
2016P (a)	2,100,000	0.65		
2016D (a)	2,100,000	0.65		
2016S	(641,775)		3	4
2016S, Silver	(419,256)		14	16

a. Not issued for circulation. b. To celebrate the 50th anniversary of the Kennedy half dollar, the U.S. Mint issued an Uncirculated two-coin set featuring a Kennedy half dollar from Philadelphia and one from Denver. c. Featured in the 2014 half dollar silver-coin collection released by the U.S. Mint to commemorate the 50th anniversary of the Kennedy half dollar. d. First gold half dollar offered by the U.S. Mint. It commemorates the 50th anniversary of the first release of the Kennedy half dollar in 1964.

	Mintage	SP-67	SP-70
2016W, Gold (a)	65,509	$650	$700

a. In 2016 the Mint issued a centennial version of the Liberty Walking half dollar in gold.

	Mintage	MS-63	PF-63	PF-65
2017P (a)	1,800,000	$0.65		
2017D (a)	2,900,000	0.65		
2017S	(621,384)		$3	$4
2017S, Silver	(404,994)		14	16
2018P (a)	4,800,000	0.65		
2018D (a)	6,100,000	0.65		

	Mintage	MS-63	PF-63	PF-65
2018S	(535,221)		$3	$4
2018S, Silver	(350,820)		14	16
2019P (a)		$0.65		
2019D (a)		0.65		
2019S			3	4
2019S, Silver (b)			14	16

a. Not issued for circulation. b. In 2019, an Enhanced Reverse Proof half dollar from the San Francisco Mint was included in the Apollo 11 50th Anniversary Half Dollar Set.

The silver dollar was authorized by Congress April 2, 1792. Its weight was specified at 416 grains and its fineness at .8924. The first issues appeared in 1794, and until 1804 all silver dollars had the value stamped on the edge: HUNDRED CENTS, ONE DOLLAR OR UNIT. After a lapse in coinage of the silver dollar during the period 1804 to 1835, coins were made with either plain (1836 only) or reeded edges and the value was placed on the reverse side.

Mintages shown here are as reported by the Mint for calendar years and do not necessarily refer to the dates on the coins.

The weight was changed by the law of January 18, 1837, to 412-1/2 grains, fineness .900. The coinage was discontinued by the Act of February 12, 1873, and reauthorized by the Act of February 28, 1878. The silver dollar was again discontinued after 1935, and since then copper-nickel and other base-metal pieces have been coined for circulation. (See also "$1 American Silver Eagle Coins" on page 244.)

FLOWING HAIR (1794–1795)

AG-3 About Good: Clear enough to identify.

G-4 Good: Date and letters legible. Main devices outlined, but lacking in detail.

VG-8 Very Good: Major details discernible. Letters well formed but worn.

F-12 Fine: Hair ends distinguishable. Top hair lines visible, but otherwise worn smooth.

VF-20 Very Fine: Some detail visible in hair in center. Other details more bold.

EF-40 Extremely Fine: Hair well defined but with some wear.

AU-50 About Uncirculated: Slight trace of wear on tips of highest curls; breast feathers usually weak.

MS-60 Uncirculated: No trace of wear. Light blemishes.

	Mintage	AG-3	G-4	VG-8	F-12	VF-20	EF-40	AU-50	MS-60
1794	1,758	$30,000	$50,000	$85,000	$105,000	$145,000	$250,000	$425,000	—
1795	160,295	750	1,500	1,750	2,500	4,500	9,500	15,000	$50,000

DRAPED BUST (1795–1804)
Small Eagle Reverse (1795–1798)

AG-3 About Good: Clear enough to identify.

G-4 Good: Bust outlined, no detail. Date legible, some leaves evident.

VG-8 Very Good: Drapery worn except deepest folds. Hair lines smooth.

F-12 Fine: All drapery lines distinguishable. Some detail visible in hair lines near cheek and neck.

VF-20 Very Fine: Left side of drapery worn smooth.

EF-40 Extremely Fine: Drapery distinctly visible. Hair well outlined and detailed.

AU-50 About Uncirculated: Slight trace of wear on the bust shoulder and hair to left of forehead, as well as on eagle's breast and top edges of wings.

MS-60 Uncirculated: No trace of wear. Light blemishes.

	Mintage	AG-3	G-4	VG-8	F-12	VF-20	EF-40	AU-50	MS-60
1795, Bust Type. .	42,738	$650	$1,450	$1,650	$2,750	$3,750	$8,000	$12,000	$35,000
1796	79,920	650	1,450	1,650	2,750	3,750	8,000	12,000	36,000
1797	7,776	650	1,450	1,650	2,750	3,750	8,000	12,000	42,000
1798	327,536	700	1,550	1,750	2,850	4,000	9,500	14,500	65,000

Heraldic Eagle Reverse (1798–1804)

G-4 Good: Letters and date legible. E PLURIBUS UNUM illegible.
VG-8 Very Good: Motto partially legible. Only deepest drapery details visible. All other lines smooth.
F-12 Fine: All drapery lines distinguishable. Some detail visible in hair lines near cheek and neck.
VF-20 Very Fine: Left side of drapery worn smooth.
EF-40 Extremely Fine: Drapery distinct. Hair well detailed.
AU-50 About Uncirculated: Slight trace of wear on the bust shoulder and hair to left of forehead, as well as on eagle's breast and top edges of wings.
MS-60 Uncirculated: No trace of wear. Light blemishes.

	Mintage	G-4	VG-8	F-12	VF-20	EF-40	AU-50	MS-60
1798, Heraldic Eagle	*	$650	$850	$1,200	$1,850	$3,000	$5,750	$17,500
1799	423,515	650	850	1,200	1,850	3,000	5,750	17,500
1800	220,920	650	850	1,200	1,850	3,000	5,750	17,500
1801	54,454	650	900	1,300	2,000	3,500	5,750	18,500
1802	41,650	650	850	1,250	1,850	3,250	5,750	17,500
1803	85,634	750	1,000	1,350	2,000	3,500	7,500	20,000
1804, Variety 1, 0 Above Cloud (a)					Proof: $3,500,000			
1804, Variety 2, 0 Above Space Between Clouds (a).					Proof: $3,000,000			

* Included in number above. **a.** Numerous counterfeits exist.

GOBRECHT (1836–1839)

Silver dollars of 1836, 1838, and 1839 were mostly made as patterns and restrikes, but some dated 1836 were made for general circulation.

	VF-20	EF-40	AU-50	PF-60
1836, C. GOBRECHT F. on base. Reverse eagle flying upward amid stars. Plain edge. Although scarce, this is the most common variety and was issued for circulation as regular coinage....................	$7,000	$10,000	$12,500	$18,500
1838, Similar obverse, designer's name omitted, stars added around border. Reverse eagle flying left in plain field. Reeded edge................	9,500	15,000	16,500	20,000
1839, Obverse as above. Reverse eagle in plain field. Reeded edge. Issued for circulation as regular coinage...........	8,500	12,000	12,500	16,500

LIBERTY SEATED (1840–1873)

Starting again in 1840, silver dollars were issued for general circulation, continuing to about 1850, after which their main use was in the export trade to China. The seated figure of Liberty was adopted for the obverse, and a heraldic eagle for the reverse.

VG-8 Very Good: Any three letters of LIBERTY at least two-thirds complete.
F-12 Fine: All seven letters of LIBERTY visible, though weak.
VF-20 Very Fine: LIBERTY strong, but slight wear visible on its ribbon.
EF-40 Extremely Fine: Horizontal lines of shield complete. Eagle's eye plain.
AU-50 About Uncirculated: Traces of light wear on only the high points of the design. Half of mint luster present.
MS-60 Uncirculated: No trace of wear. Light marks or blemishes.
PF-60 Proof: Several contact marks, hairlines, or light rubs possible on surface. Luster possibly dull and eye appeal lacking.
PF-63 Choice Proof: Reflective surfaces with only a few blemishes in secondary focal places. No major flaws.

No Motto (1840–1865)

Location of mintmark, when present, is on reverse, below eagle.

See next page for chart.

143

	Mintage	VG-8	F-12	VF-20	EF-40	AU-50	MS-60	PF-60	PF-63
1840 61,005		$250	$300	$400	$600	$900	$3,500	$9,500	$17,000
1841 173,000		250	300	350	475	800	1,850	17,500	35,000
1842 184,618		250	300	350	450	700	1,900	10,000	22,500
1843 165,100		250	300	350	425	750	1,850	8,500	20,000
1844 20,000		250	350	450	600	1,100	4,000	7,000	20,000
1845 24,500		250	350	425	650	1,100	5,000	8,000	19,000
1846 110,600		250	300	350	450	750	1,800	6,500	18,000
1846O 59,000		250	300	350	550	1,000	5,000		
1847 140,750		250	300	350	400	650	2,250	8,250	16,500
1848 15,000		350	450	500	1,100	1,550	4,750	8,250	19,000
1849 62,600		250	300	375	450	700	2,000	9,500	21,000
1850 7,500		450	575	700	1,300	2,250	4,500	8,750	16,000
1850O 40,000		250	375	650	1,250	2,500	8,000		
1851 1,300		7,500	8,500	9,500	15,000	20,000	27,500	16,000	22,000
1852 1,100		2,500	6,000	7,500	12,500	21,500	25,000	17,500	23,000
1853 46,110		400	500	600	850	1,100	2,500	15,000	23,000
1854 33,140		1,400	2,000	2,750	3,500	5,000	7,500	7,500	12,000
1855 26,000		1,100	1,500	2,250	3,250	4,500	7,500	7,500	11,500
1856 63,500		500	650	850	1,250	1,800	2,500	3,750	8,500
1857 94,000		500	650	850	1,250	2,250	3,000	3,250	8,000
1858 . . . . . . (210).		2,250	3,000	3,500	4,500	6,000		6,000	8,000
1859 . . . . . . (800). 255,700		300	350	450	600	850	2,000	1,500	3,000
1859O 360,000		250	300	350	400	600	1,500		
1859S 20,000		500	700	800	1,200	2,700	7,500		
1860 . . . . (1,330). 217,600		275	300	350	450	700	1,800	1,500	3,000
1860O 515,000		250	300	350	400	600	1,500		
1861 . . . . . . (1,000). 77,500		600	750	800	1,600	2,250	2,500	1,500	3,000
1862 . . . . . . (550). 11,540		500	700	1,100	1,900	2,500	5,000	1,500	3,000
1863 . . . . . . (460). 27,200		750	1,000	1,000	1,250	2,100	2,750	1,500	3,000
1864 . . . . . . (470). 30,700		375	550	650	950	1,850	2,750	1,500	3,000
1865 . . . . . . (500). 46,500		450	550	700	1,200	1,850	3,500	1,500	3,000

With Motto IN GOD WE TRUST (1866–1873)

Motto IN GOD WE TRUST on Reverse (1866–1873)

	Mintage	VG-8	F-12	VF-20	EF-40	AU-50	MS-60	PF-60	PF-63
1866 . . . . . . (725). 48,900		$250	$325	$450	$650	$950	$1,800	$1,450	$2,750
1867 . . . . . . (625). 46,900		250	325	450	550	900	1,650	1,450	2,750
1868 . . . . . . (600). 162,100		250	325	450	550	775	2,000	1,450	2,750
1869 . . . . . . (600). 423,700		250	325	450	500	800	1,650	1,450	2,750

	Mintage	VG-8	F-12	VF-20	EF-40	AU-50	MS-60	PF-60	PF-63
1870 . . . (1,000). . . 415,000		$250	$325	$350	$600	$650	$1,500	$1,450	$2,750
1870CC 11,758		800	800	1,250	3,500	6,000	20,000		
1870S 175,000		250,000	350,000	450,000	800,000	1,250,000			
1871 . . . . . (960). .1,073,800		250	325	350	400	600	1,500	1,450	2,750
1871CC 1,376		2,750	3,750	5,000	10,000	17,500	55,000		
1872 . . . . . (950). .1,105,500		250	325	350	400	600	1,500	1,450	2,750
1872CC 3,150		1,650	2,000	3,000	4,500	7,000	20,000		
1872S 9,000		450	600	700	1,250	2,500	5,750		
1873 . . . . . (600). . . 293,000		250	325	350	400	600	1,500	1,450	2,750
1873CC 2,300		8,000	12,500	15,000	20,000	37,500	100,000		

TRADE DOLLARS (1873–1885)

This trade dollar was issued for circulation in the Orient to compete with dollar-size coins of other countries. It weighed 420 grains compared to 412-1/2 grains, the weight of the regular silver dollar.

VG-8 Very Good: About half of mottoes IN GOD WE TRUST (on Liberty's pedestal) and E PLURIBUS UNUM (on obverse ribbon) visible. Rim on both sides well defined.

F-12 Fine: Mottoes and LIBERTY legible but worn.

EF-40 Extremely Fine: Mottoes and LIBERTY sharp. Only slight wear on rims.

AU-50 About Uncirculated: Slight trace of wear on Liberty's left breast and left knee and on hair above ear, as well as on eagle's head, knee, and wing tips.

MS-60 Uncirculated: No trace of wear. Light blemishes.

MS-63 Choice Uncirculated: Some distracting contact marks or blemishes in prime focal areas. Impaired luster possible.

PF-63 Choice Proof: Reflective surfaces with only a few blemishes in secondary focal places. No major flaws.

1875-S, S Over CC

	Mintage	VG-8	F-12	EF-40	AU-50	MS-60	MS-63	PF-63
1873 . . . . (600). 396,900		$125	$135	$200	$375	$800	$2,000	$2,200
1873CC 124,500		250	350	1,100	1,750	5,500	15,000	
1873S 703,000		125	135	205	325	1,000	2,750	
1874 . . . . (700). 987,100		125	135	205	300	850	1,650	2,200
1874CC 1,373,200		225	275	650	850	2,000	4,000	
1874S 2,549,000		125	135	200	275	700	1,200	
1875 . . . . (700). 218,200		225	350	550	850	1,750	3,000	2,200
1875CC 1,573,700		250	300	450	550	1,500	3,250	
1875S 4,487,000		125	135	200	275	700	1,100	
1875S, S Over CC . . . . *		200	275	650	900	4,000	10,000	
1876 . . . . . . (1,150). 455,000		125	135	200	275	700	1,100	2,200
1876CC 509,000		300	400	850	1,200	5,500	13,500	

* Included in number above.

Chart continued on next page.

	Mintage	VG-8	F-12	EF-40	AU-50	MS-60	MS-63	PF-63
1876S 5,227,000		$125	$135	$200	$275	$700	$1,100	
1877 . . . . (510). . . . 3,039,200		125	135	200	275	700	1,150	$2,200
1877CC 534,000		325	425	800	1,250	2,750	6,500	
1877S 9,519,000		125	135	200	275	700	1,100	
1878 . . . . (900).				800				2,200
1878CC **(a)** 97,000		550	850	2,750	4,500	12,500	25,000	
1878S 4,162,000		125	135	200	275	700	1,100	
1879 . . . . . . (1,541).				800				2,200
1880 . . . . . . (1,987).				850				2,200
1881 . . . . (960).				850				2,200
1882 . . . . . . (1,097).				850				2,200
1883 . . . . (979).				850				2,200
1884 **(b)** . . . . . . (10).								350,000
1885 **(b)** . . . . (5).								1,500,000

a. 44,148 trade dollars were melted on July 19, 1878. Many of these may have been 1878-CC. **b.** The trade dollars of 1884 and 1885 were unknown to collectors until 1908. None are listed in the Mint director's report, and numismatists believe that they are not a part of the regular Mint issue.

MORGAN (1878–1921)

George T. Morgan, formerly a pupil of William Wyon at the Royal Mint in London, designed the new dollar. His initial M is found at the truncation of the neck, at the last tress. It also appears on the reverse on the left-hand loop of the ribbon.

Sharply struck prooflike coins have a highly reflective surface and usually command substantial premiums.

VF-20 Very Fine: Two thirds of hair lines from top of forehead to ear visible. Ear well defined. Feathers on eagle's breast worn.

EF-40 Extremely Fine: All hair lines strong and ear bold. Eagle's feathers all plain but with slight wear on breast and wing tips.

AU-50 About Uncirculated: Slight trace of wear on the bust shoulder and hair left of forehead, and on eagle's breast and top edges of wings.

MS-60 Uncirculated: No trace of wear. Full mint luster present, but may be noticeably marred by scuff marks or bag abrasions.

MS-63 Choice Uncirculated: No trace of wear; full mint luster; few noticeable surface marks.

MS-64 Uncirculated: A few scattered contact marks. Good eye appeal and attractive luster.

MS-65 Gem Uncirculated: Only light, scattered contact marks that are not distracting. Strong luster, good eye appeal.

8 Tail Feathers, 1878, Philadelphia Only
Mintmark location on reverse, below wreath.

SILVER AND RELATED DOLLARS

Most Proof Morgan dollars, where indicated in mintage records (quantity shown in parentheses), are valued by coin dealers approximately as follows:
Proof-60 – $600; Proof-63 – $1,400; Proof-65 – $3,000.

Most Uncirculated silver dollars have scratches or nicks because of handling of mint bags in shipping and storage. Coin dealers usually pay more than the listed prices for choice sharply struck pieces with full brilliance and without blemishes.

	Mintage	VF-20	EF-40	AU-50	MS-60	MS-63	MS-65
1878, 8 Feathers........(500).....*749,500*		$55	$60	$75	$135	$185	$650
1878, 7 Feathers........(250)...*9,759,300*		30	31	40	60	100	500
1878, 7/8 Clear Doubled Feathers..........*		30	31	37	125	175	1,000
1878CC.....................2,212,000		80	95	120	300	350	950
1878S.......................9,774,000		30	31	35	45	55	175
1879..............(1,100)..14,806,000		20	22	30	40	55	350
1879CC, CC Over CC..............756,000		175	475	1,350	3,500	5,000	15,000
1879O.....................2,887,000		20	26	29	65	175	1,500
1879S.......................9,110,000		20	22	29	40	45	90
1880..............(1,355)..12,600,000		22	24	29	35	55	350
1880CC...................495,000		140	170	220	400	450	700
1880O.....................5,305,000		22	25	29	65	250	8,500
1880S.......................8,900,000		20	22	28	35	40	90
1881..................(984)...9,163,000		20	22	28	35	45	325
1881CC........................296,000		250	265	285	380	425	550
1881O.....................5,708,000		22	24	27	35	42	625
1881S.......................12,760,000		20	22	27	35	40	90
1882..............(1,100)..11,100,000		20	22	27	35	45	200
1882CC.....................1,133,000		65	80	100	150	185	285
1882O.....................6,090,000		22	24	28	35	45	425
1882S.......................9,250,000		20	22	27	38	40	95
1883..............(1,039)..12,290,000		20	22	27	38	45	100
1883CC.....................1,204,000		65	80	100	150	185	275
1883O.....................8,725,000		20	22	27	35	40	90
1883S.......................6,250,000		20	30	75	650	2,000	16,500
1884..................(875)..14,070,000		20	22	27	35	45	165
1884CC.....................1,136,000		90	110	115	150	185	275
1884O.....................9,730,000		20	22	27	35	40	90
1884S.......................3,200,000		22	32	175	7,000	35,000	150,000
1885..................(930)..17,787,000		20	22	27	35	42	90
1885CC........................228,000		450	460	465	575	625	700
1885O.....................9,185,000		20	22	27	35	40	90
1885S.......................1,497,000		30	37	60	175	250	1,000
1886..................(886)..19,963,000		20	22	27	35	40	90
1886O.....................10,710,000		25	30	50	750	2,100	100,000
1886S........................750,000		50	75	100	250	350	1,250
1887..................(710)..20,290,000		20	22	27	35	40	90
1887O.....................11,550,000		20	22	28	50	100	1,100
1887S.......................1,771,000		20	22	27	90	180	1,050
1888..................(833)..19,183,000		20	22	27	35	42	115
1888O.....................12,150,000		20	22	29	40	45	275
1888S........................657,000		95	110	120	240	300	1,800
1889..................(811)..21,726,000		20	22	28	35	40	150
1889CC........................350,000		800	2,000	5,000	18,000	38,000	165,000
1889O.....................11,875,000		20	22	27	130	250	2,250

* Included in number above.

Chart continued on next page. **147**

	Mintage	VF-20	EF-40	AU-50	MS-60	MS-63	MS-65
1889S	700,000	$40	$45	$70	$180	$300	$1,000
1890 (590)	16,802,000	20	22	27	35	45	600
1890CC	2,309,041	65	90	140	360	700	2,000
1890O	10,701,000	20	22	29	50	65	800
1890S	8,230,373	20	22	26	40	65	650
1891 (650)	8,693,556	20	22	28	38	125	1,750
1891CC	1,618,000	65	90	130	380	550	2,250
1891O	7,954,529	20	22	27	120	250	3,000
1891S	5,296,000	20	24	28	55	100	750
1892 (1,245)	1,036,000	28	32	55	225	375	2,200
1892CC	1,352,000	160	275	450	950	1,650	4,250
1892O	2,744,000	20	25	45	200	300	2,000
1892S	1,200,000	75	225	1,250	27,500	55,000	115,000
1893 (792)	378,000	140	165	250	600	850	2,750
1893CC	677,000	425	875	1,800	3,300	6,250	50,000
1893O	300,000	225	350	525	2,250	5,000	120,000
1893S	100,000	4,000	6,500	16,000	125,000	200,000	350,000
1894 (972)	110,000	700	750	850	2,500	4,000	22,500
1894O	1,723,000	30	55	135	1,000	3,750	40,000
1894S	1,260,000	60	95	300	600	900	3,750
1895 (880)		27,500 (a)	32,500 (a)	37,500 (a)	45,000 (a)	55,000 (a)
1895O	450,000	230	375	700	11,500	42,500	135,000
1895S	400,000	550	750	1,200	3,250	4,500	13,500
1896 (762)	9,976,000	20	22	27	35	42	1,000
1896O	4,900,000	26	28	100	1,100	4,500	100,000
1896S	5,000,000	32	125	500	1,750	2,750	8,500
1897 (731)	2,822,000	20	22	27	35	45	150
1897O	4,004,000	20	30	60	750	3,250	30,000
1897S	5,825,000	20	22	29	55	85	350
1898 (735)	5,884,000	20	22	27	35	45	125
1898O	4,440,000	20	22	27	35	40	90
1898S	4,102,000	28	30	55	200	325	1,100
1899 (846)	330,000	100	130	145	200	200	550
1899O	12,290,000	20	22	28	35	40	90
1899S	2,562,000	26	35	90	300	400	1,350
1900 (912)	8,830,000	20	22	27	35	40	90
1900O	12,590,000	20	22	27	37	40	90
1900S	3,540,000	28	30	50	205	275	1,300
1901 (813)	6,962,000	32	60	160	2,450	10,000	300,000
1901O	13,320,000	24	26	29	37	40	95
1901S	2,284,000	28	35	125	350	600	1,500
1902 (777)	7,994,000	24	28	30	55	85	235
1902O	8,636,000	22	24	29	35	40	95
1902S	1,530,000	90	140	165	285	450	1,400
1903 (755)	4,652,000	32	33	35	45	55	145
1903O	4,450,000	240	245	250	300	325	425
1903S	1,241,000	110	220	1,200	3,750	6,000	8,000
1904 (650)	2,788,000	25	28	30	85	165	1,250

a. Values are for Proofs.

	Mintage	VF-20	EF-40	AU-50	MS-60	MS-63	MS-65
19040	3,720,000	$28	$30	$33	$40	$45	$90
1904S	2,304,000	50	130	335	1,700	3,200	6,000
1921	44,690,000	18	20	22	28	40	90
1921D	20,345,000	18	20	22	28	45	145
1921S	21,695,000	18	20	22	28	45	425

PEACE (1921–1935)

Anthony de Francisci, a medalist, designed this dollar. His monogram is located in the field of the coin under the neck of Liberty.

VF-20 Very Fine: Hair over eye well worn. Some strands over ear well defined. Some eagle feathers on top and outside edge of right wing visible.

EF-40 Extremely Fine: Hair lines over brow and ear are strong, though slightly worn. Outside wing feathers at right and those at top visible but faint.

AU-50 About Uncirculated: Slight trace of wear. Most luster present, although marred by contact marks.

MS-60 Uncirculated: No trace of wear. Full mint luster, but possibly noticeably marred by stains, surface marks, or bag abrasions.

MS-63 Choice Uncirculated: Some distracting contact marks or blemishes in prime focal areas. Impaired luster possible.

MS-64 Uncirculated: A few scattered contact marks. Good eye appeal and attractive luster.

MS-65 Gem Uncirculated: Only light, scattered, non-distracting contact marks. Strong luster, good eye appeal.

PF-65 Choice Proof: Satin surfaces, no noticeable blemishes or flaws.

Mintmark location on reverse, below ONE.

Most Uncirculated silver dollars have scratches or nicks because of handling of mint bags in shipping and storage. Coin dealers usually pay more than the listed prices for choice sharply struck pieces with full brilliance and without blemishes.

	Mintage	VF-20	EF-40	AU-50	MS-60	MS-63	MS-65	PF-65
1921	1,006,473	$70	$75	$80	$200	$300	$1,250	$75,000
1922	51,737,000	17	18	19	25	28	70	100,000
1922D	15,063,000	17	18	19	28	45	375	
1922S	17,475,000	17	18	19	28	55	750	
1923	30,800,000	17	18	19	25	28	70	
1923D	6,811,000	17	18	22	32	85	650	
1923S	19,020,000	17	18	19	29	45	1,350	
1924	11,811,000	17	18	19	25	28	70	
1924S	1,728,000	17	18	33	150	300	4,000	
1925	10,198,000	17	18	19	25	28	70	
1925S	1,610,000	17	18	22	43	160	15,000	
1926	1,939,000	17	18	20	30	50	250	

Chart continued on next page.

	Mintage	VF-20	EF-40	AU-50	MS-60	MS-63	MS-65
1926D	2,348,700	$17	$19	$25	$50	$130	$600
1926S	6,980,000	17	19	25	35	55	550
1927	848,000	21	24	25	45	120	1,050
1927D	1,268,900	21	24	45	100	250	1,650
1927S	866,000	22	25	45	125	350	4,500
1928	360,649	180	210	250	325	500	2,000
1928S	1,632,000	22	25	35	100	325	12,500
1934	954,057	22	25	30	75	125	475
1934D	1,569,500	22	25	30	90	200	800
1934S	1,011,000	22	100	275	1,600	3,250	5,500
1935	1,576,000	22	25	30	50	75	375
1935S	1,964,000	22	30	50	175	300	750

EISENHOWER (1971–1978)
Eagle Reverse (1971–1974)

Honoring both President Dwight D. Eisenhower and the first landing of man on the moon, this design is the work of Chief Engraver Frank Gasparro, whose initials are on the truncation of the President's neck and below the eagle. The reverse is an adaptation of the official *Apollo 11* insignia.

Mintmark location is above date.

	Mintage	EF-40	MS-63	PF-63	PF-65
1971, Copper-Nickel Clad	47,799,000	$1.10	$1.75		
1971D, Copper-Nickel Clad	68,587,424	1.10	1.50		
1971S, Silver Clad	(4,265,234) 6,868,530		7.50	$7.50	$12.00
1972, Copper-Nickel Clad	75,890,000	1.10	1.50		
1972D, Copper-Nickel Clad	92,548,511	1.10	1.50		
1972S, Silver Clad	(1,811,631) 2,193,056		7.50	7.50	12.00
1973, Copper-Nickel Clad **(a)**	2,000,056	1.10	3.00		
1973D, Copper-Nickel Clad **(a)**	2,000,000	1.10	3.00		
1973S, Copper-Nickel Clad	(2,760,339)			2.50	7.00
1973S, Silver Clad	(1,013,646) 1,883,140		7.50	22.00	27.00
1974, Copper-Nickel Clad	27,366,000	1.10	1.25		
1974D, Copper-Nickel Clad	45,517,000	1.10	1.25		
1974S, Copper-Nickel Clad	(2,612,568)			2.50	3.75
1974S, Silver Clad	(1,306,579) 1,900,156		7.50	10.00	13.00

a. 1,769,258 of each sold only in sets and not released for circulation. Unissued coins destroyed at mint.

Bicentennial (1776–1976)

Obverse   Reverse Variety 2   Reverse Variety 1

Variety 1: Design in low relief, bold lettering on reverse.
Variety 2: Sharp design, delicate lettering on reverse.

	Mintage	EF-40	MS-63	PF-63	PF-65
1776–1976, Copper-Nickel Clad, Variety 1	4,019,000	$1.10	$0.00		
1776–1976, Copper-Nickel Clad, Variety 2	113,318,000	1.10	1.50		
1776–1976D, Copper-Nickel Clad, Variety 1	21,048,710	1.10	1.50		
1776–1976D, Copper-Nickel Clad, Variety 2	82,179,564	1.10	1.50		
1776–1976S, Copper-Nickel Clad, Variety 1	(2,845,450)			$3.00	$5.50
1776–1976S, Copper-Nickel Clad, Variety 2	(4,149,730)			2.50	3.75
1776–1976S, Silver Clad, Variety 1	11,000,000		7.50		
1776–1976S, Silver Clad, Variety 1	(4,000,000)			9.00	11.00

Eagle Reverse Resumed (1977–1978)

	Mintage	EF-40	MS-63	PF-63	PF-65
1977, Copper-Nickel Clad	12,596,000	$1.10	$1.50		
1977D, Copper-Nickel Clad	32,983,006	1.10	1.50		
1977S, Copper-Nickel Clad	(3,251,152)			$2.50	$4.25
1978, Copper-Nickel Clad	25,702,000	1.10	1.50		
1978D, Copper-Nickel Clad	33,012,890	1.10	1.50		
1978S, Copper-Nickel Clad	(3,127,781)			2.50	4.75

SUSAN B. ANTHONY (1979–1999)

Filled S   Clear S

	Mintage	MS-63
1979P, Narrow Rim	360,222,000	$1.10
1979P, Wide Rim	*	27.00
1979D	288,015,744	1.10
1979S	109,576,000	1.10

* Included in number above.

Chart continued on next page.

	Mintage	MS-65	PF-63	PF-65
1979S, Proof, Type 1	(3,677,175)		$2.50	$4
1979S, Proof, Type 2	*		20.00	40
1980P	27,610,000	$1.10		
1980D	41,628,708	1.10		
1980S	20,422,000	1.10		
1980S, Proof	(3,554,806)		2.50	3
1981P	3,000,000	2.00		

	Mintage	MS-65	PF-63	PF-65
1981D	3,250,000	$2.00		
1981S	3,492,000	2.00		
1981S, Proof, Type 1	(4,063,083)		$2.50	$4
1981S, Proof, Type 2	*		35.00	75
1999P	29,592,000	2.50		
1999P, Proof	(750,000)		13.00	16
1999D	11,776,000	2.50		

* Included in number above.

SACAGAWEA (2000–2008)

The design of this coin was selected in national competition from among 120 submissions that were considered by a panel appointed by Treasury Secretary Robert Rubin. The adopted motif depicts Sacagawea, a young Native American Shoshone, as rendered by artist Glenna Goodacre. On her back she carries Jean Baptiste, her infant son. The reverse shows an eagle in flight, designed by Mint engraver Thomas D. Rogers Sr.

The composition exemplifies the spirit of Liberty, Peace, and Freedom shown by Sacagawea in her conduct as interpreter and guide to explorers Meriwether Lewis and William Clark during their famed journey westward from St. Louis to the Pacific.

These coins have a distinctive golden color and a plain edge to distinguish them from other denominations or coins of a similar size. The change in composition and appearance was mandated under the United States Dollar Coin Act of 1997.

Several distinctive finishes can be identified on the Sacagawea dollars as a result of the Mint attempting to adjust the dies, blanks, strikes, or finishing to produce coins with minimal spotting and a better surface color. One group of 5,000 pieces dated 2000 with a special finish were presented to sculptor Glenna Goodacre in payment for the obverse design. Unexplained error coins made from mismatched dies (a State quarter obverse combined with a Sacagawea dollar reverse) are extremely rare.

	Mintage	MS-65	PF-63	PF-65
2000P	767,140,000	$1.10		
2000D	518,916,000	1.10		
2000S	(4,097,904)		$3	$5
2001P	62,468,000	1.10		
2001D	70,939,500	1.10		
2001S	(3,183,740)		7	9
2002P (a)	3,865,610	1.25		
2002D (a)	3,732,000	1.25		
2002S	(3,211,995)		3	5
2003P (a)	3,080,000	1.50		
2003D (a)	3,080,000	1.50		
2003S	(3,298,439)		3	5

	Mintage	MS-65	PF-63	PF-65
2004P (a)	2,660,000	$1.50		
2004D (a)	2,660,000	1.50		
2004S	(2,965,422)		$3	$5
2005P (a)	2,520,000	1.50		
2005D (a)	2,520,000	1.50		
2005S	(3,344,679)		3	5
2006P (a)	4,900,000	1.50		
2006D (a)	2,800,000	1.50		
2006S	(3,054,436)		3	5
2007P (a)	3,640,000	1.50		
2007D (a)	3,920,000	1.50		
2007S	(2,577,166)		3	5

a. Not issued for circulation.

	Mintage	MS-65	PF-63	PF-65
2008P (a)	1,820,000	$2		
2008D (a)	1,820,000	2		

a. Not issued for circulation.

	Mintage	MS-65	PF-63	PF-65
2008S	(2,169,561)		$6	$8

PRESIDENTIAL (2007–2016)

Four different coins, each bearing the image of a former U.S. president, were issued each year in the order that the presidents served. The size and composition of these coins is the same as that of the Native American dollars that are also made each year. A companion series of ten-dollar gold bullion coins (listed in the Bullion section) honors the spouse of each president.

Date, Mintmark, and Motto Incused on Edge (Motto Moved to Obverse in 2009)

Presidential Dollars Reverse

	Mintage	MS-65	PF-65
2007P, Washington	176,680,000	$1.10	
2007D, Washington	163,680,000	1.10	
2007S, Washington	(3,965,989)		$2
2007P, J. Adams	112,420,000	1.10	
2007D, J. Adams	112,140,000	1.10	
2007S, J. Adams	(3,965,989)		2

	Mintage	MS-65	PF-65
2007P, Jefferson	100,800,000	$1.10	
2007D, Jefferson	102,810,000	1.10	
2007S, Jefferson	(3,965,989)		$2
2007P, Madison	84,560,000	1.10	
2007D, Madison	87,780,000	1.10	
2007S, Madison	(3,965,989)		2

	Mintage	MS-65	PF-65
2008P, Monroe	64,260,000	$1.10	
2008D, Monroe	60,230,000	1.10	
2008S, Monroe	(3,083,940)		$2
2008P, J.Q. Adams	57,540,000	1.10	
2008D, J.Q. Adams	57,720,000	1.10	
2008S, J.Q. Adams	(3,083,940)		2

	Mintage	MS-65	PF-65
2008P, Jackson	61,180,000	$1.10	
2008D, Jackson	61,070,000	1.10	
2008S, Jackson	(3,083,940)		$2
2008P, Van Buren	51,520,000	1.10	
2008D, Van Buren	50,960,000	1.10	
2008S, Van Buren	(3,083,940)		2

Note: Errors have been reported in the Presidential dollar series, including coins minted without edge lettering. Depending on their rarity, dealers may pay a premium for such errors.

	Mintage	MS-65	PF-65
2009P, Harrison........	43,260,000	$1.10	
2009D, Harrison	55,160,000	1.10	
2009S, Harrison	(2,809,452)		$2
2009P, Tyler	43,540,000	1.10	
2009D, Tyler	43,540,000	1.10	
2009S, Tyler	(2,809,452)		2

	Mintage	MS-65	PF-65
2009P, Polk...........	46,620,000	$1.10	
2009D, Polk...........	41,720,000	1.10	
2009S, Polk...........	(2,809,452)		$2
2009P, Taylor	41,580,000	1.10	
2009D, Taylor	36,680,000	1.10	
2009S, Taylor	(2,809,452)		2

	Mintage	MS-65	PF-65
2010P, Fillmore........	37,520,000	$1.10	
2010D, Fillmore........	36,960,000	1.10	
2010S, Fillmore........	(2,224,613)		$2
2010P, Pierce	38,220,000	1.10	
2010D, Pierce	38,360,000	1.10	
2010S, Pierce	(2,224,613)		2

	Mintage	MS-65	PF-65
2010P, Buchanan	36,820,000	$1.10	
2010D, Buchanan	36,540,000	1.10	
2010S, Buchanan	(2,224,613)		$2
2010P, Lincoln	49,000,000	1.10	
2010D, Lincoln	48,020,000	1.10	
2010S, Lincoln	(2,224,613)		3

	Mintage	MS-65	PF-65
2011P, A. Johnson	35,560,000	$1.10	
2011D, A. Johnson	37,100,000	1.10	
2011S, A. Johnson	(1,972,863)		$2
2011P, Grant..........	38,080,000	1.10	
2011D, Grant..........	37,940,000	1.10	
2011S, Grant..........	(1,972,863)		2

	Mintage	MS-65	PF-65
2011P, Hayes	37,660,000	$1.10	
2011D, Hayes	36,820,000	1.10	
2011S, Hayes	(1,972,863)		$2
2011P, Garfield........	37,100,000	1.10	
2011D, Garfield........	37,100,000	1.10	
2011S, Garfield	(1,972,863)		2

	Mintage	MS-65	PF-65
2012P, Arthur (a)	6,020,000	$1.10	
2012D, Arthur (a)	4,060,000	1.10	
2012S, Arthur	(1,438,743)		$3
2012P, Cleveland, Variety 1 (a)	5,460,000	1.10	
2012D, Cleveland, Variety 1 (a)	4,060,000	1.10	
2012S, Cleveland, Variety 1	(1,438,743)		0

a. Not issued for circulation.

	Mintage	MS-65	PF-65
2012P, Harrison (a)	5,640,000	$1.10	
2012D, Harrison (a)	4,200,000	1.10	
2012S, Harrison	(1,438,743)		$3
2012P, Cleveland, Variety 2 (a)	10,680,000	1.10	
2012D, Cleveland, Variety 2 (a)	3,920,000	1.10	
2012S, Cleveland, Variety 2	(1,438,743)		3

	Mintage	MS-65	PF-65
2013P, McKinley (a)	4,760,000	$1.10	
2013D, McKinley (a)	3,365,100	1.10	
2013S, McKinley	(1,488,798)		$2
2013P, T. Roosevelt (a)	5,310,700	1.10	
2013D, T. Roosevelt (a)	3,920,000	1.10	
2013S, T. Roosevelt	(1,503,943)		2

a. Not issued for circulation.

	Mintage	MS-65	PF-65
2013P, Taft (a)	4,760,000	$1.10	
2013D, Taft (a)	3,360,000	1.10	
2013S, Taft	(1,488,798)		$2
2013P, Wilson (a)	4,620,000	1.10	
2013D, Wilson (a)	3,360,000	1.10	
2013S, Wilson	(1,488,798)		2

	Mintage	MS-65	PF-65
2014P, Harding (a)	6,160,000	$1.10	
2014D, Harding (a)	3,780,000	1.10	
2014S, Harding	(1,373,569)		$3
2014P, Coolidge (a)	4,480,000	1.10	
2014D, Coolidge (a)	3,780,000	1.10	
2014S, Coolidge	(1,373,569)		3

a. Not issued for circulation.

	Mintage	MS-65	PF-65
2014P, Hoover (a)	4,480,000	$1.10	
2014D, Hoover (a)	3,780,000	1.10	
2014S, Hoover	(1,373,569)		$3
2014P, F.D. Roosevelt (a)	4,760,000	1.10	
2014D, F.D. Roosevelt (a)	3,920,000	1.10	
2014S, F.D. Roosevelt	(1,392,619)		3

	Mintage	MS-65	PF-65
2015P, Truman **(a)**	4,900,000	$1.10	
2015P, Truman, Rev Pf	(16,812)		$18
2015D, Truman **(a)**	3,500,000	1.10	
2015S, Truman	(1,272,462)		3
2015P, Eisenhower **(a)**	4,900,000	1.10	
2015P, Eisenhower, Ref Pf	(16,744)		18
2015D, Eisenhower **(a)**	3,645,998	1.10	
2015S, Eisenhower	(1,272,462)		3

a. Not issued for circulation.

	Mintage	MS-65	PF-65
2015P, Kennedy **(a)**	6,160,000	$1.10	
2015P, Kennedy, Rev Pf	(49,051)		$18
2015D, Kennedy **(a)**	5,180,000	1.10	
2015S, Kennedy	(1,272,462)		3
2015P, L. Johnson **(a)**	7,840,000	1.10	
2015P, L. Johnson, Rev Pf	(23,905)		18
2015D, L. Johnson **(a)**	4,200,000	1.10	
2015S, L. Johnson	(1,272,462)		3

	Mintage	MS-65	PF-65
2016P, Nixon **(a)**	5,460,000	$1.10	
2016D, Nixon **(a)**	4,340,000	1.10	
2016S, Nixon	(1,196,582)		$3
2016P, Ford **(a)**	5,460,000	1.10	
2016P, Ford **(a)**	5,040,000	1.10	

a. Not issued for circulation.

	Mintage	MS-65	PF-65
2016S, Ford	(1,196,582)		$3
2016P, Reagan **(a)**	7,140,000	$1.10	
2016D, Reagan **(a)**	5,880,000	1.10	
2016S, Reagan	(1,196,582)		3
2016S, Reagan, Rev Pf	(47,447)		18

NATIVE AMERICAN (2009 TO DATE)

Obverse	Three Sisters (2009)	Great Law of Peace (2010)	Wampanoag Treaty (2011)

	Mintage	MS-65	PF-65
2009P, Three Sisters	39,200,000	$1.25	
2009D, Three Sisters	35,700,000	1.25	
2009S, Three Sisters	(2,179,867)		$3
2010P, Great Law	32,060,000	1.75	
2010D, Great Law	48,720,000	1.75	
2010S, Great Law	(1,689,216)		3

	Mintage	MS-65	PF-65
2011P, Wampanoag	29,400,000	$2.00	
2011D, Wampanoag	48,160,000	2.00	
2011S, Wampanoag	(1,673,010)		$3
2012P, Trade Routes	2,800,000	1.75	
2012D, Trade Routes	3,080,000	1.75	
2012S, Trade Routes	(1,189,445)		7

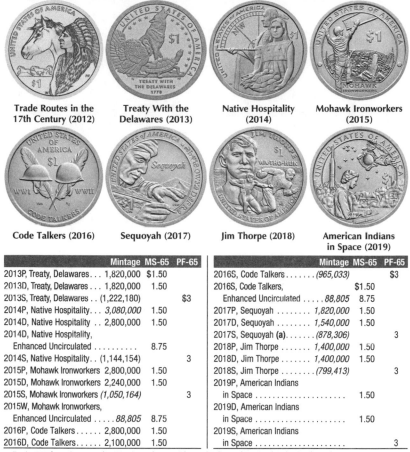

Trade Routes in the 17th Century (2012)

Treaty With the Delawares (2013)

Native Hospitality (2014)

Mohawk Ironworkers (2015)

Code Talkers (2016)

Sequoyah (2017)

Jim Thorpe (2018)

American Indians in Space (2019)

	Mintage	MS-65	PF-65
2013P, Treaty, Delawares...	1,820,000	$1.50	
2013D, Treaty, Delawares...	1,820,000	1.50	
2013S, Treaty, Delawares..	(1,222,180)		$3
2014P, Native Hospitality...	*3,080,000*	1.50	
2014D, Native Hospitality..	2,800,000	1.50	
2014D, Native Hospitality, Enhanced Uncirculated..........		8.75	
2014S, Native Hospitality..	(1,144,154)		3
2015P, Mohawk Ironworkers	2,800,000	1.50	
2015D, Mohawk Ironworkers	2,240,000	1.50	
2015S, Mohawk Ironworkers	*(1,050,164)*		3
2015W, Mohawk Ironworkers, Enhanced Uncirculated.....	*88,805*	8.75	
2016P, Code Talkers......	2,800,000	1.50	
2016D, Code Talkers......	2,100,000	1.50	

	Mintage	MS-65	PF-65
2016S, Code Talkers.......	*(965,033)*		$3
2016S, Code Talkers, Enhanced Uncirculated.....	*88,805*	8.75	
2017P, Sequoyah........	*1,820,000*	1.50	
2017D, Sequoyah........	*1,540,000*	1.50	
2017S, Sequoyah (a).......	*(878,306)*		3
2018P, Jim Thorpe.......	*1,400,000*	1.50	
2018D, Jim Thorpe.......	*1,400,000*	1.50	
2018S, Jim Thorpe........	*(799,413)*		3
2019P, American Indians in Space.....................		1.50	
2019D, American Indians in Space.....................		1.50	
2019S, American Indians in Space.....................			3

a. For its 225th anniversary, the Mint issued a special set of Enhanced Uncirculated coins from the San Francisco Mint; they are not included here.

AMERICAN INNOVATION (2018–2032)

In 2018, the U.S. Mint inaugurated a new, 15-year coin series: the American Innovation $1 Coin Program. Each of the golden dollars in the program features a reverse design that "symbolizes quintessentially American traits—the willingness to explore, to discover, and to create one's own destiny." Four new designs, in Uncirculated and Proof finishes, are issued each year from 2019 through 2032—one for each state, in the order in which the states ratified the Constitution or were admitted to the Union, and then for the District of Columbia and each of the five U.S. territories (Puerto Rico, Guam, American Samoa, the U.S. Virgin Islands, and the Northern Mariana Islands). Like all dollar coins minted after 2011, they are issued for numismatic sales only; none are distributed for circulation.

	Mintage	MS-65	PF-65
2018P, American Innovators	$1.50		
2018D, American Innovators	1.50		
2018S, American Innovators			$3
2019P, Delaware	1.50		
2019D, Delaware	1.50		
2019S, Delaware			3
2019S, Reverse Proof, Delaware			5
2019P, Georgia	1.50		
2019D, Georgia	1.50		
2019S, Georgia			3

	Mintage	MS-65	PF-65
2019S, Reverse Proof, Georgia			$5
2019P, New Jersey	$1.50		
2019D, New Jersey	1.50		
2019S, New Jersey			3
2019S, Reverse Proof, New Jersey			5
2019P, Pennsylvania	1.50		
2019D, Pennsylvania	1.50		
2019S, Pennsylvania			3
2019S, Reverse Proof, Pennsylvania			5

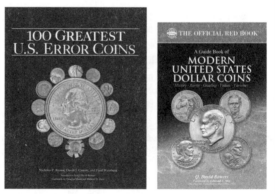

The Coinage Act of 1792 established the independent monetary system of the United States, with the dollar as its basic monetary unit. Silver dollar coins were made starting in 1794. Coinage of a gold dollar coin, however, was not authorized until the Act of March 3, 1849. Its weight was set at 25.8 grains, fineness .900.

The first type, struck until 1854, is known as the Liberty Head. In 1854 the gold dollar was made larger in diameter and thinner, while keeping the same weight. Along with that modification, the design was changed to a female wearing a feather headdress, generally referred to as the Indian Princess Head type. In 1856 this was changed slightly by enlarging the size of the head.

LIBERTY HEAD (1849–1854)

VF-20 Very Fine: LIBERTY on headband complete and legible. Knobs on coronet defined.
EF-40 Extremely Fine: Slight wear on Liberty's hair. Knobs on coronet sharp.
AU-50 About Uncirculated: Trace of wear on headband. Nearly full luster.
AU-55 Choice About Uncirculated: Evidence of friction on design high points.
MS-60 Uncirculated: No trace of wear. Light marks and blemishes.
MS-63 Choice Uncirculated: Some distracting contact marks or blemishes in prime focal areas. Impaired luster possible.

	Mintage	VF-20	EF-40	AU-50	AU-55	MS-60	MS-63
1849, Open Wreath,							
No L on Truncation 688,567		$160	$180	$225	$275	$550	$1,000
1849, Close Wreath . . . . *	145	180	165	175	325	900
1849C, Open Wreath 11,634	150,000	200,000	250,000	300,000			
1849C, Close Wreath. . . . . *	700	1,350	1,750	2,750	6,500	11,500
1849D 21,588	1,150	1,500	1,750	2,500	3,500	8,750
1849O 215,000	150	180	250	400	750	2,300
1850 481,953	145	160	170	200	250	550
1850C 6,966	850	1,350	2,250	2,850	5,500	18,000
1850D 8,382	1,150	1,500	2,250	3,500	7,000	22,500
1850O 14,000	225	400	600	750	2,000	4,500
1851 3,317,671	145	160	170	175	200	375
1851C 41,267	975	1,100	1,450	1,600	2,400	4,750
1851D 9,882	1,100	1,500	1,750	2,500	3,750	10,000
1851O 290,000	150	170	180	240	500	1,350
1852 2,045,351	145	160	170	175	200	375
1852C 9,434	950	1,200	1,500	2,000	3,250	8,000
1852D 6,360	1,000	1,400	1,850	2,750	5,500	25,000
1852O 140,000	150	200	250	475	800	2,500
1853 4,076,051	145	160	170	175	200	375
1853C 11,515	975	1,350	1,750	2,250	3,500	10,000
1853D 6,583	1,150	1,450	2,000	3,000	5,500	17,500
1853O 290,000	145	175	200	250	450	1,400
1854 855,502	145	160	170	175	200	375
1854D 2,935	1,500	2,500	4,250	5,000	7,000	22,500
1854S 14,632	225	320	460	850	1,850	5,000

* Included in number above.

INDIAN PRINCESS HEAD,
SMALL HEAD (1854–1856)

VF-20 Very Fine: Feather-curl tips on headdress outlined but details worn.

EF-40 Extremely Fine: Slight wear on tips of feather curls on headdress.

AU-50 About Uncirculated: Trace of wear on feathers, nearly full luster.

AU-55 Choice About Uncirculated: Evidence of friction on design high points. Most of original mint luster present.

MS-60 Uncirculated: No trace of wear. Light marks and blemishes.

MS-63 Choice Uncirculated: Some distracting contact marks or blemishes in prime focal areas. Impaired luster possible.

PF-63 Choice Proof: Reflective surfaces with only a few blemishes in secondary focal areas. No major flaws.

	Mintage	VF-20	EF-40	AU-50	AU-55	MS-60	MS-63	PF-63
1854	783,943	$250	$300	$425	$500	$850	$3,250	$125,000
1855	758,269	250	300	425	500	850	3,250	110,000
1855C	9,803	1,000	2,500	6,000	9,000	18,000		
1855D	1,811	7,500	17,500	20,000	25,000	40,000	70,000	
1855O	55,000	350	475	1,350	1,750	5,000	22,000	
1856S	24,600	575	900	1,500	2,100	5,500	17,500	

INDIAN PRINCESS HEAD,
LARGE HEAD (1856–1889)

VF-20 Very Fine: Slight detail in curled feathers in headdress. Details worn smooth at eyebrow, hair below headdress, and behind ear and bottom curl.

EF-40 Extremely Fine: Slight wear above and to right of eye and on top of curled feathers.

AU-50 About Uncirculated: Trace of wear on feathers, nearly full luster.

AU-55 Choice About Uncirculated: Evidence of friction on design high points. Most of original mint luster present.

MS-60 Uncirculated: No trace of wear. Light marks and blemishes.

MS-63 Choice Uncirculated: Some distracting contact marks or blemishes in prime focal areas. Impaired luster possible.

PF-63 Choice Proof: Reflective surfaces with only a few blemishes in secondary focal places. No major flaws.

	Mintage	VF-20	EF-40	AU-50	AU-55	MS-60	MS-63	PF-63
1856	1,762,936	$180	$190	$200	$225	$325	$450	$20,000
1856D	1,460	3,500	5,000	6,500	7,500	20,000	45,000	
1857	774,789	180	190	200	225	275	450	8,500
1857C	13,280	1,050	1,350	2,250	2,750	7,000		
1857D	3,533	1,100	1,500	3,000	4,000	8,000		
1857S	10,000	375	450	850	1,100	3,500	14,000	
1858	117,995	200	215	220	225	245	700	5,000
1858D	3,477	800	1,500	2,250	3,000	5,500	16,500	

| 1873, Close 3 | | | | 1873, Open 3 | | | |

	Mintage	VF-20	EF-40	AU-50	AU-55	MS-60	MS-63	PF-63
1858S 10,000		$275	$375	$1,000	$1,300	$4,000	$12,500	
1859 . . . . (80) 168,244		180	200	220	225	250	550	$7,500
1859C 5,235		800	1,150	2,250	2,750	5,500	19,000	
1859D 4,952		950	1,300	2,100	2,500	6,750	15,000	
1859S 15,000		225	275	875	1,150	3,500	10,000	
1860 . . . . (154) 36,514		180	200	220	225	300	750	6,500
1860D 1,566		1,850	2,750	5,500	6,750	13,000	40,000	
1860S 13,000		275	375	575	775	2,000	4,500	
1861 . . . . (349) 527,150		180	200	220	225	350	500	4,500
1861D *1,250*		15,000	25,000	30,000	35,000	60,000	100,000	
1862 . . . . (35) . . .1,361,355		180	200	220	225	300	475	5,000
1863 . . . . (50) 6,200		700	1,200	2,250	2,800	4,000	7,500	7,500
1864 . . . . (50) 5,900		275	375	625	825	1,000	2,500	7,500
1865 . . . . (25) 3,700		300	400	650	850	1,100	2,600	7,500
1866 . . . . (30) 7,100		300	375	550	750	800	2,000	7,500
1867 . . . . (50) 5,200		300	375	500	650	900	1,850	7,500
1868 . . . . (25) 10,500		225	325	375	550	750	1,500	7,500
1869 . . . . (25) 5,900		275	375	500	600	775	1,350	7,500
1870 . . . . (35) 6,300		225	325	375	475	650	1,450	7,500
1870S 3,000		375	550	1,000	1,200	1,850	5,000	
1871 . . . . (30) 3,900		200	325	375	475	600	1,100	6,500
1872 . . . . (30) 3,500		200	325	375	475	675	1,500	7,500
1873, Close 3 . . . (25) 1,800		300	600	675	775	1,150	2,750	10,000
1873, Open 3 123,300		165	185	200	205	225	400	
1874 . . . . (20) 198,800		165	185	200	205	225	400	7,500
1875 . . . . (20) 400		2,750	3,750	4,750	5,000	8,000	12,500	15,000
1876 . . . . (45) 3,200		190	275	375	425	500	950	5,500
1877 . . . . (20) 3,900		190	275	375	425	500	1,100	5,000
1878 . . . . (20) 3,000		190	275	375	425	500	950	4,500
1879 . . . . (30) 3,000		190	225	250	275	350	800	4,500
1880 . . . . (36) 1,600		190	200	220	235	350	750	4,000
1881 . . . . (87) 7,620		190	200	220	235	350	550	4,000
1882 . . . . (125) 5,000		190	225	250	275	350	550	4,500
1883 . . . . (207) 10,800		180	200	225	235	350	550	4,000
1884 . . . . (1,006) 5,230		180	200	225	235	350	550	4,000
1885 . . . . (1,105) 11,156		180	225	250	275	350	550	3,750
1886 . . . . (1,016) 5,000		180	200	220	225	350	500	3,750
1887 . . . . (1,043) 7,500		180	200	220	225	350	500	3,750
1888 . . . . (1,079) 15,501		180	200	220	225	325	500	3,750
1889 . . . . (1,779) 28,950		180	200	220	225	300	400	3,750

Although authorized by the Act of April 2, 1792, coinage of quarter eagles ($2.50 gold coins) was not begun until 1796.

CAPPED BUST TO RIGHT (1796–1807)

F-12 Fine: Hair worn smooth on high spots. E PLURIBUS UNUM on ribbon weak but legible.
VF-20 Very Fine: Some wear on high spots.
EF-40 Extremely Fine: Only slight wear on Liberty's hair and cheek.
AU-50 About Uncirculated: Trace of wear on cap, hair, cheek, and drapery.
AU-55 Choice About Uncirculated: Evidence of friction on design high points. Some original mint luster.
MS-60 Uncirculated: No trace of wear. Light blemishes.

No Stars on Obverse (1796)

Stars on Obverse (1796–1807)

	Mintage	F-12	VF-20	EF-40	AU-50	AU-55	MS-60
1796, No Stars on Obverse 963	$42,500	$55,000	$80,000	$105,000	$135,000	$200,000
1796, Stars on Obverse 432	45,000	57,500	70,000	85,000	100,000	150,000
1797 427	10,000	15,000	27,500	45,000	75,000	145,000
1798 1,094	3,000	6,500	11,000	20,000	25,000	75,000
1802 3,035	3,000	5,000	11,000	15,000	16,500	25,000
1804, 13-Star Reverse . . . . *	37,500	55,000	100,000	125,000	200,000	
1804, 14-Star Reverse 3,327	4,500	7,000	10,000	13,000	16,000	25,000
1805 1,781	3,000	5,000	10,000	13,000	16,000	25,000
1806, 6/4, 8 Stars Left, 5 Right 1,136	3,500	5,500	10,000	13,000	16,000	23,000
1806, 6/5, 7 Stars Left, 6 Right 480	4,500	6,500	12,000	15,000	30,000	60,000
1807 6,812	3,000	5,000	10,000	13,000	16,000	25,000

* Included in number below.

DRAPED BUST TO LEFT, LARGE SIZE (1808)

F-12 Fine: E PLURIBUS UNUM on reverse, and LIBERTY on headband, legible but weak.
VF-20 Very Fine: Motto and LIBERTY clear.
EF-40 Extremely Fine: All details of hair plain.
AU-50 About Uncirculated: Trace of wear above eye, on top of cap, and on cheek and hair.
AU-55 Choice About Uncirculated: Evidence of friction on design high points. Some original mint luster present.
MS-60 Uncirculated: No trace of wear. Light blemishes.

	Mintage	F-12	VF-20	EF-40	AU-50	AU-55	MS-60
1808 2,710	$17,500	$30,000	$50,000	$75,000	$95,000	$135,000

CAPPED HEAD TO LEFT (1821–1834)

Those dated 1829 to 1834 are smaller in diameter than the 1821 to 1827 pieces.

Large Diameter

Reduced Diameter

	Mintage	F-12	VF-20	EF-40	AU-50	AU-55	MS-60
1821	6,448	$4,500	$6,000	$10,000	$12,000	$15,000	$25,000
1824, 4 Over 1	2,600	4,500	6,000	8,500	12,000	15,000	26,500
1825	4,434	5,000	6,500	8,500	12,000	15,000	22,500
1826, 6 Over 6	760	6,000	8,000	11,000	17,500	25,000	55,000
1827	2,800	4,500	6,500	8,500	10,000	15,000	22,000
1829	3,403	4,000	5,000	7,500	10,000	13,000	16,500
1830	4,540	4,000	5,000	7,500	10,000	13,000	16,500
1831	4,520	4,000	5,000	7,500	10,000	13,000	16,500
1832	4,400	4,000	5,000	7,500	10,000	13,000	16,500
1833	4,160	4,000	5,000	7,500	10,000	13,000	16,500
1834, With Motto	4,000	15,000	25,000	35,000	45,000	65,000	85,000

CLASSIC HEAD, NO MOTTO ON REVERSE (1834–1839)

In 1834, the quarter eagle was redesigned. A ribbon binding the hair, bearing the word LIBERTY, replaced the Liberty cap. The motto was omitted from the reverse.

F-12 Fine: LIBERTY on headband legible and complete. Curl under ear outlined but no detail.

VF-20 Very Fine: LIBERTY plain; detail in hair curl.

EF-40 Extremely Fine: Small amount of wear on top of hair and below L in LIBERTY. Wear evident on wing.

AU-50 About Uncirculated: Trace of wear on coronet and hair above ear.

AU-55 Choice About Uncirculated: Evidence of friction on design high points. Some of original mint luster present.

MS-60 Uncirculated: No trace of wear. Light blemishes.

MS-63 Choice Uncirculated: Some distracting contact marks or blemishes in prime focal areas. Impaired luster possible.

Mintmark location.

	Mintage	F-12	VF-20	EF-40	AU-50	AU-55	MS-60	MS-63
1834, No Motto	112,234	$250	$375	$600	$800	$1,100	$2,500	$7,000
1835	131,402	250	375	600	800	1,100	2,500	8,500
1836	547,986	250	375	600	800	1,100	2,500	7,000
1837	45,080	325	550	750	1,100	1,500	3,500	10,500
1838	47,030	300	500	650	1,050	1,350	2,750	7,500
1838C	7,880	1,500	3,250	5,000	7,000	8,500	20,000	35,000
1839	27,021	450	750	1,200	2,000	3,000	5,500	27,500
1839C	18,140	1,250	2,500	4,250	6,500	8,000	20,000	50,000
1839D	13,674	1,750	2,750	5,000	6,500	10,000	25,000	45,000
1839O	17,781	550	1,200	2,250	3,250	5,000	8,500	25,000

LIBERTY HEAD (1840–1907)

Mintmark location.

	Mintage	VF-20	EF-40	AU-50	AU-55	MS-60	MS-63
1840	18,859	$600	$750	$1,800	$2,500	$5,000	$10,000
1840C	12,822	1,200	2,500	2,750	3,500	7,500	20,000
1840D	3,532	2,000	6,000	7,000	9,000	26,500	
1840O	33,580	350	850	1,500	2,000	6,500	20,000

Chart continued on next page.   **163**

	Mintage	VF-20	EF-40	AU-50	AU-55	MS-60	MS-63
1841	(unknown)	$45,000	$80,000	$100,000	$125,000		
1841C	10,281	1,100	1,500	3,250	3,500	$11,000	
1841D	4,164	1,600	3,750	6,000	7,500	21,500	$40,000
1842	2,823	1,000	2,500	4,500	5,750	13,500	
1842C	6,729	1,550	2,500	4,500	6,250	16,000	
1842D	4,643	1,850	4,000	6,500	8,250	27,500	
1842O	19,800	300	850	1,500	2,200	7,000	18,500
1843	100,546	250	300	500	750	1,650	4,500
1843C, Large Date	23,076	1,000	1,350	2,250	2,700	5,500	14,000
1843C, Small Date	2,988	1,850	3,750	5,750	8,500	16,500	
1843D	36,209	1,250	1,750	2,250	2,750	4,500	20,000
1843O	364,002	250	300	350	400	1,000	4,500
1844	6,784	300	500	1,650	1,800	5,000	
1844C	11,622	1,250	2,000	3,750	4,500	12,500	32,500
1844D	17,332	1,350	1,850	2,500	2,750	5,000	18,000
1845	91,051	275	300	350	400	950	3,500
1845D	19,460	1,250	1,650	2,200	3,000	6,500	30,000
1845O	4,000	1,000	2,000	5,000	7,750	18,000	
1846	21,598	275	300	500	750	3,500	17,500
1846C	4,808	1,300	2,250	4,250	5,500	12,500	25,000
1846D	19,303	1,300	2,000	2,750	3,500	7,000	24,000
1846O	62,000	275	325	750	950	3,000	13,500
1847	29,814	275	400	550	650	2,500	5,500
1847C	23,226	1,150	1,550	2,100	3,000	4,500	11,000
1847D	15,784	1,250	1,750	2,250	3,500	5,500	16,500
1847O	124,000	275	300	750	1,250	3,000	13,500
1848	6,500	375	650	1,650	1,800	4,000	12,000

CAL. Gold Quarter Eagle (1848)

In 1848, about 230 ounces of gold were sent to Secretary of War William L. Marcy by Colonel R.B. Mason, military governor of California. The gold was turned over to the Mint and made into quarter eagles. The distinguishing mark CAL. was punched above the eagle on the reverse side while the coins were in the die.

CAL. Above Eagle on Reverse (1848)

	Mintage	VF-20	EF-40	AU-50	AU-55	MS-60	MS-63
1848, CAL. Above Eagle	1,389	$25,000	$30,000	$40,000	$45,000	$65,000	$85,000
1848C	16,788	1,050	1,650	2,500	3,000	8,000	
1848D	13,771	1,350	2,000	2,850	3,250	6,500	23,500
1849	23,294	300	500	650	750	1,750	5,000
1849C	10,220	1,300	2,000	4,000	4,500	11,000	35,000
1849D	10,945	1,500	2,250	2,750	3,000	10,000	26,000
1850	252,923	250	275	300	375	675	2,500
1850C	9,148	1,150	2,000	2,750	3,250	8,500	27,500
1850D	12,148	1,200	1,800	3,000	3,500	10,000	32,000

QUARTER EAGLES ($2.50)

	Mintage	VF-20	EF-40	AU-50	AU-55	MS-60	MS-63	PF-63
1850O	84,000	$225	$350	$700	$850	$3,000	$10,000	
1851	1,372,748	200	225	275	285	350	850	
1851C	14,923	1,100	1,600	2,500	2,750	6,000	25,000	
1851D	11,264	1,250	1,850	3,000	3,500	7,500	25,000	
1851O	148,000	250	300	500	650	3,000	10,000	
1852	1,159,681	200	225	250	285	325	850	
1852C	9,772	1,050	1,650	3,000	3,500	8,000	25,000	
1852D	4,078	1,200	2,500	4,750	5,500	12,000	35,000	
1852O	140,000	275	300	650	750	3,500	8,500	
1853	1,404,668	200	225	250	285	315	750	
1853D	3,178	1,500	2,650	3,750	4,500	11,000	37,500	
1854	596,258	200	225	250	285	325	850	
1854C	7,295	1,150	1,750	3,250	4,500	8,000	30,000	
1854D	1,760	2,500	5,000	7,500	9,500	21,000	50,000	
1854O	153,000	300	325	350	400	1,000	6,000	
1854O	246	165,000	250,000	325,000				
1855	235,480	200	225	275	285	325	1,000	
1855C	3,677	1,850	3,000	4,500	5,500	14,500	30,000	
1855D	1,123	2,750	5,500	10,000	14,500	37,500	65,000	
1856	384,240	200	225	250	275	300	1,000	$45,000
1856C	7,913	1,150	1,850	3,000	3,500	8,500	23,000	
1856D	874	6,500	12,000	22,500	27,500	60,000	100,000	
1856O	21,100	275	550	1,000	1,250	5,500	20,000	
1856S	72,120	300	325	600	750	3,000	7,500	
1857	214,130	200	225	250	285	300	1,000	37,000
1857D	2,364	1,350	2,000	3,000	3,500	8,500	22,000	
1857O	34,000	250	325	750	900	3,000	10,000	
1857S	69,200	250	350	700	850	3,500	10,000	
1858	47,377	250	240	275	300	850	2,500	25,000
1858C	9,056	1,100	1,750	2,750	3,250	6,000	20,000	
1859	(80)	39,364	225	235	285	325	1,000	2,250	15,000
1859D	2,244	1,400	2,250	3,000	4,000	12,500	45,000	
1859S	15,200	300	750	1,650	1,850	3,500	12,500	
1860	(112)	22,563	225	250	325	350	750	2,000	15,000
1860C	7,469	1,200	1,850	2,500	5,000	13,000	25,000	
1860S	35,600	325	450	1,000	1,150	3,000	10,000	
1861	(90)	1,283,788	200	225	275	300	600	1,250	15,000
1861S	24,000	350	650	2,500	3,000	5,000	12,000	
1862, 2 Over 1	*	650	1,350	2,500	3,500	6,500	10,000	
1862	(35)	98,508	300	400	1,250	1,550	3,500	11,000	13,500
1862S	8,000	1,200	1,800	3,000	4,000	12,500	25,000	
1863, Proof only (30)								55,000
1863S	10,800	375	1,500	3,250	4,000	11,000	20,000	
1864	(50)	2,774	5,500	15,000	27,500	35,000	75,000		12,500
1865	(25)	1,520	3,500	7,500	15,000	16,000	35,000		12,500
1865S	23,376	450	850	1,500	1,350	3,000	10,000	
1866	(30)	3,080	750	2,500	4,000	5,500	10,000	20,000	12,500
1866S	38,960	300	500	1,000	1,550	4,500	15,000	
1867	(50)	3,200	300	550	1,100	1,250	4,000	8,500	12,500
1867S	28,000	250	400	1,000	1,350	3,000	9,000	
1868	(25)	3,600	250	350	450	675	1,650	5,000	12,500

* Included in number below.

Chart continued on next page.

	Mintage	VF-20	EF-40	AU-50	AU-55	MS-60	MS-63	PF-63
1868S 34,000		$250	$300	$750	$950	$2,500	$8,000	
1869 . . . .(25). 4,320		250	400	450	850	2,250	7,500	$12,500
1869S 29,500		250	450	550	1,000	2,750	6,000	
1870 . . . .(35). 4,520		225	350	600	900	2,750	6,500	12,500
1870S 16,000		225	350	550	1,150	3,000	11,000	
1871 . . . .(30). 5,320		225	425	425	600	1,500	3,000	12,500
1871S 22,000		225	300	425	600	1,500	3,000	
1872 . . . .(30). 3,000		300	550	750	1,650	3,200	10,000	12,500
1872S 18,000		225	300	600	1,200	3,000	8,000	
1873 . . . .(25). 178,000		225	240	315	325	400	900	12,500
1873S 27,000		225	300	500	750	1,800	5,500	
1874 . . . .(20). 3,920		225	275	450	700	1,500	4,500	15,000
1875 . . . .(20). 400		4,250	6,500	8,000	9,500	18,000	30,000	25,000
1875S 11,600		225	300	500	850	2,500	6,000	
1876 . . . .(45). 4,176		350	550	600	1,100	2,250	4,500	8,500
1876S 5,000		225	400	600	1,300	2,000	6,750	
1877 . . . .(20). 1,632		300	650	800	1,250	2,250	6,500	8,500
1877S 35,400		225	275	300	325	425	1,750	
1878 . . . .(20). 286,240		225	240	275	300	350	650	10,000
1878S 178,000		225	240	275	300	350	1,250	
1879 . . . .(30). 88,960		225	240	275	300	350	750	8,500
1879S 43,500		225	240	275	300	800	3,250	
1880 . . . .(36). 2,960		325	350	500	650	1,000	2,500	6,500
1881 . . . .(51). 640		1,250	2,000	4,500	5,000	7,500	15,000	6,500
1882 . . . .(67). 4,000		225	300	325	375	600	2,000	5,000
1883 . . . .(82). 1,920		450	850	1,850	2,250	3,500	5,000	5,000
1884 . . . .(73). 1,950		225	300	425	575	1,000	2,500	5,000
1885 . . . .(87). 800		1,200	1,800	2,250	2,500	4,000	6,500	5,000
1886 . . . .(88). 4,000		225	300	325	375	750	2,500	5,000
1887 . . . .(122). 6,160		225	300	315	325	575	1,000	4,750
1888 . . . .(97). 16,001		225	240	275	325	375	550	4,750
1889 . . . .(48). 17,600		225	240	275	325	375	600	4,750
1890 . . . .(93). 8,720		225	240	275	325	375	1,000	4,750
1891 . . . .(80). 10,960		225	240	275	325	375	900	4,750
1892 . . . .(105). 2,440		245	265	275	325	450	1,500	4,750
1893 . . . .(106). 30,000		225	240	275	325	375	550	4,750
1894 . . . .(122). 4,000		250	275	325	350	425	1,250	4,750
1895 . . . .(119). 6,000		225	240	285	325	375	1,000	4,750
1896 . . . .(132). 19,070		225	240	250	275	375	525	4,750
1897 . . . .(136). 29,768		225	240	275	305	350	425	4,750
1898 . . . .(165). 24,000		225	240	275	305	350	425	4,750
1899 . . . .(150). 27,200		210	240	275	305	350	425	4,750
1900 . . . .(205). 67,000		200	225	260	265	275	350	4,500
1901 . . . .(223). 91,100		200	225	260	265	275	350	4,500
1902 . . . .(193). . . .133,540		200	225	260	265	275	350	4,500
1903 . . . .(197). . . .201,060		200	225	260	265	275	350	4,500
1904 . . . .(170). . . .160,790		200	225	260	265	275	350	4,500
1905 . . . .(144). . . .217,800		200	225	260	265	275	350	4,500
1906 . . . .(160). . . .176,330		200	225	260	265	275	350	4,500
1907 . . . .(154). . . .336,294		200	225	260	265	275	350	4,500

INDIAN HEAD (1908–1929)

American sculptor Bela Lyon Pratt, a former student of Augustus Saint-Gaudens, designed this coin and the similar five-dollar gold piece. It features no raised rim, and the main devices and legends are in sunken relief below the surface of the coin. President Theodore Roosevelt, who sought to improve the overall aesthetic quality of American coinage, was enthusiastic about the innovative new design. Collectors and the public were not as pleased. Some feared that the recessed design would collect dirt and germs—an unfounded concern. Over time the design has been recognized as a classic, and part of the early 20th-century renaissance of American coinage.

VF-20 Very Fine: Hair-cord knot distinct. Feathers at top of head clear. Cheekbone worn.
EF-40 Extremely Fine: Cheekbone, war bonnet, and headband feathers slightly worn.
AU-50 About Uncirculated: Trace of wear on cheekbone and headdress.
MS-60 Uncirculated: No trace of wear. Light blemishes.
MS-63 Choice Uncirculated: Some distracting contact marks or blemishes in prime focal areas. Impaired luster possible.
MS-64 Uncirculated: A few scattered contact marks visible. Good eye appeal and attractive luster.
Matte PF-63 Choice Proof: Few blemishes in secondary focal areas. No major flaws. Matte surfaces.

Mintmark location is on reverse, to left of arrows.

	Mintage	VF-20	EF-40	AU-50	MS-60	MS-63	MS-64	MATTE PF-63
1908 . . . . (236) 564,821		$215	$225	$250	$275	$500	$800	$7,500
1909 . . . . (139) 441,760		215	225	250	300	800	1,350	7,500
1910 . . . . (682) 492,000		215	225	250	285	600	900	7,500
1911 . . . . (191) 704,000		215	225	250	300	450	800	7,500
1911D 55,680		2,250	2,500	3,250	6,000	10,000	15,000	
1912 . . . . (197) 616,000		215	225	250	450	800	1,600	7,500
1913 . . . . (165) 722,000		215	225	250	350	400	700	7,500
1914 . . . . (117) 240,000		225	245	265	500	1,600	3,000	7,500
1914D 448,000		215	225	250	300	700	1,250	
1915 . . . . (100) 606,000		215	225	250	300	375	700	8,500
1925D 578,000		215	225	250	275	375	525	
1926 446,000		215	225	250	275	375	525	
1927 , ...388,000		215	225	250	275	375	525	
1928 416,000		215	225	250	275	375	525	
1929 532,000		215	225	250	275	375	525	

The three-dollar gold piece was authorized by the Act of February 21, 1853. Coinage was struck beginning in 1854. It was never popular and saw very little circulation.

VF-20 Very Fine: Eyebrow, hair about forehead and ear, and bottom curl all worn smooth. Faint details visible on curled feather-ends of headdress.

EF-40 Extremely Fine: Light wear above and to right of eye, and on top of curled feathers.

AU-50 About Uncirculated: Trace of wear on top of curled feathers and to right of eye.

AU-55 Choice About Uncirculated: Evidence of friction on design high points. Much of original mint luster present.

MS-60 Uncirculated: No trace of wear. Light blemishes.

MS-63 Choice Uncirculated: Some distracting contact marks or blemishes in prime focal areas. Impaired luster possible.

Mintmark location is on reverse, below wreath.

PF-63 Choice Proof: Reflective surfaces with only a few blemishes in secondary focal places. No major flaws.

	Mintage	VF-20	EF-40	AU-50	AU-55	MS-60	MS-63	PF-63
1854	138,618	$700	$750	$800	$1,250	$1,750	$3,000	$55,000
1854D	1,120	14,500	24,500	35,000	37,500	60,000		
1854O	24,000	1,250	2,000	2,750	3,500	25,000	65,000	
1855	50,555	700	750	800	1,100	1,750	3,250	30,000
1855S	6,600	950	2,150	4,000	7,500	25,000	65,000	
1856	26,010	700	750	850	1,250	2,000	5,000	25,000
1856S	34,500	750	1,000	2,250	4,000	8,500	22,500	
1857	20,891	700	800	1,000	1,500	2,500	6,000	25,000
1857S	14,000	775	1,500	3,500	6,000	15,000	45,000	
1858	2,133	925	1,650	2,500	3,500	7,250	17,500	18,500
1859	(80).... 15,558	700	900	1,000	1,500	2,250	6,000	15,000
1860	(119).... 7,036	725	1,000	1,300	1,650	2,500	5,500	10,000
1860S	7,000	850	2,000	5,000	7,500	17,500		
1861	(113).... 5,959	1,000	1,500	2,500	3,500	5,500	9,000	12,000
1862	(35).... 5,750	1,250	2,350	2,500	3,500	5,500	9,000	12,000
1863	(39).... 5,000	1,000	2,000	2,750	3,750	5,750	9,000	12,000
1864	(50).... 2,630	1,100	2,250	4,000	4,250	5,500	9,000	12,000
1865	(25).... 1,140	2,000	3,250	6,500	7,500	10,000	17,500	15,000
1866	(30).... 4,000	850	1,000	1,350	1,750	3,000	7,000	12,000
1867	(50).... 2,600	1,000	1,250	2,000	1,750	3,500	10,000	12,000
1868	(25).... 4,850	850	1,000	1,350	1,750	2,750	7,000	12,000
1869	(25).... 2,500	850	1,000	1,500	850	3,000	10,000	12,000
1870	(35).... 3,500	900	1,250	1,500	1,750	3,000	10,000	12,000
1870S (unique)	—							
1871	(30).... 1,300	900	1,250	1,500	1,750	3,200	8,500	14,000
1872	(30).... 2,000	900	1,200	2,000	1,750	3,500	8,500	12,000
1873, Open 3 (Original)	(25)....		10,000	13,500				40,000
1873, Close 3		3,500	4,500	7,500	12,500	24,000	40,000	40,000
1874	(20).... 41,800	650	750	800	900	1,500	3,000	22,000
1875, Proof only	(20)....			40,000	50,000			100,000
1876, Proof only	(45)....			15,000	20,000			40,000
1877	(20).... 1,468	3,000	6,000	6,500	10,000	18,500	35,000	15,000
1878	(20).... 82,304	650	750	800	900	1,500	2,600	15,000
1879	(30).... 3,000	750	925	1,500	1,850	2,100	5,000	12,000
1880	(36).... 1,000	1,000	1,500	2,500	1,900	3,250	6,000	12,000
1881	(54)....500	1,850	3,000	5,000	6,000	10,000	14,000	12,000
1882	(76).... 1,500	1,000	1,250	1,650	1,750	2,500	6,000	10,000
1883	(89)....900	1,200	1,750	2,250	2,500	3,000	6,500	10,000
1884	(106).... 1,000	1,250	1,650	2,500	2,750	3,000	7,500	10,000
1885	(110)....800	1,250	2,000	2,500	2,750	3,500	10,000	12,000
1886	(142).... 1,000	1,000	1,600	2,250	2,500	3,250	10,000	10,000
1887	(160).... 6,000	725	1,000	1,500	1,750	2,500	4,000	10,000
1888	(291).... 5,000	700	1,000	1,150	1,300	2,200	3,000	10,000
1889	(129).... 2,300	700	1,000	1,150	1,300	2,350	3,250	10,000

STELLA (1879–1880)

These pattern coins were first suggested by the Hon. John A. Kasson, then U.S. envoy extraordinary and minister plenipotentiary to Austria-Hungary. It was through the efforts of Dr. W.W. Hubbell, who patented the alloy goloid (used in making another pattern piece, the goloid metric dollar) that we have these beautiful and interesting coins.

The four-dollar Stella—so called because of the five-pointed star on the reverse—was envisioned by Kasson as America's answer to various foreign gold coins popular in the international market. The British sovereign, Italy's 20 lire, and the 20 pesetas of Spain were three such coins: each smaller than a U.S. five-dollar gold piece, they were used widely in international trade.

The Stella was one of many proposals made to Congress for an international trade coin, and one of only several that made it to pattern coin form (others include the 1868 five dollar and 1874 Bickford ten dollar).

Odds were stacked against the Stella from the start. The denomination of four U.S. dollars didn't match any of the coin's European counterparts, and at any rate the U.S. double eagle (twenty-dollar coin)—already used in international commerce—was a more convenient medium of exchange. The Stella was never minted in quantities for circulation.

There are two distinct types in both years of issue. Charles E. Barber is thought to have designed the Flowing Hair type, and George T. Morgan the Coiled Hair. They were struck as patterns in gold, aluminum, copper, and white metal. Only those struck in gold are listed.

Flowing Hair   **Coiled Hair**

	Mintage	EF-40	AU-50	PF-60	PF-63	PF-65
1879, Flowing Hair . . . . (425+)	$70,000	$80,000	$100,000	$130,000	$165,000
1879, Coiled Hair *(12 known)*			200,000	350,000	750,000
1880, Flowing Hair *(17 known)*	85,000	95,000	115,000	155,000	325,000
1880, Coiled Hair *(8 known)*			350,000	650,000	1,000,000

While the 1856 Flying Eagle cent, the 1879 and 1880 four-dollar Stellas, and a few other patterns are listed in this book, there are more than 1,800 other trial pieces that were minted from 1792 to the present. These are listed in Whitman's *United States Pattern Coins* book and are a fascinating numismatic specialty. Most patterns are rare, and most were made in Proof formats.

The half eagle (five-dollar gold coin) was the first gold coin struck for the United States. It was authorized to be coined by the Act of April 2, 1792. The first type weighed 135 grains, of .91667 fineness. The weight was changed by the Act of June 28, 1834, to 129 grains, of .899225 fineness. Fineness became .900 by the Act of January 18, 1837.

CAPPED BUST TO RIGHT (1795–1807)

F-12 Fine: Liberty's hair worn smooth but with distinct outline. For heraldic type, E PLURIBUS UNUM faint but legible.
VF-20 Very Fine: Slight to noticeable wear on high spots such as hair, turban, and eagle's head and wings.
EF-40 Extremely Fine: Slight wear on hair and highest part of cheek.
AU-50 About Uncirculated: Trace of wear on cap, hair, cheek, and drapery.
MS-60 Uncirculated: No trace of wear. Light blemishes.
MS-63 Choice Uncirculated: Some distracting marks or blemishes in focal areas. Impaired luster possible.

Small Eagle Reverse (1795–1798)

1795 Obverse

1795 Reverse

1796, 6 Over 5   1797, 15 Stars   1797, 16 Stars

	Mintage	F-12	VF-20	EF-40	AU-50	AU-55	MS-60	MS-63
1795, Small Eagle	8,707	$15,000	$20,000	$25,000	$32,000	$45,000	$60,000	$125,000
1796, 6 Over 5	6,196	16,500	23,500	30,000	50,000	60,000	95,000	185,000
1797, 15 Stars	3,609	22,500	30,000	50,000	90,000	100,000	200,000	
1797, 16 Stars	*	22,500	30,000	50,000	90,000	100,000	200,000	
1798, Small Eagle (6 known)		85,000	125,000	250,000	650,000	850,000	—	

* Included in number above.

Heraldic Eagle Reverse (1795–1807)

	Mintage	F-12	VF-20	EF-40	AU-50	AU-55	MS-60	MS-63
1795, Heraldic Eagle	*	$7,500	$15,000	$25,000	$40,000	$55,000	$75,000	$125,000
1797, 7 Over 5	*	15,000	25,000	30,000	50,000	85,000	125,000	
1798, Large 8, 13-Star Reverse	24,867	3,000	4,000	6,000	8,500	11,000	20,000	
1798, Large 8, 14-Star Reverse	**	3,000	4,500	8,000	15,000	20,000	55,000	
1799	7,451	2,500	3,750	5,500	9,000	12,000	18,000	45,000
1800	37,628	2,500	3,750	5,500	7,500	8,500	11,000	25,000

* Included in number below. ** Included in number above.

	Mintage	F-12	VF-20	EF-40	AU-50	AU-55	MS-60	MS-63
1802, 2 Over 1 53,176		$2,750	$3,500	$5,500	$7,500	$8,500	$11,000	$25,000
1803, 3 Over 2 33,506		2,750	3,500	5,500	7,500	8,500	11,000	25,000
1804 30,475		2,750	3,500	5,500	7,500	8,500	11,000	25,000
1805 33,183		2,750	3,500	5,500	7,500	8,500	11,000	25,000
1806 64,093		2,750	3,500	5,500	7,500	8,500	11,000	25,000
1807 32,488		2,750	3,500	5,500	7,500	8,500	11,000	25,000

DRAPED BUST TO LEFT (1807–1812)

F-12 Fine: LIBERTY on cap legible but partly weak.
VF-20 Very Fine: Headband edges slightly worn. LIBERTY bold.
EF-40 Extremely Fine: Slight wear on highest portions of hair; 80% of major curls plain.
AU-50 About Uncirculated: Trace of wear above eye and on top of cap, cheek, and hair.
AU-55 Choice About Uncirculated: Evidence of friction on design high points. Some mint luster present.
MS-60 Uncirculated: No trace of wear. Light blemishes.

MS-63 Choice Uncirculated: Some distracting contact marks or blemishes in prime focal areas. Impaired luster possible.

	Mintage	F-12	VF-20	EF-40	AU-50	AU-55	MS-60	MS-63
1807 51,605		$2,000	$3,000	$4,000	$6,000	$7,000	$9,500	$20,000
1808, All kinds. 55,578								
1808, 8 Over 7		2,250	3,500	4,500	7,000	9,000	12,000	25,000
1808		2,000	3,000	4,000	6,000	7,000	9,500	20,000
1809, 9 Over 8 33,875		2,000	3,000	4,000	6,000	7,000	9,500	20,000
1810 100,287		2,000	3,000	4,000	6,000	7,000	9,500	20,000
1811 99,581		2,000	3,000	4,000	6,000	7,000	9,500	20,000
1812 58,087		2,000	3,000	4,000	6,000	7,000	9,500	20,000

CAPPED HEAD TO LEFT (1813–1834)

Large Diameter   Reduced Diameter

Large Diameter (1813–1829)

	Mintage	F-12	VF-20	EF-40	AU-50	AU-55	MS-60	MS-63
1813 95,428		$2,500	$3,000	$4,500	$6,500	$7,500	$9,000	$15,000
1814, 4 Over 3 15,454		3,500	5,000	6,000	8,500	10,000	15,000	25,000
1815 .635		35,000	65,000	145,000	175,000	200,000	225,000	300,000
1818 48,588		3,500	5,000	8,500	11,000	13,000	16,000	32,500
1819 51,723		6,500	10,000	25,000	35,000	40,000	50,000	65,000
1820 263,806		4,000	5,500	9,500	11,500	14,000	16,000	30,000
1821 34,641		20,000	30,000	50,000	75,000	100,000	150,000	250,000
1822 *(3 known)* 17,796				4,000,000				
1823 14,485		3,500	5,000	10,000	12,000	15,000	20,000	40,000

Chart continued on next page.   **171**

	Mintage	F-12	VF-20	EF-40	AU-50	AU-55	MS-60	MS-63
1824 17,340		$4,000	$6,000	$24,000	$30,000	$35,000	$45,000	$65,000
1825, 5 Over Partial 4 29,060		4,000	6,000	20,000	25,000	30,000	40,000	60,000
1825, 5 Over 4 (2 known) . . . . *				350,000				
1826 18,069		4,000	6,200	15,000	20,000	25,000	30,000	52,000
1827 24,913		7,500	12,500	22,000	30,000	35,000	45,000	70,000
1828, 8 Over 7 (5 known) . . . .**		15,000	25,000	50,000	65,000	80,000	150,000	250,000
1828 28,029		14,000	20,000	30,000	40,000	50,000	90,000	175,000
1829, Large Date. 57,442		12,500	25,000	50,000	65,000	75,000	120,000	275,000

* Included in number above. ** Included in number below.

Reduced Diameter (1829–1834)

	Mintage	F-12	VF-20	EF-40	AU-50	AU-55	MS-60	MS-63
1829, Small Date. . . . .*		$25,000	$45,000	$60,000	$85,000	$100,000	$150,000	$225,000
1830 126,351		12,500	24,000	30,000	35,000	40,000	52,500	75,000
1831 140,594		12,500	24,000	30,000	35,000	40,000	52,500	75,000
1832, Curved-Base 2,								
12 Stars (5 known) 157,487		75,000	110,000	175,000	250,000			
1832, Square-Base 2, 13 Stars . . . . . **		12,500	24,000	30,000	35,000	40,000	52,500	75,000
1833 193,630		12,500	24,000	30,000	35,000	40,000	52,500	75,000
1834 50,141		12,500	24,000	30,000	35,000	40,000	52,500	75,000

* Included in mintage for 1829, Large Date (previous chart). ** Included in number above.

CLASSIC HEAD, NO MOTTO (1834–1838)

	Mintage	F-12	VF-20	EF-40	AU-50	AU-55	MS-60	MS-63
1834 657,460		$400	$475	$600	$900	$1,100	$3,000	$7,500
1835 371,534		400	475	600	1,000	1,200	3,200	7,500
1836 553,147		400	475	600	1,000	1,200	3,200	9,500
1837 207,121		400	500	650	1,300	1,500	3,500	15,000
1838 286,588		400	475	600	1,250	1,500	3,500	9,000
1838C 17,179		1,250	3,000	7,000	10,000	15,000	45,000	150,000
1838D 20,583		1,350	3,500	5,500	9,000	16,500	25,000	55,000

LIBERTY HEAD (1839–1908)
Variety 1 – No Motto Above Eagle (1839–1866)

VF-20 Very Fine: LIBERTY on coronet bold. Major lines show in curls on neck.

EF-40 Extremely Fine: Details clear in curls on neck. Slight wear on top and lower part of coronet and on hair.

AU-50 About Uncirculated: Trace of wear on coronet and hair above eye.

AU-55 Choice About Uncirculated: Evidence of friction on design high points. Some original mint luster.

MS-60 Uncirculated: No trace of wear. Light blemishes.

MS-63 Choice Uncirculated: Some distracting contact marks or blemishes in prime focal areas. Impaired luster possible.

Mintmark: 1839, above date;
1840–1908, below eagle.

PF-63 Choice Proof: Attractive reflective surfaces with only a few blemishes in secondary focal places. No major flaws.

1842, Large Date	Small Letters			Large Letters			
Mintage	VF-20	EF-40	AU-50	AU-55	MS-60	MS-63	PF-63
1839 118,143	$500	$850	$1,500	$1,850	$5,500	$20,000	
1839C 17,205	1,750	3,250	7,000	10,000	18,500	42,500	
1839D 18,939	2,250	3,500	7,500	12,000	20,000		
1840 137,382	400	450	750	950	2,500	6,750	
1840C 18,992	1,550	2,750	4,500	5,500	15,000	40,000	
1840D 22,896	1,350	2,250	4,250	5,250	10,000	30,000	
1840O 40,120	450	750	1,500	2,250	7,000	27,500	
1841 15,833	400	700	1,200	1,350	3,000	8,500	
1841C 21,467	1,350	1,850	3,500	4,500	12,000	30,000	
1841D 29,392	1,350	2,000	5,500	4,000	8,000	20,000	
1842, Small Letters 27,578	400	450	2,000	2,500	8,500	15,000	
1842, Large Letters . . . . *	525	1,100	1,850	3,000	7,500	16,000	
1842C, Small Date 27,432	6,500	13,500	20,000	25,000	60,000		
1842C, Large Date . . . . *	1,350	1,700	2,750	3,250	9,500	25,000	
1842D, Small Date 59,608	1,350	1,600	2,500	3,500	10,000	25,000	
1842D, Large Date . . . . *	1,950	4,250	8,500	12,500	32,500		
1842O 16,400	750	2,500	7,000	8,000	15,000	32,500	
1843 611,205	400	425	425	475	1,200	7,500	
1843C 44,277	1,350	1,750	2,750	3,500	7,500	22,500	
1843D 98,452	1,450	1,700	2,250	2,750	7,000	16,500	
1843O, Small Letters 19,075	450	1,150	1,500	2,700	14,000	32,500	
1843O, Large Letters 82,000	425	875	1,250	2,500	8,500	18,000	
1844 340,330	400	415	425	500	1,500	6,000	
1844C 23,631	1,650	2,500	3,750	4,500	11,000	25,000	
1844D 88,982	1,400	1,800	2,500	2,750	7,000	20,000	
1844O 364,600	400	450	600	650	3,250	15,000	
1845 417,099	400	450	475	500	1,500	7,000	
1845D 90,629	1,350	1,800	2,150	2,750	6,750	18,500	
1845O 41,000	550	850	2,000	2,500	7,500	22,500	
1846, Large Date 395,942	400	415	425	500	1,650	8,500	
1846, Small Date . . . . *	400	500	550	650	1,350	7,500	
1846C 12,995	1,450	2,500	3,500	4,500	12,500	40,000	
1846D 80,294	1,550	1,800	2,500	3,250	7,500	15,000	
1846O 58,000	450	700	2,500	2,500	7,500	20,000	
1847 915,981	385	400	425	450	1,350	4,000	
1847C 84,151	1,300	1,750	2,400	2,750	7,500	23,500	
1847D 64,405	1,350	1,800	2,500	3,000	6,000	12,500	
1847O 12,000	2,250	5,000	8,500	9,000	18,000		
1848 260,775	385	400	425	450	1,450	8,000	
1848C 64,472	1,450	1,650	2,500	2,750	12,500	32,500	
1848D 47,465	1,350	2,100	2,750	3,000	9,000	20,000	
1849 133,070	385	425	475	600	2,000	8,500	
1849C 64,823	1,350	1,600	2,500	2,650	7,500	15,000	
1849D 39,036	1,400	2,000	2,500	2,750	9,500	20,000	
1850 64,491	385	450	675	825	2,500	14,000	

* Included in number above.

Chart continued on next page.

	Mintage	VF-20	EF-40	AU-50	AU-55	MS-60	MS-63	PF-63
1850C	63,591	$1,450	$1,650	$2,250	$2,750	$7,500	$15,000	
1850D	43,984	1,400	1,800	3,000	3,500	16,500		
1851	377,505	385	450	425	450	1,750	7,000	
1851C	49,176	1,350	1,700	2,450	2,800	8,000	30,000	
1851D	62,710	1,350	1,700	2,250	2,750	9,000	17,500	
1851O	41,000	650	1,100	3,750	4,500	9,000	16,500	
1852	573,901	385	425	500	575	1,200	4,000	
1852C	72,574	1,500	1,650	2,250	2,650	4,500	16,500	
1852D	91,584	1,400	1,750	2,250	3,000	7,000	18,000	
1853	305,770	385	400	425	450	1,050	5,000	
1853C	65,571	1,450	2,000	2,500	3,000	5,000	18,000	
1853D	89,678	1,350	2,000	2,750	3,500	5,250	14,000	
1854	160,675	385	400	425	450	1,500	6,000	
1854C	39,283	1,350	1,850	3,000	3,500	9,000	28,000	
1854D	56,413	1,400	1,800	3,000	3,250	6,000	20,000	
1854O	46,000	425	550	1,050	1,500	5,000	16,500	
1854S *(2 known)*	268		2,000,000					
1855	117,098	385	400	425	450	1,500	5,500	
1855C	39,788	1,350	1,650	2,250	3,000	9,000	32,500	
1855D	22,432	1,350	2,000	2,250	3,000	9,500	27,500	
1855O	11,100	800	2,100	3,000	4,500	15,000		
1855S	61,000	500	750	1,550	2,500	9,000		
1856	197,990	385	400	425	450	1,650	5,500	—
1856C	28,457	1,350	1,700	2,250	2,650	13,000	35,000	
1856D	19,786	1,350	1,850	2,750	3,000	7,500	25,000	
1856O	10,000	700	1,250	3,250	4,500	9,500		
1856S	105,100	500	600	800	1,100	4,500	18,500	
1857	98,188	350	400	425	450	1,500	5,500	—
1857C	31,360	1,350	1,800	2,450	2,650	5,250	22,500	
1857D	17,046	1,500	1,850	2,650	3,500	8,000	30,000	
1857O	13,000	700	1,250	3,000	3,750	10,000	35,000	
1857S	87,000	450	500	750	1,350	7,500	20,000	
1858	15,136	475	550	600	750	2,400	6,000	—
1858C	38,856	1,350	1,850	2,750	3,250	6,500	22,500	
1858D	15,362	1,400	1,800	2,650	3,250	8,000	23,000	
1858S	18,600	1,000	2,250	3,500	5,500	22,500		
1859 (80)	16,734	400	500	1,100	1,500	4,500	12,500	$40,000
1859C	31,847	1,350	1,750	2,500	3,250	8,500	27,000	
1859D	10,366	1,550	2,000	2,500	3,500	7,000	30,000	
1859S	13,220	1,100	2,500	3,250	4,500	20,000		
1860 (62)	19,763	450	500	850	1,300	2,500	10,000	30,000
1860C	14,813	1,700	2,250	3,250	4,500	8,000	15,000	
1860D	14,635	1,500	2,000	2,750	3,500	10,000	35,000	
1860S	21,200	1,500	2,500	4,500	7,500	22,500		
1861 (66)	688,084	385	415	425	600	1,300	5,000	30,000
1861C	6,879	4,000	6,500	8,500	10,000	20,000	65,000	
1861D	1,597	20,000	30,000	37,500	45,000	60,000	115,000	
1861S	18,000	2,250	3,500	6,500	8,500			
1862 (35)	4,430	1,500	3,000	5,500	4,500	25,000	28,000	30,000
1862S	9,500	3,000	5,000	6,500	10,000	32,500		
1863 (30)	2,442	2,500	5,500	11,000	15,000	37,500		25,000
1863S	17,000	2,250	3,500	8,500	12,500	30,000		
1864 (50)	4,170	1,200	2,000	6,500	7,500	15,000		25,000
1864S	3,888	12,000	25,000	45,000	55,000			
1865 (25)	1,270	4,500	8,500	12,500	16,500	25,000		25,000
1865S	27,612	1,750	2,500	5,000	6,000	10,000	20,000	
1866S	9,000	1,200	3,000	8,000	10,000	25,000		

Variety 2 – Motto Above Eagle (1866–1908)

VF-20 Very Fine: Half of hair lines above coronet missing. Hair curls under ear evident, but worn. Motto and its ribbon sharp.

EF-40 Extremely Fine: Small amount of wear on top of hair and below L in LIBERTY. Wear evident on wing tips and neck of eagle.

AU-50 About Uncirculated: Trace of wear on tip of coronet and hair above eye.

AU-55 Choice About Uncirculated: Evidence of friction on design high points. Some original mint luster present.

MS-60 Uncirculated: No trace of wear. Light blemishes.

MS-63 Choice Uncirculated: Some distracting contact marks or blemishes in prime focal areas. Impaired luster possible.

PF-63 Choice Proof: Reflective surfaces with only a few blemishes in secondary focal places. No major flaws.

	Mintage	VF-20	EF-40	AU-50	AU-55	MS-60	MS-63	PF-63
1866 . . . . (30). 6,700		$700	$1,500	$2,000	$3,000	$10,000		$17,500
1866S 34,920		1,000	2,000	5,500	7,000	17,500		
1867 . . . . (50). 6,870		700	1,500	2,500	3,000	7,500		17,500
1867S 29,000		800	1,500	5,500	7,500	20,000		
1868 . . . . (25). 5,700		500	650	1,850	2,500	8,500		17,500
1868S 52,000		425	950	2,200	2,750	12,500		
1869 . . . . (25). 1,760		650	2,000	3,000	4,000	10,000		17,500
1869S 31,000		400	1,050	2,400	3,500	15,000		
1870 . . . . (35). 4,000		550	1,250	2,000	3,500	11,000		17,500
1870CC 7,675		12,500	25,000	35,000	45,000	85,000		
1870S 17,000		750	1,750	4,000	6,500	17,500		
1871 . . . . (30). 3,200		625	1,250	2,000	2,500	6,500		17,500
1871CC 20,770		3,500	6,500	10,000	17,500	45,000	$70,000	
1871S 25,000		400	700	2,000	2,400	10,000		
1872 . . . . (30). 1,660		750	1,200	2,500	3,500	7,500	12,500	17,500
1872CC 16,980		2,500	4,500	12,000	17,500	40,000		
1872S 36,400		550	650	1,900	2,750	8,000		
1873 . . . . (25). 112,505		285	300	315	325	700	2,750	17,500
1873CC 7,416		5,500	10,000	20,000	25,000	55,000		
1873S 31,000		450	900	2,000	2,750	15,000		
1874 . . . . (20). 3,488		425	1,100	1,500	2,000	7,500	15,000	20,000
1874CC 21,198		1,750	3,500	7,500	10,000	27,500		
1874S 16,000		450	1,400	2,250	4,000	13,500		
1875 . . . . (20). 200		50,000	65,000	100,000	150,000			75,000
1875CC 11,828		3,000	5,000	10,000	17,500	35,000		
1875S 9,000		850	2,000	3,000	4,500	12,500		
1876 . . . . (45). 1,432		1,250	2,500	2,500	4,000	10,000	17,500	13,500
1876CC 6,887		3,000	5,500	9,000	14,000	35,000		
1876S 4,000		2,250	4,500	6,500	8,500	18,000		
1877 . . . . (20). 1,132		1,500	2,500	4,000	4,500	8,000	15,000	13,500
1877CC 8,680		2,250	3,000	7,750	12,500	35,000		
1877S 26,700		285	500	1,000	1,500	5,500	13,000	
1878 . . . . (20). 131,720		285	300	315	325	375	1,500	20,000
1878CC 9,054		3,500	5,750	12,500	15,000	55,000		
1878S 144,700		285	300	315	325	375	2,750	
1879 . . . . (30). 301,920		285	300	315	325	375	1,350	13,000
1879CC 17,281		1,250	1,100	2,750	3,500	17,500		
1879S 426,200		285	300	315	350	750	1,500	
1880 . . . . (36). . . 3,166,400		285	300	315	325	325	450	12,000
1880CC 51,017		700	875	1,000	2,750	8,500	30,000	
1880S 1,348,900		285	300	315	325	325	450	

Chart continued on next page.   **175**

	Mintage	VF-20	EF-40	AU-50	AU-55	MS-60	MS-63	PF-63
1881 . . . . (42) 5,708,760		$285	$300	$315	$325	$325	$400	$12,000
1881CC 13,886		1,200	2,500	5,000	7,500	16,500	40,000	
1881S 969,000		285	300	315	325	325	475	
1882 . . . . (48) 2,514,520		285	300	315	325	325	375	11,000
1882CC 82,817		650	1,000	1,500	2,500	7,500	30,000	
1882S 969,000		285	300	315	325	325	450	
1883 . . . . (61) 233,400		285	300	315	325	375	1,000	11,000
1883CC 12,598		1,250	2,000	3,250	4,500	14,000		
1883S 83,200		285	300	315	325	450	1,800	
1884 . . . . (48) 191,030		285	300	315	325	325	1,200	11,000
1884CC 16,402		700	1,250	3,500	5,000	16,500		
1884S 177,000		285	300	315	325	325	1,100	
1885 . . . . (66) 601,440		285	300	315	325	325	700	10,000
1885S 1,211,500		285	300	315	325	325	450	
1886 . . . . (72) 388,360		285	300	315	325	325	675	10,000
1886S 3,268,000		285	300	315	325	325	375	
1887, Proof only (87)								35,000
1887S 1,912,000		285	300	315	325	325	475	
1888 . . . . (95) 18,201		285	300	315	325	400	1,100	10,000
1888S 293,900		285	300	315	325	550	2,000	
1889 . . . . (45) 7,520		285	300	315	325	600	1,800	10,000
1890 . . . . (88) 4,240		285	300	325	750	1,500	3,500	10,000
1890CC 53,800		600	675	800	1,000	1,500	6,000	
1891 . . . . (53) 61,360		285	300	315	325	375	1,200	9,500
1891CC 208,000		550	650	750	1,000	1,200	2,500	
1892 . . . . (92) 753,480		285	300	315	325	350	450	9,500
1892CC 82,968		550	650	750	850	1,500	5,000	
1892O 10,000		1,200	1,500	2,000	2,500	3,500	15,000	
1892S 298,400		285	300	315	325	375	1,500	
1893 . . . . (77) 1,528,120		285	290	300	315	325	375	9,500
1893CC 60,000		500	550	650	850	2,000	6,000	
1893O 110,000		285	425	450	475	700	4,000	
1893S 224,000		285	300	315	325	325	600	
1894 . . . . (75) 957,880		285	300	315	325	325	400	9,500
1894O 16,600		285	425	450	475	850	6,000	
1894S 55,900		285	300	315	350	1,500	6,000	
1895 . . . . (81) 1,345,855		285	290	300	315	325	375	9,500
1895S 112,000		285	300	315	350	1,850	3,500	
1896 . . . . (103) 58,960		285	300	315	325	325	500	8,500
1896S 155,400		285	300	315	375	750	3,500	
1897 . . . . (83) 867,800		285	290	300	315	325	375	8,500
1897S 354,000		285	300	315	350	550	3,250	
1898 . . . . (75) 633,420		285	300	315	325	325	500	8,500
1898S 1,397,400		285	300	315	325	350	800	
1899 . . . . (99) 1,710,630		285	290	300	315	325	375	8,500
1899S 1,545,000		285	300	315	325	325	600	
1900 . . . . (230) 1,405,500		285	290	300	315	325	375	8,500
1900S 329,000		285	300	315	325	350	600	
1901 . . . . (140) 615,900		285	290	300	315	325	375	8,500
1901S, 1 Over 0 3,648,000		285	300	315	325	350	750	
1901S . . . . *		285	290	300	315	325	375	
1902 . . . . (162) 172,400		285	290	300	315	325	375	8,500
1902S 939,000		285	290	300	315	325	375	
1903 . . . . (154) 226,870		285	290	300	315	325	375	8,500
1903S 1,855,000		285	290	300	315	325	375	

* Included in number above.

	Mintage	VF-20	EF-40	AU-50	AU-55	MS-60	MS-63	PF-63
1904 . . . . (136).	.392,000	$285	$290	$300	$315	$325	$375	$8,500
1904S	.97,000	285	300	315	325	500	2,250	
1905 . . . . . . (108).	.302,200	285	290	300	315	325	375	8,500
1905S	.880,700	285	300	315	325	450	1,000	
1906 . . . . (85).	.348,735	285	290	300	315	325	375	8,500
1906D	.320,000	285	290	300	315	325	375	
1906S	.598,000	285	300	315	325	435	600	
1907 . . . . (92).	.626,100	285	300	315	325	350	375	8,500
1907D	.888,000	285	300	315	325	350	375	
1908	.421,874	285	300	315	325	350	375	

INDIAN HEAD (1908–1929)

This type conforms in design to the quarter eagle of the same date. The sunken-relief designs and lettering make the Indian Head a unique series, along with the quarter eagle, in United States coinage.

VF-20 Very Fine: Noticeable wear on large middle feathers and tip of eagle's wing.

EF-40 Extremely Fine: Cheekbone, war bonnet, and headband feathers slightly worn. Feathers on eagle's upper wing show considerable wear.

AU-50 About Uncirculated: Trace of wear on cheekbone and headdress.

AU-55 Choice About Uncirculated: Evidence of friction on design high points. Much of original mint luster present.

MS-60 Uncirculated: No trace of wear. Light blemishes.

MS-63 Choice Uncirculated: Some distracting contact marks or blemishes in prime focal areas. Impaired luster possible.

Mintmark Location

Matte PF-63 Choice Proof: Matte surfaces with few blemishes in secondary focal places. No major flaws.

Coin dealers usually pay higher prices than those listed for scarcer coins with well-struck mintmarks

	Mintage	VF-20	EF-40	AU-50	AU-55	MS-60	MS-63	MATTE PF-63
1908 . . . . (167).	.577,845	$300	$325	$350	$365	$350	$700	$10,000
1908D	.148,000	300	325	350	365	450	700	
1908S	.82,000	450	500	750	900	1,500	6,000	
1909 . . . . (78). . . .	.627,060	300	325	350	365	350	725	10,000
1909D	3,423,560	300	325	350	365	350	675	
1909O	.34,200	3,250	5,000	8,500	10,000	27,500	65,000	
1909S	.297,200	300	325	350	365	1,500	7,500	
1910 . . . . (250).	.604,000	300	325	350	365	475	850	10,000
1910D	.193,600	300	325	350	365	475	1,750	
1910S	.770,200	300	325	375	425	750	6,500	
1911 . . . . (139).	.915,000	300	325	350	365	475	750	10,000
1911D	.72,500	425	650	1,200	1,250	5,500	30,000	
1911S	1,416,000	300	325	375	500	650	2,500	
1912 . . . . (144).	.790,000	300	325	350	365	475	800	10,000
1912S	.392,000	300	325	375	475	1,100	11,000	
1913 . . . . (99).	.915,901	300	325	350	365	475	650	10,000
1913S	.408,000	300	325	375	550	1,750	10,000	
1914 . . . . (125).	.247,000	300	325	350	365	475	1,200	10,000
1914D	.247,000	300	325	350	365	475	1,500	
1914S	.263,000	300	325	375	450	1,250	5,500	
1915 . . . . (75).	.588,000	300	325	350	365	475	800	10,000
1915S	.164,000	300	325	375	400	1,750	8,500	
1916S	.240,000	300	325	375	400	550	3,000	
1929	.662,000	10,000	12,500	15,000	17,500	25,000	32,500	

Coinage authorization, specified weights, and fineness of the eagle coins conform to those of the half eagle. The Small Eagle reverse was used until 1797, when the large, Heraldic Eagle replaced it.

CAPPED BUST TO RIGHT (1795–1804)

F-12 Fine: Details on turban and head obliterated.

VF-20 Very Fine: Hair lines in curls on neck and details under turban and over forehead worn but distinguishable.

EF-40 Extremely Fine: Definite wear on hair to left of eye and strand of hair across and around turban, as well as on eagle's wing tips.

AU-50 About Uncirculated: Trace of wear on cap, hair, cheek, and drapery.

AU-55 Choice About Uncirculated: Evidence of friction on design high points. Most of original mint luster present.

MS-60 Uncirculated: No trace of wear. Light blemishes.

MS-63 Choice Uncirculated: Some distracting contact marks or blemishes in prime focal areas. Impaired luster possible.

Small Eagle Reverse (1795–1797)

	Mintage	F-12	VF-20	EF-40	AU-50	AU-55	MS-60	MS-63
1795	5,583	$22,500	$27,500	$40,000	$45,000	$55,000	$80,000	$200,000
1796	4,146	25,000	27,000	40,000	50,000	57,500	87,500	225,000
1797, Small Eagle	3,615	32,500	40,000	60,000	85,000	115,000	150,000	

Heraldic Eagle Reverse (1797–1804)

	Mintage	F-12	VF-20	EF-40	AU-50	AU-55	MS-60	MS-63
1797, Large Eagle	10,940	$7,500	$12,000	$15,000	$25,000	$30,000	$40,000	$100,000
1798, 8 Over 7, 9 Stars Left, 4 Right	900	10,000	15,000	25,000	37,500	55,000	105,000	200,000
1798, 8 Over 7, 7 Stars Left, 6 Right	842	25,000	35,000	55,000	85,000	125,000	250,000	
1799	37,449	7,000	8,500	12,000	15,000	16,000	22,500	50,000
1800	5,999	7,000	8,500	12,000	15,000	16,000	22,500	60,000
1801	44,344	7,000	8,500	12,000	15,000	16,000	22,500	50,000
1803	15,017	7,000	8,500	12,000	15,000	16,000	22,500	50,000
1804	3,757	14,000	18,500	25,000	35,000	47,500	65,000	150,000

LIBERTY HEAD, NO MOTTO ABOVE EAGLE (1838–1866)

In 1838 the weight and diameter of the eagle were reduced and the obverse and reverse were redesigned. Liberty now faced left and the word LIBERTY was placed on the coronet.

VF-20 Very Fine: Hair lines above coronet partly worn. Curls under ear worn but defined.

EF-40 Extremely Fine: Small amount of wear on top of hair and below L in LIBERTY. Wear evident on wing tips and neck of eagle.

AU-50 About Uncirculated: Trace of wear on tip of coronet and hair above eye.

AU-55 Choice About Uncirculated: Evidence of friction on design high points. Some of original mint luster present.

MS-60 Uncirculated: No trace of wear. Light blemishes.

Mintmark is on reverse, below eagle.

MS-63 Choice Uncirculated: Some distracting contact marks or blemishes in prime focal areas. Impaired luster possible.

PF-63 Choice Proof: Attractive reflective surfaces with only a few blemishes in secondary focal places. No major flaws.

	Mintage	VF-20	EF-40	AU-50	AU-55	MS-60	MS-63	PF-63
1838	7,200	$2,750	$7,000	$13,500	$20,000	$55,000	$75,000	
1839, Large Letters	25,801	1,250	3,250	4,500	7,500	22,500	65,000	
1839, Small Letters	12,447	2,500	6,500	8,500	12,500	30,000	80,000	
1840	47,338	800	1,050	1,350	1,800	7,000		
1841	63,131	800	825	1,100	1,800	5,500	22,000	
1841O	2,500	2,750	7,500	15,000	17,500	35,000		
1842	81,507	800	875	1,200	1,500	10,000	22,500	
1842O	27,400	1,000	1,250	2,500	5,500	25,000		
1843	75,462	800	825	1,250	2,500	12,000		
1843O	175,162	800	825	1,250	2,500	8,500	45,000	
1844	6,361	1,500	3,000	4,500	5,500	14,000		
1844O	118,700	825	1,000	1,250	3,000	8,750		
1845	26,153	800	1,100	1,650	2,500	11,000		
1845O	47,500	850	1,250	2,250	5,500	11,000	35,000	
1846	20,095	800	1,000	3,500	4,000	15,000		
1846O	81,780	950	1,500	2,500	3,500	10,000	25,000	
1847	862,258	700	750	850	875	2,500	15,000	
1847O	571,500	800	850	950	1,200	4,000	22,500	
1848	145,484	700	750	850	875	3,500	15,000	
1848O	35,850	950	2,000	2,750	4,000	12,500	20,000	
1849	653,618	700	750	850	875	2,500	12,000	
1849O	23,900	1,350	2,250	4,000	6,500	20,000		
1850	291,451	725	750	850	875	3,000	13,000	
1850O	57,500	950	950	2,250	2,500	13,000		
1851	176,328	700	1,350	800	950	3,000	15,000	
1851O	263,000	825	875	1,100	1,750	4,500	20,000	
1852	263,106	700	750	800	875	2,250	16,000	
1852O	18,000	1,200	2,000	4,000	7,500	32,500		
1853, 3 Over 2	201,253	800	1,000	1,500	1,750	10,000		
1853	*	700	750	800	875	2,000	13,000	
1853O	51,000	950	1,200	1,500	3,000	8,500		
1854	54,250	700	750	800	950	3,500		
1854O	52,500	800	1,100	1,350	2,000	6,500	25,000	
1854S	123,826	800	1,000	1,350	2,500	6,500	25,000	
1855	121,701	700	750	800	875	3,000	12,000	
1855O	18,000	900	2,500	4,750	7,000	18,000		

* Included in number above.

Chart continued on next page.

	Mintage	VF-20	EF-40	AU-50	AU-55	MS-60	MS-63	PF-63
1855S	9,000	$2,250	$2,500	$4,500	$7,500	$19,000		
1856	60,490	700	750	800	875	2,500	$12,000	
1856O	14,500	1,000	2,000	2,750	5,000	20,000		
1856S	68,000	800	825	1,250	1,750	6,500		
1857	16,606	700	800	1,250	1,750	8,500		
1857O	5,500	1,500	2,750	4,500	7,500	20,000		
1857S	26,000	1,100	1,400	1,500	2,250	7,000	13,000	
1858	2,521	3,500	6,000	8,500	10,500	25,000		$75,000
1858O	20,000	950	1,250	2,000	2,000	6,000	25,000	
1858S	11,800	1,100	2,750	4,500	6,000	22,000		
1859	(80)	16,013	800	825	1,100	1,500	6,000	12,000	45,000
1859O	2,300	3,250	7,500	13,500	20,000	40,000		
1859S	7,000	1,500	3,500	11,000	12,500	30,000		
1860	(50)	15,055	750	800	1,100	1,250	5,000	12,000	31,000
1860O	11,100	1,100	1,950	2,750	4,500	12,000		
1860S	5,000	2,000	4,000	8,500	12,500	27,500		
1861	(69)	113,164	750	800	1,100	1,500	4,000	12,000	30,000
1861S	15,500	2,500	6,000	8,500	12,000	30,000		
1862	(35)	10,960	800	1,500	3,500	4,500	12,000	18,000	30,000
1862S	12,500	1,500	3,000	5,500	12,000	26,500		
1863	(30)	1,218	2,750	10,000	20,000	25,000	35,000	50,000	30,000
1863S	10,000	4,000	7,500	10,000	15,000	35,000		
1864	(50)	3,530	1,250	4,000	6,500	8,500	15,000		30,000
1864S	2,500	35,000	75,000	125,000	175,000			
1865	(25)	3,980	2,500	4,000	10,000	13,500	25,000	40,000	30,000
1865S	16,700	3,000	6,000	11,000	15,000	32,000	50,000	
1866S	8,500	2,000	5,500	11,000	16,500	30,000		

LIBERTY HEAD, MOTTO ABOVE EAGLE (1866–1907)

VF-20 Very Fine: Half of hair lines over coronet visible. Curls under ear worn but defined. IN GOD WE TRUST and its ribbon sharp.

EF-40 Extremely Fine: Small amount of wear on top of hair and below L in LIBERTY. Wear evident on wing tips and neck of eagle.

AU-50 About Uncirculated: Trace of wear on hair above eye and on coronet.

AU-55 Choice About Uncirculated: Evidence of friction on design high points. Some of original mint luster present.

Mintmark is on reverse, below eagle.

MS-60 Uncirculated: No trace of wear. Light blemishes.

MS-63 Choice Uncirculated: Some distracting marks or blemishes in focal areas. Impaired luster possible.

PF-63 Choice Proof: Reflective surfaces with only a few blemishes in secondary focal areas. No major flaws.

	Mintage	VF-20	EF-40	AU-50	AU-55	MS-60	MS-63	PF-63
1866	(30)	3,750	$1,100	$2,000	$3,250	$8,000	$25,000		$27,500
1866S	11,500	1,500	3,000	4,750	7,000	17,500		
1867	(50)	3,090	1,350	2,250	4,500	7,500	25,000		27,500
1867S	9,000	2,500	4,500	5,500	7,000	25,000		
1868	(25)	10,630	650	1,000	1,200	2,000	10,000		27,500
1868S	13,500	1,250	1,750	2,500	4,500	13,000		
1869	(25)	1,830	1,100	2,750	3,500	4,750	25,000		27,500
1869S	6,430	1,350	2,500	4,000	8,000	13,000		
1870	(35)	3,990	825	1,350	1,850	5,500	20,000		25,000
1870CC	5,908	27,500	45,000	65,000	100,000			
1870S	8,000	1,200	2,500	3,500	4,500	20,000		
1871	(30)	1,790	1,000	2,000	3,500	4,000	11,000		25,000
1871CC	8,085	3,500	10,000	15,000	20,000	45,000		

	Mintage	VF-20	EF-40	AU-50	AU-55	MS-60	MS-63	PF-63
1871S 16,500		$1,200	$1,450	$3,000	$4,500	$15,000		
1872 . . . . (30) 1,620		1,400	3,000	5,500	6,500	10,000	$23,000	$25,000
1872CC 4,600		6,500	8,500	17,500	25,000	45,000		
1872S 17,300		750	1,200	1,500	2,000	12,000		
1873 . . . . (25) 800		6,500	14,000	22,500	30,000	50,000		27,500
1873CC 4,543		10,000	20,000	35,000	55,000	125,000		
1873S 12,000		1,000	2,000	3,000	4,500	20,000		
1874 . . . . (20) 53,140		600	650	675	725	1,000	4,000	27,500
1874CC 16,767		2,500	4,000	8,500	15,000	55,000		
1874S 10,000		1,000	1,550	2,500	5,000	25,000		
1875 . . . . (20) 100		55,000	100,000	200,000	250,000			115,000
1875CC 7,715		4,000	7,500	13,000	27,500	70,000	100,000	
1876 . . . . (45) 687		3,000	6,500	15,000	25,000	50,000		22,000
1876CC 4,696		4,000	8,500	13,500	25,000	40,000		
1876S 5,000		1,250	2,500	4,500	6,000	22,000		
1877 . . . . (20) 797		3,000	5,000	7,250	8,500	30,000		22,000
1877CC 3,332		5,500	8,000	15,000	20,000	35,000		
1877S 17,000		700	950	1,100	2,500	18,000		
1878 . . . . (20) 73,780		600	605	615	620	700	3,250	22,000
1878CC 3,244		5,000	9,500	16,500	30,000	45,000		
1878S 26,100		675	750	800	1,300	7,500	20,000	
1879 . . . . (30) 384,740		600	605	615	620	650	2,000	18,500
1879CC 1,762		8,500	16,500	30,000	37,500	75,000		
1879O 1,500		6,500	12,000	15,000	25,000	50,000		
1879S 224,000		600	615	625	635	800	3,500	
1880 . . . . (36) . . .1,644,840		600	605	615	620	650	1,000	18,500
1880CC 11,190		1,400	2,000	3,000	4,000	15,000		
1880O 9,200		1,100	1,500	3,000	3,750	12,500		
1880S 506,250		600	605	615	620	650	1,000	
1881 . . . . (40) . . .3,877,220		600	605	615	620	650	850	18,500
1881CC 24,015		1,200	1,850	2,000	2,750	5,000	25,000	
1881O 8,350		900	1,100	2,200	3,250	8,500		
1881S 970,000		600	605	615	620	650	1,000	
1882 . . . . (40) . . .2,324,440		600	605	615	620	650	700	15,000
1882CC 6,764		1,250	2,500	3,500	7,000	22,500	50,000	
1882O 10,820		850	1,100	1,500	2,500	5,500	25,000	
1882S 132,000		600	605	615	620	650	1,500	
1883 . . . . (40) 208,700		600	605	615	620	650	1,000	15,000
1883CC 12,000		1,200	1,500	3,000	4,500	25,000		
1883O 800		6,500	18,000	30,000	40,000	75,000		
1883S 38,000		600	605	615	620	800	6,000	
1884 . . . . (45) 76,860		600	605	615	620	700	3,000	15,000
1884CC 9,925		1,200	2,000	3,500	5,000	10,000		
1884S 124,250		600	605	615	620	650	2,500	
1885 . . . . (65) 253,462		600	605	615	620	650	1,250	12,500
1885S 228,000		600	605	615	620	650	850	
1886 . . . . (60) 236,100		600	605	615	620	650	1,500	12,500
1886S 826,000		600	605	615	620	650	700	
1887 . . . . (80) 53,600		600	605	615	620	700	4,000	12,000
1887S 817,000		600	605	615	620	600	1,000	
1888 . . . . (75) 132,921		600	605	615	620	650	2,250	12,000
1888O 21,335		600	605	615	675	800	4,000	
1888S 648,700		600	605	615	620	650	800	
1889 . . . . (45) 4,440		650	625	750	1,000	2,500	5,500	12,000
1889S 425,400		600	605	615	620	650	850	
1890 . . . . (63) 57,980		600	605	615	620	650	2,500	10,000
1890CC 17,500		1,000	1,050	1,300	1,850	3,000	12,000	
1891 . . . . (48) 91,820		600	605	615	620	650	1,250	10,000

Chart continued on next page.

	Mintage	VF-20	EF-40	AU-50	AU-55	MS-60	MS-63	PF-63
1891CC 103,732		$950	$1,050	$1,100	$1,350	$2,000	$5,500	
1892 . . . . (72) 797,480		600	605	615	620	650	700	$10,000
1892CC 40,000		950	1,050	1,200	1,500	3,500	17,500	
1892O 28,688		650	700	725	750	900	5,000	
1892S 115,500		600	605	615	620	700	1,500	
1893 . . . . (55) 1,840,840		600	605	615	620	650	700	10,000
1893CC 14,000		1,100	1,350	2,000	3,500	12,000	15,000	
1893O 17,000		650	700	750	775	1,000	4,000	
1893S 141,350		600	605	615	620	650	1,200	
1894 . . . . (43) 2,470,735		600	605	615	620	650	700	10,000
1894O 107,500		600	600	625	675	750	3,500	
1894S 25,000		650	700	750	850	2,500	10,000	
1895 . . . . (56) 567,770		600	615	625	630	650	700	10,000
1895O 98,000		600	600	625	635	725	4,250	
1895S 49,000		650	700	725	750	1,500	5,000	
1896 . . . . (78) 76,270		600	605	615	620	650	950	10,000
1896S 123,750		600	605	615	620	1,500	5,500	
1897 . . . . (69) 1,000,090		600	605	615	620	650	700	10,000
1897O 42,500		600	605	615	620	750	4,500	
1897S 234,750		600	605	615	620	650	3,500	
1898 . . . . (67) 812,130		600	605	615	620	650	700	10,000
1898S 473,600		600	605	615	620	650	1,250	
1899 . . . . (86) 1,262,219		600	605	615	620	650	700	10,000
1899O 37,047		600	605	615	620	800	4,500	
1899S 841,000		600	605	615	620	650	1,200	
1900 . . . . (120) 293,840		600	605	615	620	650	700	10,000
1900S 81,000		600	605	615	620	800	3,000	
1901 . . . . (85) 1,718,740		600	605	615	620	650	700	10,000
1901O 72,041		600	605	615	620	700	2,250	
1901S 2,812,750		600	605	615	620	650	700	
1902 . . . . (113) 82,400		600	605	615	620	650	950	10,000
1902S 469,500		600	605	615	620	650	700	
1903 . . . . (96) 125,830		600	605	615	620	650	700	10,000
1903O 112,771		600	605	615	620	700	1,500	
1903S 538,000		600	605	615	620	650	700	
1904 . . . . (108) 161,930		600	605	615	620	650	1,200	10,000
1904O 108,950		600	605	615	635	700	2,000	
1905 . . . . (86) 200,992		600	605	615	620	650	700	10,000
1905S 369,250		600	605	615	620	675	2,250	
1906 . . . . (77) 165,420		600	605	615	620	650	800	10,000
1906D 981,000		600	605	615	620	650	700	
1906O 86,895		600	605	615	620	700	3,000	
1906S 457,000		600	605	615	620	750	2,000	
1907 . . . . (74) 1,203,899		600	605	615	620	650	700	10,000
1907D 1,030,000		600	605	615	620	650	1,200	
1907S 210,500		600	605	615	650	750	2,250	

INDIAN HEAD (1907–1933)

VF-20 Very Fine: Bonnet feathers worn near band. Wear visible on high points of hair.

EF-40 Extremely Fine: Slight wear on cheekbone and headdress feathers. Slight wear visible on eagle's eye and left wing.

AU-50 About Uncirculated: Trace of wear on hair above eye and on forehead.

AU-55 Choice About Uncirculated: Evidence of friction on design high points. Much of original mint luster present.

MS-60 Uncirculated: No trace of wear. Light blemishes.

MS-63 Choice Uncirculated: Some distracting contact marks or blemishes in prime focal areas. Impaired luster possible.

Matte PF-63 Choice Proof: Matte surfaces with few blemishes in secondary focal places. No major flaws.

No Motto
Mintmark is above left tip of branch on 1908-D No Motto.

With Motto IN GOD WE TRUST
Mintmark is at left of arrow points.

Gem Uncirculated (MS-65) coins are rare, and dealers usually pay substantial premiums for them.

	Mintage	VF-20	EF-40	AU-50	AU-55	MS-60	MS-63
1907, Wire Rim, Periods	500	$12,500	$15,000	$17,500	$19,000	$23,000	$35,000
1907, Rounded Rim, Periods Before and After •E•PLURIBUS•UNUM•	50	32,500	35,000	45,000	50,000	75,000	100,000
1907, No Periods	239,406	600	625	650	675	000	1,250
1908, No Motto	33,500	600	650	700	775	975	3,250
1908D, No Motto	210,000	625	800	825	875	1,000	5,000

Variety 2 – Motto on Reverse (1908–1933)

	Mintage	VF-20	EF-40	AU-50	AU-55	MS-60	MS-63	MATTE PF-63
1908 ...... (116)	341,370	$600	$625	$650	$675	$650	$1,000	$15,000
1908D	836,500	600	625	650	675	875	2,500	
1908S	59,850	800	825	850	950	2,500	9,500	
1909 ..... (74)	184,789	600	625	650	675	700	1,200	17,500
1909D	121,540	600	625	650	675	1,000	2,250	
1909S	292,350	600	625	650	675	1,200	3,250	
1910 ...... (204)	318,500	600	625	650	675	700	850	15,000
1910D	2,356,640	600	625	650	675	700	750	
1910S	811,000	600	625	650	675	750	4,500	
1911 ...... (95)	505,500	600	625	650	675	700	800	15,000
1911D	30,100	900	1,250	1,500	2,200	6,500	22,500	
1911S	51,000	600	700	650	700	2,000	7,000	
1912 ..... (83)	405,000	600	625	650	675	700	800	15,000
1912S	300,000	600	625	650	700	1,000	4,000	
1913 ...... (71)	442,000	600	625	650	675	700	850	15,000
1913S	66,000	750	775	850	1,000	3,500	15,000	
1914 ...... (50)	151,000	600	625	650	675	700	1,100	15,000
1914D	343,500	600	625	650	675	700	1,000	
1914S	208,000	600	625	650	700	1,250	4,000	
1915 ...... (75)	351,000	600	625	650	675	700	1,100	17,500
1915S	59,000	600	700	750	900	4,000	14,000	
1916S	138,500	600	625	650	700	950	4,500	
1920S	126,500	12,500	18,500	25,000	27,500	40,000	70,000	
1926	1,014,000	600	625	650	660	675	700	
1930S	96,000	10,000	15,000	20,000	22,500	30,000	35,000	
1932	4,463,000	600	625	650	660	675	700	
1933	312,500	85,000	100,000	125,000	135,000	150,000	185,000	

This largest denomination of all regular United States issues was authorized to be coined by the Act of March 3, 1849. The coin's weight was set at 516 grains, and its fineness at .900. A single twenty-dollar gold specimen of 1849 resides in the Smithsonian.

LIBERTY HEAD (1850–1907)

VF-20 Very Fine: LIBERTY on crown bold; prongs on crown defined; lower half worn flat. Hair worn about ear.

EF-40 Extremely Fine: Trace of wear on rounded prongs of crown and down hair curls. Minor bagmarks.

AU-50 About Uncirculated: Trace of wear on hair over eye and on coronet.

AU-55 Choice About Uncirculated: Evidence of friction on design high points. Some of original mint luster present.

MS-60 Uncirculated: No trace of wear. Light blemishes.

MS-63 Choice Uncirculated: Some distracting marks or blemishes in focal areas. Impaired luster possible.

PF-63 Choice Proof: Reflective surfaces with only a few blemishes in secondary focal areas. No major flaws.

Without Motto on Reverse (1850–1866)

Mintmark is below eagle.

	Mintage	VF-20	EF-40	AU-50	AU-55	MS-60	MS-63	PF-63
1850	1,170,261	$1,650	$2,250	$3,500	$4,500	$120,000	$40,000	
18500	141,000	3,500	6,000	10,000	25,000	45,000		
1851	2,087,155	1,450	1,500	1,625	2,000	3,500	17,000	
18510	315,000	2,000	3,500	5,000	7,500	20,000		
1852	2,053,026	1,450	1,500	1,625	2,000	3,000	12,500	
18520	190,000	1,700	2,500	4,500	6,500	25,000	35,000	
1853	1,261,326	1,450	1,500	1,625	2,000	3,500	20,000	
18530	71,000	2,000	4,500	8,500	12,000	25,000		
1854	757,899	1,450	1,500	1,625	2,500	6,500	20,000	
18540	3,250	80,000	150,000	250,000	300,000			
1854S	141,468	1,650	2,000	6,500	10,000	22,500	35,000	
1855	364,666	1,450	1,500	2,000	2,500	7,000	40,000	
18550	8,000	10,000	25,000	30,000	50,000	85,000		
1855S	879,675	1,450	1,650	1,700	2,000	5,500	15,000	
1856	329,878	1,450	1,500	2,000	3,000	6,000	25,000	
18560	2,250	125,000	200,000	300,000	325,000			
1856S	1,189,750	1,600	1,625	1,635	2,000	4,500	12,500	
1857	439,375	1,450	1,500	1,600	2,000	5,500	25,000	
18570	30,000	3,000	6,500	10,000	15,000	35,000	150,000	
1857S **(a)**	970,500	1,600	1,625	1,650	2,000	3,000	6,000	
1858	211,714	1,600	2,000	1,700	3,000	4,500	25,000	
18580	35,250	3,000	6,500	15,000	20,000	35,000		
1858S	846,710	1,600	1,650	1,750	2,000	7,500		
1859 . . . . (80)	43,597	1,650	2,000	3,250	10,000	22,500		$100,000
18590	9,100	4,000	17,500	30,000	45,000	80,000		
1859S	636,445	1,600	1,625	1,635	2,500	8,500	35,000	
1860 . . . . (59)	577,611	1,600	1,625	1,635	2,000	3,000	10,000	75,000
18600	6,600	8,500	25,000	37,500	45,000	100,000		
1860S	544,950	1,600	1,635	1,675	2,500	5,500	10,000	

a. Different size mintmarks exists; the Large S variety is rarest.

DOUBLE EAGLES ($20)

	Mintage	VF-20	EF-40	AU-50	AU-55	MS-60	MS-63	PF-63
1861 . . . . (66)	2,976,387	$1,500	$1,625	$1,635	$2,000	$2,750	$10,000	$75,000
1861O	17,741	10,000	30,000	45,000	55,000	125,000		
1861S	768,000	1,500	1,650	2,000	2,500	10,000	25,000	
1862 . . . . (35)	92,098	3,000	6,500	8,500	12,500	25,000	27,500	50,000
1862S	854,173	1,500	1,625	1,650	2,500	8,000	30,000	
1863 . . . . (30)	142,760	2,000	3,000	6,500	10,000	20,000	50,000	50,000
1863S	966,570	1,350	1,500	1,650	2,500	6,500	22,500	
1864 . . . . (50)	204,235	2,250	3,500	4,000	6,500	15,000		47,500
1864S	793,660	1,350	1,500	1,650	2,000	6,500	25,000	
1865 . . . . (25)	351,175	1,650	1,650	1,650	2,000	4,500	15,000	47,500
1865S	1,042,500	1,550	1,625	1,650	1,700	4,500	10,000	
1866S	120,000	6,500	14,500	30,000	45,000	115,000		

Motto Above Eagle (1866–1907)
Value TWENTY D. (1866–1876)

	Mintage	VF-20	EF-40	AU-50	AU-55	MS-60	MS-63	PF-63
1866 . . . . (30)	698,745	$1,275	$1,325	$2,000	$3,000	$6,500	$35,000	$42,500
1866S	842,250	1,400	1,500	2,000	5,000	15,000		
1867 . . . . (50)	251,015	1,275	1,300	1,350	2,000	3,500	20,000	42,500
1867S	920,750	1,275	1,300	1,350	1,500	8,000		
1868 . . . . (25)	98,575	1,500	1,600	2,000	4,000	12,500	40,000	42,500
1868S	837,500	1,275	1,300	1,350	1,600	8,500	30,000	
1869 . . . . (25)	175,130	1,275	1,300	1,350	2,500	8,000	25,000	42,500
1869S	686,750	1,275	1,300	1,350	1,425	6,500	32,500	
1870 . . . . (35)	155,150	1,275	1,300	1,750	2,500	12,000	35,000	42,500
1870CC	3,789	150,000	225,000	300,000	325,000			
1870S	982,000	1,275	1,300	1,350	1,425	3,500	22,500	
1871 . . . . (30)	80,120	1,275	1,325	1,350	1,425	5,000	16,000	40,000
1871CC	17,387	10,000	22,500	40,000	50,000	80,000		
1871S	928,000	1,275	1,300	1,350	1,425	3,250	16,000	
1872 . . . . (30)	251,850	1,275	1,300	1,350	1,425	2,500	16,500	40,000
1872CC	26,900	2,750	5,000	10,000	15,000	50,000		
1872S	780,000	1,275	1,300	1,350	1,425	2,250	15,500	
1873 . . . . (25)	1,709,800	1,275	1,300	1,350	1,425	1,450	3,500	42,500
1873CC	22,410	2,750	7,000	12,500	17,500	32,500		
1873S	1,040,600	1,275	1,300	1,350	1,425	1,750	12,500	
1874 . . . . (20)	366,780	1,275	1,300	1,350	1,425	2,000	12,000	42,500
1874CC	115,085	2,000	2,500	4,500	6,500	20,000	45,000	
1874S	1,214,000	1,275	1,300	1,350	1,425	1,600	16,000	
1875 . . . . (20)	295,720	1,275	1,300	1,350	1,425	1,600	4,500	67,500
1875CC	111,151	2,000	2,500	3,000	4,000	8,500	15,000	
1875S	1,230,000	1,275	1,300	1,350	1,425	1,450	7,000	
1876 . . . . (45)	583,860	1,275	1,300	1,350	1,425	1,450	6,500	42,500
1876CC	138,441	2,250	3,000	3,500	4,500	8,500	25,000	
1876S	1,597,000	1,275	1,300	1,350	1,425	1,500	3,500	

Value TWENTY DOLLARS (1877–1907)

	Mintage	VF-20	EF-40	AU-50	AU-55	MS-60	MS-63	PF-63
1877 . . . . (20) . .	397,650	$1,275	$1,285	$1,310	$1,315	$1,325	$8,500	$30,000
1877CC	42,565	2,250	3,000	6,000	5,500	20,000		
1877S	1,735,000	1,275	1,285	1,310	1,315	1,325	10,000	
1878 . . . . (20) . .	543,625	1,275	1,285	1,310	1,315	1,325	6,500	30,000
1878CC	13,180	3,500	6,000	10,000	15,000	35,000		
1878S	1,739,000	1,275	1,285	1,310	1,315	1,325	10,000	
1879 . . . . (30) . .	207,600	1,275	1,285	1,310	1,315	1,500	10,000	30,000
1879CC	10,708	4,500	8,500	15,000	16,500	45,000		
1879O	2,325	20,000	32,500	45,000	45,000	100,000	150,000	
1879S	1,223,800	1,275	1,285	1,310	1,315	1,500	25,000	
1880 . . . . (36) . . .	51,420	1,275	1,285	1,310	1,315	4,000	16,500	30,000
1880S	836,000	1,275	1,285	1,310	1,315	1,450	11,000	
1881 . . . . (61) . . .	2,199	12,500	20,000	32,500	35,000	85,000		30,000
1881S	727,000	1,275	1,285	1,310	1,315	1,450	14,500	
1882 . . . . (59) . . .	571	20,000	40,000	65,000	75,000	100,000	175,000	30,000
1882CC	39,140	2,000	2,500	3,500	4,000	12,000	55,000	
1882S	1,125,000	1,275	1,285	1,310	1,315	1,325	10,000	
1883, Proof only . . . (92)								50,000
1883CC	59,962	2,000	2,500	3,500	4,000	7,500	25,000	
1883S	1,189,000	1,275	1,285	1,310	1,315	1,325	5,500	
1884, Proof only . . . (71)								45,000
1884CC	81,139	2,000	2,500	3,500	4,000	7,500	30,000	
1884S	916,000	1,275	1,285	1,310	1,315	1,325	2,250	
1885 . . . . (77)	751	15,000	20,000	35,000	40,000	55,000	87,500	35,000
1885CC	9,450	3,000	5,500	10,000	15,000	25,000	75,000	
1885S	683,500	1,275	1,285	1,310	1,315	1,325	2,250	
1886 . . . . (106) . . .	1,000	25,000	45,000	55,000	65,000	90,000	125,000	30,000
1887, Proof only . . (121)		1,275						45,000
1887S	283,000	1,275	1,285	1,310	1,315	1,325	12,000	
1888 . . . . (105) . .	226,161	1,275	1,285	1,310	1,315	1,500	6,500	27,500
1888S	859,600	1,275	1,285	1,310	1,315	1,325	2,500	
1889 . . . . (41) . . .	44,070	1,275	1,285	1,310	1,315	1,325	9,000	27,500
1889CC	30,945	2,000	2,000	2,500	4,000	8,500	16,500	
1889S	774,700	1,275	1,285	1,310	1,315	1,325	2,000	
1890 . . . . (55) . . .	75,940	1,275	1,285	1,310	1,315	1,325	5,000	27,500
1890CC	91,209	2,000	1,900	2,100	2,350	6,500	25,000	
1890S	802,750	1,275	1,285	1,310	1,315	1,325	2,750	
1891 . . . . (52) . . .	1,390	10,000	16,500	25,000	35,000	55,000	100,000	27,500
1891CC	5,000	5,500	10,000	11,500	20,000	30,000	40,000	
1891S	1,288,125	1,275	1,285	1,310	1,315	1,325	1,650	
1892 . . . . (93) . . .	4,430	1,750	2,350	3,750	6,500	15,000	27,000	27,500

	Mintage	VF-20	EF-40	AU-50	AU-55	MS-60	MS-63	PF-63
1892CC 27,265		$2,250	$2,500	$3,000	$5,000	$10,000	$27,500	
1892S 930,150		1,275	1,285	1,310	1,315	1,325	1,650	
1893 . . . . (59) 344,280		1,275	1,285	1,310	1,315	1,325	1,650	$27,500
1893CC 18,402		2,000	2,500	3,500	4,500	8,500	30,000	
1893S 996,175		1,275	1,285	1,310	1,315	1,325	2,200	
1894 . . . . (50) 1,368,940		1,275	1,285	1,310	1,315	1,325	1,500	27,500
1894S 1,048,550		1,275	1,285	1,310	1,315	1,325	2,000	
1895 . . . . (51) 1,114,605		1,275	1,285	1,310	1,315	1,325	1,450	27,500
1895S 1,143,500		1,275	1,285	1,310	1,315	1,325	1,500	
1896 . . . . (128) 792,535		1,275	1,285	1,310	1,315	1,325	1,500	27,500
1896S 1,403,925		1,275	1,285	1,310	1,315	1,325	1,550	
1897 . . . . (86) 1,383,175		1,275	1,285	1,310	1,315	1,325	1,450	27,500
1897S 1,470,250		1,275	1,285	1,310	1,315	1,325	1,500	
1898 . . . . (75) 170,395		1,275	1,285	1,310	1,315	1,325	4,000	27,500
1898S 2,575,175		1,275	1,285	1,310	1,315	1,325	150	
1899 . . . . (84) 1,669,300		1,275	1,285	1,310	1,315	1,325	1,350	27,500
1899S 2,010,300		1,275	1,285	1,310	1,315	1,325	1,500	
1900 . . . . (124) 1,874,460		1,275	1,285	1,310	1,315	1,325	1,350	27,500
1900S 2,459,500		1,275	1,285	1,310	1,315	1,325	1,800	
1901 . . . . (96) 111,430		1,275	1,285	1,310	1,315	1,325	1,350	27,500
1901S 1,596,000		1,275	1,285	1,310	1,315	1,325	2,500	
1902 . . . . (114) 31,140		1,275	1,285	1,310	1,315	1,325	9,000	27,500
1902S 1,753,625		1,275	1,285	1,310	1,315	1,325	2,000	
1903 . . . . (158) 287,270		1,275	1,285	1,310	1,315	1,325	1,350	27,500
1903S 954,000		1,275	1,285	1,310	1,315	1,325	1,500	
1904 . . . . (98) 6,256,699		1,275	1,285	1,310	1,315	1,325	1,350	27,500
1904S 5,134,175		1,275	1,285	1,310	1,315	1,325	1,350	
1905 . . . . (92) 58,919		1,275	1,285	1,300	1,450	1,750	7,500	27,500
1905S 1,813,000		1,275	1,285	1,310	1,315	1,325	2,500	
1906 . . . . (94) 69,596		1,275	1,285	1,310	1,315	1,325	5,000	27,500
1906D 620,250		1,275	1,285	1,310	1,315	1,325	3,000	
1906S 2,065,750		1,275	1,285	1,310	1,315	1,325	2,000	
1907 . . . . (78) 1,451,786		1,275	1,285	1,310	1,315	1,325	1,350	27,500
1907D 842,250		1,275	1,285	1,310	1,315	1,325	2,500	
1907S 2,165,800		1,275	1,285	1,310	1,315	1,325	2,200	

SAINT-GAUDENS (1907–1933)

The twenty-dollar gold piece designed by Augustus Saint-Gaudens is considered by many to be the most beautiful United States coin. The first coins issued were slightly more than 12,000 high-relief pieces struck for general circulation. The relief is much higher than that of later issues and the date 1907 is in Roman numerals. A few of the Proof coins were made using the lettered-edge collar from the Ultra High Relief version. These can be distinguished by a pronounced bottom left serif on the N in UNUM, and other minor differences. Flat-relief double eagles were issued later in 1907 with Arabic numerals, and continued through 1933.

The field of the rare, Ultra High Relief experimental pieces is extremely concave and connects directly with the edge without any border, giving it a sharp knifelike appearance. Liberty's skirt shows two folds on the side of her right leg; the Capitol building in the background at left is very small; the sun, on the reverse side, has 14 rays, as opposed to the regular high-relief coins, which have only 13 rays extending from the sun. High-relief Proofs are trial or experimental pieces.

VF-20 Very Fine: Minor wear on Liberty's legs and toes. Eagle's left wing and breast feathers worn.
EF-40 Extremely Fine: Drapery lines on chest visible. Wear on left breast, knee, and below. Eagle's feathers on breast and right wing bold.
AU-50 About Uncirculated: Trace of wear on nose, breast, and knee. Wear visible on eagle's wings.
AU-55 Choice About Uncirculated: Evidence of friction on design high points. Most of mint luster remains.
MS-60 Uncirculated: No trace of wear. Light marks or blemishes.
MS-63 Select Uncirculated: Some distracting contact marks or blemishes in prime focal areas. Impaired luster possible.
Matte PF-63 Choice Proof: Matte surfaces with only a few blemishes in secondary focal places. No major flaws.

Ultra High Relief Pattern, MCMVII (1907)

	PF-67
1907, Ultra High Relief, Plain Edge *(unique)*.	—
1907, Ultra High Relief, Lettered Edge.	—

No Motto IN GOD WE TRUST (1907–1908) and With Motto IN GOD WE TRUST (1908–1933)

High Relief, MCMVII (1907)

	Mintage	VF-20	EF-40	AU-50	AU-55	MS-60	MS-63	PF
1907, High Relief, Roman Numerals (MCMVII), Wire Rim	12,367	$6,000	$8,000	$9,000	$9,500	$12,500	$18,000	—

Arabic Numerals (1907–1933)

No Motto (1907–1908)

With Motto IN GOD
WE TRUST (1908–1933)

Mintmark is on obverse, above date.

1909, 9 Over 8

	Mintage	VF-20	EF-40	AU-50	AU-55	MS-60	MS-63	MATTE PF-63
1907	361,667	$1,250	$1,275	$1,285	$1,300	$1,450	$1,500	
1908	4,271,551	1,250	1,275	1,285	1,300	1,325	1,350	
1908D	663,750	1,250	1,275	1,285	1,300	1,325	1,350	
1908, With Motto (101)	156,258	1,250	1,275	1,285	1,300	1,300	1,600	$22,500
1908D, With Motto	349,500	1,250	1,275	1,285	1,300	1,300	1,600	
1908S, With Motto	22,000	1,700	2,500	4,000	4,500	8,500	15,000	
1909, 9 Over 8	*	1,250	1,275	1,285	1,300	1,325	2,750	
1909 (67)	161,282	1,250	1,275	1,285	1,300	1,325	2,200	22,500
1909D	52,500	1,500	1,600	1,650	1,675	2,000	4,500	
1909S	2,774,925	1,250	1,275	1,285	1,300	1,325	1,350	
1910 (167)	482,000	1,250	1,275	1,285	1,300	1,325	1,350	22,500
1910D	429,000	1,250	1,275	1,285	1,300	1,325	1,350	
1910S	2,128,250	1,250	1,275	1,285	1,300	1,325	1,350	
1911 (100)	197,250	1,250	1,275	1,285	1,300	1,325	1,650	22,500
1911D	846,500	1,250	1,275	1,285	1,300	1,325	1,350	
1911C	775,750	1,250	1,275	1,285	1,300	1,325	1,350	
1912 (74)	149,750	1,250	1,275	1,285	1,300	1,325	1,750	22,500
1913 (58)	168,780	1,250	1,275	1,285	1,300	1,325	2,000	22,500
1913D	393,500	1,250	1,275	1,285	1,300	1,325	1,600	
1913S	34,000	1,450	1,500	1,550	1,600	1,750	3,250	
1914 (70)	95,250	1,250	1,275	1,285	1,300	1,325	2,000	22,500
1914D	453,000	1,250	1,275	1,285	1,300	1,325	1,350	
1914S	1,498,000	1,250	1,275	1,285	1,300	1,325	1,350	
1915 (50)	152,000	1,250	1,275	1,285	1,300	1,325	1,900	25,000
1915S	567,500	1,250	1,275	1,285	1,300	1,325	1,350	
1916S	796,000	1,250	1,275	1,285	1,300	1,325	1,500	
1920	228,250	1,250	1,275	1,285	1,300	1,325	1,600	
1920S	558,000	14,000	20,000	25,000	27,500	40,000	70,000	
1921	528,500	25,000	35,000	45,000	55,000	85,000	200,000	
1922	1,375,500	1,250	1,275	1,285	1,300	1,325	1,350	
1922S	2,658,000	1,550	1,600	1,650	1,700	2,000	3,000	
1923	566,000	1,250	1,275	1,285	1,300	1,325	1,350	
1923D	1,702,250	1,250	1,275	1,285	1,300	1,325	1,350	
1924	4,323,500	1,250	1,275	1,285	1,300	1,325	1,350	
1924D	3,049,500	1,900	2,000	2,100	2,450	3,250	5,500	
1924S	2,927,500	1,900	1,950	2,000	2,350	3,250	7,500	
1925	2,831,750	1,250	1,275	1,285	1,300	1,325	1,350	
1925D	2,938,500	1,650	1,900	2,250	2,800	3,750	7,500	
1925S	3,776,500	1,800	2,250	2,850	3,250	7,850	13,000	
1926	816,750	1,250	1,275	1,285	1,300	1,325	1,350	
1926D	481,000	6,000	8,750	9,500	10,000	11,000	12,500	
1926S	2,041,500	1,850	2,000	2,350	2,750	3,000	4,000	
1927	2,946,750	1,250	1,275	1,285	1,300	1,325	1,350	
1927D	180,000		300,000	350,000	400,000	500,000	850,000	
1927S	3,107,000	4,000	7,000	9,000	12,500	20,000	40,000	
1928	8,816,000	1,250	1,275	1,285	1,300	1,325	1,350	
1929	1,779,750	7,500	10,000	12,000	13,000	17,500	30,000	
1930S	74,000	25,000	35,000	40,000	45,000	50,000	75,000	
1931	2,938,250	7,500	15,000	20,000	22,500	27,000	50,000	
1931D	106,500	7,500	15,000	20,000	25,000	27,500	60,000	
1932	1,101,750	7,500	15,000	20,000	22,500	27,500	60,000	
1933	445,500			None placed in circulation.				

* Included in number below.

Collecting United States commemorative coins is like gathering snapshots for an album of important events, places, and people in the nation's history. Because they represent so many different aspects of America—from wars and Olympic games to presidents and historical landmarks, every collector can assemble a set with its own special significance.

All U.S. commemorative coins are issued as legal tender, though in all cases the precious metal of the coins surpasses their face values. The weight and fineness for commemoratives follow those of standard-issue gold, silver, and clad coins.

CLASSIC COMMEMORATIVE SILVER AND GOLD

(1892–1893) World's Columbian Exposition Half Dollar

	Distribution	AU-50	MS-60	MS-63	MS-65
1892, World's Columbian Exposition half dollar............	950,000	$12	$18	$43	$250
1893, Same type.................................	1,550,405	12	18	43	250

(1893) World's Columbian Exposition, Isabella Quarter Dollar

	Distribution	AU-50	MS-60	MS-63	MS-65
1893, World's Columbian Exposition, Chicago, quarter dollar ..	24,214	$240	$275	$320	$1,000

(1900) Lafayette Dollar

	Distribution	AU-50	MS-60	MS-63	MS-65
1900, Lafayette silver dollar	36,026	$300	$600	$1,100	$4,500

(1903) Louisiana Purchase Exposition

	Distribution	AU-50	MS-60	MS-63	MS-65
1903, Louisiana Purchase / Thomas Jefferson gold dollar	17,500	$350	$425	$560	$900
1903, Louisiana Purchase / William McKinley gold dollar	17,500	350	420	475	875

(1904–1905) Lewis and Clark Exposition

	Distribution	AU-50	MS-60	MS-63	MS-65
1904, Lewis and Clark Exposition gold dollar	10,025	$600	$700	$800	$2,500
1905, Lewis and Clark Exposition gold dollar	10,041	550	675	800	3,500

(1915) Panama-Pacific Exposition

	Distribution	AU-50	MS-60	MS-63	MS-65
1915S, Panama-Pacific Exposition half dollar	27,134	$250	$350	$550	$800
1915S, Panama-Pacific Exposition gold dollar	15,000	375	425	500	950
1915S, Panama-Pacific Exposition gold $2.50	6,749	1,100	1,500	2,750	3,500
1915S, Panama-Pacific Exposition gold $50 Round	483	37,000	50,000	70,000	150,000

Entry continued on next page.

191

(1915) Panama-Pacific Exposition

	Distribution	AU-50	MS-60	MS-63	MS-65
1915S, Panama-Pacific Exposition gold $50 Octagonal 645	$37,000	$47,000	$67,500	$150,000

(1916–1917) McKinley Memorial

	Distribution	AU-50	MS-60	MS-63	MS-65
1916, McKinley Memorial gold dollar. *15,000*	$325	$400	$450	$825
1917, McKinley Memorial gold dollar. *5,000*	360	450	500	900

(1918) Illinois Centennial

	Distribution	AU-50	MS-60	MS-63	MS-65
1918, Illinois Centennial half dollar 100,058	$90	$100	$120	$240

(1920) Maine Centennial

	Distribution	AU-50	MS-60	MS-63	MS-65
1920, Maine Centennial half dollar 50,028	$85	$100	$115	$250

(1920–1921) Pilgrim Tercentenary

With 1921 in Field
on Obverse

	Distribution	AU-50	MS-60	MS-63	MS-65
1920, Pilgrim Tercentenary half dollar..................	152,112	$55	$65	$70	$130
1921, Same, With Date Added in Field	20,053	110	120	135	180

(1921) Missouri Centennial

With 2★4 in Field

	Distribution	AU-50	MS-60	MS-63	MS-65
1921, Missouri Centennial half dollar, "2★4" in Field	9,400	$400	$475	$700	$1,200
1921, Missouri Centennial half dollar, Plain................	11,400	270	325	550	1,000

(1921) Alabama Centennial

Without 2X2 in Field

	Distribution	AU-50	MS-60	MS-63	MS-65
1921, Alabama Centennial half dollar, With "2X2" in Field of Obverse.....	6,006	$190	$220	$290	$950
1921, Alabama Centennial half dollar, Plain........................	16,014	110	140	285	735

Star in Field

(1922) Grant Memorial

	Distribution	AU-50	MS-60	MS-63	MS-65
1922, Grant Memorial, With Star* half dollar	4,256	$650	$850	$1,100	$4,000
1922, Same type, No Star in Obverse Field	67,405	75	85	110	375
1922, Grant Memorial, With Star* gold dollar	5,016	950	1,000	1,200	1,500
1922, Grant Memorial, No Star in Obverse Field	5,016	900	950	1,000	1,400

* Fake stars usually have a flattened spot on the reverse.

(1923) Monroe Doctrine Centennial

	Distribution	AU-50	MS-60	MS-63	MS-65
1923S, Monroe Doctrine Centennial half dollar	274,077	$38	$55	$85	$650

(1924) Huguenot-Walloon Tercentenary

	Distribution	AU-50	MS-60	MS-63	MS-65
1924, Huguenot-Walloon Tercentenary half dollar	142,080	$85	$90	$110	$175

(1925) Lexington-Concord Sesquicentennial

	Distribution	AU-50	MS-60	MS-63	MS-65
1925, Lexington-Concord Sesquicentennial half dollar.......	162,013	$50	$60	$70	$250

(1925) Stone Mountain Memorial

	Distribution	AU-50	MS-60	MS-63	MS-65
1925, Stone Mountain Memorial half dollar..............	1,314,709	$30	$37	$55	$125

(1925) California Diamond Jubilee

	Distribution	AU-50	MS-60	MS-63	MS-65
1925S, California Diamond Jubilee half dollar..............	86,594	$110	$130	$140	$350

(1925) Fort Vancouver Centennial

	Distribution	AU-50	MS-60	MS-63	MS-65
1925, Fort Vancouver Centennial half dollar	14,994	$210	$235	$260	$425

(1926) Sesquicentennial of American Independence

	Distribution	AU-50	MS-60	MS-63	MS-65
1926, Sesquicentennial of American Independence half dollar	141,120	$50	$65	$85	$1,250
1926, Sesquicentennial of American Independence gold $2.50.....	46,019	280	325	400	1,400

(1926–1939) Oregon Trail Memorial

	Distribution	AU-50	MS-60	MS-63	MS-65
1926, Oregon Trail Memorial half dollar...................	47,955	$95	$110	$125	$160
1926S, Same type, S Mint.............................	83,055	95	110	125	160
1928, Oregon Trail Memorial half dollar (same as 1926).......	6,028	100	110	125	180
1933D, Oregon Trail Memorial half dollar	5,008	240	250	275	325
1934D, Oregon Trail Memorial half dollar	7,006	120	130	135	210
1936, Oregon Trail Memorial half dollar...................	10,006	105	115	125	170
1936S, Same type, S Mint.............................	5,006	110	120	125	170
1937D, Oregon Trail Memorial half dollar	12,008	110	125	135	170
1938, Oregon Trail Memorial half dollar (same as 1926).......	6,006				
1938D, Same type, D Mint	6,005	*Set:*	375	400	600
1938S, Same type, S Mint.............................	6,006				
1939, Oregon Trail Memorial half dollar (same as 1926).......	3,004				
1939D, Same type, D Mint	3,004	*Set:*	1,000	1,100	1,300
1939S, Same type, S Mint.............................	3,005				
Oregon Trail Memorial half dollar, single type coin		95	110	130	160

(1927) Vermont Sesquicentennial

	Distribution	AU-50	MS-60	MS-63	MS-65
1927, Vermont Sesquicentennial (Battle of Bennington) half dollar ..	28,142	$170	$175	$200	$350

COMMEMORATIVES

(1928) Hawaiian Sesquicentennial

	Distribution	AU-50	MS-60	MS-63	MS-65
1928, Hawaiian Sesquicentennial half dollar	10,008	$1,200	$1,475	$1,700	$2,800
1928, Hawaiian Sesquicentennial, Sandblast Proof Presentation Piece	(50)			15,000	20,000

(1934) Maryland Tercentenary

	Distribution	AU-50	MS-60	MS-63	MS-65
1934, Maryland Tercentenary half dollar	25,015	$90	$105	$110	$150

(1934–1938) Texas Independence Centennial

	Distribution	AU-50	MS-60	MS-63	MS-65
1934, Texas Independence Centennial half dollar	61,463	$90	$100	$110	$140
1935, Texas Independence Centennial half dollar (same as 1934)	9,996				
1935D, Same type, D Mint	10,007	Set:	300	325	450
1935S, Same type, S Mint	10,008				
1936, Texas Independence Centennial half dollar (same as 1934)	8,911				
1936D, Same type, D Mint	9,039	Set:	300	325	450
1936S, Same type, S Mint	9,055				
1937, Texas Independence Centennial half dollar (same as 1934)	6,571				
1937D, Same type, D Mint	6,605	Set:	300	325	450
1937S, Same type, S Mint	6,637				

Chart continued on next page.

	Distribution	AU-50	MS-60	MS-63	MS-65
1938, Texas Independence Centennial half dollar (same as 1934)..... 3,780					
1938D, Same type, D Mint 3,775	Set:	$460	$480	$850
1938S, Same type, S Mint................................. 3,814					
Texas Independence Centennial half dollar, single type coin		$90	100	110	140

(1934–1938) Daniel Boone Bicentennial   **1934 Added on Reverse**

	Distribution	AU-50	MS-60	MS-63	MS-65
1934, Daniel Boone Bicentennial half dollar................... 10,007		$90	$100	$110	$120
1935, Daniel Boone Bicentennial half dollar................... 10,010					
1935D, Same type, D Mint 5,005	Set:		300	325	375
1935S, Same type, S Mint................................. 5,005					
1935, Same as 1934 but Small 1934 on reverse................ 10,008					
1935D, Same type, D Mint 2,003	Set:		500	550	1,100
1935S, Same type, S Mint................................. 2,004					
1936, Daniel Boone Bicentennial half dollar (same as preceding) 12,012					
1936D, Same type, D Mint 5,005	Set:		300	350	500
1936S, Same type, S Mint................................. 5,006					
1937, Daniel Boone Bicentennial half dollar (same as preceding) 9,810					
1937D, Same type, D Mint 2,506	Set:		310	500	700
1937S, Same type, S Mint................................. 2,506					
1938, Daniel Boone Bicentennial half dollar (same as preceding) 2,100					
1938D, Same type, D Mint 2,100	Set:		650	750	1,000
1938S, Same type, S Mint................................. 2,100					
Daniel Boone Bicentennial half dollar, single type coin		90	100	110	115

(1935) Connecticut Tercentenary

	Distribution	AU-50	MS-60	MS-63	MS-65
1935, Connecticut Tercentenary half dollar................. 25,018	$150	$160	$180	$300

COMMEMORATIVES

**(1935–1939)
Arkansas Centennial**

	Distribution	AU-50	MS-60	MS-63	MS-65
1935, Arkansas Centennial half dollar 13,012					
1935D, Same type, D Mint 5,505		*Set:*	$200	$205	$330
1935S, Same type, S Mint. 5,506					
1936, Arkansas Centennial half dollar (same as 1935 but 1936 on rev) 9,660					
1936D, Same type, D Mint 9,660		*Set:*	200	210	350
1936S, Same type, S Mint. 9,662					
1937, Arkansas Centennial half dollar (same as 1936) 5,505					
1937D, Same type, D mint 5,505		*Set:*	225	240	500
1937S, Same type, S mint. 5,506					
1938, Arkansas Centennial half dollar (same as 1935) 3,156					
1938D, Same type, D Mint 3,155		*Set:*	300	325	750
1938S, Same type, S Mint. 3,156					
1939, Arkansas Centennial half dollar (same as 1935) 2,104					
1939D, Same type, D Mint 2,104		*Set:*	475	550	1,600
1939S, Same type, S Mint. 2,105					
Arkansas Centennial half dollar, single type coin		$60	65	70	150

**(1936) Arkansas
Centennial – Robinson**

	Distribution	AU-50	MS-60	MS-63	MS-65
1936, Arkansas Centennial (Robinson) half dollar 25,265	$70	$80	$100	$140

**(1935) Hudson, New
York, Sesquicentennial**

	Distribution	AU-50	MS-60	MS-63	MS-65
1935, Hudson, New York, Sesquicentennial half dollar 10,008	$500	$575	$650	$775

(1935–1936) California-Pacific International Exposition

	Distribution	AU-50	MS-60	MS-63	MS-65
1935S, California-Pacific International Exposition half dollar . . . 70,132		$65	$70	$75	$90
1936D, California-Pacific International Exposition half dollar . . . 30,092		65	70	75	95

(1935) Old Spanish Trail

	Distribution	AU-50	MS-60	MS-63	MS-65
1935, Old Spanish Trail half dollar. 10,008		$750	$800	$900	$950

(1936) Providence, Rhode Island, Tercentenary

	Distribution	AU-50	MS-60	MS-63	MS-65
1936, Providence, Rhode Island, Tercentenary half dollar 20,013					
1936D, Same type, D Mint 15,010		*Set:*	$200	$225	$300
1936S, Same type, S Mint. 15,011					
Providence, Rhode Island, Tercentenary half dollar, single type coin . . .		$60	65	75	100

(1936) Cleveland Centennial / Great Lakes Exposition

	Distribution	AU-50	MS-60	MS-63	MS-65
1936, Cleveland Centennial / Great Lakes Exposition half dollar	50,030	$65	$75	$80	$100

(1936) Wisconsin Territorial Centennial

	Distribution	AU-50	MS-60	MS-63	MS-65
1936, Wisconsin Territorial Centennial half dollar	25,015	$110	$120	$130	$160

(1936) Cincinnati Music Center

	Distribution	AU-50	MS-60	MS-63	MS-65
1936, Cincinnati Music Center half dollar	5,005				
1936D, Same type, D Mint	5,005	*Set:*	$650	$750	$950
1936S, Same type, S Mint.	5,006				
Cincinnati Music Center half dollar, single type coin		$190	220	250	325

(1936) Long Island Tercentenary

	Distribution	AU-50	MS-60	MS-63	MS-65
1936, Long Island Tercentenary half dollar	81,826	$50	$60	$65	$130

(1936) York County, Maine, Tercentenary

	Distribution	AU-50	MS-60	MS-63	MS-65
1936, York County, Maine, Tercentenary half dollar.	25,015	$105	$110	$120	$175

(1936) Bridgeport, Connecticut, Centennial

	Distribution	AU-50	MS-60	MS-63	MS-65
1936, Bridgeport, Connecticut, Centennial half dollar	25,015	$80	$85	$90	$125

(1936) Lynchburg, Virginia, Sesquicentennial

	Distribution	AU-50	MS-60	MS-63	MS-65
1936, Lynchburg, Virginia, Sesquicentennial half dollar.	20,013	$160	$170	$180	$210

(1936) Elgin, Illinois, Centennial

	Distribution	AU-50	MS-60	MS-63	MS-65
1936, Elgin, Illinois, Centennial half dollar	20,015	$125	$130	$150	$170

(1936) Albany, New York, Charter

	Distribution	AU-50	MS-60	MS-63	MS-65
1936, Albany, New York, Charter half dollar	17,671	$150	$160	$175	$210

(1936) San Francisco – Oakland Bay Bridge Opening

	Distribution	AU-50	MS-60	MS-63	MS-65
1936S, San Francisco–Oakland Bay Bridge Opening half dollar . .	71,424	$115	$120	$135	$170

(1936) Delaware Tercentenary

	Distribution	AU-50	MS-60	MS-63	MS-65
1936, Delaware Tercentenary half dollar	20,993	$145	$165	$180	$200

(1936) Columbia, South Carolina, Sesquicentennial

	Distribution	AU-50	MS-60	MS-63	MS-65
1936, Columbia, South Carolina, Sesquicentennial half dollar 9,007					
1936D, Same type, D Mint 8,009	*Set:*	$475	$500	$600
1936S, Same type, S Mint 8,007					
Columbia, South Carolina, Sesquicentennial half dollar, single type coin	$120	140	150	175

(1936) Battle of Gettysburg Anniversary

	Distribution	AU-50	MS-60	MS-63	MS-65
1936, Battle of Gettysburg Anniversary half dollar 26,928	$350	$375	$400	$600

(1936) Norfolk, Virginia, Bicentennial

	Distribution	AU-50	MS-60	MS-63	MS-65
1936, Norfolk, Virginia, Bicentennial half dollar 16,936	$220	$225	$250	$275

COMMEMORATIVES

(1937) Roanoke Island, North Carolina, 350th Anniversary

	Distribution	AU-50	MS-60	MS-63	MS-65
1937, Roanoke Island, North Carolina, 350th Anniversary half dollar	29,030	$90	$95	$115	$170

(1937) Battle of Antietam Anniversary

	Distribution	AU-50	MS-60	MS-63	MS-65
1937, Battle of Antietam Anniversary half dollar	18,028	$400	$450	$475	$500

(1938) New Rochelle, New York, 250th Anniversary

	Distribution	AU-50	MS-60	MS-63	MS-65
1938, New Rochelle, New York, 250th Anniversary half dollar	15,266	$210	$225	$250	$300

(1946) Iowa Centennial

	Distribution	AU-50	MS-60	MS-63	MS-65
1946, Iowa Centennial half dollar	100,057	$50	$60	$70	$90

(1946–1951) Booker T. Washington Memorial

	Distribution	AU-50	MS-60	MS-63	MS-65
1946, Booker T. Washington Memorial half dollar **(a)** 700,546					
1946D, Same type, D Mint 50,000		*Set:*	$40	$48	$110
1946S, Same type, S Mint................................. 500,279					
1947, Booker T. Washington Memorial half dollar (same as 1946) 6,000					
1947D, Same type, D Mint 6,000		*Set:*	55	110	140
1947S, Same type, S Mint................................. 6,000					
1948, Booker T. Washington Memorial half dollar (same as 1946) 8,005					
1948D, Same type, D Mint 8,005		*Set:*	55	120	155
1948S, Same type, S Mint................................. 8,005					
1949, Booker T. Washington Memorial half dollar (same as 1946) 6,004					
1949D, Same type, D Mint 6,004		*Set:*	90	120	300
1949S, Same type, S Mint................................. 6,004					
1950, Booker T. Washington Memorial half dollar (same as 1946) 6,004					
1950D, Same type, D Mint 6,004		*Set:*	55	105	185
1950S, Same type, S Mint................................. 62,091					
1951, Booker T. Washington Memorial half dollar (same as 1946) .. 210,082					
1951D, Same type, D Mint 7,004		*Set:*	60	105	165
1951S, Same type, S Mint................................. 7,004					
Booker T. Washington Memorial, single type coin		$10	12	15	35

a. Minted; quantity melted unknown.

(1951–1954) Carver/Washington Commemorative

	Distribution	AU-50	MS-60	MS-63	MS-65
1951, Carver/Washington half dollar 20,018					
1951D, Same type, D Mint 10,004		*Set:*	$45	$70	$225
1951S, Same type, S Mint........................... 10,004					
1952, Carver/Washington half dollar (same as 1951) 1,106,292					
1952D, Same type, D Mint 8,006		*Set:*	55	70	190
1952S, Same type, S Mint........................... 8,006					

	Distribution	AU-50	MS-60	MS-63	MS-65
1953, Carver/Washington half dollar (same as 1951) 8,003					
1953D, Same type, D Mint 8,003		*Set:*	$60	$75	$170
1953S, Same type, S Mint. 88,020					
1954, Carver/Washington half dollar (same as 1951) 12,006					
1954D, Same type, D Mint 12,006		*Set:*	50	60	130
1954S, Same type, S Mint. 42,024					
Carver/Washington half dollar, single type coin		$10	12	15	40

MODERN COMMEMORATIVES

(1982) George Washington 250th Anniversary of Birth

	Distribution	MS-67	PF-67
1982D, George Washington 250th Anniversary silver half dollar 2,210,458		$7	
1982S, Same type, S Mint, Proof. . . . . (4,894,044)			$7

(1983–1984) Los Angeles Olympiad

	Distribution	MS-67	PF-67
1983P, Discus Thrower silver dollar 294,543		$15	
1983D, Same type, D Mint 174,014		15	
1983S, Same type, S Mint. . . . . (1,577,025) 174,014		15	$16

Entry continued on next page. **207**

(1983–1984) Los Angeles Olympiad

	Distribution	MS-67	PF-67
1984P, Olympic Coliseum silver dollar	217,954	$15	
1984D, Same type, D Mint	116,675	15	
1984S, Same type, S Mint	(1,801,210) 116,675	15	$16
1984P, Olympic Torch Bearers gold $10	(33,309)		600
1984D, Same type, D Mint	(34,533)		600
1984S, Same type, S Mint	(48,551)		600
1984W, Same type, W Mint	(381,085) 75,886	600	600

(1986) Statue of Liberty Centennial

	Distribution	MS-67	PF-67
1986D, Statue of Liberty Centennial clad half dollar	928,008	$2.50	
1986S, Same type, S Mint, Proof	(6,925,627)		$2.50
1986P, Statue of Liberty Centennial silver dollar	723,635	15.00	
1986S, Same type, S Mint, Proof	(6,414,638)		15.00
1986W, Statue of Liberty Centennial gold $5	(404,013) 95,248	300.00	300.00

(1987) U.S. Constitution Bicentennial

	Distribution	MS-67	PF-67
1987P, U.S. Constitution Bicentennial silver dollar	451,629	$15	
1987S, Same type, S Mint, Proof	(2,747,116)		$15
1987W, U.S. Constitution Bicentennial gold $5	(651,659) 214,225	300	300

(1988) Seoul Olympiad

	Distribution	MS-67	PF-67
1988D, Seoul Olympiad silver dollar	191,368	$15	
1988S, Same type, S Mint, Proof	(1,359,366)		$15
1988W, Seoul Olympiad gold $5	(281,465) 62,913	300	300

(1989) Congress Bicentennial

	Distribution	MS-67	PF-67
1989D, Congress Bicentennial clad half dollar	163,753	$4	
1989S, Same type, S Mint, Proof	(767,897)		$4
1989D, Congress Bicentennial silver dollar	135,203	16	
1989S, Same type, S Mint, Proof	(762,198)		18
1989W, Congress Bicentennial gold $5	(164,690) 46,899	300	300

(1990) Eisenhower Centennial

	Distribution	MS-67	PF-67
1990W, Eisenhower Centennial silver dollar	241,669	$22	
1990P, Same type, P Mint, Proof	(1,144,461)		$18

(1991) Mount Rushmore Golden Anniversary

	Distribution	MS-67	PF-67
1991D, Mount Rushmore Golden Anniversary clad half dollar 172,754		$10	
1991S, Same type, S Mint, Proof. . . . . (753,257)			$8
1991P, Mount Rushmore Golden Anniversary silver dollar. 133,139		22	
1991S, Same type, S Mint, Proof. . . . . (738,419)			20
1991W, Mount Rushmore Golden Anniversary gold $5 . . . . (111,991) 31,959		300	300

(1991) Korean War Memorial

	Distribution	MS-67	PF-67
1991D, Korean War Memorial silver dollar. 213,049		$20	
1991P, Same type, P Mint, Proof. . . . . (618,488)			$18

(1991) United Service Organizations

	Distribution	MS-67	PF-67
1991D, USO silver dollar... 124,958		$20	
1991S, Same type, S Mint, Proof..........................(321,275)			$18

(1992) XXV Olympiad

	Distribution	MS-67	PF-67
1992P, XXV Olympiad clad half dollar 161,607		$4	
1992S, Same type, S Mint, Proof..........................(519,645)			$4
1992D, XXV Olympiad silver dollar.................................... 187,552		20	
1992S, Same type, S Mint, Proof..........................(504,505)			18
1992W, XXV Olympiad gold $5 ....(77,313) 27,732		300	300

(1992) White House 200th Anniversary

	Distribution	MS-67	PF-67
1992D, White House 200th Anniversary silver dollar	123,803	$20	
1992W, Same type, W Mint, Proof	(375,851)		$18

(1992) Christopher Columbus Quincentenary

	Distribution	MS-67	PF-67
1992D, Christopher Columbus Quincentenary clad half dollar	135,702	$8	
1992S, Same type, S Mint, Proof	(390,154)		$7
1992D, Christopher Columbus Quincentenary silver dollar	106,949	23	
1992P, Same type, P Mint, Proof	(385,241)		20
1992W, Christopher Columbus Quincentenary gold $5	(79,730) 24,329	300	300

(1993) Bill of Rights

	Distribution	MS-67	PF-67
1993W, Bill of Rights silver half dollar	193,346	$13	
1993S, Same type, S Mint, Proof	(586,315)		$10
1993D, Bill of Rights silver dollar	98,383	24	
1993S, Same type, S Mint, Proof	(534,001)		20
1993W, Bill of Rights gold $5	(78,651) 23,266	300	300

(1991–1995) 50th Anniversary of World War II

	Distribution	MS-67	PF-67
(1993P) 1991–1995 World War II clad half dollar	(317,396) 197,072	$9	$10

(1991–1995) 50th Anniversary of World War II

	Distribution	MS-67	PF-67
(1993D) 1991–1995 World War II silver dollar..................................... 107,240		$30	
(1993W) Same type, W Mint, Proof ....(342,041)			$28
(1993W) 1991–1995 World War II gold $5....................(67,026) 23,672		300	300

(1994) World Cup Tournament

	Distribution	MS-67	PF-67
1994D, World Cup Tournament clad half dollar................................ 168,208		$6	
1994P, Same type, P Mint, Proof...........................(609,354)			$6
1994D, World Cup Tournament silver dollar.................................... 81,524		20	
1994S, Same type, S Mint, Proof...........................(577,090)			20
1994W, World Cup Tournament gold $5 ....(89,614) 22,447		300	300

(1993 [1994]) Thomas Jefferson

	Distribution	MS-67	PF-67
1993 (1994) Thomas Jefferson silver dollar, P Mint......................... 266,927		$18	
1993 (1994) Same type, S Mint, Proof.......................(332,891)			$17

(1994) Vietnam Veterans Memorial

	Distribution	MS-67	PF-67
1994W, Vietnam Veterans Memorial silver dollar............................ 57,290		$35	
1994P, Same type, P Mint, Proof.........................(227,671)			$40

(1994) U.S. Prisoner of War Museum

	Distribution	MS-67	PF-67
1994W, U.S. Prisoner of War Museum silver dollar 54,893		$40	
1994P, Same type, P Mint, Proof.........................(224,449)			$35

(1994) Women in Military Service Memorial

	Distribution	MS-67	PF-67
1994W, Women in Military Service Memorial silver dollar	69,860	$22	
1994P, Same type, P Mint, Proof. . . . . (241,278)			$26

(1994) U.S. Capitol Bicentennial

	Distribution	MS-67	PF-67
1994D, U.S. Capitol Bicentennial silver dollar	68,332	$20	
1994S, Same type, S Mint, Proof. . . . . (279,579)			$20

(1995) Civil War Battlefield Preservation

	Distribution	MS-67	PF-67
1995S, Civil War Battlefield Preservation clad half dollar.	119,520	$16	
1995S, Same type, Proof. . . . . (330,002)			$18

Entry continued on next page.

(1995) Civil War Battlefield Preservation

	Distribution	MS-67	PF-67
1995P, Civil War Battlefield Preservation silver dollar	45,866	$38	
1995S, Same type, S Mint, Proof	(437,114)		$30
1995W, Civil War Battlefield Preservation gold $5	12,735	325	
1995W, Same type, Proof	(55,246)		300

(1995) XXVI Olympiad

	Distribution	MS-67	PF-67
1995S, XXVI Olympiad, Basketball clad half dollar	171,001	$12	
1995S, Same type, Proof	(169,655)		$12
1995S, XXVI Olympiad, Baseball clad half dollar	164,605	11	
1995S, Same type, Proof	(118,087)		14
1996S, XXVI Olympiad, Swimming clad half dollar	49,533	60	
1996S, Same type, Proof	(114,315)		16

	Distribution	MS-67	PF-67
1996S, XXVI Olympiad, Soccer clad half dollar	52,836	$35	
1996S, Same type, Proof	(112,412)		$35
1995D, XXVI Olympiad, Gymnastics silver dollar	42,497	26	
1995P, Same type, P Mint, Proof	(182,676)		20
1995D, XXVI Olympiad, Paralympics silver dollar	28,649	40	
1995P, Same type, P Mint, Proof	(138,337)		22
1995D, XXVI Olympiad, Track and Field silver dollar	24,976	45	
1995P, Same type, P Mint, Proof	(136,935)		25
1995D, XXVI Olympiad, Cycling silver dollar	19,662	60	
1995P, Same type, P Mint, Proof	(118,795)		28
1996D, XXVI Olympiad, Tennis silver dollar	15,983	90	
1996P, Same type, P Mint, Proof	(92,016)		48
1996D, XXVI Olympiad, Paralympics silver dollar	14,497	100	
1996P, Same type, P Mint, Proof	(84,280)		30
1996D, XXVI Olympiad, Rowing silver dollar	16,258	110	
1996P, Same type, P Mint, Proof	(131,090)		40
1996D, XXVI Olympiad, High Jump silver dollar	15,697	120	
1996P, Same type, P Mint, Proof	(124,502)		30
1995W, XXVI Olympiad, Torch Runner gold $5	14,675	325	
1995W, Same type, Proof	(57,442)		330
1995W, XXVI Olympiad, Stadium gold $5	10,579	340	
1995W, Same type, Proof	(43,124)		330
1996W, XXVI Olympiad, Flag Bearer gold $5	9,174	340	
1996W, Same type, Proof	(32,886)		330
1996W, XXVI Olympiad, Cauldron gold $5	9,210	450	
1996W, Same type, Proof	(38,555)		330

(1995) Special Olympics World Games

	Distribution	MS-67	PF-67
1995W, Special Olympics World Games silver dollar	89,301	$18	
1995P, Same type, P Mint, Proof	(351,764)		$20

(1996) National Community Service

	Distribution	MS-67	PF-67
1996S, National Community Service silver dollar.............................. 23,500		$55	
1996S, Same type, Proof.......................................(101,543)............			$22

(1996) Smithsonian Institution 150th Anniversary

	Distribution	MS-67	PF-67
1996D, Smithsonian Institution 150th Anniversary silver dollar 31,320		$40	
1996P, Same type, P Mint, Proof...........................(129,152)............			$28
1996W, Smithsonian Institution 150th Anniversary gold $5...................... 9,068		300	
1996W, Same type, Proof ....(21,772)............			300

(1997) U.S. Botanic Garden

	Distribution	MS-67	PF-67
1997P, U.S. Botanic Garden silver dollar 58,505		$18	
1997P, Same type, Proof...................................(189,671)............			$28

COMMEMORATIVES

(1997) Jackie Robinson

	Distribution	MS-67	PF-67
1997S, Jackie Robinson silver dollar	30,180	$48	
1997S, Same type, Proof	(110,002)		$42
1997W, Jackie Robinson gold $5	5,174	775	
1997W, Same type, Proof	(24,072)		380

(1997) Franklin D. Roosevelt

	Distribution	MS-67	PF-67
1997W, Franklin D. Roosevelt gold $5	11,894	$330	
1997W, Same type, Proof	(29,474)		$300

(1997) National Law Enforcement Officers Memorial

	Distribution	MS-67	PF-67
1997P, National Law Enforcement Officers Memorial silver dollar	28,575	$80	
1997P, Same type, Proof	(110,428)		$40

(1998) Robert F. Kennedy

	Distribution	MS-67	PF-67
1998S, Robert F. Kennedy silver dollar 106,422		$22	
1998S, Same type, Proof. . . . . (99,020)			$32

(1998) Black Revolutionary War Patriots

	Distribution	MS-67	PF-67
1998S, Black Revolutionary War Patriots silver dollar 37,210		$45	
1998S, Same type, Proof. . . . . (75,070)			$35

(1999) Dolley Madison

	Distribution	MS-67	PF-67
1999P, Dolley Madison silver dollar. 89,104		$22	
1999P, Same type, Proof. . . . . (224,403)			$22

COMMEMORATIVES

(1999) George Washington Death Bicentennial

	Distribution	MS-67	PF-67
1999W, George Washington Death Bicentennial gold $5	22,511	$300	
1999W, Same type, Proof	(41,693)		$300

(1999) Yellowstone National Park

	Distribution	MS-67	PF-67
1999P, Yellowstone National Park silver dollar	82,563	$28	
1999P, Same type, Proof	(187,595)		$30

(2000) Library of Congress Bicentennial

	Distribution	MS-67	PF-67
2000P, Library of Congress Bicentennial silver dollar	53,264	$17	
2000P, Same type, Proof	(198,503)		$18
2000W, Library of Congress Bicentennial bimetallic (gold/platinum) $10	7,261	950	
2000W, Same type, Proof	(27,445)		700

(2000) Leif Ericson Millennium

	Distribution	MS-67	PF-67
2000P, Leif Ericson Millennium silver dollar	28,150	$48	
2000P, Same type, Proof.	(144,748)		$35

(2001) American Buffalo Commemorative

	Distribution	MS-67	PF-67
2001D, American Buffalo silver dollar	227,131	$90	
2001P, Same type, P Mint, Proof.	(272,869)		$80

(2001) Capitol Visitor Center

	Distribution	MS-67	PF-67
2001P, U.S. Capitol Visitor Center clad half dollar	99,157	$10	
2001P, Same type, Proof.	(77,962)		$14

(2001) Capitol Visitor Center

	Distribution	MS-67	PF-67
2001P, U.S. Capitol Visitor Center silver dollar	35,380	$20	
2001P, Same type, Proof	(143,793)		$28
2001W, U.S. Capitol Visitor Center gold $5	6,761	400	
2001W, Same type, Proof	(27,652)		300

(2002) Salt Lake Olympic Games

	Distribution	MS-67	PF-67
2002P, Salt Lake Olympic Games silver dollar	40,257	$24	
2002P, Same type, Proof	(166,864)		$22
2002W, Salt Lake Olympic Games gold $5	10,585	300	
2002W, Same type, Proof	(32,877)		300

(2002) West Point Bicentennial

See next page for chart.

225

	Distribution	MS-67	PF-67
2002W, West Point Bicentennial silver dollar	103,201	$18	
2002W, Same type, Proof	(288,293)		$26

(2003) First Flight Centennial

	Distribution	MS-67	PF-67
2003P, First Flight Centennial clad half dollar	57,122	$10	
2003P, Same type, Proof	(109,710)		$12
2003P, First Flight Centennial silver dollar	53,533	28	
2003P, Same type, Proof	(190,240)		30
2003W, First Flight Centennial gold $10	10,009	600	
2003W, Same type, Proof	(21,676)		600

(2004) Thomas Alva Edison

	Distribution	MS-67	PF-67
2004P, Thomas Alva Edison silver dollar	92,510	$20	
2004P, Same type, Proof	(211,055)		$20

(2004) Lewis and Clark Bicentennial

	Distribution	MS-67	PF-67
2004P, Lewis and Clark Bicentennial silver dollar 142,015		$20	
2004P, Same type, Proof..............................(351,989)			$20

(2005) Chief Justice John Marshall

	Distribution	MS-67	PF-67
2005P, Chief Justice John Marshall silver dollar 67,096		$26	
2005P, Same type, Proof..............................(196,753)			$22

(2005) Marine Corps 230th Anniversary

	Distribution	MS-67	PF-67
2005P, Marine Corps 230th Anniversary silver dollar....................... 49,671		$36	
2005P, Same type, Proof..............................(548,810)			$33

(2006) Benjamin Franklin "Scientist"

	Distribution	MS-67	PF-67
2006P, Benjamin Franklin "Scientist" silver dollar	58,000	$22	
2006P, Same type, Proof	(142,000)		$22

(2006) Benjamin Franklin "Founding Father"

	Distribution	MS-67	PF-67
2006P, Benjamin Franklin "Founding Father" silver dollar	58,000	$20	
2006P, Same type, Proof	(142,000)		$20

(2006) San Francisco Old Mint Centennial

	Distribution	MS-67	PF-67
2006S, San Francisco Old Mint Centennial silver dollar	67,100	$27	
2006S, Same type, Proof	(160,870)		$25
2006S, San Francisco Old Mint Centennial gold $5	17,500	300	
2006S, Same type, Proof	(44,174)		300

(2007) Jamestown 400th Anniversary

	Distribution	MS-67	PF-67
2007P, Jamestown 400th Anniversary silver dollar	81,034	$22	
2007P, Same type, Proof	(260,363)		$22
2007W, Jamestown 400th Anniversary gold $5	10,623	300	
2007W, Same type, Proof	(47,123)		300

(2007) Little Rock Central High School Desegregation

	Distribution	MS-67	PF-67
2007P, Little Rock Central High School Desegregation silver dollar	124,678	$20	
2007P, Same type, Proof	(66,093)		$18

(2008) Bald Eagle Recovery and National Emblem

	Distribution	MS-67	PF-67
2008S, Bald Eagle Recovery and National Emblem clad half dollar	120,180	$10	
2008S, Same type, Proof	(220,577)		$12

Entry continued on next page.

(2008) Bald Eagle Recovery and National Emblem

	Distribution	MS-67	PF-67
2008P, Bald Eagle Recovery and National Emblem silver dollar.................. 119,204		$20	
2008P, Same type, Proof................................(294,601)			$18
2008W, Bald Eagle Recovery and National Emblem gold $5 19,009		300	
2008W, Same type, Proof ....(59,269)			300

(2009) Louis Braille Bicentennial

	Distribution	MS-67	PF-67
2009P, Louis Braille Bicentennial silver dollar 82,639		$19	
2009P, Same type, Proof................................(135,235)			$18

(2009) Abraham Lincoln Bicentennial

	Distribution	MS-67	PF-67
2009P, Abraham Lincoln Bicentennial silver dollar 125,000		$24	
2009P, Same type, Proof................................(325,000)			$28

COMMEMORATIVES

	Distribution	MS-67	PF-67
2010W, American Veterans Disabled for Life silver dollar	78,301	$25	
2010W, Same type, Proof	(202,770)		$23
2010P, Boy Scouts of America Centennial silver dollar	105,020	20	
2010P, Same type, Proof	(244,963)		22
2011S, Medal of Honor silver dollar	44,752	32	
2011P, Same type, P Mint, Proof	(112,883)		32
2011P, Medal of Honor gold $5	8,233	340	
2011W, Same type, W Mint, Proof	(17,999)		300
2011D, U.S. Army clad half dollar	39,442	25	
2011S, Same type, S Mint, Proof	(68,332)		35
2011S, U.S. Army silver dollar	43,512	32	
2011P, Same type, P Mint, Proof	(119,829)		30
2011P, U.S. Army gold $5	8,052	300	
2011W, Same type, W Mint, Proof	(17,148)		300
2012W, Infantry Soldier silver dollar	44,348	28	
2012W, Same type, Proof	(161,151)		34
2012P, Star-Spangled Banner silver dollar	41,686	30	
2012P, Same type, Proof	(169,065)		30
2012W, Star-Spangled Banner gold $5	7,027	330	
2012W, Same type, Proof	(18,313)		300
2013W, Girl Scouts of the U.S.A. Centennial silver dollar	37,462	26	
2013W, Same type, Proof	(86,355)		30
2013D, 5-Star Generals clad half dollar	38,095	15	
2013S, Same type, S Mint, Proof	(47,326)		24
2013W, 5-Star Generals silver dollar	34,638	40	
2013P, Same type, P Mint, Proof	(69,283)		38
2013P, 5-Star Generals gold $5	5,667	375	
2013W, Same type, W Mint, Proof	(15,844)		345
2014D, National Baseball Hall of Fame clad half dollar	176,446	18	
2014S, Same type, S Mint, Proof	(257,173)		16
2014P, National Baseball Hall of Fame silver dollar	131,924	35	
2014P, Same type, Proof	(268,076)		40
2014W, National Baseball Hall of Fame gold $5	17,677	360	
2014W, Same type, Proof	(32,427)		360
2014P, Civil Rights Act of 1964 silver dollar	24,720	40	
2014P, Same type, Proof	(61,992)		45
2015D, U.S. Marshals Service 225th Anniversary clad half dollar	30,231	14	
2015S, Same type, S Mint, Proof	(76,549)		16
2015P, U.S. Marshals Service 225th Anniversary silver dollar	38,149	35	
2015P, Same type, Proof	(124,329)		40
2015W, U.S. Marshals Service 225th Anniversary gold $5	6,743	330	
2015W, Same type, Proof	(24,959)		335
2015P, March of Dimes 75th Anniversary silver dollar	24,742	35	
2015W, Same type, W Mint, Proof	(132,030)		30
2016P, Mark Twain silver dollar	*26,281*	30	
2016P, Same type, Proof	*(78,536)*		30

Chart continued on next page.

	Distribution	MS-67	PF-67
2016W, Mark Twain $5 gold coin	5,695	$320	
2016W, Same type, Proof	(13,266)		$325
2016D, National Park Service 100th Anniversary half dollar	21,019	15	
2016S, Same type, S Mint, Proof	(54,844)		18
2016P, National Park Service 100th Anniversary silver dollar	20,994	30	
2016P, Same type, Proof	(77,309)		28
2016W, National Park Service 100th Anniversary $5 gold coin	5,150	325	
2016W, Same type, Proof	(19,506)		325
2017P, Lions Club International Century of Service silver dollar	17,247	35	
2017P, Same type, Proof	(68,519)		32
2017S, Boys Town Centennial half dollar	15,525	20	
2017D, Same type, D Mint, Proof	(23,164)		22
2017P, Boys Town Centennial silver dollar	12,234	35	
2017P, Same type, Proof	(31,610)		38
2017W, Boys Town Centennial $5 gold coin	2,947	325	
2017W, Same type, Proof	(7,347)		335
2018P, World War I Centennial silver dollar	22,340	35	
2018P, Same type, Proof	(127,848)		40
2018D, Breast Cancer Awareness half dollar	11,301	15	
2018S, Same type, S Mint, Proof	(22,393)		18
2018P, Breast Cancer Awareness silver dollar	12,526	35	
2018P, Same type, Proof	(34,543)		40
2018W, Breast Cancer Awareness $5 gold coin	4,477	325	
2018W, Same type, Proof	(10,387)		335
2019D, Apollo 11 50th Anniversary clad half dollar			
2019S, Same type, S Mint, Proof			
2019P, Apollo 11 50th Anniversary silver dollar			
2019P, Same type, Proof			
2019W, Apollo 11 50th Anniversary $5 gold coin			
2019W, Same type, Proof			
2019P, Apollo 11 50th Anniversary 5-oz. Proof silver dollar			
2019D, American Legion 100th Anniversary clad half dollar			
2019S, Same type, S Mint, Proof			
2019P, American Legion 100th Anniversary silver dollar			
2019P, Same type, Proof			
2019W, American Legion 100th Anniversary $5 gold coin			
2019W, Same type, Proof			

GOVERNMENT COMMEMORATIVE SETS

Values are for commemorative coins and sets in all of their original packaging.

	Value
(1983–1984) Los Angeles Olympiad	
1983 and 1984 Proof dollars	$32
1983 and 1984 6-coin set. One each of 1983 and 1984 dollars, both Proof and Unc. gold $10 **(a)**	1,260
1983 3-piece collector set. 1983 P, D, and S Uncirculated dollars	50
1984 3-piece collector set. 1984 P, D, and S Uncirculated dollars	50
1983 and 1984 gold and silver Uncirculated set. One each of 1983 and 1984 Uncirculated dollar and one 1984 Uncirculated gold $10	630

a. Packaged in cherrywood box.

	Value
(1983–1984) Los Angeles Olympiad (continued)	
1983 and 1984 gold and silver Proof set. One each of 1983 and 1984	
Proof dollars and one 1984 Proof gold $10	$630
(1986) Statue of Liberty	
2-coin set. Proof silver dollar and clad half dollar	16
3-coin set. Proof silver dollar, clad half dollar, and gold $5	315
2-coin set. Uncirculated silver dollar and clad half dollar	16
2-coin set. Uncirculated and Proof gold $5	620
3-coin set. Uncirculated silver dollar, clad half dollar, and gold $5	315
6-coin set. One each of Proof and Uncirculated half dollar, silver dollar, and gold $5 **(a)**	620
(1987) Constitution	
2-coin set. Uncirculated silver dollar and gold $5	315
2-coin set. Proof silver dollar and gold $5	315
4-coin set. One each of Proof and Uncirculated silver dollar and gold $5 **(a)**	640
(1988) Seoul Olympiad	
2-coin set. Uncirculated silver dollar and gold $5	315
2-coin set. Proof silver dollar and gold $5	315
4-coin set. One each of Proof and Uncirculated silver dollar and gold $5 **(a)**	640
(1989) Congress	
2-coin set. Proof clad half dollar and silver dollar	23
3-coin set. Proof clad half dollar, silver dollar, and gold $5	325
2-coin set. Uncirculated clad half dollar and silver dollar	20
3-coin set. Uncirculated clad half dollar, silver dollar, and gold $5	325
6-coin set. One each of Proof and Uncirculated clad half dollar, silver dollar, and gold $5 **(a)**	640
(1991) Mount Rushmore	
2-coin set. Uncirculated clad half dollar and silver dollar	32
2-coin set. Proof clad half dollar and silver dollar	28
3-coin set. Uncirculated clad half dollar, silver dollar, and gold $5	330
3-coin set. Proof half dollar, silver dollar, and gold $5	325
6-coin set. One each of Proof and Uncirculated clad half dollar, silver dollar, and gold $5 **(a)**	660
(1992) XXV Olympiad	
2-coin set. Uncirculated clad half dollar and silver dollar	27
2-coin set. Proof clad half dollar and silver dollar	25
3-coin set. Uncirculated clad half dollar, silver dollar, and gold $5	330
3-coin set. Proof half dollar, silver dollar, and gold $5	330
6-coin set. One each of Proof and Uncirculated clad half dollar, silver dollar, and gold $5 **(a)**	660
(1992) Christopher Columbus	
2-coin set. Uncirculated clad half dollar and silver dollar	32
2-coin set. Proof clad half dollar and silver dollar	27
3-coin set. Uncirculated clad half dollar, silver dollar, and gold $5	330
3-coin set. Proof half dollar, silver dollar, and gold $5	330
6-coin set. One each of Proof and Uncirculated clad half dollar, silver dollar, and gold $5 **(a)**	660
(1993) Bill of Rights	
2-coin set. Uncirculated silver half dollar and silver dollar	36
2-coin set. Proof silver half dollar and silver dollar	30
3-coin set. Uncirculated silver half dollar, silver dollar, and gold $5	335
3-coin set. Proof half dollar, silver dollar, and gold $5	330
6-coin set. One each of Proof and Uncirculated silver half dollar, silver dollar, and gold $5 **(a)**	665
"Young Collector" set. Silver half dollar	10
Educational set. Silver half dollar and James Madison medal	15
Proof silver half dollar and 25-cent stamp	10

a. Packaged in cherrywood box.

Chart continued on next page.

	Value
(1993) World War II	
2-coin set. Uncirculated clad half dollar and silver dollar...........................	$38
2-coin set. Proof clad half dollar and silver dollar	40
3-coin set. Uncirculated clad half dollar, silver dollar, and gold $5	335
3-coin set. Proof clad half dollar, silver dollar, and gold $5......................	340
6-coin set. One each of Proof and Uncirculated clad half dollar, silver dollar, and gold $5 **(a)**	675
"Young Collector" set. Clad half dollar...................................	10
Victory Medal set. Uncirculated clad half dollar and reproduction medal	10
(1993) Thomas Jefferson	
"Coinage and Currency" 3-piece set (issued in 1994). Silver dollar, Jefferson nickel, and $2 note	40
(1994) World Cup Soccer	
2-coin set. Uncirculated clad half dollar and silver dollar..........................	26
2-coin set. Proof clad half dollar and silver dollar	26
3-coin set. Uncirculated clad half dollar, silver dollar, and gold $5	335
3-coin set. Proof clad half dollar, silver dollar, and gold $5......................	335
6-coin set. One each of Proof and Uncirculated clad half dollar, silver dollar, and gold $5 **(a)**.........	670
"Young Collector" set. Uncirculated clad half dollar............................	5
"Special Edition" set. Proof clad half dollar and silver dollar	27
(1994) U.S. Veterans	
3-coin set. Uncirculated POW, Vietnam, and Women in Military Service silver dollars	100
3-coin set. Proof POW, Vietnam, and Women in Military Service silver dollars.....................	95
(1995) Special Olympics	
2-coin set. Proof Special Olympics silver dollar, 1995-S Kennedy half dollar.....................	50
(1995) Civil War Battlefield Preservation	
2-coin set. Uncirculated clad half dollar and silver dollar..........................	52
2-coin set. Proof clad half dollar and silver dollar	50
3-coin set. Uncirculated clad half dollar, silver dollar, and gold $5	380
3-coin set. Proof clad half dollar, silver dollar, and gold $5......................	350
6-coin set. One each of Proof and Uncirculated clad half dollar, silver dollar, and gold $5 **(a)**.........	730
"Young Collector" set. Uncirculated clad half dollar............................	20
2-coin "Union" set. Clad half dollar and silver dollar	60
3-coin "Union" set. Clad half dollar, silver dollar, and gold $5.....................	350
(1995–1996) Centennial Olympic Games	
4-coin set #1. Uncirculated half dollar (Basketball), dollars (Gymnastics, Paralympics), gold $5 (Torch Bearer)	410
4-coin set #2. Proof half dollar (Basketball), dollars (Gymnastics, Paralympics), gold $5 (Torch Bearer)..	385
4-coin set #3. Proof half dollar (Baseball), dollars (Cyclist, Track Runner), gold $5 (Olympic Stadium) ..	390
2-coin set #1: Proof silver dollars (Gymnastics, Paralympics)	45
"Young Collector" set. Uncirculated Basketball, Baseball, Swimming, or Soccer half dollar..........	—
1995–1996 16-coin Uncirculated set. One each of all Uncirculated coins **(a)**	2,250
1995–1996 16-coin Proof set. One each of all Proof coins **(a)**	1,650
1995–1996 8-coin Proof silver dollars set.	250
1995–1996 32-coin set. One each of all Uncirculated and Proof coins **(a)**	3,900
(1996) National Community Service	
Proof silver dollar and Saint-Gaudens stamp....................................	30
(1996) Smithsonian Institution 150th Anniversary	
2-coin set. Proof silver dollar and gold $5....................................	330
4-coin set. One each of Proof and Uncirculated silver dollar and gold $5 **(a)**.....................	660
"Young Collector" set. Proof silver dollar....................................	30
(1997) U.S. Botanic Garden	
"Coinage and Currency" set. Uncirculated silver dollar, Jefferson nickel, and $1 note...............	100

a. Packaged in cherrywood box.

	Value
(1997) Jackie Robinson	
2-coin set. Proof silver dollar and gold $5	$425
4-coin set. One each of Proof and Uncirculated silver dollar and gold $5 **(a)**.	1,250
3-piece "Legacy" set. Baseball card, pin, and gold $5 **(a)**.	400
(1997) Franklin D. Roosevelt	
2-coin set. One each of Proof and Uncirculated gold $5	630
(1997) National Law Enforcement Officers Memorial	
Insignia set. Silver dollar, lapel pin, and patch.	75
(1998) Robert F. Kennedy	
2-coin set. RFK silver dollar and JFK silver half dollar	140
2-coin set. Proof and Uncirculated RFK silver dollars.	55
(1998) Black Revolutionary War Patriots	
2-coin set. Proof and Uncirculated silver dollars	80
"Young Collector" set. Uncirculated silver dollar	50
Black Revolutionary War Patriots set. Silver dollar and four stamps.	55
(1999) Dolley Madison Commemorative	
2-coin set. Proof and Uncirculated silver dollars	44
(1999) George Washington Death	
2-coin set. One each of Proof and Uncirculated gold $5	600
(1999) Yellowstone National Park	
2-coin set. One each of Proof and Uncirculated silver dollars	58
(2000) Leif Ericson Millennium	
2-coin set. Proof silver dollar and Icelandic 1,000 kronur	65
(2000) Millennium Coin and Currency Set	
3-piece set. Uncirculated 2000 Sacagawea dollar; Uncirculated 2000 Silver Eagle;	
George Washington $1 note, series 1999	75
(2001) American Buffalo	
2-coin set. One each of Proof and Uncirculated silver dollar	170
"Coinage and Currency" set. Uncirculated American Buffalo silver dollar, face reprint of 1899	
$5 Indian Chief Silver Certificate, 1987 Chief Red Cloud 10¢ stamp, 2001 Bison 21¢ stamp	100
(2001) U.S. Capitol Visitor Center	
3-coin set. Proof clad half dollar, silver dollar, and gold $5.	340
(2002) Salt Lake Olympic Games	
2-coin set. Proof silver dollar and gold $5.	325
4-coin set. One each of Proof and Uncirculated silver dollar and gold $5	650
(2003) First Flight Centennial	
3-coin set. Proof clad half dollar, silver dollar, and gold $10.	645
(2003) Legacies of Freedom™	
Uncirculated 2003 $1 American Eagle silver bullion coin and an Uncirculated 2002 £2 Silver Britannia coin	40
(2004) Thomas A. Edison	
Edison set. Uncirculated silver dollar and light bulb.	30
(2004) Lewis and Clark	
Coin and Pouch set. Proof silver dollar and beaded pouch.	40
"Coinage and Currency" set. Uncirculated silver dollar, Sacagawea golden dollar, two 2005 nickels,	
replica 1901 $10 Bison note, silver-plated Peace Medal replica, three stamps, two booklets	40
(2004) Westward Journey Nickel Series™	
Westward Journey Nickel Series™ Coin and Medal set. Proof Sacagawea golden dollar,	
two 2004 Proof nickels, silver-plated Peace Medal replica	40

a. Packaged in cherrywood box.

Chart continued on next page.

	Value

(2005) Westward Journey Nickel Series™
Westward Journey Nickel Series™ Coin and Medal set. Proof Sacagawea golden dollar,
two 2005 Proof nickels, silver-plated Peace Medal replica $25

(2005) Chief Justice John Marshall
"Coin and Chronicles" set. Uncirculated silver dollar, booklet, BEP intaglio portrait 30

(2005) American Legacy
American Legacy Collection. Proof Marine Corps dollar, Proof John Marshall dollar, 11-piece Proof set . . . 60

(2005) Marine Corps 230th Anniversary
Marine Corps Uncirculated silver dollar and stamp set 40

(2006) Benjamin Franklin
"Coin and Chronicles" set. Uncirculated "Scientist" silver dollar, four stamps,
Poor Richard's Almanack replica, intaglio print 30

(2006) American Legacy
American Legacy Collection. Proof 2006P Benjamin Franklin, Founding Father silver dollar; Proof
2006S San Francisco Old Mint silver dollar; Proof cent, nickel, dime, quarter, half dollar, and dollar . . 55

(2007) American Legacy
American Legacy Collection. 16 Proof coins for 2007: five state quarters; four Presidential dollars;
Jamestown and Little Rock Central High School Desegregation silver dollars; Proof cent, nickel,
dime, half dollar, and dollar. 60

(2007) Little Rock Central High School Desegregation
Little Rock Coin and Medal set. Proof 2007P silver dollar, bronze medal 80

(2008) Bald Eagle
3-piece set. Proof clad half dollar, silver dollar, and gold $5 330
Bald Eagle Coin and Medal Set. Uncirculated silver dollar, bronze medal 30
"Young Collector" set. Uncirculated clad half dollar. 12

(2008) American Legacy
American Legacy Collection. 15 Proof coins for 2008: cent, nickel, dime, half dollar, and dollar;
five state quarters; four Presidential dollars; Bald Eagle dollar. 55

(2009) Louis Braille
Uncirculated silver dollar in tri-folded package 22

(2009) Abraham Lincoln Coin and Chronicles
Four Proof 2009S cents and Abraham Lincoln Proof silver dollar. 50

(2012) Star-Spangled Banner
2-coin set. Proof silver dollar and gold $5 330

(2013) 5-Star Generals
3-coin set. Proof clad half dollar, silver dollar, and gold $5 400
Profile Collection. Uncirculated half dollar and silver dollar, replica of
1962 General MacArthur Congressional Gold Medal 60

(2013) Theodore Roosevelt Coin and Chronicles
Theodore Roosevelt Proof Presidential dollar; silver Presidential medal; National Wildlife
Refuge System Centennial bronze medal; and Roosevelt print. 125

(2013) Girl Scouts of the U.S.A.
"Young Collector" set. Uncirculated silver dollar 35

(2014) Franklin D. Roosevelt Coin and Chronicles
Franklin D. Roosevelt Proof dime and Presidential dollar; bronze Presidential
medal; silver Presidential medal; four stamps; companion booklet 50

(2014) National Baseball Hall of Fame
"Young Collector" set. Uncirculated half dollar 35

	Value
(2014) American $1 Coin and Currency Set 2014-D Native Hospitality Enhanced Uncirculated dollar and $1 Federal Reserve Note	$35
(2015) Harry S. Truman Coin and Chronicles Truman Reverse Proof Presidential dollar, silver Presidential medal, one stamp, information booklet . . .	160
(2015) Dwight D. Eisenhower Coin and Chronicles Eisenhower Reverse Proof Presidential dollar, silver Presidential medal, one stamp, information booklet	105
(2015) John F. Kennedy Coin and Chronicles Kennedy Reverse Proof Presidential dollar, silver Presidential medal, one stamp, information booklet. . .	50
(2015) Lyndon B. Johnson Coin and Chronicles Johnson Reverse Proof Presidential dollar, silver Presidential medal, one stamp, information booklet. . .	55
(2015) March of Dimes Special Silver Set Proof dime and March of Dimes silver dollar, Reverse Proof dime.	50
(2015) American $1 Coin and Currency Set 2015W Native American–Mohawk Ironworkers Enhanced Uncirculated dollar and $1 Federal Reserve Note. .	50
(2016) National Park Service 100th Anniversary 3-coin set. Proof clad half dollar, silver dollar, and gold $5	370
(2016) Ronald Reagan Coin and Chronicles Ronald Reagan Reverse Proof Presidential dollar, 2016W American Eagle silver Proof dollar, Ronald and Nancy Reagan bronze medal, engraved Ronald Reagan Presidential portrait, information booklet.	55
(2016) American $1 Coin and Currency Set 2016-S Code Talkers Enhanced Uncirculated dollar and $1 Federal Reserve Note	50
(2017) Boys Town Centennial 3-coin set. Proof clad half dollar, silver dollar, and gold $5.	395
(2018) Breast Cancer Awareness Coin and Stamp Set Breast Cancer Awareness commemorative Proof half dollar and Proof silver Breast Cancer Awareness stamp	80
(2018) World War I Centennial Silver Dollar and Air Service Medal Set World War I Centennial commemorative Proof silver dollar and Proof silver Air Service medal	80
(2018) World War I Centennial Silver Dollar and Army Medal Set World War I Centennial commemorative Proof silver dollar and Proof silver Army medal.	80
(2018) World War I Centennial Silver Dollar and Coast Guard Medal Set World War I Centennial commemorative Proof silver dollar and Proof silver Coast Guard medal	80
(2018) World War I Centennial Silver Dollar and Marine Corps Medal Set World War I Centennial commemorative Proof silver dollar and Proof silver Marine Corps medal.	80
(2018) World War I Centennial Silver Dollar and Navy Medal Set World War I Centennial commemorative Proof silver dollar and Proof silver Navy medal	80
(2019) Apollo 11 50th Anniversary Half Dollar Set Apollo 11 50th Anniversary commemorative uncirculated and Proof clad half dollars	
(2019) American Legion 100th Anniversary Three-Coin Proof Set American Legion 100th Anniversary commemorative Proof clad half dollar, silver dollar, and gold $5. . .	
(2019) American Legion 100th Anniversary Silver Dollar and American Veterans Medal Set American Legion 100th Anniversary commemorative Proof silver dollar and American Veterans medal. .	
(2019) Native American $1 Coin & Currency Set 2019-W American Indians in Space Enhanced Uncirculated dollar and $1 Federal Reserve Note	
(2019) American Innovation Uncirculated Coin Set Four Uncirculated American Innovation $1 coins.	
(2019) American Innovation $1 Proof Set Four Proof American Innovation $1 Proof coins.	

PROOF COINS AND SETS

Proof coins can usually be distinguished by their sharpness of detail, high wire edge, and extremely brilliant, mirrorlike surface. Proofs are sold by the Mint at a premium.

Proof coins were not struck during 1943–1949 or 1965–1967. Sets from 1936 through 1972 include the cent, nickel, dime, quarter, and half dollar; from 1973 through 1981 the dollar was also included. From 1999 on, Proof sets have included the year's multiple quarter dollars, and since 2000 they have included the Mint's golden dollar coins. *Values shown are for original unblemished sets.*

Figures in parentheses represent the total number of full sets minted.

	Mintage	Issue Price	Current Value		Mintage	Issue Price	Current Value
1936	(3,837)	$1.89	$4,500.00	1981S, Type 1	(4,063,083)	$11.00	$3.25
1937	(5,542)	1.89	2,000.00	1981S, Type 2	*	11.00	190.00
1938	(8,045)	1.89	825.00	1982S	(3,857,479)	11.00	3.25
1939	(8,795)	1.89	725.00	1983S	(3,138,765)	11.00	3.00
1940	(11,246)	1.89	625.00	1983S, Prestige set			
1941	(15,287)	1.89	625.00	(Olympic dollar)	(140,361)	59.00	28.00
1942, Both nickels	(21,120)	1.89	700.00	1984S	(2,748,430)	11.00	3.75
1942, One nickel	*	1.89	600.00	1984S, Prestige set			
1950	(51,386)	2.10	395.00	(Olympic dollar)	(316,680)	59.00	17.00
1951	(57,500)	2.10	375.00	1985S	(3,362,821)	11.00	2.00
1952	(81,980)	2.10	150.00	1986S	(2,411,180)	11.00	3.75
1953	(128,800)	2.10	125.00	1986S, Prestige set (Statue			
1954	(233,300)	2.10	65.00	of Liberty half, dollar)	(599,317)	48.50	17.50
1955, Box pack	(378,200)	2.10	65.00	1987S	(3,792,233)	11.00	2.50
1955, Flat pack	*	2.10	80.00	1987S, Prestige set			
1956	(669,384)	2.10	40.00	(Constitution dollar)	(435,495)	45.00	17.00
1957	(1,247,952)	2.10	18.00	1988S	(3,031,287)	11.00	3.00
1958	(875,652)	2.10	19.00	1988S, Prestige set			
1959	(1,149,291)	2.10	18.00	(Olympic dollar)	(231,661)	45.00	20.00
1960, With LgDt cent	(1,691,602)	2.10	18.00	1989S	(3,009,107)	11.00	2.75
1960, With SmDt cent	*	2.10	19.00	1989S, Prestige set			
1961	(3,028,244)	2.10	15.00	(Congressional half,			
1962	(3,218,019)	2.10	15.00	dollar)	(211,807)	45.00	21.00
1963	(3,075,645)	2.10	15.00	1990S	(2,793,433)	11.00	2.75
1964	(3,950,762)	2.10	15.00	1990S, With No S cent	(3,555)	11.00	3,100.00
1968S	(3,041,506)	5.00	4.50	1990S, With No S cent			
1969S	(2,934,631)	5.00	4.50	(Prestige set)	*	45.00	3,300.00
1970S	(2,632,810)	5.00	7.00	1990S, Prestige set			
1970S, With SmDt cent	*	5.00	55.00	(Eisenhower dollar)	(506,126)	45.00	17.50
1971S	(3,220,733)	5.00	2.25	1991S	(2,610,833)	11.00	2.50
1972S	(3,260,996)	5.00	2.75	1991S, Prestige set (Mt.			
1973S	(2,760,339)	7.00	5.00	Rushmore half, dollar)	(256,954)	59.00	28.00
1974S	(2,612,568)	7.00	6.50	1992S	(2,675,618)	11.00	2.50
1975S, With 1976 quarter,				1992S, Prestige set			
half, and dollar	(2,845,450)	7.00	6.00	(Olympic half, dollar)	(183,293)	56.00	31.00
1976S	(4,149,730)	7.00	5.75	1992S, Silver	(1,009,586)	21.00	13.00
1976S, 3-piece set	(3,998,621)	15.00	14.50	1992S, Silver Premier set	(308,055)	37.00	14.50
1977S	(3,251,152)	9.00	4.50	1993S	(2,409,394)	12.50	3.25
1978S	(3,127,781)	9.00	4.00	1993S, Prestige set (Bill			
1979S, Type 1	(3,677,175)	9.00	5.25	of Rights half, dollar)	(224,045)	57.00	22.50
1979S, Type 2	*	9.00	31.00	1993S, Silver	(570,213)	21.00	17.00
1980S	(3,554,806)	10.00	3.00	1993S, Silver Premier set	(191,140)	37.50	23.00

* Included in number above.

PROOF AND MINT SETS

	Mintage	Issue Price	Current Value
1994S . . . . (2,308,701)		$12.50	$3.25
1994S, Prestige set (World Cup half, dollar) . . . . . . (175,893)		57.00	22.50
1994S, Silver . . . . (636,009)		21.00	16.00
1994S, Silver Premier set (149,320)		37.50	22.50
1995S . . . . (2,010,384)		12.50	6.00
1995S, Prestige set (Civil War half, dollar) . . . . . . (107,112)		57.00	56.00
1995S, Silver . . . . (549,878)		21.00	35.00
1995S, Silver Premier set (130,107)		37.50	35.00
1996S . . . . (1,695,244)		12.50	5.00
1996S, Prestige set (Olympic half, dollar) . . . . (55,000)		57.00	225.00
1996S, Silver . . . . (623,655)		21.00	17.50
1996S, Silver Premier set (151,366)		37.50	20.00
1997S . . . . (1,975,000)		12.50	5.00
1997S, Prestige set (Botanic dollar) . . . . (80,000)		48.00	39.00
1997S, Silver . . . . (605,473)		21.00	21.00
1997S, Silver Premier set (136,205)		37.50	24.00
1998S . . . . (2,086,507)		12.50	6.50
1998S, Silver . . . . (638,134)		21.00	14.50
1998S, Silver Premier set (240,658)		37.50	18.50
1999S, 9-pc set . . . . . . (2,543,401)		19.95	5.25
1999S, 5-pc qtr set. . . . (1,169,958)		13.95	2.75
1999S, Silver 9-pc set . . . (804,565)		31.95	65.00
2000S, 10-pc set . . . . . (3,082,572)		19.95	3.75
2000S, 5-pc qtr set. . . . . . (937,600)		13.95	1.75
2000S, Silver 10-pc set . . (965,421)		31.95	26.00
2001S, 10-pc set . . . . . (2,294,909)		19.95	6.75
2001S, 5-pc qtr set. . . . . . (799,231)		13.95	2.75
2001S, Silver 10-pc set . . (889,697)		31.95	31.00
2002S, 10-pc set . . . . . (2,319,766)		19.95	4.75
2002S, 5-pc qtr set. . . . . . (764,479)		13.95	2.75
2002S, Silver 10-pc set . . (892,229)		31.95	26.00
2003S, 10-pc set . . . . . (2,172,684)		19.95	4.00
2003S, 5-pc qtr set. . . . (1,235,832)		13.95	1.75
2003S, Silver 10-pc set (1,125,755)		31.95	26.00
2004S, 11-pc set . . . . . (1,789,488)		22.95	7.00
2004S, 5-pc qtr set. . . . . . (951,196)		15.95	3.00
2004S, Silver 11-pc set (1,175,934)		37.50	26.00
2004S, Silver 5-pc qtr set (593,852)		23.95	16.50
2005S, 11-pc set . . . . . (2,275,000)		22.95	3.00
2005S, 5-pc qtr set. . . . . . (987,960)		15.95	1.75
2005S, Silver 11-pc set (1,069,679)		37.95	26.00
2005S, Silver 5-pc qtr set (608,970)		23.95	16.50
2006S, 10-pc set . . . . . (2,000,428)		22.95	5.00
2006S, 5-pc qtr set. . . . . . (882,000)		15.95	2.00
2006S, Silver 10-pc set (1,054,008)		37.95	26.00
2006S, Silver 5-pc qtr set (531,000)		23.95	16.50
2007S, 14-pc set . . . . . (1,702,116)		26.95	10.00
2007S, 5-pc qtr set. . . . . . (672,662)		$13.95	$4.75
2007S, 4-pc Pres set . . (1,285,972)		14.95	4.00
2007S, Silver 14-pc set . . (875,050)		44.95	32.00
2007S, Silver 5-pc qtr set (672,662)		25.95	16.50
2008S, 14-pc set . . . . . (1,382,017)		26.95	18.00
2008S, 5-pc qtr set. . . . . . (672,438)		13.95	14.00
2008S, 4-pc Pres set . . . . (836,730)		14.95	8.00
2008S, Silver 14-pc set . . (763,887)		44.95	30.00
2008S, Silver 5-pc qtr set (429,021)		25.95	15.00
2009S, 18-pc set . . . . . (1,482,502)		29.95	16.00
2009S, 6-pc qtr set. . . . . . (630,976)		14.95	3.50
2009S, 4-pc Pres set . . . . (629,585)		14.95	5.00
2009S, Silver 18-pc set . . (697,365)		52.95	34.00
2009S, Silver 6-pc qtr set (299,183)		29.95	19.00
2009S, 4-pc Lincoln Bicentennial set . . . . . . (201,107)		7.95	6.00
2010S, 14-pc set . . . . . (1,100,015)		31.95	24.00
2010S, 5-pc qtr set. . . . . . (276,296)		14.95	8.50
2010S, 4-pc Pres set . . . . (535,397)		15.95	10.00
2010S, Silver 14-pc set . . (585,401)		56.95	34.00
2010S, Silver 5-pc qtr set (274,034)		32.95	16.50
2011S, 14-pc set . . . . . (1,098,835)		31.95	23.00
2011S, 5-pc qtr set. . . . . . (152,302)		14.95	9.00
2011S, 4-pc Pres set . . . . (299,853)		19.95	18.50
2011S, Silver 14-pc set . . (574,175)		67.95	40.00
2011S, Silver 5-pc qtr set (147,901)		39.95	16.50
2012S, 14-pc set . . . . . (794,002)		31.95	80.00
2012S, 5-pc qtr set. . . . . . (148,498)		14.95	10.00
2012S, 4-pc Pres set . . . . (249,265)		18.95	45.00
2012S, Silver 14-pc set . . (395,443)		67.95	165.00
2012S, Silver 8-pc Limited Edition set . . . . . (44,952)		149.95	160.00
2012S, Silver 5-pc qtr set (162,448)		41.95	18.50
2013S, 14-pc set . . . . . . (802,460)		31.95	22.50
2013S, 5-pc qtr set. . . . . . (128,377)		14.95	9.00
2013S, 4-pc Pres set . . . . (266,677)		18.95	12.00
2013S, Silver 14-pc set . . (419,720)		67.95	48.00
2013S, Silver 8-pc Limited Edition set . . . . . (47,971)		139.95	80.00
2013S, Silver 5-pc qtr set (138,451)		41.95	18.50
2014S, 14-pc set . . . . . (680,977)		31.95	23.00
2014S, 5-pc qtr set. . . . . . (109,423)		14.95	9.50
2014S, 4-pc Pres set . . . . (218,976)		18.95	12.00
2014S, Silver 14-pc set . . (404,665)		67.95	38.00
2014S, Silver 8-pc Limited Edition set . . . . . (41,609)		139.95	110.00
2014S, Silver 5-pc qtr set (111,172)		41.95	21.00
2015S, 14-pc set . . . . (662,854)		32.95	24.00
2015S, 5-pc qtr set. . . . . . (99,466)		14.95	8.00
2015S, 4-pc Pres set . . . . (222,068)		18.95	12.00
2015S, Silver 14-pc set . . (387,310)		53.95	38.00

Chart continued on next page.

239

Year	Mintage	Issue Price	Current Value
2015S, Silver 5-pc qtr set *(103,311)*		$31.95	$20.00
2016S, 13-pc set *(595,184)*		31.95	32.00
2016S, 5-pc qtr set *(91,754)*		14.95	8.00
2016S, 3-pc Pres set *(231,559)*		17.95	15.00
2016S, Silver 13-pc set *(369,849)*		52.95	45.00
2016S, Silver 8-pc Limited Edition set *(49,647)*		139.95	90.00
2016S, Silver 5-pc qtr set *(95,649)*		31.95	30.00
2017S, 10-pc set *(568,681)*		31.95	30.00
2017S, 5-pc qtr set *(85,238)*		14.95	10.00
2017S, Silver 10-pc set *(358,093)*		52.95	45.00
2017S, Silver 5-pc qtr set *(84,258)*		31.95	20.00
2017S, Silver 8-pc Limited Edition set *(48,901)*		139.95	90.00

Year	Mintage	Issue Price	Current Value
2018S, 10-pc set *(490,414)*		$27.95	
2018S, 5-pc qtr set *(80,812)*		15.95	
2018S, Silver 10-pc set *(308,999)*		49.95	
2018S, Silver 5-pc qtr set *(74,874)*		33.95	
2018S, 50th Anniv silver 10-pc RevPf set *(199,116)*		54.95	
2018S, Silver 8-pc Limited Edition set *(41,821)*		144.95	
2019S, 10-pc set			
2019S, 5-pc qtr set		15.95	
2019S, Silver 10-pc set			
2019S, Silver 5-pc qtr set		36.95	
2019S, Silver 8-pc Limited Edition set			

UNCIRCULATED MINT SETS

Official Mint Sets are specially packaged by the government for sale to collectors. They contain Uncirculated specimens of each year's coins for every denomination issued from each mint. Scts from 1947 through 1958 contain two examples of each regular-issue coin. No official sets were produced in 1950, 1982, or 1983. Privately assembled sets are valued according to individual coin prices. Only official sets are included in the following list. Unlike the Proof sets, these are normal coins intended for circulation and are not minted with any special consideration for quality. From 1942 to 1946, groups of two coins from each mint were sold in a cloth shipping bag with only minimal protection. Very few of those mailing packages were saved by collectors.

	Mintage	Issue Price	Current Value
1947 P-D-S	*5,000*	$4.87	$1,200
1948 P-D-S	*6,000*	4.92	825
1949 P-D-S	*5,000*	5.45	950
1951 P-D-S	8,654	6.75	760
1952 P-D-S	11,499	6.14	700
1953 P-D-S	15,538	6.14	575
1954 P-D-S	25,599	6.19	310
1955 P-D-S	49,656	3.57	250
1956 P-D	45,475	3.34	250
1957 P-D	34,324	4.40	250
1958 P-D	50,314	4.43	250
1959 P-D	187,000	2.40	35
1960 P-D	260,485	2.40	26
1961 P-D	223,704	2.40	28
1962 P-D	385,285	2.40	28
1963 P-D	606,612	2.40	24
1964 P-D	1,008,108	2.40	24

	Mintage	Issue Price	Current Value
1965*	2,360,000	$4.00	$6.00
1966*	2,261,583	4.00	5.50
1967*	1,863,344	4.00	7.00
1968 P-D-S	2,105,128	2.50	4.00
1969 P-D-S	1,817,392	2.50	4.00
1970 P-D-S	2,038,134	2.50	12.00
1971 P-D-S	2,193,396	3.50	2.50
1972 P-D-S	2,750,000	3.50	2.50
1973 P-D-S	1,767,691	6.00	8.00
1974 P-D-S	1,975,981	6.00	3.75
1975 P-D	1,921,488	6.00	5.00
1776–1976, 3-piece set	4,908,319	9.00	12.00
1976 P-D	1,892,513	6.00	6.00
1977 P-D	2,006,869	7.00	4.00
1978 P-D	2,162,609	7.00	4.00
1979 P-D	2,526,000	8.00	4.00
1980 P-D-S	2,815,066	9.00	5.00

* Special Mint Set.

	Mintage	Issue Price	Current Value
1981 P-D-S	2,908,145	$11.00	$6.00
1984 P-D	1,832,857	7.00	2.50
1985 P-D	1,710,571	7.00	2.50
1986 P-D	1,153,536	7.00	4.50
1987 P-D	2,890,758	7.00	2.50
1988 P-D	1,646,204	7.00	2.50
1989 P-D	1,987,915	7.00	2.25
1990 P-D	1,809,184	7.00	2.25
1991 P-D	1,352,101	7.00	2.50
1992 P-D	1,500,143	7.00	2.50
1993 P-D	1,297,431	8.00	3.00
1994 P-D	1,234,813	8.00	2.25
1995 P-D	1,038,787	8.00	3.00
1996 P-D, Plus			
1996W dime	1,457,949	8.00	10.00
1997 P-D	960,473	8.00	3.25
1998 P-D	1,187,325	8.00	2.50
1999 P-D (18 pieces)	1,243,867	14.95	5.00
2000 P-D (20 pieces)	1,490,160	14.95	5.00
2001 P-D (20 pieces)	1,116,915	14.95	5.00
2002 P-D (20 pieces)	1,139,388	14.95	5.00

	Mintage	Issue Price	Current Value
2003 P-D (20 pieces)	1,001,532	$14.95	$5.50
2004 P-D (22 pieces)	842,507	16.95	5.50
2005 P-D (22 pieces)	1,160,000	16.95	5.50
2006 P-D (20 pieces)	847,361	16.95	5.50
2007 P-D (28 pieces)	895,628	22.95	13.00
2008 P-D (28 pieces)	745,464	22.95	20.00
2009 P-D (36 pieces)	784,614	27.95	16.00
2010 P-D (28 pieces)	583,897	31.95	16.00
2011 P-D (28 pieces)	533,529	31.95	16.00
2012 P-D (28 pieces)	392,224	27.95	45.00
2013 P-D (28 pieces)	376,844	27.95	16.00
2014 P-D (28 pieces)	314,060	27.95	18.00
2015 P-D (28 pieces)	314,029	28.95	19.00
2016 P-D (28 pieces)	296,582	27.95	23.00
2017 P-D (28 pieces)	286,813	26.95	22.00
2017S, 225th Anniversary Enhanced Uncirculated Set (10 pieces)	210,419	29.95	
2018 P-D (20 pieces)	240,770	20.95	
2019 P-D (28 pieces)			

Note: Sets issued from 2005 to 2010 have a special Satin Finish that is somewhat different from the finish on Uncirculated coins made for general circulation.

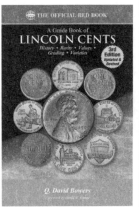

AMERICA THE BEAUTIFUL™ SILVER BULLION COINS

Weight and purity incused on edge.
Actual size 3 inches.

	Mintage	MS	SP
25¢ 2010(P), Hot Springs National Park (Arkansas)	33,000	$95	
25¢ 2010P, Hot Springs National Park (Arkansas)	(26,788)		$135
25¢ 2010(P), Yellowstone National Park (Wyoming)	33,000	110	
25¢ 2010P, Yellowstone National Park (Wyoming)	(26,711)		135
25¢ 2010(P), Yosemite National Park (California)	33,000	110	
25¢ 2010P, Yosemite National Park (California)	(26,716)		135
25¢ 2010(P), Grand Canyon National Park (Arizona)	33,000	95	
25¢ 2010(P), Grand Canyon National Park (Arizona)	(25,967)		135
25¢ 2010(P), Mount Hood National Park (Oregon)	33,000	95	
25¢ 2010P, Mount Hood National Park (Oregon)	(26,637)		110
25¢ 2011(P), Gettysburg National Military Park (Pennsylvania)	126,700	95	
25¢ 2011P, Gettysburg National Military Park (Pennsylvania)	(24,625)		135
25¢ 2011(P), Glacier National Park (Montana)	126,700	95	
25¢ 2011P, Glacier National Park (Montana)	(20,805)		135
25¢ 2011P, Olympic National Park (Washington)	104,900	95	
25¢ 2011P, Olympic National Park (Washington)	(18,345)		135
25¢ 2011P, Vicksburg National Military Park (Mississippi)	58,100	95	
25¢ 2011P, Vicksburg National Military Park (Mississippi)	(18,528)		135
25¢ 2011P, Chickasaw National Recreation Area (Oklahoma)	48,700	95	
25¢ 2011P, Chickasaw National Recreation Area (Oklahoma)	(16,746)		135
25¢ 2012(P), El Yunque National Forest (Puerto Rico)	24,000	120	
25¢ 2012P, El Yunque National Forest (Puerto Rico)	(17,314)		200
25¢ 2012(P), Chaco Culture National Historical Park (New Mexico)	24,400	125	
25¢ 2012P, Chaco Culture National Historical Park (New Mexico)	(17,146)		175
25¢ 2012P, Acadia National Park (Maine)	25,400	175	
25¢ 2012P, Acadia National Park (Maine)	(14,978)		375
25¢ 2012(P), Hawai'i Volcanoes National Park (Hawaii)	20,000	200	
25¢ 2012P, Hawai'i Volcanoes National Park (Hawaii)	(14,863)		500
25¢ 2012(P), Denali National Park and Preserve (Alaska)	20,000	120	
25¢ 2012P, Denali National Park and Preserve (Alaska)	(15,225)		250
25¢ 2013(P), White Mountain National Forest (New Hampshire)	35,000	95	
25¢ 2013P, White Mountain National Forest (New Hampshire)	(20,530)		125
25¢ 2013(P), Perry's Victory and International Peace Memorial (Ohio)	30,000	95	
25¢ 2013P, Perry's Victory and International Peace Memorial (Ohio)	(17,707)		105
25¢ 2013(P), Great Basin National Park (Nevada)	30,000	95	
25¢ 2013P, Great Basin National Park (Nevada)	(17,792)		105
25¢ 2013(P), Ft McHenry Nat'l Monument and Historic Shrine (Maryland)	30,000	95	
25¢ 2013P, Ft McHenry Nat'l Monument and Historic Shrine (Maryland)	(19,802)		105

Note: The U.S. Mint produces the America the Beautiful™ 5-oz. silver coins in bullion and numismatic versions. The bullion version, which lacks the P mintmark, has a brilliant Uncirculated finish and is sold only through dealers. The numismatic version, with the P mintmark, has a matte or burnished finish (although it is not marketed by the Mint as "Burnished"). These coins, designated Specimens (SP) by grading services, are sold directly to the public.

	Mintage	MS	SP
25¢ 2013(P), Mount Rushmore National Memorial (South Dakota)	35,000	$95	
25¢ 2013P, Mount Rushmore National Memorial (South Dakota)	(23,547)		$105
25¢ 2014(P), Great Smoky Mountains National Park (Tennessee)	33,000	95	
25¢ 2014P, Great Smoky Mountains National Park (Tennessee)	(24,710)		105
25¢ 2014(P), Shenandoah National Park (Virginia)	25,000	95	
25¢ 2014P, Shenandoah National Park (Virginia)	(28,451)		105
25¢ 2014(P), Arches National Park (Utah)	22,000	95	
25¢ 2014(P), Arches National Park (Utah)	(28,424)		105
25¢ 2014(P), Great Sand Dunes National Park (Colorado)	22,000	95	
25¢ 2014(P), Great Sand Dunes National Park (Colorado)	(24,103)		105
25¢ 2014(P), Everglades National Park (Florida)	34,000	95	
25¢ 2014(P), Everglades National Park (Florida)	(22,732)		105
25¢ 2015(P), Homestead Nat'l Monument of America (Nebraska)	35,000	95	
25¢ 2015P, Homestead Nat'l Monument of America (Nebraska)	(21,286)		105
25¢ 2015(P), Kisatchie National Forest (Louisiana)	42,000	95	
25¢ 2015P, Kisatchie National Forest (Louisiana)	(19,449)		105
25¢ 2015(P), Blue Ridge Parkway (North Carolina)	45,000	95	
25¢ 2015P, Blue Ridge Parkway (North Carolina)	(17,461)		105
25¢ 2015(P), Bombay Hook National Wildlife Refuge (Delaware)	46,000	95	
25¢ 2015P, Bombay Hook National Wildlife Refuge (Delaware)	(17,309)		105
25¢ 2015(P), Saratoga National Historical Park (New York)	45,000	95	
25¢ 2015P, Saratoga National Historical Park (New York)	(17,563)		105
25¢ 2016P, Shawnee National Forest (Illinois)	105,000	95	
25¢ 2016P, Shawnee National Forest (Illinois)	(18,781)		105
25¢ 2016(P), Cumberland Gap National Historical Park (Kentucky)	75,000	95	
25¢ 2016P, Cumberland Gap National Historical Park (Kentucky)	(18,713)		105
25¢ 2016P, Harpers Ferry National Historical Park (West Virginia)	75,000	95	
25¢ 2016P, Harpers Ferry National Historical Park (West Virginia)	(18,896)		105
25¢ 2016(P), Theodore Roosevelt National Park (North Dakota)	40,000	95	
25¢ 2016P, Theodore Roosevelt National Park (North Dakota)	(18,917)		105
25¢ 2016(P), Fort Moultrie at Fort Sumter National Monument (SC)	35,000	95	
25¢ 2016P, Fort Moultrie at Fort Sumter National Monument (SC)	(17,882)		105
25¢ 2017(P), Effigy Mounds National Monument (Iowa)	35,000	95	
25¢ 2017P, Effigy Mounds National Monument (Iowa)	(17,251)		105
25¢ 2017(P), Frederick Douglass National Historic Site (DC)	20,000	95	
25¢ 2017P, Frederick Douglass National Historic Site (DC)	(17,678)		105
25¢ 2017(P), Ozark National Scenic Riverways (Missouri)	20,000	95	
25¢ 2017P, Ozark National Scenic Riverways (Missouri)	(17,694)		105
25¢ 2017(P), Ellis Island (Statue of Liberty National Monument) (NJ)	40,000	95	
25¢ 2017P, Ellis Island (Statue of Liberty National Monument) (NJ)	(17,670)		105
25¢ 2017(P), George Rogers Clark National Historical Park (Indiana)	35,000	95	
25¢ 2017P, George Rogers Clark National Historical Park (Indiana)	(14,731)		105
25¢ 2018(P), Pictured Rocks National Lakeshore (Michigan)	30,000	95	
25¢ 2018(P), Pictured Rocks National Lakeshore (Michigan)	(17,773)		105
25¢ 2018(P), Apostle Islands National Lakeshore (Wisconsin)	30,000	95	
25¢ 2018(P), Apostle Islands National Lakeshore (Wisconsin)	(16,801)		105
25¢ 2018(P), Voyageurs National Park (Minnesota)	30,000	95	
25¢ 2018P, Voyageurs National Park (Minnesota)	(16,225)		105
25¢ 2018P, Cumberland Island National Seashore (Georgia)	52,500	95	
25¢ 2018P, Cumberland Island National Seashore (Georgia)	(15,437)		105
25¢ 2018(P), Block Island National Wildlife Refuge (Rhode Island)	80,000	95	

Note: The U.S. Mint produces the America the Beautiful™ 5-oz. silver coins in bullion and numismatic versions. The bullion version, which lacks the P mintmark, has a brilliant Uncirculated finish and is sold only through dealers. The numismatic version, with the mintmark, has a matte or burnished finish (although it is not marketed by the Mint as "Burnished"). These coins, designated Specimens (SP) by grading services, are sold directly to the public.

Chart continued on next page.   243

	Mintage	MS	SP
25¢, 2018P, Block Island National Wildlife Refuge (Rhode Island) . . . .*(15,152)*			105
25¢, 2019(P), Lowell National Historical Park (Massachusetts)		$95	
25¢, 2019(P), Lowell National Historical Park (Massachusetts)			105
25¢, 2019(P), American Memorial Park (Northern Mariana Islands)		95	
25¢, 2019(P), American Memorial Park (Northern Mariana Islands)			105
25¢, 2019(P), War in the Pacific National Historical Park (Guam)		95	
25¢, 2019P, War in the Pacific National Historical Park (Guam)			105
25¢, 2019(P), Frank Church River of No Return National Wilderness (Idaho)		95	
25¢, 2019P, Frank Church River of No Return National Wilderness (Idaho)			105
25¢, 2019(P), San Antonio Missions National Historical Park (Texas)		95	
25¢, 2019P, San Antonio Missions National Historical Park (Texas)			105

Note: The U.S. Mint produces the America the Beautiful™ 5-oz. silver coins in bullion and numismatic versions. The bullion version, which lacks the P mintmark, has a brilliant Uncirculated finish and is sold only through dealers. The numismatic version, with the mintmark, has a matte or burnished finish (although it is not marketed by the Mint as "Burnished"). These coins, designated Specimens (SP) by grading services, are sold directly to the public.

$1 AMERICAN SILVER EAGLE COINS

Values below are based on spot silver value of $15.00 per ounce.

	Mintage	Unc.	PF		Mintage	Unc.	PF
$1 1986 5,393,005		$25		$1 1996 3,603,386		$45	
$1 1986S . . . .(1,446,778)			$40	$1 1996P . . . . (500,000)			$40
$1 1987 11,442,335		20		$1 1997 4,295,004		20	
$1 1987S . . . . (904,732)			40	$1 1997P . . . . (435,368)			43
$1 1988 5,004,646		20		$1 1998 4,847,549		20	
$1 1988S . . . . (557,370)			40	$1 1998P . . . . (450,000)			40
$1 1989 5,203,327		18		$1 1999 7,408,640		20	
$1 1989S . . . . (617,694)			40	$1 1999P . . . . (549,769)			40
$1 1990 5,840,210		18		$1 2000(W) 9,239,132		20	
$1 1990S . . . . (695,510)			40	$1 2000P . . . . (600,000)			40
$1 1991 7,191,066		18		$1 2001(W) 9,001,711		18	
$1 1991S . . . . (511,925)			40	$1 2001W . . . . (746,398)			40
$1 1992 5,540,068		18		$1 2002(W) 10,539,026		18	
$1 1992S . . . . (498,654)			40	$1 2002W . . . . (647,32)			40
$1 1993 6,763,762		18		$1 2003(W) 8,495,008		18	
$1 1993P . . . . (405,913)			55	$1 2003W . . . . (747,831)			40
$1 1994 4,227,319		30		$1 2004(W) 8,882,754		18	
$1 1994P . . . . (372,168)			115	$1 2004W . . . . (801,602)			40
$1 1995 4,672,051		25		$1 2005(W) 8,891,025		18	
$1 1995P . . . . (438,511)			40	$1 2005W . . . . (816,663)			40
$1 1995W . . . . (30,125)			3,000	$1 2006(W) 10,676,522		18	

SILVER BULLION

	Mintage	Unc.	PF
$1 2006W, Burnished	468,020	$40	
$1 2006W	(1,092,477)		$40
$1 2006P, Reverse Proof	(248,875)		125
$1 2007(W)	9,028,036	18	
$1 2007W, Burnished	621,333	20	
$1 2007W	(821,759)		40
$1 2008(W)	20,583,000	18	
$1 2008W, Burnished	533,757	28	
$1 2008W, Burnished, Reverse of 2007	47,000	375	
$1 2008W	(700,979)		40
$1 2009(W) (a)	30,459,000	18	
$1 2010(W)	34,764,500	18	
$1 2010W	(849,861)		40
$1 2011(W)(S)	40,020,000	18	
$1 2011W, Burnished	409,776	23	
$1 2011S, Burnished	99,882	150	
$1 2011W	(947,355)		40
$1 2011P, Reverse Proof	(99,882)		200
$1 2012(W)(S)	33,742,500	18	
$1 2012W, Burnished	226,120	41	
$1 2012W	(869,386)		40
$1 2012S, Reverse Proof	(224,981)		75
$1 2012S	(285,184)		40
$1 2013(W)(S)	42,675,000	18	
$1 2013W, Burnished	222,091	$26	
$1 2013W, Enhanced	281,310	62	
$1 2013W	(934,812)		$40
$1 2013W, Reverse Proof	(281,310)		55
$1 2014(W)(S)	44,006,000	18	
$1 2014W, Burnished	253,169	26	
$1 2014W	(944,757)		40
$1 2015(W)(S)	47,000,000	18	
$1 2015W, Burnished	223,879	26	
$1 2015W	(707,518)		40
$1 2016(W)(S)	37,701,500	18	
$1 2016W, Burnished	216,501	26	
$1 2016W	(651,453)		40
$1 2017(W)(S)	18,065,500	18	
$1 2017W, Burnished	176,739	26	
$1 2017W	(440,596)		40
$1 2017S	(123,799)		85
$1 2018(W)(S)	15,700,000	18	
$1 2018W, Burnished	137,306	26	
$1 2018W	(402,669)		40
$1 2018-S	(202,712)		40
$1 2019(W)(S)		18	
$1 2019W, Burnished		30	
$1 2019W			40
$1 2019S			40

Note: "Burnished" refers to special American Eagle Uncirculated coins in silver, gold, and platinum sold directly by the U.S. Mint. Similar in appearance to ordinary Uncirculated American Eagle bullion coins, these coins can be distinguished by the presence of a mintmark and the use of burnished coin blanks. (Proof coins also have a mintmark but have highly reflective, mirrorlike surfaces.) **a.** No Proof dollars were made in 2009. Beware of alterations made privately outside the Mint.

Anniversary Sets

1997 Impressions of Liberty Set **(a)**	$2,400
2006 20th Anniversary Silver Coin Set. Uncirculated, Proof, Reverse Proof	175
2006W 20th Anniversary 1-oz. Gold- and Silver-Dollar Set. Uncirculated	1,275
2011 25th Anniversary Five-Coin Set. 2011W Uncirculated, Proof; 2011P Reverse Proof; 2011S Uncirculated; 2011 Bullion	460
2012 75th Anniversary of San Francisco Mint Two-Piece Set. S-Mint Proof and Reverse Proof silver dollars	105
2013 75th Anniversary of West Point Depository Two-Coin Set. W-Mint Enhanced Uncirculated and Reverse Proof silver dollars	95

a. See under "Gold Bullion Sets."

AMERICAN GOLD EAGLE COINS

Bullion values are based on spot gold at $1,250 per ounce.

$5 Tenth-Ounce Gold

	Mintage	Unc.	PF
$5 MCMLXXXVI (1986)....	912,609	$155	
$5 MCMLXXXVII (1987)...	580,266	155	
$5 MCMLXXXVIII (1988)...	159,500	155	
$5 MCMLXXXVIII (1988)P.	(143,881)		$165
$5 MCMLXXXIX (1989)....	264,790	145	
$5 MCMLXXXIX (1989)P...	(84,647)		165
$5 MCMXC (1990).......	210,210	155	
$5 MCMXC (1990)P	(99,349)		165
$5 MCMXCI (1991)	165,200	155	
$5 MCMXCI (1991)P	(70,334)		165
$5 1992	209,300	145	
$5 1992P	(64,874)		165
$5 1993	210,709	145	
$5 1993P	(58,649)		165
$5 1994	206,380	145	
$5 1994W............	(62,849)		165
$5 1995	223,025	145	
$5 1995W............	(62,667)		165
$5 1996	401,964	145	
$5 1996W............	(57,047)		165
$5 1997	528,266	145	
$5 1997W............	(34,977)		165
$5 1998	1,344,520	145	
$5 1998W............	(39,395)		165
$5 1999	2,750,338	145	
$5 1999W............	(48,428)		165
$5 1999W, Unc. Made from unpolished Proof dies..	14,500	620	
$5 2000	569,153	145	
$5 2000W............	(49,971)		165
$5 2001	269,147	145	
$5 2001W............	(37,530)		165
$5 2002	230,027	145	
$5 2002W............	(40,864)		165
$5 2003	245,029	145	
$5 2003W	(40,027)		$165
$5 2004	250,016	$145	
$5 2004W............	(35,131)		165
$5 2005	300,043	145	
$5 2005W............	(49,265)		165
$5 2006	285,006	145	
$5 2006W, Burnished	20,643	155	
$5 2006W............	(47,277)		165
$5 2007	190,010	145	
$5 2007W, Burnished	22,501	160	
$5 2007W............	(58,553)		165
$5 2008	305,000	155	
$5 2008W, Burnished	12,657	255	
$5 2008W............	(28,116)		165
$5 2009	270,000	155	
$5 2010	435,000	155	
$5 2010W............	(54,285)		165
$5 2011	350,000	155	
$5 2011W............	(42,697)		165
$5 2012	290,000	155	
$5 2012W............	(20,637)		165
$5 2013	555,000	155	
$5 2013W............	(21,738)		165
$5 2014	545,000	155	
$5 2014W............	(22,725)		165
$5 2015	980,000	155	
$5 2015W............	(26,769)		165
$5 2016	925,000	155	
$5 2016W............	(38,889)		165
$5 2017	395,000	155	
$5 2017W............	(20,969)		165
$5 2018	230,000	155	
$5 2018W............	(21,734)		165
$5 2019		155	
$5 2019W.................			165

$10 Quarter-Ounce Gold

	Mintage	Unc.	PF
$10 MCMLXXXVI (1986)...	726,031	$370	
$10 MCMLXXXVII (1987)..	269,255	380	
$10 MCMLXXXVIII (1988)...	49,000	$550	
$10 MCMLXXXVIII (1988)P..	(98,028)		$375

	Mintage	Unc.	PF
$10 MCMLXXXIX (1989)....	81,789	$550	
$10 MCMLXXXIX (1989)P..	(54,170)		$375
$10 MCMXC (1990).......	41,000	600	
$10 MCMXC (1990)P.....	(62,674)		375
$10 MCMXCI (1991).....	36,100	600	
$10 MCMXCI (1991)P	(50,839)		375
$10 1992	59,546	455	
$10 1992P	(46,269)		375
$10 1993	71,864	455	
$10 1993P	(46,464)		375
$10 1994	72,650	455	
$10 1994W	(48,172)		375
$10 1995	83,752	455	
$10 1995W	(47,526)		375
$10 1996	60,318	455	
$10 1996W	(38,219)		375
$10 1997	108,805	355	
$10 1997W	(29,805)		375
$10 1998	309,829	355	
$10 1998W	(29,503)		375
$10 1999	564,232	355	
$10 1999W	(34,417)		375
$10 1999W, Unc. Made from unpolished Proof dies..	10,000	1,150	
$10 2000	128,964	355	
$10 2000W	(36,036)		375
$10 2001	71,280	455	
$10 2001W	(25,613)		375
$10 2002	62,027	455	
$10 2002W	(29,242)		375
$10 2003	74,029	355	
$10 2003W	(30,292)		375
$10 2004	72,014	355	

	Mintage	Unc.	PF
$10 2004W	(28,839)		$375
$10 2005	72,015	$355	
$10 2005W	(37,207)		375
$10 2006	60,004	355	
$10 2006W, Burnished	15,188	475	
$10 2006W	(36,127)		375
$10 2007	34,004	455	
$10 2007W, Burnished	12,766	475	
$10 2007W	(46,189)		375
$10 2008	70,000	350	
$10 2008W, Burnished	8,883	1,100	
$10 2008W	(18,877)		375
$10 2009	110,000	355	
$10 2010	86,000	355	
$10 2010W	(44,057)		375
$10 2011	80,000	355	
$10 2011W	(28,782)		375
$10 2012	90,000	355	
$10 2012W	(13,926)		375
$10 2013	114,500	355	
$10 2013W	(12,782)		375
$10 2014	90,000	355	
$10 2014W	(14,790)		375
$10 2015	158,000	355	
$10 2015W	(15,775)		375
$10 2016	152,000	355	
$10 2016W	(24,405)		375
$10 2017	64,000	355	
$10 2017W	(14,513)		375
$10 2018	62,000	355	
$10 2018W	(12,351)		375
$10 2019		355	
$10 2019W			375

$25 Half-Ounce Gold

	Mintage	Unc.	PF
$25 MCMLXXXVI (1986)...	599,566	$685	
$25 MCMLXXXVII (1987)..	131,255	860	
$25 MCMLXXXVII (1987)P	(143,398)		$725
$25 MCMLXXXVIII (1988)...	45,000	1,285	
$25 MCMLXXXVIII (1988)P..	(76,528)		725
$25 MCMLXXXIX (1989)...	44,829	1,260	
$25 MCMLXXXIX (1989)P..	(44,798)		725
$25 MCMXC (1990).......	31,000	1,460	
$25 MCMXC (1990)P.....	(51,636)		725
$25 MCMXCI (1991)	24,100	2,360	
$25 MCMXCI (1991)P	(53,125)		725
$25 1992	54,404	760	
$25 1992P	(40,976)		725
$25 1993	73,324	685	
$25 1993P	(43,819)		725
$25 1994	62,400	685	
$25 1994W	(44,584)		725
$25 1995	53,474	910	
$25 1995W	(45,388)	725	

	Mintage	Unc.	PF
$25 1996	39,287	$935	
$25 1996W	(35,058)		$725
$25 1997	79,605	685	
$25 1997W	(26,344)		725
$25 1998	169,029	685	
$25 1998W	(25,374)		725
$25 1999	263,013	685	
$25 1999W	(30,427)		725
$25 2000	79,287	685	
$25 2000W	(32,028)		725
$25 2001	48,047	835	
$25 2001W	(23,240)		725
$25 2002	70,027	685	
$25 2002W	(26,646)		725
$25 2003	79,029	685	
$25 2003W	(28,270)		725
$25 2004	98,040	685	
$25 2004W	(27,330)		725
$25 2005	80,023	685	

Chart continued on next page.

	Mintage	Unc.	PF
$25 2005W	(34,311)		$725
$25 2006	66,005	$685	
$25 2006W, Burnished	15,164	785	
$25 2006W	(34,322)		725
$25 2007	47,002	685	
$25 2007W, Burnished	11,455	835	
$25 2007W	(44,025)		725
$25 2008	61,000	685	
$25 2008W, Burnished	15,682	810	
$25 2008W	(22,602)		725
$25 2009	110,000	685	
$25 2010	81,000	685	
$25 2010W	(44,527)		725
$25 2011	70,000	685	
$25 2011W	(26,781)		725
$25 2012	43,000	685	

	Mintage	Unc.	PF
$25 2012W	(12,919)		$725
$25 2013	57,000	$685	
$25 2013W	(12,716)		725
$25 2014	35,000	685	
$25 2014W	(14,693)		725
$25 2015	78,000	685	
$25 2015W	(15,820)		725
$25 2016	71,000	685	
$25 2016W	(23,578)		725
$25 2017	37,000	685	
$25 2017W	(12,715)		725
$25 2018	32,000	685	
$25 2018W	(9,533)		725
$25 2019		685	
$25 2019W			725

$50 One-Ounce Gold

	Mintage	Unc.	PF
$50 MCMLXXXVI (1986)	1,362,650	$1,390	
$50 MCMLXXXVI (1986)W	(446,290)		$1,425
$50 MCMLXXXVII (1987)	1,045,500	1,390	
$50 MCMLXXXVII (1987)W	(147,498)		1,425
$50 MCMLXXXVIII (1988)	465,000	1,390	
$50 MCMLXXXVIII (1988)W	(87,133)		1,425
$50 MCMLXXXIX (1989)	415,790	1,390	
$50 MCMLXXXIX (1989)W	(54,570)		1,425
$50 MCMXC (1990)	373,210	1,390	
$50 MCMXC (1990)W	(62,401)		1,425
$50 MCMXCI (1991)	243,100	1,390	
$50 MCMXCI (1991)W	(50,411)		1,425
$50 1992	275,000	1,390	
$50 1992W	(44,826)		1,425
$50 1993	480,192	1,390	
$50 1993W	(34,369)		1,425
$50 1994	221,633	1,390	
$50 1994W	(46,674)		1,425
$50 1995	200,636	1,390	
$50 1995W	(46,368)		1,425
$50 1996	189,148	1,390	
$50 1996W	(36,153)		1,425
$50 1997	664,508	1,390	
$50 1997W	(32,999)		1,425
$50 1998	1,468,530	1,390	
$50 1998W	(25,886)		1,425
$50 1999	1,505,026	1,390	
$50 1999W	(31,427)		1,425
$50 2000	433,319	1,390	
$50 2000W	(33,007)		1,425
$50 2001	143,605	1,390	
$50 2001W	(24,555)		1,425
$50 2002	222,029	1,390	
$50 2002W	(27,499)		1,425
$50 2003	416,032	1,390	
$50 2003W	(28,344)		1,425

	Mintage	Unc.	PF
$50 2004	417,019	$1,390	
$50 2004W	(28,215)		$1,425
$50 2005	356,555	1,390	
$50 2005W	(35,246)		1,425
$50 2006	237,510	1,390	
$50 2006W, Burnished	45,053	1,425	
$50 2006W	(47,092)		1,425
$50 2006W, Reverse Proof	(9,996)		2,150
$50 2007	140,016	1,390	
$50 2007W, Burnished	18,066	1,450	
$50 2007W	(51,810)		1,425
$50 2008	710,000	1,390	
$50 2008W, Burnished	11,908	1,875	
$50 2008W	(30,237)		1,675
$50 2009	1,493,000	1,390	
$50 2010	1,125,000	1,390	
$50 2010W	(59,480)		1,425
$50 2011	857,000	1,390	
$50 2011W, Burnished	8,729	1,710	
$50 2011W	(48,306)		1,425
$50 2012	675,000	1,390	
$50 2012W, Burnished	6,118	1,750	
$50 2012W	(23,805)		1,425
$50 2013	758,500	1,390	
$50 2013W, Burnished	7,293	1,450	
$50 2013W	(24,709)		1,425
$50 2014	425,000	1,390	
$50 2014W, Burnished	7,902	1,450	
$50 2014W	(28,703)		1,425
$50 2015	594,000	1,390	
$50 2015W, Burnished	6,533	1,450	
$50 2015W	(32,652)		1,425
$50 2016	817,500	1,390	
$50 2016W, Burnished	6,887	1,450	
$50 2016W	(41,621)		1,425
$50 2017	228,500	1,390	

	Mintage	Unc.	PF
$50 2017W, Burnished	8,076	$1,700	
$50 2017W	(19,056)		$1,425
$50 2018	191,000	1,390	
$50 2018W, Burnished	8,076	1,450	

	Mintage	Unc.	PF
$50 2018W	(14,517)		$1,425
$50 2019		$1,390	
$50 2019W, Burnished		1,450	
$50 2019			1,425

Gold Bullion Sets

	PF
1987 Gold Set. $50, $25	$2,450
1988 Gold Set. $50, $25, $10, $5	2,990
1989 Gold Set. $50, $25, $10, $5	2,990
1990 Gold Set. $50, $25, $10, $5	2,990
1991 Gold Set. $50, $25, $10, $5	2,990
1992 Gold Set. $50, $25, $10, $5	2,990
1993 Gold Set. $50, $25, $10, $5	2,990
1993 Bicentennial Gold Set. $25, $10, $5, $1 silver eagle, and medal	1,420
1994 Gold Set. $50, $25, $10, $5	2,990
1995 Gold Set. $50, $25, $10, $5	2,990
1995 Anniversary Gold Set. $50, $25, $10, $5, and $1 silver eagle	5,990
1996 Gold Set. $50, $25, $10, $5	2,990
1997 Gold Set. $50, $25, $10, $5	2,990
1997 Impressions of Liberty Set. $100 platinum, $50 gold, $1 silver	2,795
1998 Gold Set. $50, $25, $10, $5	2,990
1999 Gold Set. $50, $25, $10, $5	2,990

	PF
2000 Gold Set. $50, $25, $10, $5	$2,990
2001 Gold Set. $50, $25, $10, $5	2,990
2002 Gold Set. $50, $25, $10, $5	2,990
2003 Gold Set. $50, $25, $10, $5	2,990
2004 Gold Set. $50, $25, $10, $5	2,990
2005 Gold Set. $50, $25, $10, $5	2,990
2006 Gold Set. $50, $25, $10, $5	2,990
2007 Gold Set. $50, $25, $10, $5	2,990
2008 Gold Set. $50, $25, $10, $5	2,990
2010 Gold Set. $50, $25, $10, $5 **(a)**	2,990
2011 Gold Set. $50, $25, $10, $5	2,990
2012 Gold Set. $50, $25, $10, $5	2,990
2013 Gold Set. $50, $25, $10, $5	2,990
2014 Gold Set. $50, $25, $10, $5	2,990
2015 Gold Set. $50, $25, $10, $5	2,990
2016 Gold Set. $50, $25, $10, $5	2,990
2017 Gold Set. $50, $25, $10, $5	2,990
2018 Gold Set. $50, $25, $10, $5	2,990
2019 Gold Set. $50, $25, $10, $5	2,990

a. The U.S. Mint did not issue a 2009 gold set.

2006 20th Anniversary Sets

2006W $50 Gold Set. Uncirculated, Proof, Reverse Proof	$4,965
2006W 1-oz. Gold and Silver Coin Set. Burnished	1,465

Gold Bullion Burnished Sets 2006–2008

	Unc.
2006W Burnished Gold Set. $50, $25, $10, $5	$2,840
2007W Burnished Gold Set. $50, $25, $10, $5	2,920
2008W Burnished Gold Set. $50, $25, $10, $5	4,022

AMERICAN BUFFALO .9999 FINE GOLD BULLION COINS

	Mintage	Unc.	PF
$5 2008W, Burnished	17,429	$345	

	Mintage	Unc.	PF
$5 2008W	(18,884)		$320

Chart continued on next page

	Mintage	Unc.	PF
$10 2008W, Burnished 9,949		$875	
$10 2008W . . . . (13,125)			$700
$25 2008W, Burnished 16,908		910	
$25 2008W . . . . (12,169)			960
$50 2006 337,012		1,375	
$50 2006W . . . . (246,267)			1,450
$50 2007 136,503		1,375	
$50 2007W . . . . (58,998)			1,450
$50 2008 189,500		1,800	
$50 2008W . . . . (18,863)			2,000
$50 2008W, Burnished 9,074		2,150	
$50 2009 200,000		1,400	
$50 2009W . . . . (49,388)			1,450
$50 2010 209,000		1,400	
$50 2010W . . . . (38,895)			1,450
$50 2011 250,000		1,400	
$50 2011W . . . . (28,693)			1,450
$50 2012 100,000		$1,400	
$50 2012W . . . . (19,765)			$1,450
$50 2013 198,500		1,400	
$50 2013W . . . . (18,594)			1,475
$50 2013W, Reverse Proof (47,836)			1,450
$50 2014 180,500		1,400	
$50 2014W . . . . (20,557)			1,450
$50 2015 223,500		1,400	
$50 2015W . . . . (21,878)			1,450
$50 2016 211,000		1,400	
$50 2016W . . . . (21,878)			1,450
$50 2017 99,500		1,400	
$50 2017W . . . . (15,810)			1,450
$50 2018 121,500		1,400	
$50 2018W . . . . (15,741)			1,450
$50 2019		1,400	
$50 2019W			1,450

American Buffalo Gold Bullion Sets

	Unc.	PF
2008W Four-coin set ($5, $10, $25, $50)	$3,980	$2,000
2008W Four-coin set ($5, $10, $25, $50), Burnished	4,280	
2008W Double Prosperity Set. Uncirculated $25 Buffalo and $25 American Gold Eagle coins . .	1,685	

FIRST SPOUSE $10 GOLD BULLION COINS
Half-Ounce 24-Karat Gold

| Martha Washington | Abigail Adams | Jefferson's Liberty | Dolley Madison |

	Mintage	Unc.	PF
$10 2007W, Martha Washington . . . . (19,167) 17,661		$685	$695
$10 2007W, Abigail Adams . . . . (17,149) 17,142		685	695
$10 2007W, Thomas Jefferson's Liberty . . . . (19,815) 19,823		685	695
$10 2007W, Dolley Madison . . . . (17,943) 12,340		685	695
$10 2008W, Elizabeth Monroe . . . . (7,800) 4,462		685	695
$10 2008W, Louisa Adams . . . . (6,581) 3,885		685	695
$10 2008W, Andrew Jackson's Liberty . . . . (7,684) 4,609		685	695
$10 2008W, Martin Van Buren's Liberty . . . . (6,807) 3,826		685	695
$10 2009W, Anna Harrison . . . . (6,251) 3,645		685	700
$10 2009W, Letitia Tyler . . . . (5,296) 3,240		685	730
$10 2009W, Julia Tyler . . . . (4,844) 3,143		685	730
$10 2009W, Sarah Polk . . . . (5,151) 3,489		685	695

	Mintage	Unc.	PF
$10 2009W, Margaret Taylor	(4,936)	3,627	$685	$695
$10 2010W, Abigail Fillmore	(6,130)	3,482	685	710
$10 2010W, Jane Pierce	(4,775)	3,338	685	695
$10 2010W, James Buchanan's Liberty	(7,110)	5,162	685	695
$10 2010W, Mary Lincoln	(6,861)	3,695	685	695
$10 2011W, Eliza Johnson	(3,887)	2,905	685	695
$10 2011W, Julia Grant	(3,943)	2,892	685	695
$10 2011W, Lucy Hayes	(3,868)	2,196	685	730
$10 2011W, Lucretia Garfield	(3,653)	2,168	685	695
$10 2012W, Alice Paul	(3,505)	2,798	685	695
$10 2012W, Frances Cleveland, Type 1	(3,158)	2,454	685	695
$10 2012W, Caroline Harrison	(3,046)	2,436	685	695
$10 2012W, Frances Cleveland, Type 2	(3,104)	2,425	685	695
$10 2013W, Ida Mckinley	(2,724)	2,008	685	695
$10 2013W, Edith Roosevelt	(2,840)	2,027	685	695
$10 2013W, Helen Taft	(2,598)	1,993	685	695
$10 2013W, Ellen Wilson	(2,511)	1,980	685	695
$10 2013W, Edith Wilson	(2,464)	1,974	685	695
$10 2014W, Florence Harding	(2,372)	1,944	685	695
$10 2014W, Grace Coolidge	(2,315)	1,949	685	695
$10 2014W, Lou Hoover	(2,392)	1,936	685	695
$10 2014W, Eleanor Roosevelt	(2,377)	1,886	685	695
$10 2015W, Elizabeth Truman	(2,747)	1,946	685	695
$10 2015W, Mamie Eisenhower	(2,704)	2,102	690	695
$10 2015W, Jacqueline Kennedy	(11,222)	6,771	690	695
$10 2015W, Claudia Taylor "Lady Bird" Johnson	(2,653)	1,927	690	695
$10 2016W, Pat Nixon	(2,645)	1,839	690	695
$10 2016W, Betty Ford	(2,471)	1,824	690	695
$10 2016W, Nancy Reagan	(3,548)	2,009	690	695

MMIX ULTRA HIGH RELIEF GOLD COIN (2009)

A modern version of the 1907 Ultra High Relief double eagle gold pattern was produced in 2009 at the Philadelphia Mint. It was made to demonstrate technical advances in minting techniques that make possible such a coin. The original design was never made for commercial use because it could not be made in sufficient quantities.

The design was by Augustus Saint-Gaudens. A version of it in much lower relief was used on double eagle coins minted from 1907 to 1933. To create the coin in ultra high relief, the 2009 version was made in a slightly smaller diameter, and composed of 24-karat gold, making it easier to strike and maintain the fidelity of the design. Through 21st-century technology the original Saint-Gaudens plasters were digitally mapped by the Mint and used in the die-making process. The date was changed to 2009, and four additional stars were added to represent the current 50 states. The inscription "In God We Trust" was not used on the 1907 version.

MMIX Ultra High Relief Gold Coin
Photographed at an angle to show the edge, lettered E PLURIBUS UNUM, and the depth of relief.

The MMIX Ultra High Relief gold coins are 4 mm thick and contain one ounce of .999 fine gold. All are Uncirculated (business strikes). All are made at the West Point Mint, and packaged by the Mint in a special mahogany box.

	Mintage	SP
(2009) MMIX Ultra High Relief $20 Gold Coin.	114,427	$1,600

AMERICAN LIBERTY HIGH RELIEF GOLD COINS

The first American Liberty High Relief .9999-fine gold coin, with a weight of one ounce and a face value of $100, was minted at West Point in 2015. The coin was not congressionally mandated, instead being created under authority granted to the Secretary of the Treasury by federal law. Its design was created in part to show "a 'modern' Liberty that reflects the nation's diversity."

The designs for the American Liberty High Relief gold coins are created to take full advantage of the same high-relief techniques used to create the MMIX Ultra High Relief gold coin. The series is slated to continue biennially, with a new design being issued every two years. In the years between gold issues, silver medals featuring the same designs will be issued.

2015

1792–2017W

	Mintage	Unc.	PF
$10 2018W, 1/10 oz.	(27,479)		$132
$100 2015W, 1 oz.	49,325	$1,500	
$100 1792–2017W, 1 oz.	(30,153)		1,650
$100 2019W, 1 oz.			1,650

AMERICAN PLATINUM EAGLE COINS

The one-ounce American Eagle platinum coin is designated $100 and contains one ounce of pure platinum. Fractional denominations containing 1/2 ounce, 1/4 ounce, or 1/10 ounce are called $50, $25, and $10, respectively.

Bullion values are based on spot platinum at $825 per ounce.

Obverse for Bullion and Proof, All Years

Reverse for Bullion, All Years; for Proof in 1997

1998: Eagle Over New England. "Vistas of Liberty" series.

1999: Eagle Above Southeastern Wetlands. "Vistas of Liberty" series.

2000: Eagle Above America's Heartland. "Vistas of Liberty" series.

2001: Eagle Above America's Southwest. "Vistas of Liberty" series.

2002: Eagle Fishing in America's Northwest. "Vistas of Liberty" series.

2003.

2004.

2005.

2006: Legislative Branch. "Foundations of Democracy" series. 253

2007: Executive Branch.
"Foundations of
Democracy" series.

2008: Judicial Branch.
"Foundations of
Democracy" series.

2009: To Form a More Perfect
Union. "Preamble to the
Constitution" series.

2010: To Establish Justice.
"Preamble to the
Constitution" series.

2011: To Insure Domestic
Tranquility. "Preamble to
the Constitution" series.

2012: To Provide for the
Common Defence. "Preamble
to the Constitution" series.

2013: To Promote the
General Welfare. "Preamble
to the Constitution" series.

2014: To Secure the Blessings
of Liberty to Ourselves and
Our Posterity. "Preamble to
the Constitution" series.

2015: Liberty Nurtures
Freedom. "Torches
of Liberty" series.

2016: Portrait
of Liberty. "Torches
of Liberty" series.

Common Reverse.
"Preamble to the Declaration
of Independence" series.

2018. Life.
"Preamble to the Declaration
of Independence" series.

2019. Liberty.
"Preamble to the Declaration
of Independence" series.

$10 Tenth-Ounce Platinum

	Mintage	Unc.	PF
$10 1997	70,250	$95	
$10 1997W	(36,993)		$100
$10 1998	39,525	95	
$10 1998W	(19,847)		100
$10 1999	55,955	95	
$10 1999W	(19,133)		100
$10 2000	34,027	95	
$10 2000W	(15,651)		100
$10 2001	52,017	95	
$10 2001W	(12,174)		100
$10 2002	23,005	95	
$10 2002W	(12,365)		100
$10 2003	22,007	95	
$10 2003W	(9,534)		90

	Mintage	Unc.	PF
$10 2004	15,010	$95	
$10 2004W	(7,161)		$100
$10 2005	14,013	95	
$10 2005W	(8,104)		100
$10 2006	11,001	95	
$10 2006W, Burnished	3,544	300	
$10 2006W	(10,205)		100
$10 2007	13,003	95	
$10 2007W, Burnished	5,556	150	
$10 2007W	(8,176)		100
$10 2008	17,000	95	
$10 2008W, Burnished	3,706	215	
$10 2008W	(5,138)		175

$25 Quarter-Ounce Platinum

	Mintage	Unc.	PF
$25 1997	27,100	$240	
$25 1997W	(18,628)		$260
$25 1998	38,887	240	
$25 1998W	(14,873)		260
$25 1999	39,734	240	
$25 1999W	(13,507)		260
$25 2000	20,054	240	
$25 2000W	(11,995)		260
$25 2001	21,815	240	
$25 2001W	(8,847)		260
$25 2002	27,405	240	
$25 2002W	(9,282)		260
$25 2003	25,207	240	
$25 2003W	(7,044)		260

	Mintage	Unc.	PF
$25 2004	18,010	$240	
$25 2004W	(5,193)		$260
$25 2005	12,013	240	
$25 2005W	(6,592)		260
$25 2006	12,001	240	
$25 2006W, Burnished	2,676	400	
$25 2006W	(7,813)		260
$25 2007	8,402	240	
$25 2007W, Burnished	3,690	400	
$25 2007W	(6,017)		260
$25 2007W, Frosted FREEDOM	(21)		—
$25 2008	22,800	240	
$25 2008W, Burnished	2,481	400	
$25 2008W	(4,153)		425

$50 Half-Ounce Platinum

	Mintage	Unc.	PF
$50 1997	20,500	$490	
$50 1997W	(15,431)		$510
$50 1998	32,415	490	

	Mintage	Unc.	PF
$50 1998W	(13,836)		$510
$50 1999	32,309	$490	
$50 1999W	(11,103)		510

Chart continued on next page.

	Mintage	Unc.	PF
$50 2000	18,892	$490	
$50 2000W	(11,049)		$510
$50 2001	12,815	490	
$50 2001W	(8,254)		510
$50 2002	24,005	490	
$50 2002W	(8,772)		510
$50 2003	17,409	490	
$50 2003W	(7,131)		510
$50 2004	13,236	490	
$50 2004W	(5,063)		980
$50 2005	9,013	490	
$50 2005W	(5,942)		510

	Mintage	Unc.	PF
$50 2006	9,602	$490	
$50 2006W, Burnished	2,577	650	
$50 2006W	(7,649)		$510
$50 2007	7,001	490	
$50 2007W, Burnished	3,635	575	
$50 2007W	(25,519)		510
$50 2007W, Reverse Proof			1,100
$50 2007W, Frosted FREEDOM	(21)		—
$50 2008	14,000	490	
$50 2008W, Burnished	2,253	800	
$50 2008W	(4,020)		850

$100 One-Ounce Platinum

	Mintage	Unc.	PF
$100 1997	56,000	$980	
$100 1997W	(20,851)		$1,025
$100 1998	133,002	980	
$100 1998W	(14,912)		1,025
$100 1999	56,707	980	
$100 1999W	(12,363)		1,025
$100 2000	10,003	980	
$100 2000W	(12,453)		1,025
$100 2001	14,070	980	
$100 2001W	(8,969)		1,025
$100 2002	11,502	980	
$100 2002W	(9,834)		1,025
$100 2003	8,007	980	
$100 2003W	(8,246)		1,025
$100 2004	7,009	980	
$100 2004W	(6,007)		1,025
$100 2005	6,310	980	
$100 2005W	(6,602)		1,025
$100 2006	6,000	980	
$100 2006W, Burnished	3,068	1,500	
$100 2006W	(9,152)		1,025
$100 2007	7,202	980	
$100 2007W, Burnished	4,177	1,350	

	Mintage	Unc.	PF
$100 2007W	(8,363)		$1,025
$100 2007W, Frosted FREEDOM	(12)		—
$100 2008	21,800	$980	
$100 2008W, Burnished	2,876	1,560	
$100 2008W	(4,769)		1,600
$100 2009W	(7,945)		1,025
$100 2010W	(9,871)		1,025
$100 2011W	(14,790)		1,025
$100 2012W	(10,084)		1,025
$100 2013W	(5,745)		1,025
$100 2014	16,900	950	
$100 2014W	(4,596)		1,075
$100 2015W	(3,881)		1,075
$100 2016	20,000	950	
$100 2016W	(9,151)		1,075
$100 2017	20,000	950	
$100 2017W	(8,890)		1,075
$100 2018	30,000	950	
$100 2018W	(13,086)		1,075
$100 2019		900	
$100 2019W			1,075

Platinum Bullion Sets

	Unc.	PF
1997 Platinum Set. $100, $50, $25, $10		$1,950
1998 Platinum Set. $100, $50, $25, $10		1,950
1999 Platinum Set. $100, $50, $25, $10		1,950
2000 Platinum Set. $100, $50, $25, $10		1,950
2001 Platinum Set. $100, $50, $25, $10		1,950
2002 Platinum Set. $100, $50, $25, $10		1,950
2003 Platinum Set. $100, $50, $25, $10		1,950
2004W Platinum Set. $100, $50, $25, $10		1,950
2005W Platinum Set. $100, $50, $25, $10		1,950
2006W Platinum Set. $100, $50, $25, $10		1,950

Prices are for original Uncirculated or Proof pieces with box and papers.

	Unc.	PF
2006W Platinum Burnished Set. $100, $50, $25, $10	$2,400	
2007W Platinum Set. $100, $50, $25, $10		$1,950
2007W Platinum Burnished Set. $100, $50, $25, $10	2,280	
2008W Platinum Set. $100, $50, $25, $10		1,950
2008W Platinum Burnished Set. $100, $50, $25, $10	2,400	

Prices are for original Uncirculated or Proof pieces with box and papers.

American Eagle 10th Anniversary Platinum Set

	Unc.
Two-coin set containing one Proof platinum half-ounce and one Enhanced Reverse Proof half-ounce dated 2007W. Housed in hardwood box with mahogany finish	$1,140

AMERICAN PALLADIUM EAGLE COINS (2017 TO DATE)

Designer Adolph A. Weinman; composition .9995 palladium; net weight 1 oz. pure palladium; diameter 32.7 mm; reeded edge; mints: Philadelphia, West Point.

The American Palladium Eagle features a high-relief obverse design derived from artist Adolph Weinman's Winged Liberty dime of 1916 to 1945. The reverse is a high-relief version of Weinman's 1907 American Institute of Architects gold medal reverse, showing an eagle grasping a branch.

Bullion-strike coins are minted in Philadelphia on an annual basis, and distributed through the Mint's authorized purchasers. A Proof version was struck at the West Point Mint in 2018, and sold by the Mint directly to collectors.

As of this printing, the spot price of palladium is about $1,350/oz.

	Mintage	Unc.	PF
2017	*15,000*	$1,650	
2018W. . . . .*(14,986)*			$1,750
2019W.		1,500	
2019W, Reverse Proof.			1,800

Private coins were circulated in most instances because of a shortage of regular coinage. Some numismatists use the general term *private gold* to refer to coins struck outside of the United States Mint. In the sense that no state or territory had authority to coin money, *private gold* simply refers to those interesting necessity pieces of various shapes, denominations, and degrees of intrinsic worth which were circulated in isolated areas of our country by individuals, assayers, bankers, etc. Some numismatists use the words *territorial* and *state* to cover certain issues because they were coined and circulated in a territory or state. While the state of California properly sanctioned the ingots stamped by F.D. Kohler as state assayer, in no instance were any of the gold pieces struck by authority of any of the territorial governments.

The stamped ingots put out by Augustus Humbert, the United States assayer of gold, were not recognized at the United States Mint as an official issue of coins, but simply as ingots, though Humbert placed the value and fineness on the pieces as an official agent of the federal government.

TEMPLETON REID
Georgia Gold 1830

The first private gold coinage in the 19th century was struck by Templeton Reid, a jeweler and gunsmith, in Milledgeville, Georgia, in July 1830. To be closer to the mines, he moved to Gainesville, where most of his coins were made. Although weights were accurate, Reid's assays were not, and his coins were slightly short of claimed value. Accordingly, he was severely attacked in the newspapers and soon lost the public's confidence. His mint closed before the end of that October.

	VG	VF
1830, $2.50	$30,000	$70,000
1830, $5	75,000	150,000
1830, TEN DOLLARS	145,000	300,000
(No Date) TEN DOLLARS	150,000	350,000

California Gold 1849

1849 TEN DOLLAR CALIFORNIA GOLD *(unique, in Smithsonian collection)*. . . . .

THE BECHTLERS
RUTHERFORD COUNTY, NC, 1831–1852

Two skilled German metallurgists, Christopher Bechtler and his son August, and later Christopher Bechtler, Junior, a nephew of Christopher the elder, operated a private mint at Rutherfordton, North Carolina. Rutherford County, in which Rutherfordton is located, was a principal source of the nation's gold supply from 1790 to 1848.

Christopher Bechtler

	VF	EF	AU	Unc.
ONE DOLLAR CAROLINA, 28.G, N Reversed.	$1,200	$1,750	$2,750	$6,000
ONE GOLD DOLLAR N. CAROLINA, 28.G, No Star.	2,200	3,250	4,500	10,000
ONE GOLD DOLLAR N. CAROLINA, 30.G.	1,350	2,100	3,000	8,000
2.50 CAROLINA, 67.G., 21 CARATS.	3,000	5,000	6,500	11,000
2.50 CAROLINA, 70.G, 20 CARATS.	3,200	5,500	7,000	13,000
2.50 GEORGIA, 64.G, 22 CARATS.	3,500	5,750	8,000	14,000
2.50 NORTH CAROLINA, 75.G., 20 C., RUTHERFORD				
in a Circle. Border of Large Beads.	10,000	15,000	22,500	45,000
2.50 NORTH CAROLINA, 20 C. Without 75.G.	10,000	15,000	22,500	45,000

Without 150.G.

	VF	EF	AU	Unc.
5 DOLLARS NORTH CAROLINA GOLD, 150.G., 20.CARATS	$10,000	$17,000	$30,000	$50,000
Similar, Without 150.G.		—	—	
5 DOLLARS CAROLINA, RUTHERFORD, 140.G., 20 CARATS				
Plain Edge.	3,000	4,500	6,000	10,000
Reeded Edge.	8,500	15,000	20,000	32,000
5 DOLLARS CAROLINA GOLD, RUTHERF., 140.G., 20 CARATS,				
AUGUST 1, 1834	5,000	8,000	15,000	30,000
Similar, but "20" Distant From CARATS.	3,250	5,500	6,500	13,000
5 DOLLARS CAROLINA GOLD, 134.G., 21 CARATS, With Star.	3,000	4,000	5,000	8,500
5 DOLLARS GEORGIA GOLD, RUTHERFORD, 128.G., 22 CARATS	3,250	4,500	7,000	13,000
5 DOLLARS GEORGIA GOLD, RUTHERF, 128.G., 22 CARATS	3,250	4,500	7,000	13,000

August Bechtler

	VF	EF	AU	Unc.
1 DOL:, CAROLINA GOLD, 27.G., 21.C.	$800	$1,200	$1,600	$2,500
5 DOLLARS, CAROLINA GOLD, 134.G:, 21 CARATS	2,700	4,500	6,500	18,000

	VF	EF	AU	Unc.
5 DOLLARS, CAROLINA GOLD, 128.G., 22 CARATS	$6,250	$8,500	$14,000	$24,000
5 DOLLARS, CAROLINA GOLD, 141.G., 20 CARATS	5,500	8,000	13,000	22,000

NORRIS, GREGG & NORRIS
SAN FRANCISCO 1849

Numismatists consider these pieces the first of the California private gold coins. A newspaper account dated May 31, 1849, described a five-dollar gold coin struck at Benicia City, though with the imprint San Francisco, and the private stamp of Norris, Gregg & Norris.

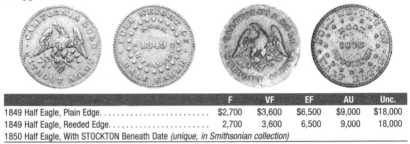

	F	VF	EF	AU	Unc.
1849 Half Eagle, Plain Edge.	$2,700	$3,600	$6,500	$9,000	$18,000
1849 Half Eagle, Reeded Edge.	2,700	3,600	6,500	9,000	18,000
1850 Half Eagle, With STOCKTON Beneath Date *(unique, in Smithsonian collection)*					

MOFFAT & CO.
SAN FRANCISCO 1849–1853

The firm of Moffat & Co. was perhaps the most important of the California private coiners. The assay office they conducted was semi-official in character, and successors to this firm later sold its facilities to the Treasury Department, which used them to create the San Francisco Mint.

In June or July, 1849, Moffat & Co. began to issue small rectangular pieces of gold in values from $9.43 to $264. The $9.43, $14.25, and $16.00 varieties are the only known types. A similar ingot was made by the firm of Meyers & Company at this same time.

	EF
$9.43 Moffat Ingot *(unique, in Smithsonian collection)*.	—
$14.25 Moffat Ingot *(unique, in Smithsonian collection)*.	—
$16.00 Moffat Ingot.	$80,000
$18.00 Meyers Ingot *(unique)*.	—

The dies for the five-dollar and ten-dollar pieces were cut by Albrecht Küner. The words MOFFAT & CO. appear on Liberty's coronet instead of the word LIBERTY as in regular United States issues.

	F	VF	EF	AU	Unc.
1849 FIVE DOL. *(all varieties)*	$900	$1,400	$1,900	$3,000	$7,000
1850 FIVE DOL. *(all varieties)*	900	1,500	2,000	3,200	8,000
1849 TEN DOL.	1,700	2,500	5,000	9,000	18,000
1849 TEN D.	1,800	2,900	6,000	11,000	22,000

UNITED STATES ASSAY OFFICE
Augustus Humbert
United States Assayer of Gold, 1851

When Augustus Humbert was appointed United States assayer, he placed his name and the government imprint on the ingots of gold issued by Moffat & Co. The assay office, a provisional government mint, was a temporary expedient to accommodate the Californians until the establishment of a permanent branch mint. The fifty-dollar gold piece was accepted as legal tender on a par with standard U.S. gold coins.

Lettered Edge Varieties

	F	VF	EF	AU	Unc.
1851 50 D C 880 THOUS., No 50 on Reverse. Sunk in Edge: AUGUSTUS HUMBERT UNITED STATES ASSAYER OF GOLD CALIFORNIA 1851	$10,000	$19,000	$34,000	$52,000	$100,000

50 on Reverse

	F	VF	EF	AU	Unc.
1851 50 D C 880 THOUS, Similar to Last Variety, but					
50 on Reverse...........................	$13,000	$23,000	$37,500	$65,000	$125,000
1851 50 D C 887 THOUS, With 50 on Reverse	12,000	20,000	35,000	55,000	110,000

Reeded Edge Varieties

	F	VF	EF	AU	Unc.
1851 FIFTY DOLLS, 880 THOUS., "Target" Reverse.......	$8,000	$12,000	$18,000	$24,000	$55,000
1851 FIFTY DOLLS, 887 THOUS., "Target" Reverse.......	8,000	12,000	18,000	24,000	55,000
1852 FIFTY DOLLS, 887 THOUS., "Target" Reverse.......	8,500	13,000	19,000	27,000	57,500

Moffat & Co. proceeded in January 1852 to issue a new ten-dollar piece bearing the stamp MOFFAT & CO.

	F	VF	EF	AU	Unc.
1852 TEN D. MOFFAT & CO.........................	$2,000	$3,600	$7,000	$19,000	$39,000

	F	VF	EF	AU	Unc.
1852 TEN DOLS. 1852, 2 Over 1............	$1,500	$2,750	$4,200	$8,000	$15,000
1852 TEN DOLS............................	1,350	2,000	3,000	6,000	13,500

	F	VF	EF	AU	Unc.
1852 TWENTY DOLS., 1852, 2 Over 1........	$4,000	$6,000	$10,000	$21,000	$57,500

United States Assay Office of Gold – 1852

The firm of Moffat & Co. was reorganized by Curtis, Perry, and Ward, who assumed the government contract to conduct the United States Assay Office of Gold.

	F	VF	EF	AU	Unc.
1852 FIFTY DOLLS., 887 THOUS.............	$7,500	$12,000	$18,000	$22,000	$46,000
1852 FIFTY DOLLS., 900 THOUS.............	8,000	13,000	20,000	25,000	50,000

	F	VF	EF	AU	Unc.
1852 TEN DOLS., 884 THOUS..........................	$1,000	$1,650	$2,500	$4,000	$9,000
1853 TEN D., 884 THOUS..........................	3,500	7,000	13,500	18,000	35,000
1853 TEN D., 900 THOUS..........................	2,000	3,000	4,000	7,000	10,000
1853 TWENTY D., 884 THOUS.	3,500	5,000	9,000	14,000	26,000
1853 TWENTY D., 900 THOUS.	1,200	1,500	2,000	3,000	6,500

Moffat & Company Gold

The last Moffat issue was an 1853 twenty-dollar piece that is very similar to the U.S. double eagle of that period. It was struck after the retirement of John L. Moffat from Moffat & Company.

	F	VF	EF	AU	Unc.
1853, TWENTY D.	$2,200	$3,500	$5,500	$9,000	$19,000

CINCINNATI MINING & TRADING CO. (1849)

The origin and location of this company are unknown. It might have been organized in Ohio, and conducted business in California.

	EF	Unc.
1849 FIVE DOLLARS	—	—
1849 TEN DOLLARS.	$450,000	—

MASSACHUSETTS AND CALIFORNIA COMPANY

This company was believed to have been organized in Northampton, Massachusetts, in May 1849. Pieces with 5D are not genuine.

	F	VF	EF
1849 FIVE D.	$65,000	$95,000	$160,000

MINERS' BANK
SAN FRANCISCO 1849

The institution of Wright & Co., exchange brokers located in Portsmouth Square, San Francisco, was known as the Miners' Bank.

A ten-dollar piece was issued in the autumn of 1849, but the coins were not readily accepted because they were worth less than face value.

	VF	EF	AU	Unc.
(1849) TEN D.	$9,000	$16,500	$24,000	$45,000

J.S. ORMSBY
SACRAMENTO 1849

The initials J.S.O., which appear on certain issues of California privately coined gold pieces, represent the firm of J.S. Ormsby & Co. The firm struck both five- and ten-dollar denominations, all undated.

	VF
(1849) 5 DOLLS *(unique)*	—
(1849) 10 DOLLS *(4 known)*	$200,000

PACIFIC COMPANY, SAN FRANCISCO 1849

The origin of the Pacific Company is uncertain. All data regarding the firm are based on conjecture.

Edgar H. Adams wrote that he believed that the coins bearing the stamp of the Pacific Company were produced by the coining firm of Broderick and Kohler. The coins were probably hand struck with the aid of a sledgehammer.

	EF
1849, 1 DOLLAR *(2 known)*	—
1849, 5 DOLLARS *(4 known)*	$200,000
1849, 10 DOLLARS *(4 known)*	300,000

F.D. KOHLER
CALIFORNIA STATE ASSAYER 1850

The State Assay Office was authorized on April 12, 1850. That year, Governor Peter Burnett appointed F.D. Kohler, who thereupon sold his assaying business to Baldwin & Co. Kohler served at both the San Francisco and Sacramento offices. The State Assay Offices were discontinued when the U.S. Assay Office was established, on February 1, 1851. Ingots ranged from $36.55 to $150.00.

	EF
$36.55 Sacramento	—
$37.31 San Francisco	—
$40.07 San Francisco	—
$45.34 San Francisco	—
$50.00 San Francisco	—
$54.09 San Francisco	—

DUBOSQ & COMPANY
SAN FRANCISCO 1850

Theodore Dubosq, a Philadelphia jeweler, took melting and coining machinery to San Francisco in 1849.

	VF
1850, FIVE D.	$150,000
1850, TEN D.	150,000

BALDWIN & CO.
SAN FRANCISCO 1850

George C. Baldwin and Thomas S. Holman were in the jewelry business in San Francisco and were known as Baldwin & Co. They were the successors to F.D. Kohler & Co., taking over its machinery and other equipment in May 1850.

	F	VF	EF	AU	Unc.
1850, FIVE DOL.	$3,750	$6,200	$12,000	$18,000	$32,000
1850, TEN DOLLARS, Horseman Type	21,000	40,000	60,000	80,000	135,000

	F	VF	EF	AU	Unc.
1851, TEN D.	$6,500	$16,000	$22,000	$37,500	$90,000

	VF	EF	AU	Unc.
1851 TWENTY D.	$125,000	$300,000	—	—

SHULTZ & COMPANY
SAN FRANCISCO 1851

The firm, located in back of Baldwin's establishment, operated a brass foundry beginning in 1851. Judge G.W. Shultz and William T. Garratt were partners in the enterprise.

	F	VF
1851, FIVE D.	$17,000	$30,000

DUNBAR & COMPANY
SAN FRANCISCO 1851

Edward E. Dunbar operated the California Bank in San Francisco. Dunbar later returned to New York City and organized the famous Continental Bank Note Co.

	VF	EF
1851, FIVE D.	$115,000	$250,000

WASS, MOLITOR & CO.
SAN FRANCISCO 1852–1855

The gold-smelting and assaying plant of Wass, Molitor & Co. was operated by two Hungarian patriots, Count S.C. Wass and A.P. Molitor. They maintained an excellent laboratory and complete apparatus for analysis and coinage of gold.

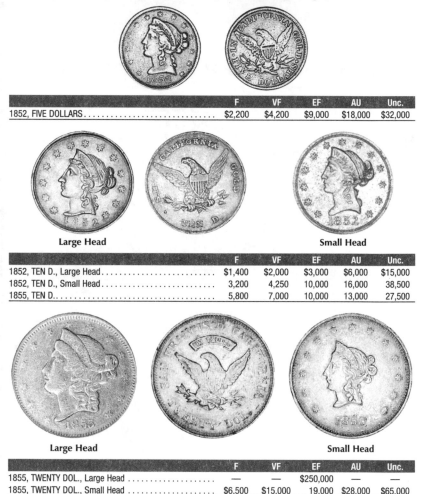

	F	VF	EF	AU	Unc.
1852, FIVE DOLLARS	$2,200	$4,200	$9,000	$18,000	$32,000

Large Head   **Small Head**

	F	VF	EF	AU	Unc.
1852, TEN D., Large Head	$1,400	$2,000	$3,000	$6,000	$15,000
1852, TEN D., Small Head	3,200	4,250	10,000	16,000	38,500
1855, TEN D.	5,800	7,000	10,000	13,000	27,500

Large Head   **Small Head**

	F	VF	EF	AU	Unc.
1855, TWENTY DOL., Large Head	—	—	$250,000	—	—
1855, TWENTY DOL., Small Head	$6,500	$15,000	19,000	$28,000	$65,000

	F	VF	EF	AU	Unc.
1855, 50 DOLLARS	$12,000	$17,000	$25,000	$47,500	$95,000

KELLOGG & CO.
SAN FRANCISCO 1854–1855

When the U.S. Assay Office ceased operations, a period ensued during which no private firm was striking gold. The new San Francisco branch mint did not produce coins for some months after Curtis & Perry took the government contract. The lack of coin was again keenly felt by businessmen, who petitioned Kellogg & Richter to "supply the vacuum" by issuing private coin. Their plea was soon answered, for on February 9, 1854, Kellogg & Co. placed their first twenty-dollar piece in circulation.

	F	VF	EF	AU	Unc.	PF
1854, TWENTY D.	$1,600	$2,200	$3,000	$5,000	$12,500	
1855, TWENTY D.	1,650	2,500	3,300	5,000	13,500	
1855, FIFTY DOLLS						$400,000

OREGON EXCHANGE COMPANY
OREGON CITY 1849
The Beaver Coins of Oregon

On February 16, 1849, the territorial legislature passed an act providing for a mint and specified five- and ten-dollar gold coins without alloy. Oregon City, the largest city in the territory with a population of about 1,000, was designated as the location for the mint. However, Oregon was then brought into the United States as a territory. When the new governor arrived on March 2, he declared the coinage act unconstitutional. Still, a local company coined these private pieces.

	F	VF	EF	AU	Unc.
1849 5 D.	$15,000	$23,000	$35,000	$70,000	—
1849 TEN.D.	37,000	70,000	135,000	200,000	—

MORMON GOLD PIECES
SALT LAKE CITY, UTAH, 1849–1860

Brigham Young was the instigator of the coinage system and personally supervised the mint, which was housed in a little adobe building in Salt Lake City. The mint was inaugurated late in 1848 as a public convenience.

	F	VF	EF	AU	Unc.
1849, TWO.AND.HALF.DO.	$6,500	$11,000	$18,000	$30,000	$50,000
1849, FIVE.DOLLARS	5,000	10,000	15,000	20,000	40,000

	F	VF	EF
1849, TEN.DOLLARS	$125,000	$200,000	$300,000
1849, TWENTY.DOLLARS.	55,000	90,000	130,000

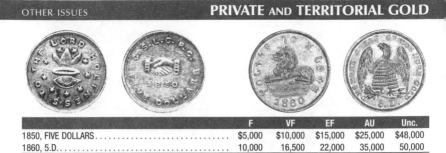

	F	VF	EF	AU	Unc.
1850, FIVE DOLLARS...........................	$5,000	$10,000	$15,000	$25,000	$48,000
1860, 5.D....................................	10,000	16,500	22,000	35,000	50,000

COLORADO GOLD PIECES
Clark, Gruber & Co.
Denver 1860–1861

Clark, Gruber & Co. was a well-known private minting firm in Denver, Colorado, in the early 1860s.

	F	VF	EF	AU	Unc.
1860, 2 1/2 D	$850	$1,200	$1,800	$2,750	$6,500
1860, FIVE D	950	1,500	2,100	3,750	7,000

	F	VF	EF	AU	Unc.
1860, TEN D	$4,500	$7,000	$11,000	$17,500	$30,000
1860, TWENTY D.	30,000	70,000	125,000	200,000	350,000

	F	VF	EF	AU	Unc.
1861, 2 1/2 D..................................	$900	$1,400	$2,100	$3,500	$7,000
1861, FIVE D.	1,200	1,800	2,600	4,700	17,000
1861, TEN D....................................	1,250	1,900	2,750	4,800	14,000

	F	VF	EF	AU
1861, TWENTY D.	$10,000	$20,000	$32,000	$50,000

John Parsons & Company
Tarryall Mines – Colorado, 1861

Very little is known regarding the mint of John Parsons and Co., although it is reasonably certain that it operated in the South Park section of Park County, Colorado, near the original town of Tarryall, in the summer of 1861.

	VF
(1861) Undated 2 1/2 D.	$120,000
(1861) Undated FIVE D.	150,000

J.J. Conway & Co.
Georgia Gulch, Colorado, 1861

Records show that the Conway mint operated for a short while in 1861. As in all gold mining areas, the value of gold dust caused disagreement among the merchants and the miners. The firm of J.J. Conway & Co. solved this difficulty by bringing out its gold pieces in August 1861.

	VF
(1861) Undated 2 1/2 DOLL'S	$85,000
(1861) Undated FIVE DOLLARS	125,000
(1861) Undated TEN DOLLARS	—

CALIFORNIA SMALL-DENOMINATION GOLD

There was a scarcity of small coins during the California Gold Rush and, starting in 1852, quarter, half, and dollar pieces were privately minted from native gold to alleviate the shortage. The need and acceptability of these pieces declined after 1856 and they then became popular as souvenirs. Authentic pieces all have CENTS, DOLLAR, or an abbreviation thereof on the reverse. The tokens are much less valuable. Modern restrikes and replicas (often having a bear in the design) have no numismatic value.

The values in the following charts are only for coins made before 1883 with the denomination on the reverse expressed as CENTS, DOL., DOLL., or DOLLAR.

Quarter Dollar – Octagonal

	EF-40	AU-50	MS-60
Liberty Head	$75	$100	$170
Indian Head	90	125	175
Washington Head	350	600	850

Quarter Dollar – Round

	EF-40	AU-50	MS-60
Liberty Head	$75	$100	$170
Indian Head	80	110	200
Washington Head	350	550	750

Half Dollar – Octagonal

	EF-40	AU-50	MS-60
Liberty Head	$75	$100	$175
Liberty Head / Eagle	500	700	1,100
Indian Head	85	125	270

Half Dollar – Round

	EF-40	AU-50	MS-60
Liberty Head	$85	$125	$225
Indian Head	75	110	185

Dollar – Octagonal

	EF-40	AU-50	MS-60
Liberty Head	$200	$300	$650
Liberty Head / Eagle	800	1,500	2,200
Indian Head	250	400	800

Dollar – Round

	EF-40	AU-50	MS-60
Liberty Head	$900	$1,350	$2,000
Indian Head	950	1,400	2,250

HARD TIMES TOKENS (1832–1844)

During the financial crises of 1832 to 1844 many government coins were hoarded, and privately made tokens were used out of necessity. The so-called Hard Times tokens of this period were slightly smaller and lighter than normal large cents. They were made of copper or brass and are of two general groups: political tokens whose theme centered on President Andrew Jackson's fight against the Bank of the United States, and tradesmen's cards, issued by merchants. Many different designs and varieties exist.

	VF	EF
Hard Times Tokens, 1832–1844, most common pieces	$12	$24

CIVIL WAR TOKENS (1860s)

Civil War tokens are generally divided into two groups: tradesmen's tokens, and anonymously issued pieces with political or patriotic themes. They came into existence only because of the scarcity of government coins and disappeared as soon as the bronze coins of 1864 met the public demand for small copper change.

These tokens vary greatly in composition and design. A number were more or less faithful imitations of the copper-nickel cent. A few of this type have the word NOT in very small letters above the words ONE CENT.

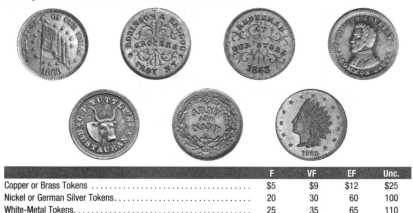

	F	VF	EF	Unc.
Copper or Brass Tokens	$5	$9	$12	$25
Nickel or German Silver Tokens	20	30	60	100
White-Metal Tokens	25	35	65	110
Copper-Nickel Tokens	30	50	80	125
Silver Tokens	80	150	225	400

Values shown are for the most common tokens in each composition.

In April 1899 control of the Philippine Islands was officially transferred from Spain to the United States, as a condition of the treaty ending the Spanish-American War. In July 1901 a civilian government (led by American judge William Howard Taft) replaced the islands' military administration; one of its first tasks was to sponsor a new territorial coinage that was compatible with the old Spanish issues, but also legally exchangeable for American money at the rate of two Philippine pesos to the U.S. dollar. The resulting coins—which bear the legend UNITED STATES OF AMERICA but are otherwise quite different in design from regular U.S. coins—today can be found in many collections, having been brought to the States as souvenirs by service members after World War II or otherwise saved.

The coins, introduced in 1903, also bear the Spanish names for the islands: FILIPINAS. Following Spanish custom, the dollar-sized peso was equivalent to 100 centavos. Silver fractions were minted in denominations of fifty, twenty, and ten centavos, and minor coins (in copper-nickel and bronze) included the five-cent piece, the centavo, and the half centavo.

Dies for the coins were made at the Philadelphia Mint. From 1903 to 1908 the coins were struck at the Philadelphia Mint (with no mintmark) and the San Francisco Mint (with an S mintmark). From 1909 through 1919, they were struck only at San Francisco. In the first part of 1920, one-centavo coins were struck in San Francisco; later in the year, a new mint facility was opened in Manila, and from that point into the early 1940s Philippine coins of one, five, ten, twenty, and fifty centavos were struck there. The coins produced at the Manila Mint in 1920, 1921, and 1922 bore no mintmark. No Philippine coins were struck in 1923 or 1924. The Manila Mint reopened in 1925; from then through 1941 its coinage featured an M mintmark.

Rising silver prices forced a reduction in the fineness and weight for each silver denomination beginning in 1907, and subsequent issues are smaller in diameter. The smaller size of the new silver issues led to confusion between the silver twenty-centavo piece and the copper-nickel five-centavo piece, resulting in a mismatching of dies for these two denominations in 1918 and again in 1928. A solution was found by reducing the diameter of the five-centavo piece beginning in 1930.

Japanese military forces advanced on the Philippines in 1942, prompting the civil government to remove much of the Philippine treasury's bullion to the United States. Nearly 16 million pesos' worth of silver remained, mostly in the form of one-peso pieces of 1907 through 1912. These coins were hastily crated and dumped into Manila's Caballo Bay to prevent their capture by Japan, then at war with the United States. The Japanese occupied the Philippines and did manage to recover some of the sunken coins (probably fewer than a half million). After the war, over the course of several years, more than 10 million of the submerged silver pesos were retrieved under the direction of the U.S. Treasury and, later, the Central Bank of the Philippines. Most of them show evidence of prolonged salt-water immersion, with dark corrosion that resists cleaning. This damage to so many coins has added to the scarcity of high-grade pre-war silver pesos.

Later during World War II, in 1944 and 1945, the U.S. Mint struck coins for the Philippines at its Philadelphia, Denver, and San Francisco mints.

The Philippines became an independent republic after the war, on July 4, 1946. Today the coins of 1903 to 1945, including a set of commemoratives issued in 1936, remain as interesting mementoes of a colorful chapter in U.S. history and numismatics.

The following are general descriptions of Philippine issues by type. For detailed date-by-date charts with mintages and retail values, see the *Guide Book of United States Coins, Deluxe Edition.*

BRONZE COINAGE UNDER U.S. SOVEREIGNTY (1903–1936)

Half Centavo   One Centavo

The bronze half centavo was struck from 1903 through 1908 (except for 1907), with some dates struck in Proof format only. Dealer buy prices for the most common pieces are $0.50 in EF to $12 in MS-63; for the most common Proofs, $25 to $70, depending on quality. The rarest Proof is the 1905, generally worth $60 to $175.

The bronze centavo was struck from 1903 through 1936. Dealers buy the most common pieces for $0.25 in VF to $10 in MS-63. The 1918-S, Large S, variety is the rarity of the series, valued from $75 (VF) to $850 (MS-63). Proofs were struck several years in the early 1900s; the most common Proofs bring buy prices of $40 to $80.

COPPER-NICKEL COINAGE UNDER U.S. SOVEREIGNTY
(1903–1935)

Large-Size Five Centavos   Reduced-Size Five Centavos
(1903–1928)   (1930–1935)

Copper-nickel five-centavo coins were struck by the millions in various years from 1903 through 1935. The most common dates are bought by dealers for $0.25 to $0.50 in VF, and for $10 to $20 in MS-63. The rare dates are the 1916-S ($20 to $500) and the 1918-S mule with the small-date reverse of the 20-centavo die ($200 to $3,500). Proofs were struck in some years of the early 1900s; the most common Proofs are bought by dealers for $50 to $85, depending on their state of preservation.

SILVER COINAGE UNDER U.S. SOVEREIGNTY (1903–1935)

Basic Design for Ten-, Twenty-, and
Fifty-Centavo and 1 Peso Pieces
(Large-size fifty centavos shown.)

Silver ten-centavo coins were struck by the millions in various years from 1903 through 1935. The most common dates are bought by dealers for their silver bullion value in VF, and for $15 to $20 in MS-63. The rarest dates are the 1909-S ($10 to $500) and the 1915-S ($9 to $220). Proofs were struck in some years of the early 1900s; the most common Proofs are bought by dealers for $20 to $50, depending on their state of preservation.

Silver twenty-centavo coins were struck in quantity in various years from 1903 through 1929. The most common dates are bought by dealers for their silver bullion value in VF, and for $25 to $30 in MS-63. There are several rarer dates in the series; the 1903-S, 1915-S, and the 1928-M mule (with a reverse of the 1903–1928 five-centavo die) are bought for $5 (VF) to $600 (MS-63). Proofs were struck in some years of the early 1900s; the most common Proofs are bought by dealers for $25 to $70, depending on their state of preservation.

Silver fifty-centavo coins were struck in quantity in various years from 1903 through 1921. The most common dates are bought by dealers for their silver bullion value in VF, and for $25 to $35 in MS-63. The rarest collectible date in the series, the 1905-S, is bought for $8 in VF but up to $800 in MS-63. Proofs were struck in some years of the early 1900s; the most common Proofs are bought by dealers for $40 to $50, depending on their state of preservation.

Silver pesos were struck in quantity in various years from 1903 through 1912. The most common dates are bought by dealers for their silver bullion value in VF, and for $50 to $60 in MS-63. There are several rarities in the series; the rarest, the 1906-S, is bought for $700 in VF and $12,000 or more in MS-63. Proofs were struck in some years of the early 1900s; the most common Proofs are bought by dealers for $80 to $100, depending on their state of preservation.

COINAGE UNDER THE COMMONWEALTH (1937–1945)

Basic Reverse Design for Commonwealth Coinage
(1936 peso shown.)

By 1935 the momentum for Philippine independence justified the creation of a Philippine Commonwealth, with full independence planned by 1946. Circulating coins struck for the commonwealth (1937–1945) featured the same basic obverse designs as those struck under U.S. sovereignty (1903–1936), and shared a common reverse design of an eagle-surmounted shield (the coat of arms of the commonwealth). All are fairly common, with mintages ranging from the millions to tens of millions, and dealer buy prices ranging from $0.05 to $2 in VF.

A set of three 1936-dated commemorative silver coins was issued to mark the beginning of the commonwealth. The fifty-centavo coin and one of the pesos feature busts of Philippine president Manuel L. Quezon and of outgoing U.S. governor-general Frank Murphy. The other peso has busts of Quezon and U.S. president Franklin D. Roosevelt. The fifty-centavo coin has a buy price of about $70 in MS-63, and the pesos of about $100 each.

These charts show the bullion values of common-date circulation-strike silver and gold coins. These are intrinsic values and do not reflect any numismatic premium a coin might have. The weight listed under each denomination is its actual silver weight (ASW) or actual gold weight (AGW). Dealers generally purchase common silver coins at around 15% below bullion value, and sell them at around 15% above bullion value. Nearly all U.S. gold coins have an additional numismatic premium beyond their bullion content. Gold bullion values here are based on AGW only; consult a coin dealer to ascertain current buy and sell prices.

Bullion Values of Silver Coins

Silver Price Per Ounce	Wartime Nickel .05626 oz.	Dime .07234 oz.	Quarter .18084 oz.	Half Dollar .36169 oz.	Silver Clad Half Dollar .14792 oz.	Silver Dollar .77344 oz.
$12	$0.68	$0.87	$2.17	$4.34	$1.78	$9.28
13	0.73	0.94	2.35	4.70	1.92	10.05
14	0.79	1.01	2.53	5.06	2.07	10.83
15	0.84	1.09	2.71	5.43	2.22	11.60
16	0.90	1.16	2.89	5.79	2.37	12.38
17	0.96	1.23	3.07	6.15	2.51	13.15
18	1.01	1.30	3.26	6.51	2.66	13.92
19	1.07	1.37	3.44	6.87	2.81	14.70
20	1.13	1.45	3.62	7.23	2.96	15.47
21	1.18	1.52	3.80	7.60	3.11	16.24
22	1.24	1.59	3.98	7.96	3.25	17.02

Bullion Values of Gold Coins

Gold Price Per Ounce	$5.00 Liberty Head 1839–1908 Indian Head 1908–1929 .24187 oz.	$10.00 Liberty Head 1838–1907 Indian Head 1907–1933 .48375 oz.	$20.00 1849–1933 .96750 oz.
$900	$217.68	$435.38	$870.75
950	229.78	459.56	919.13
1,000	241.87	483.75	967.50
1,050	253.96	507.94	1,015.88
1,100	266.06	532.13	1,064.25
1,150	278.15	556.31	1,112.63
1,200	290.24	580.50	1,161.00
1,250	302.34	604.69	1,209.38
1,300	314.43	628.88	1,257.75
1,350	326.52	653.06	1,306.13
1,400	338.62	677.25	1,354.50
1,450	350.71	701.44	1,402.88
1,500	362.81	725.63	1,451.25
1,550	374.90	749.81	1,499.63
1,600	386.99	774.00	1,548.00
1,650	399.09	798.19	1,596.38
1,700	411.18	822.38	1,644.75
1,750	423.27	846.56	1,693.13
1,800	435.37	870.75	1,741.50
1,850	447.46	894.94	1,789.88
1,900	459.55	919.13	1,838.25

Note: The U.S. bullion coins first issued in 1986 are unlike the older regular issues. They contain the following amounts of pure metal: silver $1, 1 oz.; gold $50, 1 oz.; gold $25, 1/2 oz.; gold $10, 1/4 oz.; gold $5, 1/10 oz.

The precursor to the best-selling *Guide Book of United States Coins* (the "Red Book") was *The Handbook of United States Coins With Premium List,* popularly known as the "Blue Book" because of its cover color. The mastermind behind the Blue Book was R.S. Yeoman, who had been hired by Western Publishing Company as a commercial artist in 1932. He distributed Western's Whitman line of "penny boards" to coin collectors, promoting them through department stores, along with children's books and games. He eventually arranged for Whitman to expand the line of penny boards into other denominations, giving them the reputation of a more serious numismatic endeavor rather than a "game" of filling holes with missing coins. He also developed these flat boards into a line of popular folders.

Soon Yeoman realized that coin collectors needed other resources and supplies for their hobby, and he began to compile coin mintage data and market values. This research grew into the Blue Book: now collectors had a coin-by-coin, grade-by-grade guide to the prices dealers would pay, on average, for U.S. coins. The first and second editions were both published in 1942, indicating the strong demand for this kind of hobby-related information.

In the first edition of the Red Book, published four years later, Whitman Publishing would describe the Blue Book as "a low priced standard reference book of United States coins and kindred issues" for which there had been "a long-felt need among American collectors."

The Blue Book has been published annually (except in 1944 and 1950) since its debut. Past editions offer valuable information about the hobby of yesteryear as well as developments in numismatic research and the marketplace. Old Blue Books are collectible, but they are not yet as avidly sought as the Red Book, and most editions after the 12th can be found for a few dollars in VF or better condition. Major variants were produced for the third, fourth, and ninth editions, including perhaps the only "overdate" books in American numismatic publishing. Either to conserve the previous years' covers or to correct an error in binding, the cloth on some third-edition covers was overstamped "Fourth Edition," and a number of eighth-edition covers were overstamped "Ninth Edition." The third edition was produced in several shades of blue ranging from light to dark. Some copies of the fourth edition were also produced in black cloth—the only time the Blue Book was bound in other than blue.

Valuation Guide for Select Past Editions of the Blue Book

| Edition | Date* | | VF | EF | Edition | Date* | | VF | EF |
	Title-Page	Copyright				Title-Page	Copyright		
1st	1942	1942	$50	$100	7th	1949	1948	$10	$15
2nd.......	1943	1942	25	55	8th	1950	1949	7	12
3rd	1944	1943	20	40	9th	1952	1951	4	7
4th	None	1945	20	40	10th	1953	1952	3	6
5th	None	1946	12	18	11th	1954	1953	2	4
6th	1948	1947	10	15	12th	1955	1954	2	4

* During its early years of production, the Blue Book's date presentation was not standardized. Full information is given here to aid in precise identification of early editions.

Combined with dealer's buying prices, auction data can help advanced collectors understand the modern market for high-end rarities.

It is important to understand that the following prices include a buyer's premium (a surcharge which the buyer pays the auction house over the final "hammer price," or winning bid; contemporary auction houses charge around 17.5%) and the seller's commission (a small percentage of the hammer price which the individual selling the coin pays to the auction house; this fee can sometimes be negotiated to less than 5%).

Rank	Price	Coin	Grade	Firm	Date
1	$10,016,875	$1(s), 1794, Silver Plug, B-1 BB-1	PCGS SP-66	Stack's Bowers	January 2013
2	7,590,020	$20, 1933	Gem BU	Sotheby's/Stack's	July 2002
3	4,993,750	$1(s), 1794 PCGS	MS-66+	Sotheby's/Stack's Bwrs	September 2015
4	4,582,500	Prefed, 1787, Brasher doubloon, EB on Wing	NGC MS-63	Heritage	January 2014
5	4,560,000	5¢, 1913, Liberty Head	PCGS PF-66	Stack's Bowers	August 2018
6	4,140,000	$1(s), 1804, Class I	PCGS PF-68	B&M	August 1999
7	3,960,000	$1 Trade, 1885	NGC PF-66	Heritage	January 2019
8	3,877,500	$1(s), 1804, Class I	PCGS PF-62	Heritage	August 2013
9	3,737,500	5¢, 1913, Liberty Head **(A)**	NGC PF-64	Heritage	January 2010
10	3,737,500	$1(s), 1804, Class I	NGC PF-62	Heritage	April 2008
11	3,290,000	$1(s), 1804, Class I	PCGS PF-65	Sotheby's/Stack's Bwrs	March 2017
12	3,290,000	5¢, 1913, Liberty Head **(A)**	NGC PF-64	Heritage	January 2014
13	3,172,500	5¢, 1913, Liberty Head	NGC PF-63	Heritage	April 2013
14	2,990,000	Prefed, 1787, Brasher, EB on Breast	NGC EF-45	Heritage	January 2005
15	2,990,000	$20, MCMVII, Ultra HR, LE **(B)**	PCGS PF-69	Heritage	November 2005
16	2,820,000	$1(s), 1794	PCGS MS-64	Stack's Bowers	August 2017
17	2,760,000	$20, MCMVII, Ultra HR, LE **(B)**	PCGS PF-69	Stack's Bowers	June 2012
18	2,640,000	$1(s), 1804, Class I	PCGS PF-62	Heritage	June 2018
19	2,585,000	$10, 1795, 13 Leaves, BD-4	PCGS MS-66+	Sotheby's/Stack's Bwrs	September 2015
20	2,585,000	Pattern 1¢, 1792, Birch Cent, LE, J-4	NGC MS-65RB	Heritage	January 2015
21	2,574,000	$4, 1880, Coiled Hair	NGC PF-67Cam	Bonhams	September 2013
22	2,415,000	Prefed, 1787, Brasher, EB on Wing	NGC AU-55	Heritage	January 2005
23	2,350,000	$2.50, 1808	PCGS MS-65	Sotheby's/Stack's Bwrs	May 2015
24	2,350,000	1¢, 1793, Chain AMERICA, S-4	PCGS MS-66BN	Heritage	January 2015
25	2,300,000	$1(s), 1804, Class III	PCGS PF-58	Heritage	April 2009

KEY

Price: The sale price of the coin, including the appropriate buyer's fee.

Coin: The denomination/classification, date, and description of the coin, along with pertinent catalog or reference numbers. Abbreviations include: dbln = doubloon; HR = High Relief; J = Judd; LE = Lettered Edge; Pattern = a pattern, experimental, or trial piece; Prefed = pre-federal issue; S = Sheldon. Letters in parentheses, **(A)** and **(B)**, denote instances in which multiple sales of the same coin rank within the Top 25.

Grade: The grade of the coin, plus the name of the grading firm (if independently graded). NGC = Numismatic Guaranty Corporation of America; PCGS = Professional Coin Grading Service.

Firm: The auction firm (or firms) that sold the coin. B&M = Bowers & Merena; Soth = Sotheby's; Stack's Bowers or Stack's Bwrs = Stack's Bowers Galleries (the name under which Stack's and B&M merged in 2010; also encompasses the merger of Stack's and American Numismatic Rarities in 2006).

Date: The month and year of the auction.

Auction records compiled and edited by P. Scott Rubin.

Over the years coin collectors and dealers have developed a special jargon to describe coins. Here are some terms frequently used within the hobby.

altered date—A false date on a coin; a date fraudulently changed to make a coin appear to be one of a rarer or more valuable issue.

bag mark—A surface mark, usually a small nick, acquired by a coin through contact with others in a mint bag.

blank—The formed piece of metal on which a coin design will be stamped.

bullion—Uncoined silver, gold, or platinum in the form of bars, ingots, or plate.

certified coin—A coin that has been graded, authenticated, and encapsulated in plastic by an independent third-party (neither buyer nor seller) grading service.

circulation strike—A coin intended for eventual use in commerce, as opposed to a Proof coin.

clad coinage—U.S. dimes, quarters, half dollars, and some dollars made since 1965. Each coin has a center core of pure copper and a layer of copper-nickel or silver on both sides.

die—A piece of metal engraved with a negative-image design and used for stamping coins.

die variety—Any minor alteration in the basic design of a coin type.

dipped coin—A coin that has been chemically cleaned to remove oxidation or foreign matter from its surfaces.

doubled die—A die that has been given two misaligned impressions from a hub (positive-image punch); also, a coin made from such a die.

encapsulated coin—A coin that has been authenticated, graded, and sealed in plastic by a professional third-party grading service.

error coin—A mismade coin not intended for circulation.

field—The background portion of a coin's surface not used for a design or legends.

fineness—The purity of gold, silver, or other precious metal, expressed in terms of one thousand parts. A coin of 90% pure silver is described as being .900 fine.

gem—A coin of exceptionally high quality, typically considered MS-65 or PF-65 or better.

intrinsic value—The bullion or "melt" value of the actual silver or gold in a precious-metal coin.

junk silver—Common-date silver coins in circulated grades, worth only their bullion value.

key coin—One of the scarcer or more valuable coins in a series.

legend—A principal inscription on a coin (e.g., E PLURIBUS UNUM).

luster—The brilliant or "frosty" surface quality of an Uncirculated coin.

mintmark—A small letter or other mark on a coin, indicating the mint at which it was made.

Mint set—A set of Uncirculated coins, packaged and sold by the U.S. Mint, containing one of each of the coins made for circulation at each of the mints in a particular year.

Mint State—The grade of a circulation-strike coin that has never been used in commerce, and has retained its original surface and luster; also called Uncirculated.

obverse—The front or face ("heads") side of a coin.

planchet—The blank piece of metal on which a coin design is stamped.

Proof—A coin struck for collectors by the Mint using specially polished dies and planchets.

Proof set—A set of each of the Proof coins made during a given year, packaged by the Mint and sold to collectors.

raw coin—A coin that has not been encapsulated by an independent third-party grading service.

reeded edge—The edge of a coin with grooved lines that run vertically around its perimeter, as seen on modern U.S. silver and clad coins.

reverse—The back or "tails" side of a coin.

rim—The raised outer portion of a coin that protects the design from wear.

slab—A hard plastic case containing a coin that has been graded and encapsulated by a professional grading service.

spot price—The daily quoted market value of a precious metal in bullion form.

third-party grading service—A professional firm that authenticates and grades a coin, encapsulating it in a protective hard plastic case; called *third-party* because it is neither the buyer nor the seller of the coin.

token—A privately issued piece, similar to a coin but not official legal tender, typically with an exchange value for goods or services.

type—A series of coins defined by a shared distinguishing design, composition, denomination, and other elements. For example, Barber dimes or Morgan dollars.

type set—A collection consisting of one representative coin of each type, of a particular series or period.

Uncirculated coin—A circulation-strike coin that has never been used in commerce, and has retained its original surface and luster; also called Mint State.

variety—A coin with a die characteristic that sets it apart from the normal issues of its type.

Colonial Issues

Bowers, Q. David. *Whitman Encyclopedia of Colonial and Early American Coins*. Atlanta, GA, 2009.

Cents

Bowers, Q. David. *A Guide Book of Half Cents and Large Cents*. Atlanta, GA, 2015.

Bowers, Q. David. *A Guide Book of Lincoln Cents* (2nd ed.). Atlanta, GA, 2016.

Snow, Richard. *A Guide Book of Flying Eagle and Indian Head Cents* (3rd ed.). Atlanta, GA, 2016.

Nickels and Dimes

Bowers, Q. David. *A Guide Book of Barber Silver Coins*. Atlanta, GA, 2015.

Bowers, Q. David. *A Guide Book of Buffalo and Jefferson Nickels* (2nd ed.). Pelham, AL, 2017.

Bowers, Q. David. *A Guide Book of Mercury Dimes, Standing Liberty Quarters, and Liberty Walking Half Dollars*. Atlanta, GA, 2015.

Bowers, Q. David. *A Guide Book of Shield and Liberty Head Nickels*. Atlanta, GA, 2006.

Flynn, Kevin. *The Authoritative Reference on Roosevelt Dimes*. Brooklyn, NY, 2001.

Quarter Dollars and Half Dollars

Bowers, Q. David. *A Guide Book of Barber Silver Coins*. Atlanta, GA, 2015.

Bowers, Q. David. *A Guide Book of Mercury Dimes, Standing Liberty Quarters, and Liberty Walking Half Dollars*. Atlanta, GA, 2015.

Bowers, Q. David. *A Guide Book of Washington and State Quarters* (2nd ed.). Pelham, AL, 2017.

Tomaska, Rick. *A Guide Book of Franklin and Kennedy Half Dollars* (2nd ed.). Atlanta, GA, 2012.

Silver Dollars

Bowers, Q. David. *A Guide Book of Morgan Silver Dollars* (5th ed.). Pelham, AL, 2016.

Burdette, Roger W. *A Guide Book of Peace Dollars* (3rd ed.). Atlanta, GA, 2016.

Newman, Eric P., and Kenneth E. Bressett. *The Fantastic 1804 Dollar, Tribute Edition*. Atlanta, GA, 2009.

Standish, Michael "Miles," and John B. Love. *Morgan Dollar: America's Love Affair With a Legendary Coin*. Atlanta, GA, 2014.

Gold Coins

Bowers, Q. David. *A Guide Book of Double Eagle Gold Coins*. Atlanta, GA, 2004.

Bowers, Q. David. *A Guide Book of Gold Dollars* (2nd ed.). Atlanta, GA, 2011.

Fivaz, Bill. *United States Gold Counterfeit Detection Guide*. Atlanta, GA, 2005.

Garrett, Jeff, and Ron Guth. *Encyclopedia of U.S. Gold Coins, 1795–1933* (2nd ed.). Atlanta, GA, 2008.

Commemoratives

Bowers, Q. David. *A Guide Book of United States Commemorative Coins* (2nd ed.). Pelham, AL, 2016.

Proof and Mint Sets

Lange, David W. *A Guide Book of Modern United States Proof Coin Sets* (2nd ed.). Atlanta, GA, 2010.

Bullion Coins

Mercanti, John M., with Michael Standish. *American Silver Eagles: A Guide to the U.S. Bullion Coin Program* (2nd ed.). Atlanta, GA, 2013.

Moy, Edmund C. *American Gold and Platinum Eagles: A Guide to the U.S. Bullion Coin Programs*. Atlanta, GA, 2013.

Tucker, Dennis. *American Gold and Silver: U.S. Mint Collector and Investor Coins and Medals, Bicentennial to Date*. Atlanta, GA, 2015.

Tokens and Medals

Bowers, Q. David. *A Guide Book of Civil War Tokens* (2nd ed.). Atlanta, GA, 2015.

Bowers, Q. David. *A Guide Book of Hard Times Tokens*. Atlanta, GA, 2015.

Jaeger, Katherine, and Q. David Bowers. *100 Greatest American Medals and Tokens*. Atlanta, GA, 2007.

Jaeger, Katherine. *A Guide Book of United States Tokens and Medals*. Atlanta, GA, 2008.

Tucker, Dennis. *American Gold and Silver: U.S. Mint Collector and Investor Coins and Medals, Bicentennial to Date*. Atlanta, GA, 2015.

U.S./Philippine Coins

Allen, Lyman L. *U.S. Philippine Coins*. Oakland Park, FL, 1998.

Shafer, Neil. *United States Territorial Coinage for the Philippine Islands*. Racine, WI, 1961.

Type Coins

Bowers, Q. David. *A Guide Book of United States Type Coins* (2nd ed.). Atlanta, GA, 2008.

Guth, Ron, and Jeff Garrett. *United States Coinage: A Study by Type*. Atlanta, GA, 2005.

Die Varieties

Fivaz, Bill, and J.T. Stanton. *The Cherrypickers' Guide to Rare Die Varieties (various editions and volumes)*. Atlanta, GA.

PATRIOTIC SILVER COINS OF WORLD WAR II

A new silver dime, quarter, and half dollar debuted in 1916. Today all three are widely collected as American classics. The era of these coins spanned from the Great War (1914–1918, with the United States involved in 1917 and 1918) through the Roaring Twenties, the Great Depression, and World War II. Together with an unusual silver five-cent piece and the Washington quarter, these make up the silver pocket change that most Americans spent in the 1940s. They were the patriotic silver coins of World War II.

The United States enjoyed economic prosperity after the Great War, and the following decade came to be known as the Roaring Twenties. Social, artistic, and cultural innovation bloomed, and Americans rushed to buy many modern-day luxuries. Motion pictures and radio shows entertained the nation, and electricity was brought into more and more communities. Commercial, passenger, and freight aviation took off. Sports heroes and movie stars became celebrities. Jazz music and dancing became popular as Americans put the war behind them. Women were finally allowed to vote nationwide, thanks to the 19th Amendment. The U.S. population exceeded 100 million in 1920.

Sadly, the exuberant prosperity was not to last—in 1929 the stock market crashed, and the nation (along with the rest of the world) entered a period of poverty and unemployment known as the Great Depression.

Many factors led to the economic crash at the end of the Roaring Twenties. People were consuming too much, buying expensive goods, often on installment plans and with weak credit. Businesses reinvested their record-setting profits to the point of creating a financial bubble. Banks had no guarantees in place to protect account holders, which encouraged panics (people trying to quickly withdraw all or most of their

1918: America and her allies celebrate the end of the Great War. The Roaring Twenties were on the horizon.

cash) when markets went down. Banks also loaned money recklessly through the 1920s, as speculators borrowed to invest in the hot stock market. The house of cards toppled on October 29, 1929, "Black Tuesday." On that day some 16 million stocks were traded and the market crashed. This was the biggest stock-market collapse in U.S. history, before or since. Rich and poor felt its effects. Construction came to a halt. Crop prices fell, causing hardship for farmers. As other nations fell into the same economic hole, demand for U.S. goods dried up. Soon it wasn't just poor Americans eating at soup kitchens, but previously middle-class and wealthier ones, too.

In Germany discontent had been long festering over inflation and poverty caused by the Great War. In 1939, while America was still finding its feet economically, German soldiers invaded Poland, and the Second World War began. It would continue for six grueling years, earning the horrific distinction of being the most widespread war in history. More than 100 million people were swept up in its course, with more than 30

In 1929 Paramount released "The Dance of Life," a film that captured the energy of the Jazz Age.

countries involved. The United States officially entered the war after Japan attacked the American naval base at Pearl Harbor on December 7, 1941. Industry and government spending in the war effort provided work for many unemployed Americans. After a long and horrible conflict the Allied Powers triumphed with the unconditional surrender of Germany on May 8, 1945, followed by the official signing of Japan's surrender on September 2, 1945.

People gathering outside of the New York Stock Exchange after the Great Crash of 1929.

Mercury Dimes (1916–1945)

The silver ten-cent piece of 1916 to 1945 is popularly called the "Mercury" dime, because its design resembles the ancient Roman god of commerce, financial gain, communication, and travelers. In truth, it shows Miss Liberty wearing a winged cap representing freedom of thought. The coins debuted as America was just months away from entering one war, and bowed out some 30 years later as it finished another.

In the early 1900s several of America's coins were updated with bold and artistic new designs. President Theodore Roosevelt in 1905 commissioned Augustus Saint-Gaudens, one of the country's most famous sculptors, to update U.S. coins ranging from the copper cent to the gold $20 piece. Roosevelt had seen a display of ancient Greek coins at the Smithsonian Institution in Washington, and he admired their high-relief sculpted artistry. The president believed that

President Theodore Roosevelt.

the United States should have equally impressive coins since it was the greatest nation on Earth. By 1907 Saint-Gaudens had prepared sketches, ideas, and patterns for the $10 and $20 gold coins, but he died of cancer that August, before the final products could be minted. His assistant Henry Hering finished his work and the beautiful new Saint-Gaudens "eagles" and "double eagles" (as $10 and $20 gold coins are called) were struck starting later that year. President Roosevelt then turned to Boston-area sculptor Bela Lyon Pratt to create new designs for the $2.50 and $5 gold coins, which debuted in 1908. Next a new one-cent coin by sculptor Victor David Brenner, featuring a portrait of Abraham Lincoln, came out in 1909.

Augustus Saint-Gaudens's $20 double eagle.

Indian Head $10 eagle, also by Saint-Gaudens.

By 1914, coin collectors—including members of the very active New York Numismatic Club—were tired of Charles Barber's Liberty Head design used on silver dimes, quarters, and half dollars. They wanted something new for these coins, akin to the artistic renaissance in the nation's gold coins.

U.S. Mint artists started working on new designs in 1915, and in December of that year Mint director Robert W. Woolley met with the Commission of Fine Arts to review them. Proposals by Barber were rejected, and artists Adolph Weinman, Hermon MacNeil, and Albin Polasek were invited to submit ideas. Ultimately Weinman's models were accepted for both the dime and the half dollar, and MacNeil's for the quarter dollar.

Treasury Secretary William G. McAdoo announced on May 30, 1916, that the new coin designs had been adopted. "The design of the dime," he said, "owing to the smallness of the coin, has been held quite simple. The obverse shows a head of Liberty with winged cap. The head is firm and simple in form, the profile forceful. The reverse shows a design of the bundle of rods, with battle ax, known as 'fasces,' and symbolical of unity, wherein lies the nation's strength. Surrounding the fasces is a full foliaged branch of olive, symbolical of peace."

Minting and distribution of the coins started in October 1916.

By 1914, Barber dimes had been around for more than 20 years, and America was ready for a change.

"The new dime, in my opinion, is one of the handsomest coins of the denomination that has been issued for regular circulation in this country," said Edgar H. Adams, the most honored numismatic writer and researcher of that era.

John W. Scott, a retired longtime coin dealer, said, "The new dime is the best piece of work that the United States Mint has turned out in a century."

Farran Zerbe, past president of the American Numismatic Association, announced that he was delighted with the new coin.

The Winged Liberty ("Mercury") dime replaced the old Barber coins in 1916. They would be minted into the 1940s.

Frank G. Duffield, editor of *The Numismatist* (journal of the American Numismatic Association), observed that "The girlish Miss Liberty with wings on her cap has already won a place in the numismatist's heart." He described America's dime as "a good friend to man, woman and child; it opens many doors to pleasure and amusement," and beyond its day-to-day usefulness the new dime is "a bit of art to admire as well."

Coin collectors and the general public alike admired the Mercury dime and its artistic, unusual designs. The coin would be minted continuously from 1916 to 1945 (except for the years of 1922, 1932, and 1933), with hundreds of millions produced in many of the later years. The death of President Franklin Roosevelt in 1945 would bring a new coin, the Roosevelt dime, minted to this day in his honor.

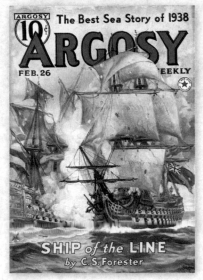

Among the "pleasures and amusements" that 10 cents would buy in the era of the Winged Liberty dime were many different magazines featuring detective stories, science fiction, adventures, humor, and other entertainment.

Adolph Weinman, designer of the Winged Liberty ("Mercury") dime.

Standing Liberty Quarters (1916–1930)

In 1916 Miss Liberty made a bold new appearance on the U.S. quarter dollar: standing in a full-length pose for the first time on an American coin. On the coin's reverse, a bald eagle, the national bird, winged its way through the sky, surrounded by stars. These powerful symbols would grace the quarter for nearly 20 years.

The Liberty Head silver coins designed by the Mint's chief engraver, Charles Barber, and first issued in 1892, were "old news" by 1914. Coin collectors wanted something fresh and more interesting for the dime, quarter, and half dollar, and they made their desire known to the U.S. Mint. Turning away from new ideas submitted by Barber, Mint Director Robert Woolley invited well-known American artists from outside the Mint to submit potential designs.

One of them, Hermon Atkins Mac-Neil, was born in Everett, Massachusetts, in 1866. By the time he was

Hermon A. MacNeil circa 1907.

asked to submit designs for the 1916 coinage, he had taught industrial art at Cornell University, studied in Europe, and created famous and influential sculptures and monuments. His ideas for the new quarter dollar were chosen and modified into what collectors today know as the Standing Liberty.

MacNeil's Standing Liberty quarter.

A 1917 war-bond poster featuring Miss Liberty in a
standing pose similar to that on the 1916 quarter dollar.

This excerpt from an article in the August 1916 issue of *The Numismatist* put the Standing Liberty quarters in the context of the ongoing war in Europe: "On the 25-cent piece, taking a new pose and gesture, [Miss Liberty] is to be seen stepping toward the country's gateway, bearing upraised a shield from which the covering is being drawn, and in her right hand the olive branch of peace. This is the coin of the preparedness movement; it indicates, as Secretary McAdoo tells us, that the country is 'awakening to its own protection.'"

The mixture of symbolism showed that the United States had peaceful intentions but was vigilant and prepared to defend itself if necessary. In 1917 this message was reinforced by giving Liberty a coat of chainmail armor under her flowing robe, partially visible over her previously bare breast.

The premonition that America would eventually have to enter the European conflict became reality a few months after the new coins came out. Congress declared war on the government of Imperial Germany in April 1917.

A Standing Liberty quarter in 1920 would get you a quart of cream from the local milkman, or a jar of marmalade. Two of them that year would buy a men's dress shirt—not of the highest quality, but decent. If you lived in Atlanta, Georgia, you could eat lunch at Thornton's Cafeteria at the corner of Luckie and Forsyth streets and get five fried oysters for 25 cents.

Ten years later, 1930 was the first full year of the Great Depression and prices went down as money became scarce. In 1930 your Standing Liberty quarter would buy five pounds of sugar or a dozen eggs (about the same price as eggs in 1900).

A milkman on his rounds in 1925.

Liberty Walking Half Dollars (1916–1947)

Adolph Alexander Weinman, the artist who created the "Mercury" dime, also designed the Liberty Walking half dollar. Weinman was born in 1870 in the Grand Duchy of Baden (later part of the German Empire). He moved to the United States at the age of 14 and began studying art in New York City. He took evening classes at Cooper Union and studied at the Art Students League of New York with sculptors Augustus Saint-Gaudens and Philip Martiny, and later served as an assistant to Charles Niehaus, Olin Warner, and Daniel Chester French before opening his own studio in 1904. By the time he made his 1916 coins, the medalist and architectural sculptor was well known for the bronze reproductions of his larger statues and artistic works.

Audrey Marie Munson was an artists' model and film actress in America during the 1900s. She was considered to be "America's First Supermodel" and was variously called "Miss Manhattan," "American Venus," the "Panama-Pacific Girl," and the "Exposition Girl." The last two nicknames came from her posing for the majority of statues created for the Panama-Pacific International Exposition of 1915. She was also the model or inspiration for more than a dozen statues in New York City. Adolph Weinman hired her as a model for some of his sculptures, including *The Setting Sun*. She was one of the inspirations for his 1916 coinage designs.

Adolph Weinman was a sculptor as well as a designer. His statue *The Setting Sun* was featured on this cover of *Sunset, The Pacific Monthly* magazine.

Weinman around 1897.

PATRIOTIC SILVER COINS OF WORLD WAR II

The obverse of the half dollar features a beautiful Miss Liberty, draped in a neo-classical gown as she strides toward the sun. Weinman's monogram can be seen beneath the tips of the eagle's wings on the reverse.

The coin was struck intermittently from 1916 to 1947, so there are some missing dates (1922, 1924, 1925, 1926, 1930, 1931, and 1932). Mintages were in the tens of millions annually through the World War II years. If your grandparents were alive during the war and the decades following, and saved some old coins in a cigar box or jewelry chest, chances are good you'll find a Liberty Walking half dollar there.

The Liberty Walking half dollar.

Weinman's *The Voice of Reason*, displayed at the Environmental Protection Agency, Ronald Reagan Building, Washington, D.C.

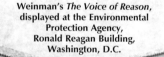

Audrey Munson posed for artist Adolph Weinman, designer of both the
Liberty Walking half dollar and the "Mercury" or Winged Liberty Head dime.

A silver half dollar represented a good sum of money in the 1930s. It would have made dinner of ground beef and potatoes for this poor family in Oklahoma during the Great Depression.

Throughout World War II, the half dollar was America's largest contemporary circulating coin. (The Peace silver dollar was last minted in 1935.) The Mercury dime was also minted through the final year of the war. The Standing Liberty quarter, although last minted in 1930, was part of everyday Americans' pocket change, as was the silver Washington quarter, which debuted in 1932.

A new silver "nickel" and a steel cent were two wartime inventions.

On October 8, 1942, ten months after the United States entered hostilities, a new composition was introduced for the five-cent coin. The alloy of 56% copper, 35% silver, and 9% manganese eliminated *nickel* from the nickel, saving some 2.4 million pounds of the important metal for strategic wartime usage. About 860 million "silver war nickels" were made from 1942 to 1945. A large letter above Monticello indicates where each coin was minted—Philadelphia (with a P), Denver (D), or San Francisco (S).

Copper was another important metal in the United States' war effort during World War II. To help save more of the metal for military use, the Treasury Department switched the Lincoln cent from bronze (made of 95% copper) to zinc-coated steel. This change was only for a single year—1943—but it helped save millions of pounds of copper for military use in cartridges and other ammunition. Though not made of silver, the coins have a beautiful silvery shine in Uncirculated condition.

P, D, and S mintmarks for Philadelphia, Denver, and San Francisco nickels.

Today it's rare to find any of the patriotic wartime silver coins in pocket change. But you can easily buy one for your collection from a coin shop, or from a coin dealer online or through the mail. These special coins are an important reminder of America's sacrifices and efforts during World War II.

The silver Washington quarter debuted in 1932. Hundreds of millions were minted during the war years. In addition to a portrait of President George Washington, designer John Flanagan's quarter featured an eagle spreading its wings and grasping a bundle of arrows atop olive branches. The symbolism was of military preparedness coupled with peaceful intentions.